Feminist Cyberspaces

Feminist Cyberspaces:
Pedagogies in Transition

Edited by

Sharon Collingwood, Alvina E. Quintana
and Caroline J. Smith

**CAMBRIDGE
SCHOLARS**

P U B L I S H I N G

Feminist Cyberspaces:
Pedagogies in Transition,
Edited by Sharon Collingwood, Alvina E. Quintana and Caroline J. Smith

This book first published 2012

Cambridge Scholars Publishing

12 Back Chapman Street, Newcastle upon Tyne, NE6 2XX, UK

British Library Cataloguing in Publication Data
A catalogue record for this book is available from the British Library

ISBN (10): 1-4438-3633-8, ISBN (13): 978-1-4438-3633-3

CONTENTS

LIST OF ILLUSTRATIONS

Figure 1: Share It! Senior seminar presentation at the University of Maryland

Figure 2: A paused clip of Dr. Scheiner Gills' podcast

Figure 3: This screen capture of the Diigo interface shows how tagging is integral to building a vocabulary of significant concepts to and by a specific group

Figure 4: Collaborative Transcultural Dialogue Artwork by LaMonique Adom, Karen Keifer-Boyd, Muwonge Kyazze, Kanuge John Bosco, Banaddo Godfrey, Nakisanze Sarah (March 2010)

Figure 5: A discussion group of avatars can be held in text chat or voice, and this can be supplemented by private instant message to individuals or to the group as a whole.

Figure 6: Students can easily upload PowerPoints to structure their in-class presentations. In this example, the student has included a gift of clothing to underscore points about Western attitudes to Muslim dress.

LIST OF TABLES

INTRODUCTION

WHY TECHNOLOGY?

SHARON COLLINGWOOD

In the summer of 2008, I attended my first conference on education and technology. Technology is not my area of specialization; I was attending because I had recently been charged with developing an online introductory women's studies course for my department. Although I had expected to feel out of place at a tech event, I was pleasantly surprised. The atmosphere at the conference was relaxed and friendly, the audiences were reasonably gender-balanced, and the presentations covered an interesting variety of subjects and technologies.

One of the many different presentations I attended was on using games in teaching. I went with an open mind, thinking that a few games scattered through the term work might well make an online course more lively. The presenter demonstrated the first game enthusiastically, propelling a little armed figure through a series of challenges; he jumped over chasms, slid under cars, dodged dangerous-looking buzz saws, and ended by combining mastery of the gameplay with assimilation of course material.

Unimpressed but still hopeful, I waited for the second game to be demonstrated. In this example, a little clown figure jumped through hoops, slid down a tightrope, and collected falling money. He, too, was successful in integrating gameplay and learning.

By the time the third example was presented and another little animated figure began his desperate dash for knowledge, the pattern was becoming clear. I had just decided to politely daydream away the remaining ten minutes of the session when an educational technology specialist in the audience stood up to berate the presenter fiercely for his unimaginative approach to instructional gaming and his total neglect of the play patterns of female gamers.

The presenter beamed benevolently at her. He answered that he did indeed have games that were designed with women in mind, and he proceeded to show us one of them. We then watched as a small but adorable baby jumped over kitchen tables, slid through windows, and saved falling puppies from disaster. The presenter, happily oblivious to the reactions of the women in the room, explained the importance of emotional connection for true immersive learning.

The session did not end well. The heated discussion that ensued was the beginning of my education on gender and gaming; I learned that linearity, risk, violence, competition, and control are understood to be essential for games designed for males, while many believe that collaboration, communication, and aesthetics are important in designing games for women (Gee and Hayes, 2010, 1-16). I found arguments that males approach the computer as a challenge to be mastered, while females see it as a tool to extend one's own power, and that while males pit themselves against the computer, females attempt to use it communicatively and cooperatively (Turkle 1997, 88). Further research revealed a growing but still relatively undeveloped discussion of the essentialist notions at the heart of the gender and technology question (Graner-Ray 2004). Gender in gaming is still a highly controversial topic, and given the low number of female game designers, it seems destined to remain so for some time to come.

Although games are only one aspect the gender and technology problem, this session proved to be very useful to me, as it alerted me to the assumptions I had brought to the conference. As a professor of women's studies, I have taught hundreds of students to look at social phenomena through the lens of gender. I think this is the most important thing I do; many students have told me that this training gives them a new understanding of their world. Yet, when presented with a demonstration of gender-biased instructional gaming, I did not question the lack of inclusivity in the construction of these exercises. Instead, I accepted that the presentation was an accurate portrayal of instructional gaming, and my response was that what was being presented was "not for me" and certainly not for my female students. Instead of looking for what could be of value for students of both genders in integrating games into my course, or asking if there were other ways to use the gaming software, I accepted that the linear, competitive, and high-pressure elements I saw were an integral part of all computer games. Even worse, I was not the one who stood to protest the obvious bias in constructing these games. Perhaps this was because I believed that computing is outside my area of expertise, or perhaps at some level I felt an unspoken, unacknowledged acceptance of this technology as "male territory." This led me to wonder what other territories I had been conceding.

Many of us who teach women's studies are tentative in our acceptance of technology, as are many of our female students. However, computing and information technology is rapidly becoming essential in both the private and the public spheres; our ability to integrate it into new ways of teaching is important, not just for the efficient communication of course content, but also for the development of skills and literacies that will assure a satisfactory level of comfort and agency in the new digital culture.

Although women and men have shown roughly equal interest in using the computer, studies demonstrate that women feel less confident in computer use and are far less likely to pursue a career in computer sciences (Hill 2010, Tam 2006). A recent publication by the American Association of University Women demonstrated that although young women's interest in careers in science, engineering, and technology in general is growing, enrollment in computer science programs is undergoing an alarming decline, dropping from a high of 36 percent of computer science bachelor's degrees awarded in the mid 1980's to 20 percent of those awarded in 2006 (Hill 2010, 37). Many reasons have been given for the gender gap; a perceived lack of interest, the prevalence of cultural stereotypes, a hostile work culture, or even the superior abilities in spatial reasoning males acquire through video games. Whatever the cause, women are not fully participating in a highly-paid technology that is rapidly restructuring our society (Tapia 2004, Walton 2009).

The lack of interest in computer science as a profession may tell us something about women's participation in digital culture. It is not necessary to have a degree in computer sciences to be active online, but it is important to be confident and comfortable; recent studies suggest that underlying attitudes may need to be addressed in order to foster full participation by women. In 2005 a survey by the Pew Internet and American Life Project established that women make up a slight majority of Internet users (Fallows 1995), and this ratio remained constant in a subsequent study in 2009 (Pew 2009). The voices being heard, however, are predominantly male. In 2007, *PC Magazine*'s list of the 50 most influential people on the web contained social activists, political commentators, social media moguls, and prominent web CEOs, but only five people on the list were women. In 2008 *Bloomberg Businessweek* listed the 25 most influential people on the web, four of whom were women (Casserly and Goudreau 2010). In 2010 *Internet Evolution*, a news and analysis macrosite, released their list of 100 influential people in business, technology, entertainment, news and commentary; there were only seven women. A new sphere of influence is rising in Internet culture, and although there are many examples of talented and successful female and feminist participants, they are still in a minority (Sweeney 2010).

Our students need the tools to understand women's involvement social media. Women are the majority in social media applications like Facebook, MySpace, and Twitter, making up 60% of all users, but men predominate on Linked In, a business-oriented social network used primarily to post curricula vitae and to trade referrals (Rapleaf 2008). This may mean that while the collaborative and open nature of social media encourages female participation with friends and family, it is men who are more successful in goal-oriented transactional networking in a wider circle of influence.

Blogging is another area where women show strong participation; over 22 million women read or publish blogs, according to a recent report by BlogHer, the preeminent women's blog aggregation site (Wright 2009, 9) and women publish 49.1% of all blogs (Sysmos 2010). Yet, as seen above, this does not translate into female participation in the wider culture. The reason for this becomes apparent in an examination of the BlogHer site itself. The majority of the blogs focus on work, parenting, and lifestyles, with far less attention paid to news and commentary. This kind of community interaction may serve in the long run to establish a network that transcends race and class divisions to serve a larger political goal; as it stands today, however, women's self-expression on the web seems to be as vulnerable to gatekeeping as it was in the traditional media, which relegated "women's interests" to the Sunday section. This is not to say that the blogs themselves are not well written, insightful, and highly relevant, but it does suggest that although women's voices are being heard on the Internet, too often we are only talking to each other. This problem was made particularly clear in the summer of 2008, when the annual BlogHer Convention in San Francisco was held the same weekend as the conference for Netroots Nation, an association of young, male, and very political bloggers. Netroots was covered in the news section of *The New York Times*, but the BlogHer convention was relegated to the lifestyles section. The uproar that ensued on the feminist blogosphere demonstrated that the *Times* coverage had hit a nerve (Traister 2008).

Another difficulty for women bloggers is in the level of discourse on the web. Internet discussions can be very confrontational, and some participants argue that this creates a climate of hostility. Maureen Dowd, one of the few female op-ed writers for *The New York Times*, accepted her online position in 1996. Six months later she was ready to quit: "I was a bundle of frayed nerves. I felt as though I were in a 'Godfather' movie, shooting and getting shot at" (Dowd 2005). She was persuaded to remain, but if an experienced journalist like Maureen Dowd can feel threatened in internet debate, how much more difficult will it be for our students? To fully participate in online commentary our students will need the rhetorical skills to successfully deal with "male" discourse and advocate for inclusionary practices.

Many women bloggers believe they are targeted for harassment more than men (Nakashima 2007). In 2007 Cathy Sierra, a nationally-known tech blogger, permanently closed her blog, citing vicious sexual harassment and threats to herself and to her family (Wagner 2007, Havenstein 2007). Other bloggers have been attacked in a similar fashion; in an interview with Gaby Wood, Jessica Valenti, founder of the feminist blog *Feministing*, describes her confrontation with misogynist attackers:

> There was one incident where I posted a video about online misogyny and saying that feminist bloggers blog under our own names all the time and say what we believe in, whereas when it comes to rapist and sexist and homophobic bloggers, they have massive anonymity to protect them. I said: if you really believe this, then have the guts to say who you are. They went nuts. They took the site down that night. I got 5,000 emails – you cunt, bitch, I'll kill you, I'll cut your breasts off...all kinds of sexually violent, scary things.

The problem of internet harassment is ongoing (Thorpe and Rogers 2011). Clearly, without our support, our students may not be able to deal with this behavior and could be silenced by it.

Blogging is more than a hobby. Some women are making a profit from their writing, others are gaining an influence in their respective professions, and still others are using blogging for charitable fundraising and social activism. The high proportion of women in social media in general is a very good sign and could have tremendous social repercussions if their voices become mainstream. The Internet itself is becoming a dominant source of information on political life; 55 percent of the American electorate took part in the 2008 presidential campaign or received news and information about it through the Internet (Smith 2009). The feminist classroom must prepare students for the rough-and-tumble nature of internet discourse.

Speaking out successfully requires good research skills and a competent handling of resources. In the past, a teacher's task was to assemble information, present it to students, and encourage them to engage with it. Due to the rapid changes in information technology, our task today is to help our students navigate a bewildering ocean of information. Library skills are of prime importance, but so is media literacy. Students need to develop an ability for critical analysis in many areas, including social media, where they will be able to use their social networking skills to engage in collaborative knowledge building. However, they must also understand how web culture works. Not all areas of discourse are as open as our students believe them to be.

Wikipedia is a case in point. A powerful social phenomenon whose borders are linguistic rather than geopolitical, Wikipedia has great potential for global collaboration and social transformation. It is ubiquitous; most searches find a Wikipedia article at the head of the results, and this is partly because some search engines rank an article not just by the number of visits but also by the number of sites linking to it. As a prime disseminator of knowledge for the online community, it has a profound cultural influence. Due to its very nature, however, Wikipedia is sometimes unreliable; articles are constantly changing, and critics fault authors and editors for neglecting verification that is not freely available online (Garfinkel 2008).

Some academics refuse to accept work based on Wikipedia, and others recommend it only as a starting point. Whether or not Wikipedia is banned, however, students often use it. A recent analysis showed that 52% of students studied used Wikipedia in course-related research, whether or not their instructor advised against it (Head 2010). Many academics argue that Wikipedia is a valuable resource that teaches students to be critical of their sources, document their own arguments, participate in an open peer review process, and fine-tune their skills in argumentation (Maehre 2009). If these scholars are right, there is much to be learned from Wikipedia, providing that our students learn to keep a critical distance from it.

Other aspects of Wikipedia are more troubling. In 2009 a study by the Wikimedia Foundation revealed that women write only 12.6 percent of all contributions. Ed Chi, a computer scientist at the Palo Alto Research Center, has studied Wikipedia extensively and supports the findings of the Wikimedia study: "The average Wikipedian is a young man in a wealthy country who's probably a grad student – somebody who's smart, literate, engaged in the world of ideas, thinking, learning, writing all the time" (Manjoo 2009). Other scholars have revealed gender differences in Wikipedia usage (Sook and Kwon, 2010). This gender imbalance is particularly disturbing if we consider the success women are having in graduate schools of many countries, where women either outnumber men or are at least approaching parity. Other social disparities are also implied in Chi's acceptance of the gender gap, and indicate that Wikipedia may well provide us with teachable moments but in more ways than its creators intend. If we should not be encouraging our students to rely on Wikipedia, we should certainly be encouraging them to write it.

There are many positive aspects to our students' use of new media. Even on sites like Facebook, where interaction is primarily social, verification is second nature; posts are often reinforced with a link to a news story, a picture, or a video. With a maximum of 140 characters per message, Twitter is teaching them concision. Blogging promotes self-analysis and social awareness. Wikipedia highlights the necessity for trust in collaborative knowledge building and the importance of maintaining one's reputation in a scholarly community. Social activism is facilitated by these and other online programs, and as students learn to use the interface, involvement becomes progressively easier to initiate. Barriers between the private and the public, between amateur and professional, and between academic and activist are being bridged by new technology.

The initial feminist objective was to get women online; this has been accomplished. Now is the time to survey the field and learn to consolidate our efforts. Our discipline has always emphasized consensus-based decision making, and outreach to the community is essential to what we do. We now have the ability to forge stronger ties between our students and the communities of practice they study, while teaching them the skills they will need to succeed in the new digital culture.

This volume is about reaching across disciplines, going out of our comfort zones, and trying something new. Many of the contributions chronicle first attempts; some have not been completely successful. We are learning as we go along.

Our collection has been structured to reflect the multifaceted nature of education today; learning takes place on a personal level, through independent study and social media, it takes place at a local level in our classrooms and lecture halls, but it is also increasingly taking place on a global scale as new technologies foster international collaboration between individuals and organizations. In addition, there is a growing acceptance of learning in the collaborative 3D classrooms of virtual worlds. These educational spaces are not mutually exclusive, as the chapters in this volume make clear.

The contributors to this collection use a variety of technologies, suited to individual teaching styles and the demands of the subject material. Most are not experts, having "tinkered" enough to begin using these tools with students, and then developing pedagogical approaches as we deepened our understanding of the technology. However, we all share an understanding of the tremendous potential of the technologies we are using, and we hope our contributions will encourage you to explore some of them for your own teaching.

Bibliography

"The 25 Most Influential People on the Internet." 2008. *Bloomberg Businessweeek*. Accessed June 25, 2010. http://images.businessweek.com/ss/08/09/0929_most_influential/index.htm?chan=technology_best+of+the+web.

Adam, Alison. 2002. "Exploring the Gender Question in Critical Information Systems." *Journal of Information Technology* 17, no. 2: 59-67.

Benkler, Yochai. 2006. *The Wealth of Networks: How Social Production Transforms Markets and Freedom.* Yale University Press, New Haven.

Carr, Diane. 2005. "Context, Gaming Pleasures and Gendered Preferences." *Simulation and Gaming* 36, no. 4: 464-482.

Casserly, Meghan and Jenna Goudreau. 2010. "Top 100 Websites For Women." *Forbes.com*, June 6. Accessed June 15, 2010. http://www.forbes.com/2010/06/23/100-best-womens-blogs-forbes-woman-time-websites.html.

Crocco, Margaret, Judith Cramer and Ellen Meier. 2008. "(Never) Mind the Gap!: Gender Equity in Social Studies Research on Technology in the Twenty-First Century." *Multicultural Education & Technology Journal* 2, no. 1: 19-36.

"Demographics of Internet Users." 2009. *Pew Internet and American Life Project*. Accessed June 25, 2010. http://pewinternet.org/ Static-Pages/Trend-Data/Whos-Online.aspx.

Dowd, Maureen. 2005. "Dish It Out, Ladies." *New York Times*, March 13. Accessed November 13, 2011. http://www.nytimes.com/2005/03/13/opinion/13dowd.html?_r=2&oref=slogin.

Fallows, Deborah. 2005. "How Women and Men Use the Internet." *Pew Internet and American Life Project*. Accessed June 22, 2010. http://www.pewinternet.org/Reports/2005/How-Women-and-Men-Use-the-Internet.aspx.

Garfinkel, Simon. 2008. "Wikipedia and the Meaning of Truth." *Technology Review* 111, no. 6: 84-86.

Gee, James and Elizabeth Hayes. *Women and Gaming: The Sims and 21st Century Learning.* New York: Palgrave.

Grainer-Ray, Sheri. 2004. *Gender Inclusive Game Design: Expanding the Market.* Hingham, Massachusetts: Charles Rivera Media.

Gray, Gaby. 2009. "The Interview: Jessica Valenti." *The Guardian,* May 9. Accessed January 25, 2010. http://www.guardian.co.uk/books/2009/may/10/jessica-valenti-feminist-blogger? INTCMP=ILCNETTXT3487.

Havenstein, Heather. 2007. "Death Threats Force Blogger to Sidelines." *Computerworld.* Accessed June 23, 2010. http://www.computerworld.com/s/article/9014647/Q_A_Death_Threats_Force_Blogger_to_Sidelines?intsrc=hm_list.

Head, Alison and Michael Eisenberg. 2010. "How Today's College Students Use Wikipedia for Course-Related Research." *First Monday* 15, no. 3 (March). Accessed June 20. http://www.uic.edu/htbin/cgiwrap/bin/ojs/index.php/fm/article/viewArticle/2830/2476.

Hill, Catherine, Christianne Corbett and Andresse St. Rose. 2010. "Why So Few? Women in Science, Technology, Engineering and Mathematics." *American Association of University Women.* Accessed June 5. http://www.aauw.org/ learn/research/whysofew.cfm.

Holland, Alison. 2002. "How the Other Half Plays." *The Age.* Accessed June 5, 2010. http://www.theage.com.au/articles/ 2002/05/25/1022243279705.html.

Lim, Sook and Nahyun Kwon. 2010. "Gender Differences in Information Behavior Concerning Wikipedia, an Unorthodox Information Source?" *Library and Information Science Research* 32, no. 3: 212-220.

Jesella, K. 2008. "Blogging's Glass Ceiling." *New York Times*, July 27. Accessed June 14, 2010. http://www.nytimes.com/2008/07/27/fashion/27blogher.html?_r=1.

Lenhart, Amanda, Kristin Purcell, Aaron Smith and Kathryn Zickuhr. 2010. "Social Media and Mobile Internet Use Among Teens and Young Adults." *Pew Internet and American Life Project.* Accessed June 15. http://www.pewinternet.org/Reports/2010/Social-Media-and-Young-Adults.aspx.

Maehre, Jeff. 2009. "What It Means to Ban Wikipedia: An Exploration of the Pedagogical Principles at Stake." *College Teacher* 57, no. 4: 229-236.

Manjoo, Farhad. 2009. "Is Wikipedia a Victim of Its Own Success?" *Time Magazine*, September 28. Accessed June 15, 2010. http://www.time.com/time/magazine/article/0,9171,1924492-2,00.html.

Mellström, Ulf. 2009. "The Intersection of Gender, Race and Cultural Boundaries, or Why Is Computer Science in Malaysia Dominated by Women?" *Social Studies of Science* 39, no. 6: 885-907.

Nakashima, Ellen. 2007. "Sexual Threats Stifle Some Bloggers." *The Washington Post,* April 30. Accessed June 20, 2010. http://www.washingtonpost.com/wpdyn/content/article/2007/04/29/AR 2007042901555.html.

"Rapleaf Study Reveals Gender and Age Data of Social Network Users." 2008. *Rapleaf.* Accessed June 25, 2010. http://www.rapleaf.com/business/ press_release/age.

Smith, Aaron. 2009. "The Internet's Role in Campaign 2008." *Pew Internet and American Life Project.* Accessed June 15, 2010. http://pewresearch.org/pubs/1192/internet-politics-campaign-2008.

Sussman, Matt. 2009. "Who Are the Bloggers? State of the Blogosphere, 2009." *Technorati.* Accessed June 24, 2010. http://technorati.com/blogging/article/ day-1-who-are-the-bloggers1/.

Sweeney, Tim. 2010. "The Internet Evolution 100." *Internet Evolution.* Accessed July 27, 2010. http://www.internetevolution.com/document.asp?doc_id=190304.

Sysmos, Inc. 2010. "Inside Blog Demographics." *Sysmos Company Blog.* Accessed June 28, 2010. http://www.sysomos.com/reports/bloggers/.

Tapia, Andrea and Lynnette Kvasny. May 22-24, 2004. "Recruitment Is Not Enough: Retention of Women and Minorities in the IT Workplace." Proceedings of the ACM SIGMIS CPR Conference, Tucson, Arizona. Accessed June 10, 2010. http://ist.psu.edu/faculty_pages/ lkvasny/publications.html.

Tam, Mo-Yin and Gilbert Bassett. 2006. "The Gender Gap in Information Technology" in *Removing Barriers: Women in Academic Science, Technology Engineering and Mathematics*, edited by Jill Bystydzienski and Sharon R. Bird, 108-22. Bloomington: Indiana University Press.

Taylor, Marisa. 2009. "Women Outnumber Men on Social-Networking." *Wall Street Journal Blogs.* Accessed June 15, 2010. http://blogs.wsj.com/digits/2009/10/07/women-outnumber-men-on-social-networking-sites/.

Thorpe, Vanessa and Richard Rogers. 2011. "Women Bloggers Call for a Stop to 'Hateful' Trolling by Misogynist Men." *The Guardian,* November 5. Accessed November 8, 2011. http://www.guardian.co.uk/ world/2011/nov/05/women-bloggers-hateful-trolling?newsfeed=true.

Traister, Rebecca. 2008. "A Blogosphere of Their Own." *Salon.com,* July 30. Accessed June 20, 2010. http://www.salon.com/life/broadsheet/2008/07/30/blogher_convention.

Turkle, Sherry. 1997. *Life on the Screen: Identity in the Age of the Internet.* New York: Simon & Schuster.

Wagner, Mitch. 2007. "Death Threats Force Designer to Cancel ETech Conference." *InformationWeek.* Accessed June 20, 2010. http://www.informationweek.com/blog/main/archives/2007/03/death_t hreats_f.html.

Walton, Marsha. 2009. "IT Jobs Offer Growth, but Women Are Bailing Out." *Women's eNews.* Accessed June 24, 2010. http://www.womensenews.org/story/women-in-science/100623/it-jobs-offer-growth-women-are-bailing-out.

Wright, M. 2009. "Women and Social Media. BlogHer, iVillage and Compass Partners." Accessed June 15, 2010. http://www.blogher.com/files/ 2009_Compass_BlogHer_Social_Media_Study_042709_FINAL.pdf.

WIDENING THE SCOPE
OF THE TRADITIONAL CLASSROOM:
TECHNOLOGY AND FEMINIST PEDAGOGY

CHAPTER ONE

FEMINIST WORLDING:
MEDIA ECOLOGIES LEARNING

KATIE KING, JARAH MOESCH,
AND THE STUDENTS OF SHARE IT!, A WOMEN'S STUDIES SENIOR
SEMINAR, UNIVERSITY OF MARYLAND, COLLEGE PARK

*In the middle of the room sat a large cardboard box overflowing with
surge protectors and extension cords, thoughtfully brought by one student
to share with the rest of us. Laptops everywhere, a large projection screen
on the wall, people flowing in and out of this feminist cyberspace created
by our students at the* Theorizing the Web *conference. Ah ha! For the first
time students got to feel out what the "People" part of the prototyping
process really meant: actual people to talk to, actual people to offer
comments and get excited, actual people to take the ideas on...Process,
process, process. This is what worlding means: activating spaces, activist
intentions, worlds everywhere.*[1] *More and more is networked among
activisms, even in this particularly disciplinary place.*

Katie: This year the senior seminar needed both of us. Jarah Moesch, a
professional technologist and multi-modal artist, and me, Katie King, a
scholar of, among other things, feminist technoscience. Together we are
prototyping a new sort of course, something the university wants to call
"scholarship and practice." Well, neither term is that easy to separate. In
fact, mixing them unexpectedly is what we wanted to do.[2]

Like our class, this essay is also a collaboration, one with Jarah, Katie,
the students of *Share It!*, using a range of social media tools, all engaged
together across time and media but also peopled face to face, spoken in
real time, distributed among internets, but also located in real space.[3] It
proceeds in sections; *gamestorming, social media learning, worn tools,
storytelling and prototyping*, and it ends with *learning to be affected:*

feminist worlding. It is interspersed with the cards our students wrote out on the last day of class to share with you, our readers. – And so, we begin.

Figure 1. Share It! Senior seminar presentation at the University of Maryland

Gamestorming

Jarah: When Katie calls me a professional technologist, that points more to the "technology" part of what I do – web development, time-based media (video, audio, performance), using and manipulating softwares – but for me the technology never stands alone. Ideas, structures, and technologies are always entangled: complicit and intrinsic to each other, a complex web of theories, histories, practices and power. They only appear separate.

I want my students to know this, to experiment, to play in a complex, thoughtful, and curious process. To this end, students in my classes spend time creating their own theoretical practice, beginning with what I affectionately call *gamestorming* – a cross between game design strategies, performance, play and brainstorming. I am a big fan of construction paper, markers, and glue. Paper gives us more ability to play; it is easier to use, to cross-off, add-on, crumple up, throw away, cut and paste, move around than the digital. It feels less permanent.

To get started this semester, we held an "activist-possibilities" card-sorting session (inspired by Mary Flanagan's *Grow A Game* cards).[4] The idea was to think through how ideas, values, and actions can come together in unexpected ways – to rely on each other for ideas, to cooperate, share, and trust within a system of feminist values and social media.

A last-day topic card:

CARD SORTING VALUES, from the *UMD Now* group:[5]
Tara Fischer, Charissa Powell, Angie Nedd

Card sorting is a great tool to encourage critical thinking, because with each switch of a card, you can form new views on the same idea, or you can go off into a different direction and come up with something new. There are endless possibilities.

Students were asked to identify a social issue they were concerned with, perhaps had done work for, or were passionate about. They each wrote their "issue" on a blank notecard. They then broke up into smaller groups and were given two decks of cards. Deck #1 included goals-based words, and deck #2 was action-based. Each group worked as a brainstorming team for each of their "issue" cards. They placed an issue card down then selected a "goals" card. They then brainstormed based on this mash-up of issue and goal. Ideas could be realistic, far-fetched, even fantastical. Then, they added a card from the "actions" deck and continued to brainstorm based on these added possibilities.

This way of entering into media making considers every action, every system, every space, as structurally embedded with beliefs and values that manifest themselves in very material ways, from a public city park to the spaces of the Internet. The same applies to uncritically using technologies to share content, learning, and teaching. By divorcing theory from practice, the classroom from the world, content from technology, students lose a huge learning opportunity, especially when it comes to feminist approaches to the world.

To communicate ideas or to create meaningful action, a media-maker must consider not only the content, but the form of the media, because interactions, the actions taken with the technology, must also create the very system that is being navigated and explored. In other words, media making enters into and incorporates digital architectures.

Mary Flanagan (2009) describes this process in relation to play:

Critical Play is built on the premise that, as with other media, games carry beliefs within their representation systems and mechanics. Artists using games as a *medium of expression*, then, manipulate elements common to games—representation systems and styles, rules of progress, codes of conduct, context of reception, winning and losing paradigms, ways of interacting in a game—for they are the material properties of games, much like marble and chisel or pen and ink bring with them their own intended possibilities, limitation, and conventions. (4)

What if students began to understand activism itself as a tool? Technology as methodology? What if intersectional feminisms were activated through creation and use of media?

If we think about students using activism as a "medium of expression" and then "manipulate" traditional activisms, such as community organizing, fundraising, lobbying, protesting, through the creation and jamming of multiple forms of media, we begin to get at a framework for gamestorming theoretical practices.

What if students began thinking, learning, teaching, and doing the technology itself in relation to the content? What if students explore, question, think about, and propose structural change based on the feminisms they have been learning about?

The purpose of gamestorming is to move beyond the norms inherent in activism and in social media and to begin thinking about other possibilities for social change. Some of the ideas generated could then be experimented with by morphing existing digital media, creating new methodologies for transmedia and transdisciplinary work.

A last day topic card:

PROTOTYPING, from the *Idea2Action* group:
Rachel Westbrook-Fritts, Carmen Atlee Loudon, Emily Hooper, Renee Leone

This class has been an excellent opportunity for us, as students, to experiment with prototyping in many senses. Not only is this class a prototype itself, but our project has also served as a crucial prototype, serving as a launching pad for future work and possibilities. In exploring US UNCUT, and documenting how an idea can be put into action and turn into a full-scale grassroots movement, we can use this prototype to not only further the movement, but also to create our own.

Social Media Learning

Katie: I was off to Sweden one week toward the last part of the course, just after spring break and just before we were scheduled to offer a workshop at the UMD *Theorizing the Web* conference.[6] Invited to help brainstorm the possibilities involved in an online distance learning gender studies curriculum, I was excited to meet with Swedish feminist tech folks, game developers, science studies grad students, feminist theorists, and British eLearning specialists. What I offered there came out of and returned back into the *Share It!* course:

> Whatever might be hopeful, innovative, exciting about offering a BA and MA in Gender Studies as a distance learning project comes in a necessarily altering infrastructure for gender studies, a very mixed bag of the commercial, of restructuring, and of the social ecological. These are what social media use to network today.
>
> I see Social Media in 2011 as FIRST an exercise in learning itself. Social media have a lot to teach us and our students about what learning is and even in five years those lessons will be of use. SECOND, social media are right now the very transmedia platforms and interfaces for all kinds of learning, formal and informal. We need to use them as such and to validate the kinds of learning that they foster, even as we also teach students now and later about their implication in systems of power. THIRD: social media are actually elements in larger ecologies which themselves "learn."
>
> Using social media for learning and directing analysis to social media at the same time are ways of understanding more clearly the many systems within which they are embedded and the forms of agency involved. These are not simply either human or technological, but rather call into question simple nature culture divisions, or human instrumentalisms, or agencies understood as forms of control and prediction.
>
> Emergence and self-organization are forms of connection that we all need to encounter and understand more carefully. They characterize the global financial systems mediated among media, some of the natural ecologies of which media are now actually elements in dynamic interaction, neurological rewards and attentions entertainment and educational media elicit, as well as operate more and more obviously as mechanisms of global social change. Social media are agencies in these in a range of striking forms today with implications for politics, ethics, and living.
>
> Just about every element of distance learning quite properly puts into perspective and could be used to make visible the very conditions of contemporary learning, how what we know about it is changing, and how it is interactive among knowledge ecologies in discontinuous layers, accretions and assemblages. Not all distance education is online or computer mediated. Not all distance education is never face to face. Not all

distance education is isolating or even individual. The value of distance education is paradoxically social, in that it rearranges who is where, with who else, and through what means.

Social media learning puts all that right up front. And despite the ways we may conceptualize social media, its ecologies are continuous with our many worlds, not something exclusively technological or even wholly media-driven. That these ecologies will change over the next five years is given. That gender studies will change over the next five years ought to be as given, as clearly dynamic and contingent.

Social media learning is thus a properly altering infrastructure for gender studies, whether for this very program or for any gender studies located anywhere today. One in which learning is the condition of both students and teachers in conditions emergent and self-organizing as global academic restructuring continues or is challenged or is altered. (*Social Media Learning: A Necessarily Altering Infrastructure for Gender Studies*)

Jarah: In my classrooms, students play, experiment, and reach out in areas they may not normally dabble in, to think, and when they want, to create. I encourage them to go beyond their comfort zone because although they may know how to use particular technologies, such as texting, social networking sites, or word processing, they also have areas of fear that prevent them from experimenting with what they think they know.

First, students come to the class with definitive attitudes about "technology" and the "Internet" – from fear around issues of privacy and safety, to believing that technology is objective and available to all, if only everyone can learn how to technically use it.

Second, although they may participate in social networking, most have never built web technologies or websites on their own. Part of this is due to the plug-n-play nature of our current web, internet, app culture, and part is due to the commodification of the Internet, all that purchasing, streaming, posting, and communicating across the walled gardens we use today.

Third, many students have never thought about how the technologies (hardware, such as the computer itself) and softwares (websites, forms, etc.) are created and deployed or what it means to participate with and through pre-determined systems of code and form. For many students, "it just works" – like turning on a faucet. Computers, phones, softwares are just accepted as is, not thought about socio-historically.

This really begins to get at my and Katie's hesitation to use the term "digital native." It is a far-too-simple term even to describe that particular age group which was born into a world filled with technology, and having grown up with it, purportedly has an easier time comprehending it and using it.

We still have to encourage them and ourselves to think critically about and to de-naturalize all our experience, teaching students to create research questions of their own which then enable them to learn, explore, and share through their own critical thinking process. To get them there, we provide a workshop atmosphere, with small working groups, and an open framework to encourage thinking.

How do you create this framework? Shift students from consumer and "sharer" to (the mindset of) system creator. Get them thinking about how an application, software, or technology is made, its purpose, and how the underlying systems and infrastructures work. Start with the search engine.

But you cannot expect a student to re-think a search engine when they come to it thinking that it is simply an objective place to search for information. They first need to understand it as a producer of specialized information, based on particular data-sets, handled by both people and algorithms, resulting in a much-manipulated stream of information. To this end, *I had our students perform as a search engine.*

We began by thinking about our own individual digital footprints. What technologies do you own and use? What online services do you use regularly? Where are you on the Internet? What happens when you use a search engine to look for yourself? Are you surprised by the results? What do these results say about you as a person? Does it describe your identity(ies)? Are there items missing? How might the missing information change how people who do not know you understand you?

Some students had written for their high-school newspapers, and these were still available. Others interned, volunteered, or worked for non-profits, so their names were affiliated with particular organizations working on singular issues. A couple were mentioned in family member obituaries. Interestingly, many students were not readily accessible via search – either because they had "locked down" their information in Facebook or did not use social networking at all, or they had a very common name or shared a name with someone more famous than themselves, so they did not appear on the first few pages.

After learning what information was publicly available about their names, they broke up into groups, with one person playing the search engine, and the others, the searchers. The searchers entered the name of the person "playing" the search engine, along with keywords to gain potential information, and the "search engine" responded with the information that they knew was actually available online. This meant for example that one student who shares a name with a semi-popular porn star had to return information about herself that was not actually about her. Students then introduced each other to the rest of class with the information they received via the search performance.

This workshop enabled students to begin thinking about the underlying systems that form our digital realities, both enabling and disallowing certain types of data to be in/visible. By investigating how we use a search engine to "ask" for information, students began to understand how and why search engines give us particular answers. We then discussed how certain bits of data were prioritized over others and what information is more visible, less visible, depending on how the information was layered and manipulated.

Such learning enables us to reconceptualize knowledges and structures, allows us to engage new ways of looking as well as to create across ecologies. Only after all of that work can we ask, what would a *feminist* search engine look like?

A last day topic card:

> STORYTELLING, from the *Queer Bloggers* group: Joanna "Jojo" Damiano, Rafaela Spencer
>
> The process of creating our blog WHAT'S HAPPENING LGBT is a story. In class we told this story through the various activities Jarah had us do such as creating a storyboard. The symposium allowed us to tell our story through a graph of progress. An excerpt of our story is how we progressed from a broad idea to a narrow idea. An even better example is our blog posts themselves.

Worn Tools

Katie: Feminist students come to a social media class with lots of worries, as do feminist teachers. *What is there to worry about?* Since it is impossible to disentangle any project for online or distance learning today from the politics of economic restructuring, must one buy into such politics when creating these courses or curricula? How does one keep from somehow disabling women's studies and its epistemological commitments when participating in these complex political and economic ecologies? I think the whole point is to make THAT central concern the very heart of any such curriculum: to use it to investigate these very issues with the tools that emerge from this nexus.

What else is there to worry about? There are undeniable gender, race, and labor gaps in technology use, a bunch of so-called digital divides.[7]

Each of these are variously organized in particular places across varying axes of: development and commercialization of broadband, computer availability, media rich and poor environments; knowledge and interest disparities commons and privatizations; as well as family and school resources, literacies and languages. As with other elements of social life, all these are unevenly distributed, subject to macro and micro political power and are agencies for oppression and liberation. Our use of unevenly distributed resources, the very material limitations on their use for distance learning, is itself a subject for intersectional feminist analysis for project-driven, policy-sensitive, constructivist practice.

Working with media is likely to be social rather than individual, context and situation dependent, and continually re-crafted in practice that is sometimes individual and often collective. The ways in which students and teachers participate in this work are not platform specific, which matters a lot when thinking over time, but instead crisscross cultural referents, technology workarounds, and media contexts. These are *constellations*, subject to experimentation by students and teachers who occupy a range of locations and collectivities amid social media ecologies.

Personally I prefer to use what I call "worn tools." That is, absolutely *not* whatever the latest this or that is. Thus in my own classes I use materials that are, first, *public* and commercially available for free, have been around a while, and are the clunkier versions of the type. I add materials to my toolkit in either bursts of dopamine driven pleasurable intensity or a little bit at a time in the evening for relaxation, maybe while listening to audiobooks. Right now I usually work with Blogger, YouTube, and Google Images, Books, Search, Maps, Documents, and Visualizations; occasionally supplemented by iTunes, Twitter, Second Life and Facebook; and other tools as they fall into my lap, like Jing or Scribd.

All of my courses now have an accompanying website that I use for multimedia class presentation (I rarely use PowerPoint).[8] I use Blogger as my website authoring convenience for classes and for talk sites when internet access is easy and I have multimedia to share. Although I began using WebCT in 2005, my university's move in 2007 to Blackboard coincided with my own disillusionment with these gated learning systems, which I abandoned then in favor of these tools I have mentioned. At that time it was difficult to use multimedia in Blackboard. Of course that is no longer true, and one of my much appreciated neighbors in the online virtual world Second Life is an award winning application developer for Blackboard, so I still hear about some of the latest bells and whistles now and then.

Nevertheless, I like being public on the web, a person professing, not in a gated learning community, and I also value that students using Blackboard mostly learn how to use Blackboard, but when they socialize via media, they can use it for many purposes. And so can their teachers.

Jarah: I love Katie's concept of the worn tool – not new, publicly available, free, an addition to the toolkit. It allows room to play with and experiment around technologies without having to be an early adopter who uses the tool "appropriately."

Blogging softwares, such as Blogger and WordPress, could easily be understood as worn tools, but in fact only a couple of our students had ever commented on any blog or had their own sites. The reason why social media knowledge is uneven is two-fold. First, individual tools are used or appropriated according to market forces and demographics, and second, our students, the so-called digital natives, are already trained on individual tools but do not necessarily understand the larger systems within which these products are deployed.

For most of them learning how to use the course blogging workspace was a difficult process. For workshopping we used a WordPress site, which I configured to allow them all to register and then to be in control over their posts in many very granular ways.

Interestingly, the most difficult part was the registration process. Only a handful of students managed to do it without having difficulties. This is not because they are not capable but because the registration process makes assumptions about who is using the form. The registration content assumed prior knowledge of blogs, using the particular language and taxonomies for speaking about blogs, which meant that our students, some of whom had no such prior knowledge, did not understand the language or the standards that were normalized in the form, making it difficult to figure out the process.

So, worn tools for one person are new tools for someone else. What I love and find easy, you may find difficult, and what I find difficult you may love and even be expert at. These knowledges get spread amongst the students as they learn and share with each other.

Once students were appropriately registered for the course workspace, it became much easier for them to do the broader, less granular posting, uploading of images, and categorization. Where WordPress's registration form failed through knowledge assumptions, it succeeded within the mechanisms of the site itself. Their use of web standards and best practices make it easier for people to use new tools since these are similar enough to students' own worn tools. Because most of our students used social networking and all used email, they already understood subject lines and attachments, including uploading images and creating blog posts.

In this particular case, students relied on us and on each other as they learned in order to become proficient with the tool. This, though, is simply training, not real learning. Students are trained on individual tools, such as how to use a search engine, or how to use a blog, but unless we teach them to think about the tools themselves and what they are doing, they will always be simply users instead of thinkers, creators, and people with the ability to create workarounds.

They do not need to become experts in particular tools; playing and experimenting are the most important part of the learning process, but they do need to be able to think conceptually about overarching systems, which will break them away from their fear of learning and succeeding at one particular tool, and instead allow them to feel comfortable not knowing how to do a particular something, and to try it anyway.

This is why I like to look at worn tools from a larger, categorical version of system standards. Instead of Blogger and WordPress, or even blogs themselves, students investigate how interactive web pages use similar standards and practices and question the larger systems of knowledge, thereby allowing them to feel comfortable testing and playing, instead of feeling "trained" for a particular tool.

If students learn and teach conceptually, for example, about how blogs, social networking, email, and even online shopping are similar in structural process then, regardless of what the particular tool is, students will feel comfortable testing, playing, trying a wide range of tools within a similar structure. Anything related to these concepts, even when shiny and new, become worn tools more readily.

A last day topic card:

COLLABORATION, from the *Sex+++* group:[9] Jana Young, Anjalee Sharma, Kara DeMillo

Through the WMST 488 senior seminar we as a group have collaborated on the micro level among ourselves. We've also collaborated on a macro level with the community at the Theorizing the Web Conference, and with class mates during the development stages, and the community at large by conducting a survey through Facebook.com and Surveymonkey.com.

Storytelling and Prototyping

Katie: I was playing around on Facebook one day last year and saw in my news feed another report about her classroom experiments posted by Cathy Davidson, co-founder of the Humanities, Arts, Science, and Technology Advanced Collaboratory (HASTAC) at Duke University.[10] Drawing on the *Learning, Freedom and the Web* project online, Davidson posted about their five-part process for collaborative construction.[11] I got so excited I decided that I had to use it in the *Share It!* course I was then designing. Indeed, as became clear later on, this process ended up not only structuring the course and being the central process Jarah and I offered our students for their use but also turned out to be the process through which we prototyped the class itself, imagining future iterations down the road. (Oh, and by the way, Jarah is a HASTAC scholar, one of their fellows in a program intended to promote innovation in learning, media, art and scholarship.)

1. **Strategy** – what's your big idea?
2. **Story** – help people understand it.
3. **Tools** – set up simple tools that make it easy for contributors to see what's happening and get involved.
4. **People** – who are you trying to reach? how can they help right now?
5. **Prototype** – build fast. test and improve it together.
   (Shake and repeat.)

This hands-on approach to learning went especially well with one of our books too. Its title, *Hanging Out, Messing Around and Geeking Out* (Ito, et al. 2009) is drawn from the *genres of participation* described by actors in this final research report of a large US MacArthur Foundation project hubbed both at the University of Southern California and at the University of California at Berkeley.[12] This meta-analysis of twenty odd collaborative research projects investigated how youth – from a range of diverse venues in the US and from the first teen years through college – use social media.

A single student, for example, could be, say, "hanging out" with various collectivities, project-driven or place-specific or interface-specific, gathering information, attending demonstrations, participating in information sharing and conversation, indeed mobilizing multiple media intensively to cross platforms, constituencies and forms, online, in mobile space, in real time, or as archived.

My own bottom-up experiences entering into gender studies from the 1970s on found resonances with this terminology. I came to the studies of gender through group practice and sharing associated first with the women's liberation movement and other progressive movements of my time and place, thus "hanging out." I entered academic practice as a student through collaborations with teachers who were academically far more sophisticated but in terms of the new knowledges often as much a beginner as I was, thus together "messing around." And finally I became a teacher myself as gender studies, women's studies, feminist studies were institutionalized and disciplined, and as theory-driven analysis was often replaced or in better circumstances, supplemented by disciplinary method-driven analysis, thus "geeking out."

As the Digital Youth Project report demonstrates, hanging out, messing around, and geeking out are ways of considering and working with the ebb and flow of intensity and possibly here. The typical and the possible are often at odds when most folks cannot participate in something that some more intensively invested group can. Expertise itself is a kind of exclusive intensity as "geeking out," but one can practice geeking out in one sort of media practice while simultaneously hanging out or messing around in others, and with various others.

Workarounds can be about getting around the rules, from those of social organization along axes of illegitimate power, to media ownership and property rights, to the gatekeeping of identities of expertise, to access to the Internet. We had some dramatic examples of workarounds recently when the government of Egypt cut off internet access, and folks used the workaround of calling friends in other countries on the phone to publish their tweets on breaking news and events.

Learning and teaching with and about social media as a feminist project collectively quite possibly works with all three of these genres of participation, and they, despite my personal trajectory here, do not reflect increasing mastery – either of a field or set of fields themselves, or by individuals initiated into that mastery – but something rather more interesting, flexible, and generative. A trajectory of mastery is precisely what it does not exclusively celebrate, but actually rearranges – with, I think, implications for better ways of understanding and teaching among feminist knowledge worlds.

Jarah: I always ask my students what they are passionate about. Then I ask them to reconceptualize how they know it. Gamestorming cards, storyboarding, and prototyping all provide frameworks for critical thought and play but how each student experiments, designs, and plays is up to them.

Storyboarding

Storyboarding in the traditional sense is a narrative taking you from start to finish: beginning, middle and end. But our students' stories were not simply one narrative; instead, they were about sites of conflict, action, erasure, told through their chosen tools, which also have stories. Understanding that these cannot be disconnected from the learning environment, the tools themselves, the institutional and social structures they are created in, all deeply impact any mapping, storyboarding or protoyping of activist projects. Here is a story link, a kind of worm-hole to seeing our students in action at their WordPress workshopping and archive site: http://femsocmedia.wordpress.com.

One student began by re-thinking the idea of the classroom to invite non-students to learn from our class. He chose to use Twitter as a platform to experiment with and began tweeting key points and ideas, furthering underused classroom knowledges. From this he joined with another student to create an online presence for campus activists to share their experiences, organizing skills, and historical information over time. The larger story is the same – rethinking the classroom – but the process of getting there has many different stories, many different paths. Experimenting with different approaches brings different, sometimes surprising, twists and results.

A last day topic card:

FEMINIST ACTIVISMS, from the *F.urthering U.nderused C.ollective K.nowledge* group:[13] Eva Steinhorn and Anton Medvedev

Course: Deanna Zandt [in *Share This!*] shows how in this social media sphere feminists are able to generate and share ideas and provides tools to do so.

Joss Hands' *@ is for activism* (2010), while not expressly related to feminist activism, shows how the anti-globalization movement employed alternative media centers (Indy Media) to spread activist updates and in, for, through non-traditional channels. Furthermore, Internet networks were essential in spreading indigenous knowledge from the Zapatistas to the world. This framework could benefit feminists working transnationally.

Our project: our website acknowledges that every generation of activists has valuable lessons to teach and creates intergenerational links between campus activists.

Learning To Be Affected: Feminist Worlding

Katie: "Bring in your laptops and share!" I ask students in all my classes, to their sometime amazement. These are my opportunities too to hang out, mess around, and geek out, to experiment in a media intensive environment, to play around and see if, say, twitter works for sharing class content or organizing projects. "Write for the Wikipedia!" I beg them, and we discuss how all sorts of women, especially those of color, people of color generally are needed to write and edit it, and how reading the history section of its articles opens onto disputes underneath what seems like authority.

"It's okay to play Angry Birds, IF that helps you to entangle yourself into our class discussion. If it doesn't, do what does." And we discuss how Cathy Davidson's new book on the sciences of attention points out that learning requires unfocusing as well as focusing.[14] It turns out, for example, that the neurotransmitter dopamine controls what one might call the gate to working memory. Steady stimulation, at even high levels of joyful play, keep this so-called gate closed and permit increasing absorption. But the gate opens whenever there is an increase or decrease of stimulation. Then new information enters for reorganization, and the gate closes again. As Davidson analyzes it, momentary delightful distractions performed periodically, say, bits of Angry Birds or Facebook, can actually increase our ability to refocus afterwards; they facilitate learning in those moments between absorptions when the "gate" opens and closes.

How do we all learn how to notice these, learn how to work well among a ranging ecology of social media, learn how to engage our very bodily sensitivities among worldly processes?

I myself practice, model, display, and talk about what Vinciane Despret (2004) and Bruno Latour (2004) call "learning to be affected." Vinciane Despret is a French philosopher of psychology who teaches us to rethink a tale of classic research methodology, the one about the so-called "Clever Hans effect." Rather than a debunking tale in which a famous horse is cleverly revealed as only appearing to do mathematical calculations, while in reality it is "merely" reading the reactions of the humans around him, Despret's retold story turns out to be about clever bodies and things which, at the very edge of apprehension, attune themselves to one another: an interactive agency we can call "learning to be affected." (2004, 113) Relaying this story[15] and adding his own patterns of meaning to it, Bruno Latour, one of the architects of so-called actor-network theory in the social studies of science, uses the idea to describe what happens when a perfume expert learns to become a "nose" (in the parlance of the trade), that is, learns to distinguish very subtle ranges of smell by training with an "odor kit," a device organized in a careful palette of small differences. Learning to be affected here entails "a dynamic trajectory by which we learn to register and become sensitive to what the world is made of" (2004, 206). Bodies and things, processes and interactivities, are all engaging together in the many possibilities across "learning to be affected." Social media learning also works across redistributed agencies, ones not located simply in the consciousness of individual humans in seeming control but rather ones emergent across media and beings and economies and neurobiological systems. Hanging out, messing around, and geeking out, with and on the part of students, teachers, and the very media themselves, names another range of possible practices, affecting and being affected.

In the language of media economies, USC scholar of film and communication Henry Jenkins (2006) calls the thought-out strategies for gathering bits of such interactivity "transmedia storytelling" (95). That term describes an artistic and/or industrial choreography of sensations, technology platforms, commercial franchises, and the various commodities themselves coming together to tell collective stories. These stories are hunted for and gathered by media users who patch together bits of such interconnecting story lines from comics, films, tv, advertising, toys, journalism, music, and internet, across vertical and horizontal forms of industry economies of integration. Cross platforming, multi-commercial appeals to all the senses are in industrial cases mined for profit. But this term has artistic resonances too, as arts and universities become intertwined with globally restructuring knowledge work.

So how then do we position social justice concerns, transdisciplinary knowledge worlds, women's studies classes and practices among these self-organizing systems in which we are embedded today? How do we teach our students about these, model and practice attunement in sensitizing and liberatory forms?

With our students we troll the web looking for "transmedia activisms" and "transdisciplinary intersectional feminisms." And we examine who "we" – beings, processes, things, practices – are becoming. We discover our own new embodiments, layered and distributed, as we discover new bits of worldliness too. Social media learning is a practice that includes us as some of the self-organizing elements in emergent worlds: across platforms, across feminisms, across stories, across activisms, across changes in which we do not own the action but in which we matter.

A last day topic card:

OFFERING, from the *UMD International Women (half the sky)* group: Maariya Bassa, Leslie Bademosi, Fatoumata Bangoura

What we offered:
• awareness of global injustices through social media outlets
• offered opportunity to volunteer with different organizations that specialized in our interests

"We are offering social media tools to spread awareness of social injustice women face all over the world.

Jarah: Katie spoke earlier about our offering to the class Cathy Davidson's five-part process for collaborative construction, as it is a useful framework for a theoretical practice. By providing a support structure for students to hang their ideas on, they are free to organize themselves across multiple platforms, engaging affectively with their own particular social activisms.

This process is similar to, but more open than, those commercial frameworks for creating interactive projects: purpose, goals, audience, functional specifications, interface design, visual design, wire framing, technical / code development, testing, launch. These are items that must be done in a very particular order to get the desired results in a flow chart for implementation: when you know the outcome you are looking for, you can build towards that idea to obtain the desired result.

In relationship to the women's studies classroom, or any disciplinary set of practices, it is similar to how, after students learn to recognize institutional and structural forms of oppression, they head off to internships with non-profit activist organizations so they can take action on "issues" that inspire them. They focus on community organizing and activism, enabling them to gain first-hand knowledge on supporting those affected by a particular issue, caused by structural oppressions. They are promised meaningful, hands-on experiences, training and skills for their resume, and the ability to take on leadership roles. While I do not dismiss this, it too is a specific disciplining framework, done in a particular order to obtain a desired result: learn through reading, writing, and discussing, then take action within what (it seems to me) is an already failing system.

By offering Cathy Davidson's process as a framework, which itself is open to change ("repeat") and also opening students to multiple modes of exploration, process, and play ("shake" as in gamestorming, performance, and genres of participation), then – using activism as a tool and technology as methodology – students create their own affective theoretical practice, one that allows them to break away from any disciplining that places them in an already failing system and allows them to re-work it from the ground up.

Dropping pathways and repeating processes are not only accepted, they are encouraged. Moving from one idea to the next, expanding and then refining, choosing different tools for different moments and needs help the student to re-know, to re-think, and to re-arrange their world.

Student's newly created theoretical practices are not completed insular projects. Instead they allow multiple worlds to coalesce, break-apart, and re-emerge, activated through our class and then shifted out into the worlds of activist practices and processes as new beginnings.

Jarah and Katie sit together, facing each other, laptops at hand. We talk and write and edit each other's stuff on Google Docs, rearranging lines and inserting words and punctuation. "I will close out the draft now, you move that around." "Which feedback card goes in this section?" Or, "Let's stop and eat!" Katie intends to redo the social media class in the next year or so, carrying what she has learned from Jarah about critical play to the next iteration. Jarah is continuing her gamestorming practices with other students and will take Katie's feminist technoscience scholarship along for the ride. As we sit and write and eat together, collaborating across spacetime, using the Internet, we begin to think about pastfutures; more iterations of our processes, based on pathways both previous and unknown. Shake and repeat.

Bibliography

Despret, Vinciane. 2004. "The Body We Care for: Figures of Anthropo-zoo-genesis." *Body & Society* 10, no. 113: 111-134.

Flanagan, Mary. 2009. *Critical Play: Radical Game Design*. Cambridge, MIT Press.

Hands, Joss. 2010. *@ is for Activism: Dissent, Resistance and Rebellion in a Digital Culture*. London: Pluto Press.

Ito, Mizuko, Heather A. Horst, Judd Antin, Megan Finn, Arthur Law, Annie Manion, Sarai Mitnick, David Schlossberg and Sarita Yardi.

2009. *Hanging Out, Messing Around and Geeking Out: Kids Living and Learning with New Media*. Cambridge: The MIT Press.

Jenkins, Henry. 2006. *Convergence Culture: Where Old and New Media Collide*. New York: NYU Press.

King, Katie. 2011. *Social Media Learning: A Necessarily Altering Infrastructure for Gender Studies*, March 29. http://socmedlearn.blogspot.com/.

Latour, Bruno. 2004. "How to Talk About the Body? The Normative Dimension of Science Studies." *Body & Society* 10, no. 2: 205-229.

Notes

[1] "Worlding" is a term shared by Donna Haraway and now others; see for example, Donna Haraway *When Species Meet* (University of Minnesota Press 2007), 19.

[2] The website for the class is located at: http://femsocmedia.blogspot.com/

[3] The title for the course is based on one of the books we used in it: Deanna Zandt, *Share This! How You Will Change the World with Social Networking* (Berrett-Koehler Publishers 2010).

[4] You can see an online version of the cards at: http://www.tiltfactor.org/grow-a-game Some discussion of the whole issue of values and gaming in relation to the cards is online at: http://www.valuesatplay.org/?page_id=6

[5] The group's website is at: http://umdnow.wordpress.com/

[6] Information about the conference is at: http://www.cyborgology.org/theorizingtheweb/index.html and our workshop site is at: http://theowebsocmed.blogspot.com/

[7] For a range of transnational divides among the digital, see the Digital Divide Institute (DDI). Online at: http://www.digitaldivide.org/

[8] Links to some of Katie's course sites online: http://katiekin.weebly.com/teaching.html

[9] This group's website is at: http://sexpositiveliberation.blogspot.com/

[10] Information about Davidson: http://hastac.org/users/cathy-davidson/

[11] Website at: http://learningfreedomandtheweb.org/ One Davidson post on the subject is online at: http://hastac.org/blogs/cathy-davidson/how-prototype-first-you-get-it-wrong

[12] The final report is online at: http://digitalyouth.ischool.berkeley.edu/ report

[13] This group's website is at: http://fumd.wordpress.com/

[14] Cathy Davidson (2011). *Now You See It: How the Brain Science of Attention Will Transform the Way We Live, Work, and Learn* (Viking Adult, 2011). See also the book's blog site online at: http://www.cathydavidson.com/

[15] Used this way, "relaying" is another term and idea shared by Donna Haraway, "SF: Science Fiction, Speculative Fabulation, String Figures, So Far: The Pilgrim Award Speech," delivered by DVD in Lublin, Poland, July 7, 2011. Video online at: http://people.ucsc.edu/~haraway/PilgrimAward.html

Chapter Two

Counterculture, Craftsmanship, and Cyberspace Connectivity: Considerations of Contemporary Feminist Zines in/as/of Art Education

Courtney Lee Weida

Girl zines provide a glimpse of the future of feminism.
—Sarah Hentges, *Pictures of Girlhood:*
Modern Female Adolescence on Film

Unlikely Introductions: My Zine Nature

I have a confession to make. I am an assistant professor, an artist, a feminist, a former K-12 educator, *and a zine writer* (or zinester). While I relish teaching formal university courses on studio art, art history, and art education theory, I also delight in the ever evocative, sometimes despairing and often hilarious subcultural world of zines as a part of art education. I love the hand-bound and taped pages, scrawled and personalized fonts, and generally intimate nature of these small books. I am inspired by their rawness and honesty as scraps of autobiographical musings and global questions pasted into the Xeroxed pages. I also enjoy submitting essays, articles, bits of art, and poetry to hand-made, communal, and youth-oriented publications.

Although it is tempting to contrast the slick, anesthetic, manufactured quality of computer-based production with the very old-fashioned, artisanal techniques and appearances of handmade zines, this can be an oversimplification. Although I would classify zines as wonderfully rugged, jagged, and sticky, they can also be digital in their formatting, fonts, and Xeroxed qualities. The zine genre occupies the space between objects that are manufactured or mass-produced and things that are crafted and one of a kind (often abbreviated online as OOAK). Zines can model, embody, and question that digital/manual balance, particularly within their discursive and communal cultures. Kylie Peppler and Yasmin Kafai (2009) have suggested that for young people, "artistic, media, and technological connections form the basis for a complex set of contemporary practices, expanding what it means to be truly fluent in today's multimedia landscape well beyond traditional forms of print literacy" (49). This chapter investigates zine processes online and on paper as artistic, literary, and pedagogical practices of feminist inquiry. Zines explore the greater political scene of gender, sexuality, and reproductive rights, *and* the realms of personal testimonials and individual experiences. Keeping in mind the persistence of zines alongside blogs and other digital media, the following sections will examine both cyberculture and craft cultures of feminist zines and their creators.

Zines on the Screen and on the Page: Examining Digital Impacts and Connections

Although many young people are blogging on Facebook, LiveJournal, and to a lesser extent, Myspace; others continue to document, draw, and collage their art and writing onto zines composed upon old-fashioned copy paper. Physically, most print zines I have encountered are comprised of standard printer paper, folded in half, and stapled. Their content often overlaps with material found in blogs, including such items as photographs, diary-like entries, poetry, art, and cut-and-pasted content from other sources. Zine researcher Alison Piepmeier (2009) has noted that while "blogs and zines are often conflated, zine creators know that the material matters, and they repeatedly identify zines as a paper medium." She also emphasizes that "blogs have not replaced zines" and observes that many young women create both zines and blogs (63). In my experience, zines encompass politics and the public sphere in their PSAs (public service announcements), community-related information, and other political content, in ways that are typically more radical and politically-engaged than many blogs may be. Comparing blogs and zines, zine historian Jennifer Bleyer (2004) has similarly observed that webpages "are pretty closely related to zines – rants, raves, diary entries, some photographs, perhaps some poetry, yet often nothing politicized" (58). In contrast, Bleyer described zines as "the intersection of art, protest, confession, and theory" (49).

Both the politicized content and the materiality of zines raise comparisons with the continuum of printed news media. Zinester and zine collector Seth Friedman (1997) has classified zines as "writing that's unlike anything else in the mainstream: more opinionated than newspaper editorials, more personal than magazine articles, more topical than books" (1). While zines focus upon materiality and political messages, they may often retreat from declarations of authorship and identity in various ways. We may note that zines are often associated with authorial contact information including only pseudonyms, defunct websites, or college email addresses. The zinester who created *What's Her Deal?* observed that her zine took 6-7 years to create, and yet she priced it for merely $1 and without any form of internet contact: "I'm not on the internet or anything." Like many other zinesters I know, she ultimately contributed this zine to a library collection where it persists in a unique archival context, as a sort of ephemera-turned-artifact. Some zines only list a physical address at a college as contact information, suggesting an authorial and artistic choice to focus upon a particular and often transitional moment in time, instead of emphasizing the identity of the artist, one's presence in cyberspace, or any lasting artistic mark on the world. In this way, I believe zines speak uniquely to tensions and dualities surrounding female authorship and artistic presence. For instance, *aberration*, a zine by a Wisconsin pre-med student named Monica, laments the writer's experience of loss and transition. Juxtaposing medical processes of digestion with fragments of a tale of urban unrequited love, she observes:

> ...he has left me behind in this city, but no: he left me as soon as he arrived. i am beginning to get used to this, now. i wonder what i will leave behind in this city: traces of rubber soles off my shoes, sloughed off on rough pavement, dollars and cents for records and cds and food and coffee and tees and zines and transportation: i am always going somewhere, never keeping still.

Zines themselves do not typically keep still, passing from reader to reader and representing the passing thoughts of transitional students and young people. Paradoxically, zine culture may outlast other print media that have moved to a digital format, as zines are material and continue to provide texture, color, and formatting that can only be experienced as part of an interaction with the hand-made object. For instance, *CHiNesE SwEAtSHoP* is a digital and print zine that was conceived as a sort of newsletter for friends of the creator. Interestingly, creator Elsie Sampson collects any ephemera at hand in order to record various musings and news items and later collages them into a print edition. Sampson also notes, problematically, some overlap of mass production of zines by hand with processes of sweatshop labor. For me, this somewhat startling point calls attention to the significant amount of personal time and effort that zines inevitably entail. One cannot create a zine without substantial labor (of love) that is non-negotiable, even if the content itself can later be scanned, advertised, and experienced through the Internet. It is difficult to document the amount of labor and profit actually involved with zine-making. Typically, this is not a focus of discussion, and their creators frequently call zines a "labor of love." However, zines are some of the only independently (or self) published works found in university libraries. These considerations are particularly relevant aspects of zines as hybrid, digital artforms.

Zine Angst: Functions, Artifacts, and Archives of Zines

If making a zine by hand entails much more effort than typing a few entries into a blog, why do young women persist in creating them? Writing about teenagers and subtle sexism, Susan Douglas (2010) has observed that "adolescents in America are expected to be restless, rebellious, defiant of adult society…but girls are supposed to conform to pre-existing (mostly male) standards of beauty and behavior, to comply, to obey…How is that for an impossible place to stand?" (53). Zines can pose a self-made space of possibility and inquiry, exhibiting alternatives to narrow concepts of fandom, teenage angst, and commercially-condoned expressions of creativity and resistance for young women. For example, *girl swirl fanzine* includes empowering calls to the reader: "Protect Yourself! Do not be another victim. Fuck shit up." *Girl swirl fanzine* also counters the "conventional wisdom" of avoiding unwanted sexual advances by shunning provocative clothing and instead gives young women fashion tips to wear sunglasses to avoid eye contact with a predator, to wear shoes that allow for running or slipping off easily, and to forget feminine modesty that might slow oneself down in a fight. Rather than emphasize safety over personal expression, the zine questions conceptions of femininity that marginalize young women and their bodies, offering alternatives.

It may be noted that while zines are often products of adolescents, there are many zines in circulation that are written by and about adults that also interrogate gender. For instance, *leeking INK* is a Baltimore zine about topics ranging from adult pregnancy, menstruation, work and travel to many other aspects of adult life. Perhaps the most prominent current resource addressing the vast range of feminist zines is digital: *The Global Grrrl Zine Network*, a web directory of zines (much like a *distro* or zine distribution service). Echoing the *Riot Girl Newsletter* and *Action Girl*

Newsletter of the 1990s, the website features self-made and published zines spanning categories of grrl, lady, queer, trans, and folk zine cultures. *The Global Grrrl Zine Network* also subtly reconfigures language and status online, with references to *webmistresses* of online zines and distros (instead of webmasters). Sherry Turkle, Director of MIT's Initiative on Community and the Self, has observed that traditionally some women "identified being a woman with all that a computer is not, and computers with all that a woman is not" (1998, 270). In digital craft communities, the assertion of female identity is often prominent in declarations of digital space such as "riot grrl," "craft grrl," or "grrl zine" online communities.

For educators, this distinction in zines underscores the potential of digital media to address gender and artistic identities. We can begin to question representation and identification in terms of virtual and physical realities.

Further, Malcolm McCullough, a writer on craft and urban computing, has examined how "networks make artifacts more transmissible, and provide more settings for comparisons and discussions of practice, than do their grassroots traditional craft counterparts" (1998, 270). In the case of zines, online networks allow readers to connect with the zinester, to explore webpages related to references in the zine, and/or to locate related zines. Many zines function as a sort of directory, containing references or detailed information about other zines and zinesters. Bleyer has similarly observed that the ways in which we subscribe to and collect zines is artistic, noting that the zines she has acquired over time are like "artifacts in my own personal museum" (49). As structures of reference and acquisition, the *Global Grrrl Zine Network* and other online directories provide a context as well as an archive for zines and bring them into conversation with one another. Further, this website exhibits the overlap and dialogue of many of the feminist zines currently in circulation and collections. Additional information defining zines and zine makers may be found in a specialized wiki, zinewiki.com, which is the Wikipedia of independent media. This site is collaborative and editable by users, a distinction that is perhaps uniquely appropriate in the context of a strong contributing zine community. Unlike Wikipedia, these sites challenge expectations of hypertext, often referring the reader not to another link or webpage on the computer screen but rather to physical zines. As I peruse these sites and discuss them with students studying education and gender theory, we find that zines can both enhance online journaling and transgress the borders of the computer screen and digital networks.

Zine Roles: Collectors and Crafters

As an educator and artist who has worked in both schools and museums, physical elements of collage and collection intrigue me within my recent readings and interpretations of zines. Zines document an assemblage of personal handwriting, traces of the tape the author used in cutting and pasting, and other visible connections of language and visual art between the zine's creator and the reader. Craft researcher Bruce Metcalf has observed a "crucial opposition stance [in that] the hand-made object is widely understood as the antithesis of mass-produced anonymity" (2007, 21). In this way, zines are distinctly personal among a range of manufactured objects that occupy the physical space of our lives. However, scanning in original zines and converting them to pdfs is one reconciliation of the computer with the hand-crafted object. Other zinesters transitioned naturally from typing and photocopying to typing and uploading. Personal voice, artworks, and confessional writing persist in both formats. Zines might be seen as digital double agents because they are part of cyberspace and yet often exhibit frameworks and sentiments that are antithetical to digital journaling.

Even the pages of physical zines may be hand-bound with yarn or thread, showing the zinester's interest in crafting materials over traditional hardware of staples or paperclips. Specifically, *aberration # 13* is hand-bound, decorated with yarn, and enclosed in a red paper cover. Zines may be linked with hand-made artists' books in this regard, which are also characterized by artistic binding, hand-made paper, and hand-written typography. In some cases, zines even use simple printmaking processes, as hand-made books often do. Within both artists' books and zine formats, there is a conscious artistic choice to create within a structure that is increasingly archaic, yet aesthetically and symbolically meaningful. Additionally, from an archival perspective, we find that hand-bound books and zines frequently outlast those that are merely stapled, demonstrating a certain concern for temporality and readership.

However, zines on the whole are not as carefully nor prescriptively created as many hand-made artists' books, and this is an important distinction that relates to their immediacy and freshness. As the Radical Art Girls stated in their 2001 zine of the same title, "art is not based in a system of competition and comparison. Some of the most stunning artwork, layout and writing I have experienced has been in zines that were copied on cheap photocopy machines and haphazardly stapled together." Zines take on a certain accidental quality, where media and message are not always clearly linked. In other words, making a zine does not require training, initiation, or education – a zinester is a simply person who creates a zine. In this way, the accidental and immediate quality of digital media is well-suited to zines. A valuing of democracy and artistic accessibility may be liberatory as well as problematic in terms of issues of artistic expression and quality. For example, artists and teachers are limited by fonts, formats, and copyright restrictions if we post art on Facebook and other sites. Meanwhile, the grassroots and offline practice of zine-making allows creators to approach authorship, creation, and the page itself as considerations to be revised and reconsidered. As a sidenote, we may also note the etymological kinship of "zinester" with other feminized terms like "spinster."

Zine Histories: Creative Lineages of Zine Writing

Part of the hybridism of zines that is of interest in feminist teaching is found not only in their innovation digitally and their historical link to other artists' books but also located in histories and traditions of feminism and open publishing. My sense is that zines are often associated with an entirely personalized and often fluid mode of self publishing, whereas many blogs, wikis, and online fora are created, maintained, and written by distinct individuals and/or groups. Despite zine conventions of "text-speak" and creative spelling, the importance of zine writing as an artistic tradition and literary form lends it credibility in the classroom. Seth Friedman observed that "it was artists and writers who took up the call of self-publishing in the early part of the twentieth century. Classic letterpress printers and A. B. Dick's mimeograph duplicators churned out Dadaist manifestos, surrealist journals, anarchic broadsheets, and 'little magazines'" (1997, 4). Zines may be seen as an extension of genres like artist sketchbooks, chapbooks, and manifestos of art history.

I have become similarly intrigued by how writer Anais Nin's printing press and diaries could be viewed on a continuum of hand-made, self-published works, alongside zines. Or we might ask students to consider activist zine writings in dialogue with Valerie Solanas' SCUM manifesto. We could also examine zines about sexuality and PSAs in comparison with Margaret Sanger's health pamphlets and/or Hildegard von Bingen's writings about the female orgasm. I have invited students within courses on women and imagery of Western civilization to consider major female figures through various forms of documentation: comparing and contrasting voice, histories, and artistic formats. Countering the "Great Women" approach to women's studies, zines often give voice to lesser known female activists and artists. Zines, like other forms of marginalized or non-mainstream writing, can introduce students to neglected issues or unexplored aspects of mainstream topics. For example, *boiling point* is a 2002 zine that represents both the benefit concerts for the Rape, Abuse + Incest National Network (RAINN) and also addresses the topic of rape personally through various literary forms. As the author writes, the zine is "by no means comprehensive. But I wanted to represent a few different types of materials on rape – essays, poems, lyrics, etc."

Within a comparison of various zines, it should also be stressed that my search for connections is not intended to conclude with a homogenized or canonical approach to zines as art and/or literature. Instead, a major strength of zines lies in their capacity to directly exhibit otherness and alternative visions from a singular maker to the reader/viewer. This is not always the case online, where individual user commentary can get lost in a sea of consensus or conflict that results from more static posted commentary. However, as Joshua Breitbart and Ana Noguiera (2004) have argued "open publishing works best when many people are posting their versions of the same event…users can build their own understanding of an event or issue…flatten[ing] the hierarchy that exists whenever specialized news producers are separated from their passive audience" (35). As an example, *mothra* is one zine that critiqued a range of media in dialogue with examples from high and low culture and art. *Mothra* examined Charlie's Angels films, along with the Powerpuff Girls cartoons, and activist movements of the Combahee River Collective. The idea of talking back to (and re-envisioning) an array of images and ideas selected from consumer culture and contemporary life is evident among many zines as feminist practice. This too may be enhanced by digital presence, for zinesters are better able to network with one another and create dialogue. As one digital example, I find sites like Adbusters, Culturejammers, and Crimethinc to be exemplary collectives around critical literacy and feminist theory. However, they sometimes remain collective and collaborative in a somewhat predetermined way, whereas zines can continue to encourage direct interaction between makers and media.

(Re)Mixing Notions of Crafts Through Digital Dialogue of Zines

Just as zines have educational potential as a part of historical inquiry into publishing and art-making, they simultaneously look forward into digital realms and contemporary practices of zine writing and distribution. With contemporary technologies and digital practices in mind, educators might characterize the zine as a cross between hand-made books and

YouTube in some respects. The creation of zines often involves techniques of mixing, sampling, and re-arranging other source content into a new composition, just as YouTube creations may alter content from existing movies and other media. Many zines include re-prints of essays, manifestos, poems, and other works by various authors (with and without permission from the original creators). A noticeable example is jt bunnell and irit reinheimer's acknowledgement in their coloring book-style zine on gender: "We would like to thank all the artists who created work that we gracefully appropriated, changed, and used as inspiration for this project. May we all appreciate, make, and share anti-copyright work." In this way, zines could be seen as an exemplary Creative Commons-friendly media format.

Educators might make classroom connections as obvious as "cut and paste" that could be reclaimed, experienced, learned, and revised in various ways. Which images are we allowed to appropriate as men, as women, as people from particular cultures and within various communities? What constitutes borrowing, and what may be considered theft? When (if ever) is it acceptable to break copyright law as activism? Simple choices of crafting a zine become highly personal and political. Along these lines, we may wish to classify zines within the category of guerilla art, art that is often found in unconventional spaces and serves to question the structure of the art world itself. Specifically and along a feminist vein, we may consider such zines in relation to the work of the Guerilla Girls, anonymous feminist artists who have created works that critique sexism in film, galleries, and museums.

Aside from the role of critic, we may also view the zinester as collector and cataloguer/archivist, for as the author of *Mister Fujiyama Loves You* notes, "we are all collectors of humorous and completely true stories." So too, the creator of *Black and Blue* often creates word collages of different artists from across time discursively, including, for example: Edward Gorey, Tim Burton, Betye Saar, Eva Hesse, Frida Kahlo, Guerilla Girls, and Hieronymus Bosch. This sort of grouping feels much like an exercise in googling or web searching, for no one art history book would contain all these art world characters. Additionally, the expectation of the popular icon is subverted to include feminist figures as artistic influences. A classification of *found* art is also applicable here, for the zinester is creating and/or reconfiguring photographic, material, and/or text-based artifacts of their lives and influences. Within both of these zines' collections of artists and/or narratives lies a sense of personalization in the practice of anthologizing, which is a sort of literary categorization, classification, and collection process. Meanwhile, zine websites like smilandactnice.com feature web design that appears rather like collaged images, showing the nostalgic aesthetic influence of the handmade upon webpage design. There is a certain subversiveness in flouting the often sleek and clean format of web design by reverting to imperfect arts and crafts sensibilities. For educators, zines can provide particularly interesting and in-depth provocations around overlapping issues of style and expression that can sometimes be overlooked in digital spaces.

Zine Currencies: Craft and Consumption

Zines not only differ from manufactured objects and spaces in terms of appearance but also within commercial contexts. While the cost of formally published books through a distributor typically separates the author from the financial arrangements of its sale, zinesters are more directly involved in pricing and profit from their zines. An unconventional approach to consumption among zinesters and their aficionados is enhanced by a common practice of not only selling zines for a low cost but also generating a system of barter or trade that most zines offer. Many zines are priced with both a dollar amount and the suggestion of a trade, underscoring the importance of their circulation over capital gains. Zines can be found at independent bookstores, record shops, youth centers, and library collections. Access to zines is integrally linked to sites of youth culture, for they are sold wherever their creators are likely to spend time. Many zine artists sell both their zines and other artistic products. For instance, a zine author named Samantha has a zine and craft company, both entitled *What's her deal?,* which reference a range of personal experiences, including racial stereotyping, social isolation, and experiences with psychiatric medication. Zine culture uniquely contributes to the creation of art by supporting its own market.

Similarly, Craftzine.com is a digital DIY (Do-It-Yourself) community that features events, community conversations, craft marketplaces, and spaces for teaching and learning. Craftzine's "community" page reads like a digital bulletin board of announcements and questions, replete with links to etsy.com where crafters can sell their work. Craftzine's "101" section of the website mirrors the naming of introductory courses and features tutorials in silkscreening, dying, Adobe Illustrator, and several practical cooking-related topics. Offering education and folk information free of charge is an additional possibility of the Internet, depending upon site hosting and advertising instead of funding from the reader. If zine content is read online or in a pdf file, print cost is no longer an issue (no pun intended). I have found that most digital zines are available on back-order, sold in a manner very similar to early editions of traditional periodicals.

Despite increased accessibility created by the growth of cybercommunities, one of the major concerns voiced by craft artists and fine artists with whom I have worked addresses their artistic ambivalence toward the consumer-driven focus that sites like etsy.com ascribe to DIY culture. We may phrase these concerns of art and education as questions: In what ways is crafting about consumption? How is the experience of barter different in the case of hand-made goods? What is a zine really worth? Some artists, designers, and zinesters may wish to remove themselves from such conversations, which can detract from the content of their work. Still other web resources like Folkvine.com playfully acknowledge the tourist aspect of folk art consumption with a gift-shop-like virtual space for zines and other artworks. The site is literally set up as if one is traveling to a home or home-like gallery, in which the motions of the mouse causes bobbleheads to bobble, lazy susans to turn, and zines that appear to shuffle and turn pages. In this way, consumer culture and local culture may overlap consciously and with a sense of criticality that we may explore and question as educators.

Unconventional Conventions: Zines Containing Gifts and Comics

Zines offer readers literal collections of objects as well as conceptual take-aways. Many zines feature add-ons, including pins, prizes, folded "cootie catchers," and other objects that offer additional materiality, connection, publicity, and presence. These additions and inclusions not only extend the nostalgic idea of the prize in children's cereals or bubble gum machines but also perhaps relate to the idea of gift-giving as social exchange. The consumer's attention is drawn to the fact that they are being given more than the product of the zine itself. The artist might, for example, include a pill or tablet as a decoration and gift. *The Radical Art Girls 2001* includes a pouch sewn into the back cover to hold actual medicine. I cannot help but be reminded of *Through the Looking Glass* and drug associations, of pills and bodies of young women. I would also pose the possibility that zines themselves can serve as remedies for other sorts of media. But perhaps such an inclusion can also act symbolically, as zines provide information, commiseration, and commentary (all metaphorical "medicine" for readers). Since many zines contain information on alternative medicines and lifestyles, these objects can even be seen as an anti-pharmaceutical statement. However, as an artist and educator, I am mostly concerned with their potential as shared artifacts between maker and reader/viewer. One of my favorite art education professors, Dr. Jessica Hoffmann Davis, invited students to create gift tributes in the form of artworks for artist educators whom they admire. This practice, modeled beautifully by zines, is one I enjoy passing along to my own students. Further, we may practice both digital and hand-held exchanges and observe the potentialities of each.

The gift aspect of a zine does not detract from its worth as a work of writing. In their great versatility as a literary form, zines may cross formatting boundaries into other areas of creative production, such as comics and graphica. For instance, *The Sex Ed Comic Project* is both a zine and a blog. Further, creators jt bunnell and irit reinheimer have generated a physical zine that is a coloring book (entitled *Girls will be boys will be girls will be...*) in the tradition of old-fashioned primers that have been artistically altered, explaining:

> So, one summer day…irit and jt decided to take action against all the rigid gender roles that had been unwillingly placed upon them and their friends. They got out all the markers, crayons, pens, pencils, and scissors they could find and created a coloring book that would change the world as they knew it.

The particular materials used by the artists serve to emphasize nostalgic, child-friendly, or "arts and crafts" sensibilities of making and learning. These formats also demonstrate humor, irony, and a resistance to standardized literary or artistic forms. Zines overlap printed genres from brochures to materials of art histories, and even guerrilla or street art, such as the Guerilla Girls' publications. Notably, the Guerilla Girls activity books are sold at *Printed Matter*, a New York independent, non-profit art space for artists' books. Similarly, physical zines are often found in independent bookstores, galleries, and other artist-centered spaces. The physical concepts of artistic materials and consumer space also define zines and the diverse culture of their readership.

Zines and the Creation of Communal Cyberspaces

Like readers of blogs, zine readers may interact with zines not only as consumers and receivers of gifts but also as fellow creators. Royce Carlson, creator of *Black and Blue* zine, routinely invites readers to take and submit pictures of activist activities in their towns for upcoming issues. This sort of participatory and documentary content among zines predicts, predates, and persists alongside community-based blogs. Jennifer

Bleyer has observed how the engendering of other zinesters is an impulse of many zines: "integral to reading zines was the implicit challenge to turn around and write them. Zines made clear that they were not another product to be consumed but were unique contributions to a vast conversation" (48). This also relates well to the formerly mentioned issue of trading or bartering zines as a method of encouraging zine practice. Barbara J. Guzzetti and Margaret Gamboa (2004) conducted research on collaborative teen zines and issues of development and education. They found that zinesters strengthened their personal relationships with collaborators, a social and intrinsic motivator in the creative process of zines. They were able to broaden "personal worlds by exchanging ideas and 'meeting' (through cyberspace or snail mail) new people" (431).

Within creative processes, collaborations are grassroots and face-to-face, but the zine itself can be disseminated and discussed digitally. I do not mean to suggest that all zines envision the feminist community as an uncomplicated ideal. One zine, *her side of the sidewalk,* carefully articulates anxiety and ambivalence around models of feminist sisterhood in contrast with her lived experience:

> Women are generally not encouraged to be supportive of one another. In order to understand the implications of this, I feel like we need to go back and look at how we, as well as other groups, have been set up to pitted against each other historically…How do we undo this training?…I struggle with the contradictions in my own relationships with women. They unravel in an astoundingly similar pattern before my eyes. What makes these close friendships so much more fragile than I had thought? We go to these meetings, sit in a circle and talk about our bonds with each other as we cut and sew the patterns of homemade menstrual pads – then we all leave and go home to our boyfriends…How do I balance the dynamic of being mostly intimate with boys while wanting to work on and acknowledge my clashes and closeness with girls. I have come to rationalize it this way: I am uncomfortable with my heterosexual tendencies.

In this way, zines can address tensions around sexuality (including heteronormative imperatives), feminism, and coalitional dynamics within elegantly authentic personal examples.

Zines may also underscore tensions around craft and gender. In *Girlhood in America: An Encyclopedia*, Miriam Forman-Brunell has noted that colonial girls were restricted to domestic skills, decorative arts, and writing within dame schools. In modern times, a certain uncomfortable relationship persists between young women's choices and agency as artists and craftswomen, and those assumption and social mores relating to their interests. Even zine communities, craft circles, or feminist groups can be subject to the same contradictions, clichés, and other problems of feminisms and community. Zines have a very honest way of addressing this historical tension, even as they support and create contemporary feminist discourses.

Furthermore, while zines look forward to digital processes, they also seem to hearken back to traditions of writing and making. I have already addressed some craft overlap in creating zines. Zinesters also often follow a traditional convention from old novels, to address the reader directly or dedicate the zine to him or her. Such is the case with *Black and Blue* and *mister Fujiyama loves you*. Both traditional handwriting and addressing one's readership are traditional, and yet these practices are reconceived in zines and zinester cyberculture as friendly, informal, and/or subversive literary gestures. This convention also highlights the practice of communication between author and writer inherent in zines, addressed throughout zines in calls for community participation and gifts to the reader mentioned earlier in this chapter.

Embodiment: Selves Embedded in the Zine

Zines are not only personalized to their readership but also may reflect the unique personal and artistic goals of the author. The creator of digital zine *Galatea's Pants* included a passage about a New Year's resolution to read her weight in books, emphasizing the felt corporeal connection between books and bodies. We may also interpret the literary weight project as a reinterpretation of female body into a measure of intellect. This gesture is also quite subversive in the face of societal associations of women's weight with shame and negative self-worth. For me, there is a certain lightness and disembodied feeling surrounding e-books and e-readers in comparison to physical books. Zines often unflinchingly reference the personality as well as the body of the zine creator, showing the ways in which representation is experienced, crafted, and realized. For example, there are complex musings around appearance and identity from the zinester of *mister fujiyama loves you* in a 2004 summer issue in which she recalls a situation that arose for a child's question: "'Mommy is that a boy or a girl?' The woman looked at me apologetically and I held up my hand to signal it was okay. I smiled at the curious child" (15). Such anecdotes of sex and gender identity are common among confessional zines and express otherness in contrast with essentializing tendencies in teen magazines and other popular media.

The online presence of zines reveals an interesting cross-section of digital platforms of expression selected by zinesters. For instance,

HipMama.com is a magazine website with distro/zine directories and links to its original zine dedicated to and written by progressive mothers. *Hip Mama* is not only a publication by Bee Lavender but also a website with a Facebook presence, Twitter account, and Café Press store. These various sites possess both overlapping blog information and additional content from community members that depends upon individual contributions. For example, the Facebook page features a community wall that is typically updated with short announcements and resources several times a week, whereas the original website tends more towards less frequent, yet more polished, pieces of writing in the form of blog posts. The expansion of motherhood-related print zines to hybrid cybercommunities reflects the various ways in which computerized experiences of writing, reading, and digital sharing is particularly appropriate and accessible for some mothers. Some zinesters-turned-bloggers, such as Rhon, midwife and author of *Zuzu and the Babycatcher*, also use their websites as makeshift bookstores to sell re-prints of zines (and interestingly express the wish to return to zine writing instead of the blogosphere when possible). The way in which a zine is digitally scanned and sent adds a layer to the original procedure of hand-photocopying a handmade object. However, one may argue women zinesters are crafting and personalizing artistic space online, much as they have done and continue to do on the physical page.

Concluding Reflections: Future Feminism and CyberZines

In closing, the educator part of me wishes to revisit and reframe the richness that exists within the hybridism of digital realms and grassroots zine communities in terms of future teaching. This consideration is not an uncomplicated topic for me. I have felt personal unease about many issues surrounding zines. For example, during the months I spend researching zines in the Barnard College collection and its comprehensive digital database, I found myself simultaneously impressed by the scope of the zines yet perplexed by the collection's affluent university setting. Somehow discussions of zines belong on the screen and in the library as much as in other spaces, and yet their particular presence there symbolically reminded me of my own uncertain attempts to reconcile the persistence of my teenage angst (extending well into my 20s and commemorated within zines I created to cope with turning thirty!) and the artistry and wisdom I hope to embrace and impart in the capacity of a university teacher educator. Some of the tensions and dichotomies surrounding zines prove productive avenues of inquiry for feminist teaching in my personal and professional experiences. These include sometimes opposing and sometimes collaborating forces such as academic discourse versus discourse that is outside of or anti-academia, youth cultures versus adult cultures, digitized and mass-produced zines versus those that are OOAK, timeless versus timely zines, and issues of the personal versus the political within zines.

If we are to take up zines in their dual roles of artifacts and practices of feminist pedagogy, we must do so within a framework that honors their histories, meanings, and potentialities (as I have begun to do here). Craft researcher Tami Katz-Frieberg has noted ways in which "strategies that in previous decades were identified with women artists attempting to liberate themselves of the male hegemony have been integrated into contemporary artmaking as…a celebration of manual production in a world that has wildly over-computerized itself" (696). In this manner, crafting zines by hand (and/or holding them in our hands and reading them) can both identify makers with a continuum of creative women in the past and also function as a subversion of mass-production through contemporary, manual artistic processes. Today's DIY culture might be viewed as a renaissance of craft itself, a celebration of the reemergence of ideals about community, feminism, and social justice, often expressed and catalogued online.

Further, women documenting, sharing, exhibiting, and selling their artwork online through zines can be viewed as another re-working of the hegemony of gender divisions in art and in technology. As I began writing this chapter, a mainstream movie about the male founder of Facebook released by Columbia Pictures was being advertised on billboards nationally. Meanwhile, recent films focusing on women artists and zinesters like *Who Does She Think She Is?* and *The Grrrly Show* remain underground, independent hits among moviegoers. I believe feminist educators should ask students to consider why and how this our present situation in popularized visions of gender and technology. As Helen Sterk and Annelies Knoppers (2009) have stated, we may come to explore questions "somewhere in between hardware and software, those two reductive senses of how humans live out gender, in a space that honors both individual humans and communal living" (xiv). My sense of zines is that they are often immensely personal and yet relatable in compelling, gendered ways. Further, many zines offer rare political context, personal expression, and a view into localized folk vision, transcribing oral information into self-published print. As Kyle Bravo notes in his 2005 book on DIY cultures, "there is an obvious hunger for DIY…people are dissatisfied with what our contemporary situation has to offer and…searching for practical, vital, and sustainable alternatives…yearning for some sort of blueprint for a better world" (1). Zines provide a compelling framework for future visions of art and feminism.

Along the same lines, Bill Brent (1997) has observed how self-publishing is a sort of antidote to the disaffection of zinesters (16). I believe that many feminist artists and educators will locate much of their activist cues by reading zines, and they will create new paradigms by generating them. One teaching strategy from Barbara Guzetti and Margaret Gamboa emphasizes the nuances of zine frameworks over actual zine-making assignments in school: "zinesters suggested that teachers can adopt a stance that promotes the ethic of zines (do it yourself) through journaling, and by allowing students to write about themselves and their experiences" (432). I would echo the impulse to encourage our students in their pursuits of personal sketchbooks, blogs, and (if they choose) zines as part of students' explorations of feminism, cyberculture, and self. I look forward to teaching and learning about the persistence of paper in zines, aided and altered by digital databases and distros.

Bibliography

Bleyer, Jennifer. 2004. "Cut-and-Paste Revolution: Notes from the Girl Zine Explosion." In *The Fire This Time: Young Activists and the New Feminism,* edited by Vivien Labaton and Dawn Lundy Martin, 42-60. New York: Anchor Books.

Bravo, Kyle. 2005. *Making Stuff and Doing Things.* Portland, OR: Microcosm.

Breitbart, Joshua and Ana Nogueira. 2004. "An Independent Media Center of One's Own: A Feminist Alternative to Corporate Media" In *The Fire This Time: Young Activists and New Feminism,* edited by Vivian Lambaton and Dawn Martin, 19-41. New York, NY: Anchor.

Brent, Bill. 1997. *Make a Zine!: A Guide to Self-Publishing Disguised as a Book on How to Produce a Zine.* Collingwood, AU: Black Books.

Douglas, Susan. 2010. *Enlightened Sexism.* New York, NY: Times Books.

Formanek-Brunell, Miriam. 2001. *Girlhood in America: An Encyclopedia.* Santa Barbara, California: ABC-CLIO.

Friedman, Seth. 1997. *The Factsheet Five Zine Reader.* New York, NY: Three Rivers Press.

Guzzetti, Barbara and Margaret Gamboa. 2004. "Zines for Social Justice: Adolescent Girls Writing on Their Own." *Reading Research Quarterly* 39, no. 4: 408-36.

Hentges, Sarah. 2005. *Pictures of Girlhood: Modern Female Adolescence on Film.* Jefferson, NC: McFarland and Company.

Kafai, Yasmin and Kylie Peppler. 2009. *The Computer Clubhouse: Constructionism and Creativity in Youth Communities.* New York, NY: Teachers College Press.

Katz-Frieberg, Tami. 2010. "Craftsmen in the Factory of Images." In *The Craft Reader*, edited by Glenn Adamson, 689-698. New York: Berg.

McCullough, Malcolm. 1998. *Abstracting Craft: The Practiced Digital Hand.* Cambridge, MA: MIT Press.

Metcalf, Bruce. 2007. "Replacing the Myth of Modernism." In *NeoCraft: Modernity and the Crafts,* edited by Sandra Alfoldy, 4-33. Halifax: The Press of the Nova Scotia College of Art and Design.

Piepmeier, Alison. 2009. *Girl Zines: Making Media, Doing Feminism.* New York, NY: New York University Press.

Sterk, Helen and Annelies Knoppers. 2009. *Gender, Culture, and Physicality: Paradoxes and Taboos.* Lanham, MD: Lexington Books.

Turkle, Sherry. 1995. *Life on the Screen: Identity in the Age of the Internet.* New York: Simon and Schuster.

Weinberger, David. 2002. *Small Pieces Loosely Joined: A Unified Theory of the Web.* Cambridge, MA: Perseus Books.

CHAPTER THREE

FROM THE CENTER:
BRIDGING THE "DIVIDE" THROUGH FEMINIST
JAIL-BASED HIV/AIDS EDUCATION
AND DIGITAL STORYTELLING

MARGARET RHEE AND ISELA GONZÁLEZ

Prelude

Digital storytelling is about having fun, interacting with others, meeting new people, being creative and learning something new. Women who are incarcerated are limited to what they can and cannot do. They are judged each and every day and it's not a good feeling. It's important that incarcerated women feel loved and cared about even under their circumstances. I myself have come a long way and know what it feels like to be dressed in jail clothing, feeling like your back is against the wall and feeling like nobody cares.

I know how it feels to be judged and put down by the system and I know what it sounds like to be told (You're never gonna make it) but guess what, none of that matters now because here I sit today with a whole new life and a new way of living my life. I told my story in a digital story and it was a great experience. I was actually able to see where I used to be and where I am today. It was a good feeling to see my life and the changes that I have made.

And what made it an even better feeling is the fact that I created my own life story in such a beautiful way.

Yes I was afraid and had worries but I found the courage to step up and show up for my life and I didn't care what people said or thought because it was my time to shine and now it's yours.
— *Breeyana Singletary, "My Face, My Voice, My Story"[1]*

Feminist New Media Interventions:
The Intersections and Our Possibilities

Why bring digital storytelling and feminist-based HIV prevention education to women-centered spaces in the San Francisco jails? In this article, we illuminate the liberatory possibilities and challenges of new media technologies and feminist HIV/AIDS pedagogy. Specifically, we provide a narrative of our current process of implementing "From the Center" (FTC), a collaborative feminist community-based participatory research (CBPR), arts, and education initiative by the San Francisco Department of Public Health, Jail Health Services, Forensic AIDS Project. Established in 1983, the Forensic AIDS Project (FAP) was the first HIV service provider in a California jail/prison. As part of Jail Health Services, a division of the San Francisco Department of Public Health, FAP has successfully implemented HIV prevention and care programs/services in the San Francisco (SF) county jails for over twenty years. Moreover, "From the Center" follows FAP's commitment for innovative and feminist-based HIV prevention education.

Our current project of implementing digital storytelling education derives from FAP's feminist CBPR project, "Jailed Women and HIV Education" (JWHE). JWHE was FAP's initial collaboration with San Francisco State University's Center for Research on Gender and Sexuality and incarcerated women of color (Fields et al. 2008). JWHE centralized the necessity to recognize incarcerated women as "experts on their own lives" (Fields et al. 2008, 81). Through JWHE CBPR workshops, incarcerated women trained in qualitative sociological research methods on HIV/AIDS issues and served simultaneously as "researcher, research assistant, participant, interviewer, teacher, student, expert." (Fields et al. 2008, 77).

Thus, we open our article with insights from writer, FAP intern, and JWHE participant Breeyana Singletary, who demonstrates the importance of digital storytelling education for formerly or currently incarcerated women. After participating in JWHE and upon release from jail, Breeyana created a digital story as a participant in The Center for Young Women's Development program in collaboration with Health Initiatives for Youth (HIFY), both located in San Francisco, CA. Currently, Breeyana has returned to work with FAP, providing her expertise and support in advocating for technological access and HIV education in this current phase of the project. Digital stories remain an innovative new educational genre, utilizing still or moving images, simple technological editing, and a focus on the personal narrative. Moreover, creating a digital story can be empowering for women of color, who are often marginalized in the larger discourse. Breeyana's perspectives and insights demonstrate how new media access to women in the SF jails can be a feminist intervention.

As Breeyana's trajectory attests, "From the Center" derives intimately from involvement and CBPR feminist principles JWHE mapped out in the SF jails. Both co-authors worked on different aspects of the project. Isela González is FAP's HIV Prevention Services Coordinator and served as JWHE co-principal investigator. Margaret Rhee worked as a graduate student research assistant on the project while obtaining her MA in Ethnic Studies from San Francisco State University. In the JWHE team's co-authored article we posed a call to action because "sexuality educators and researchers must offer incarcerated women a chance to consume, produce, and share knowledge that not only is accurate but also validates their experience as sexual beings and not just as the objects of violence, pain, and disease" (Fields et al. 2008, 82). While JWHE was completed in 2009, we wondered how technology and the arts could continue JWHE's feminist interventions and validate the experiences of currently and formerly incarcerated women. As Breeyana illustrates, digital storytelling may intervene in state-sanctioned and hegemonic representational violence against women: "The goal is for incarcerated/ HIV women and all types of women to feel and know that they are important and they do matter" (Singletary).

As feminists in our new media age, we believe women should be the authors, directors, and storytellers of our own lives. We re-imagine how new media technologies can provide a vital intervention for all women, even those whose voices are subsumed in larger hegemonic discourse. Oftentimes, incarcerated women and issues of race, class, and sexuality are unacknowledged even in interdisciplinary areas such as Ethnic, Women, and Queer Studies or in larger conversations and decisions of HIV/AIDS prevention education and new media technologies. "From the Center" derives from intersectional issues, domains, and disciplines. We hope to bridge seemingly disparate subjects: feminist praxis, HIV/AIDS education, digital storytelling, the prison industrial complex, women's studies, ethnic studies, and new media studies. Thus, we question, hope, and urge a re-articulation of women's identity, HIV/AIDS education, and the digital divide by centering the issues and concerns of incarcerated women.

In this article, we begin by highlighting the current crisis of HIV/AIDS for women and outline how new media technologies, digital storytelling, and feminism can be utilized to provide innovative HIV/AIDS education. We share how collaboration can be fruitful and challenging as "From the Center" involves academic researchers, graduate students, community providers, incarcerated and formerly incarcerated women. Subsequently, we hope to establish how providing digital media tools for incarcerated women to create and share their digital stories around HIV/AIDS can be a vital intervention in multiple ways. However, our narrative depicts our yet unrealized goal of implementing digital storytelling in the San Francisco jails. While our story may not have a definite or traditional conclusion, we are hopeful it is a narrative of movement, process, and progress, leading us to the possibility for change.

HIV/AIDS and Women: The Crisis and Necessity for Action

"From the Center" signals the need to pay attention to issues of HIV/AIDS, rates of incarceration, race, class, and gender. Specifically, HIV/AIDS prevention, support for people living with HIV/AIDS, (PLWHA) and awareness around transmission and risk for women is pressing. AIDS is the primary cause of death for 25-34 year-old African American women (Center for Disease Control and Prevention 2010). Moreover, in San Francisco, current funding cuts have significantly reduced FAP HIV prevention services for female prisoners. Within the female population of San Francisco, there are a disproportionate number of African Americans diagnosed with AIDS. Although African American women represent 8% of the female population, they account for 46% of the female AIDS cases in San Francisco (San Francisco Department of Public Health 2011) In 2008, the San Francisco Sheriff's Department reported that 67% of incarcerated women were African American, 10% Hispanic, 20% Caucasian, 4% Asian, and 4% Other. These statistics highlight the need for services for a population significantly impacted by HIV.

While preventative programs have been established to address these statistics, many are centered on an abstinence-only model and disease prevention as opposed to comprehensive health care (Labonte and Robertson 1996, 5-9). Most of these programs do not take into account socio-economic factors that shape marginalized communities and women's HIV/AIDS risk. With traditional HIV/AIDS education, the teacher and the public health official is posited as the expert. Conventional HIV/AIDS education does not support collaboration and creativity among students. Sex education videos, books, and pamphlets, are written by "experts" instead of those communities and individuals these statistics represent and reflect (Fields, *Risky Lessons: Sex Education and Social Inequality* 2008, 117). Additionally, traditional programs may not account for sexual and gender identities LGBTQ (lesbian, gay, bisexual, transgender, and queer), women's, and structural Oppressions of race, class, and ethnicity.

To address these issues, "From the Center," is a proposed model that centers on engaged pedagogy, PAR, and feminist praxis through creativity and technology. We draw from engaged pedagogical principles demonstrated in Brazilian educator Paulo Freire's central work, *Pedagogy of the Oppressed*, which dismantles teacher-student hierarchy and the "banking system," as a way to fight classroom and social inequality (Freire 2006, 73). Additionally, Brazilian theatre artist and activist Augusto Boal believes that hierarchy between stage and audience must be deconstructed (*Theatre of the Oppressed* 1979). For Boal, spectators are transformed into "spec-actors" rather than passive observers (*Theatre of the Oppressed* 1979). Moreover, our previous project centered on the foundation of participatory action research (PAR) principles as "Participatory action researchers prioritize learning for and with – not only about – disenfranchised people. Students, teachers, study participants, and researchers work together on shared concerns" (Fields, et al. 2008, 3). Feminist scholar bell hooks writes: "To have a revolutionary feminist pedagogy, we must relinquish our ties to traditional ways of teaching that reinforces domination...we must first focus on the teacher-student relationship and the issue of power" (*Teaching To Transgress* 1994, 1). Moreover, according to sociologist and JWHE co-principal investigator Jessica Fields, deconstructing power in the sex education classroom is vital:

> ...if education is an opportunity for students and teachers to face and reimagine those constraining definitions, then sex education insists upon the importance for young peoples' desires, pleasure, and power in that reimagining. (*Risky Lessons: Sex Education and Social Inequality* 2008, 5)

As Fields suggests, reimagining sex education for young people includes the importance of centralizing their own "desires, pleasures, and power." Through "From the Center" and our previous work with JWHE, we establish that HIV/AIDS education can be liberatory, comprehensive, and empowering. Shaped by radical philosophies of education, PAR, and feminist principles, "From the Center" insists that the classroom can be a space of empowerment where women can be simultaneously educators, students, and experts.

Much like feminist-based pedagogy, theorists of technology, creativity, and education centralize agency and empowerment. Educator and computer theorist Seymour Papert insists that instead of children being programmed by computers, in the LOGO environment, "the relationship is reversed: The child programs the computer. And in teaching the computer how to think, children embark on an exploration about how they themselves can think" (Papert 1980, 19). For Papert, "when a child learns to program, the process of learning is transformed. It becomes more active and self-directed. In particular, the knowledge is acquired for a recognizable personal purpose…The new knowledge is a source of power and is experienced as such from the moment it begins to form in the child's mind" (Papert 1980, 21). As Papert insists, through constructionist learning, many new media scholars provide that learning comes from doing "learning with understanding" and not memorization (Bransford, Brown, and Rodney 2000, 4). New Media scholar Michael Resnick points out in his MIT based project, *Computer Clubhouse,* that inner city youth not only have "access to new technologies" but learn in a space "where young people and adult mentors work together on projects, using new technologies to explore and experiment in new ways" (Resnick, Rusk, and Cook 1998, 2). Thus at the *Computer Clubhouse*, "young people become designers and creators, not just consumers of computer-based products" (Resnick, Rusk, and Cook 1998, 2). Moreover, Resnick writes, "Most teachers avoid situations where they are not the expert," in the importance of delineating hierarchy between mentors/mentees in lower income neighborhoods (Resnick, Rusk, and Cook 1998, 9). Historically, "women's access to science and engineering has historically been blocked by prejudice and discrimination," but for technology scholars Sherry Turkle and Papert, learning requires a pluralism: "Our central thesis is that equal access to even the most basic elements of computation requires an epistemological pluralism, accepting the validity of multiple ways of knowing and thinking" (Turkle and Papert 1990).

As a result of computational accessibility, digital storytelling remains a vital medium increasingly utilized for educational purposes. As a genre, digital storytelling combines images, narration, music, or moving image to construct powerful personal stories (Robin 2011). Moreover, the author of the story may not necessarily have to identify as an artist but someone with a story to share (Lambert 2006, 2). Perhaps most innovatively, the technological and economical form of the digital story is simple and does not need a "fancy apparatus" to produce. Oftentimes, simple editing software, images, and clips can be used to create a digital story (Banaszewski 2002).

Many classrooms in elementary, high school, college, retirement, and community-based centers have utilized the form with the Center for Digital Storytelling (CDS) in Berkeley, California leading the way (Robin 2011; *Center for Digital Storytelling* 2010). CDS provides in storytelling is for everyone, including marginalized communities (*Center for Digital Storytelling* 2010). Additionally, while not widespread, the influence of digital storytelling has been introduced to jail-based settings. For example, scholar Barbara Barry worked with imprisoned youth and digital storytelling as part of Seymour Papert's Maine Youth Center Project, which "encouraged imprisoned youth to tell stories about their experiences, thoughts and concerns. The learners constructed multiple viewpoint stories in digital video based on their own everyday life experiences then shared them with their community" (*Barbara Barry* 2010). Our focus on digital storytelling derives from some questions we pose: What might it mean, if women could create their own safer sex digital stories, videos, and media? Could technology provide an avenue to learning that is constructionist, feminist, and engaged? How might utilization of technology offer innovative ways to combat HIV transmission, stigma, and lives prematurely lost, particularly for women?

HIV/AIDS education has included digital storytelling as part of its curricula; however, it has largely been within the international context. Planned Parenthood of New York City traveled to Africa with the Margaret Sanger Center International (MSCI) and Women's Net to conduct a digital storytelling project on HIV/AIDS, reproductive health, and sexual abuse (*Planned Parenthood NYC* 2010). Additionally CDS's affiliated department, Silence Speaks, focuses on gender, sexuality, and public health education particularly HIV/AIDS (*Silence Speaks* 2010). Led by educator and artist Amy Hill, Silence Speaks provides feminist HIV/AIDS digital storytelling workshops focused in the South African context in partnership with Sonke Gender Justice Network (Sonke Gender Justice Network 2010; *Silence Speaks* 2010).

As Silence Speaks demonstrates, digital Storytelling can be an innovative means of empowering participants and providing vital educational curricula around HIV/AIDS. Amy Hill sees the value of this new instructional form for social change:

> The storytellers have offered glimpses of their lives, with the hope that their stories will have a lasting and meaningful impact on communities, organizations, and policymakers – one that leads to action and change. Sonke's vision for these stories is to make local voices and images the centerpiece of local and national efforts to promote new forms of masculinity, gender equality, and reduce stigma around HIV/AIDS. (2010)

Hill sees that stories may have a lasting impact on social change and in particular can be utilized to combat HIV/AIDS stigma. As a result of locale and Silence Speaks' commitment to feminist pedagogies and expertise in HIV/AIDS education, Amy Hill will serve as the lead digital storytelling consultant for "From the Center." Additionally, "From the Center" would be the first time CDS Silence Speaks incorporates HIV/AIDS digital storytelling in the U.S. For both FAP and CDS, "From the Center" would be the inaugural attempt of implementing digital storytelling in a jail setting.

While digital storytelling may be a new addition to FAP's curricula, some new media had already been part of the project. For example, FAP's JWHE project utilized digital tape recorders to facilitate sociological listening and interviewing. In addition, FAP utilized technology to foster better privacy for incarcerated adults through PALM IT, a computer for electronic data collection (González 2008). Instead of verbally sharing with a counselor, incarcerated adults who were voluntarily being tested for HIV entered personal sexual and HIV risk history into PALM IT. Moreover, the digital access had unexpected results for pedagogy. In one case, Isela recalls working with a woman in her mid 40's, who didn't know how to use a computer and was becoming frustrated by the process. However, after the instructor took the time to teach and explain, the woman agreed to complete PALM IT herself. After she was done, she had remarked, "I didn't know I could use a computer. I should take a class" (González 2008). Some of these opportunities empower women in a way that one would not expect.

As utilization of PALM IT depicts, digital media has unexpected results for feminist-based education for all members involved in the process. One pivotal example is Margaret's experience of working as a JWHE graduate research assistant and at the same time a burgeoning digital media artist. As Margaret is from a low income and immigrant background, she obtained her new media training at community-based organizations, such as Queer Women of Color Media Arts Project and Berkeley Community Media at the same time when working with JWHE. Through Isela's mentorship and support, Margaret utilized her nascent digital skills to help document JWHE's work at the Chicago conference on "Race, Sex, Power: New Movements in Black and Latina/o Sexualities." Margaret filmed and provided a video that depicted two formerly incarcerated women, Cat White and Allyse Gray, who presented their research findings on spirituality, women, and HIV/AIDS with Isela (Rhee 2008). Later, the video was screened in the jails and at the Center for Research on Gender and Sexuality and helped the conference presentation to move, travel, and educate. Women on the inside saw the formerly incarcerated women as leaders, researchers, and educators. Additionally, the presentation became archiveable, sharable, and accessible. The ability to film with an inexpensive DV camera was a surprising addition to feminist pedagogy that was not anticipated.

The impetus of "From the Center" demonstrates how the experience working on JWHE helps shape notions of epistemology, pedagogy, and technology. Upon graduating from San Francisco State, Margaret entered UC Berkeley as a doctoral student in Ethnic Studies and enrolled in a New Media Studies course entitled "Technologies for Creative Thinking and Learning" taught by Professor Kimiko Ryoki. While new to the field of media studies, Margaret attempted to provide a curriculum based on her experience of working with JWHE and filmmaking. With Isela's vital mentorship, Margaret felt the need to explore what digitality could mean in the context of feminist based HIV/AIDS education.

The course, involvement in JWHE, and mentorship from Isela and the class proved vital. From obtaining feedback from Professor Kimiko Ryoki, and her close friend, filmmaker and social worker, Tai Cao, Margaret learned of digital storytelling as a vital, accessible alternative to filmmaking. Upon finishing her project brief, Margaret discussed the project with Isela and FAP director Kate Monico Klein for additional feedback. Because of their shared interests in working with digital video, both Isela and Kate responded affirmatively to the potential of the project. By training and educating incarcerated women using digital storytelling, FAP would be expanding the ways in which HIV/AIDS educators teach, as well as exploring a more inclusive way of learning. Thus, "From the Center" attests to collaboration, inspiration, and the ways learning moves and is shared between women inside and outside the jails, public health educators, and graduate students.

Current Challenges and Constraints: The Need for Accessible Education

In large part, new media technologies have not been utilized in a jail setting because of institutional challenges and policies. However, the San Francisco jails previously housed theatre projects for women, such as *The Medea Project* led by award winning theatre artist and activist, Rhodessa Jones (Fraden 2001, 2). Additionally, the jail based drug treatment program, SISTER (Sisters in Sober Treatment Empowered by Recovery) – where FAP primarily works with women –previously had a program where women would tape record stories for their children, yet a computer-based digital storytelling program has never been included. As an interview with SISTER Program Manager Jacqueline Gordon explains: "it's very difficult in here, because of confidentiality. We do have media waivers. A lot of times, the women do not want to be seen, so it's kind of hard to get a lot of participation in that. You know, they don't want to be seen here in custody, so we have some who may participate, but overall, most women don't want to be seen here in custody" (2010) Compared to being filmed as a subject in a documentary, digital storytelling provides women the agency to choose and create their own images to represent themselves and the story they wish to share. To address the concern that many women may not want to be visually photographed or videotaped, digital storytelling was "From the Center's" chosen genre.

Although digital media has not been utilized in the SISTER program (located in SF County Jail #2 housing unit pod), Gordon provides that a program of digital storytelling can ultimately be vital for incarcerated women:

> I think digital storytelling can be very empowering and important. Because the population we serve, these women, mostly come from poverty. They don't really have social status in the community. Being so, they lack the opportunity to get the information they need, to help them to take care of themselves and their children. At that point, I feel their priorities is not about having fun, or education, the priority is about putting a roof over their heads, and food on the table. And so, they lack the education piece, when it comes to AIDS and HIV. Because it's not a priority. Because they are trying to survive. (Ibid.)

As many incarcerated women struggle with survival, access to education around HIV/AIDS is challenging and not a priority. Gordon believes that the jail setting may be the appropriate space to break the cycle of incarceration, poverty, and education:

> And so, I think that's a message that needs to be revealed in here, because it starts here (SF Jails). The reason I say that, is that I have 3 generations of families here. You know. It's just sad, because of the lack of education, and where their priority lies is not about educating themselves, its about providing for their kids or putting a roof over their heads, food, and clothes, and that becomes a priority, and is not necessarily education. (Ibid.)

Additionally, Gordon explains, "I think digital storytelling would be great in the pod with the community that we serve. Reason being, because it's really important for the women to hear stories, especially from women who have similar things in common and talking about their struggles and lets them know, for one, that they are not alone, and just hearing that, helps to empower them" (Ibid.).

Currently, "From the Center" has secured collaboration with CDS Silence Speaks Amy Hill, SISTER's Jackie Gordon, and most importantly, continuously reached out for the perspectives of incarcerated and formerly incarcerated women on the issue of digital storytelling. On October 26, 2009, Isela and Margaret conducted a feedback session in the SISTER's pod so women may respond and provide input on the potential of bringing digital storytelling to the San Francisco jail. Ten incarcerated women expressed enthusiasm to include their voices in the digital realm.[2] As part of our feedback session, we screened digital stories created from CDS Silence Speaks and Sonke Gender Justice Network in South Africa. After viewing the digital stories, participants wrote short responses to digital storytelling: "Anyone can do it! New Age, Hands on participation" "Digital Storytelling: It gives me a sense of attraction and excitement!" "Make your own movie, Informative." "Educational/Computer: Learning to work with different stuff, opportunity to educate others in a form of a DVD!" This feedback demonstrates FAP's proposed new media program resonates with an interest incarcerated women themselves express.

Moreover, one participant, Tina Reyes* wrote after watching "Sibongile: My Life as A Widow Living With HIV" a digital story from *Responding to Violence and HIV/AIDS: Digital Stories from South Africa*:

> I appreciated how she told her story. It may give women facing or dealing with HIV/AIDS inspiration. For instance, she stated that she was very sick when her husband died. I think she said she had a CD4 count of nine, yet she kept striving and taking her meds and was able to get well again. This may give people who are skeptical about getting on meds or taking on them regularly, a different outlook. (2009)

Tina's response illuminates how digital stories can be a means of empowerment and education for women, reducing stigma around HIV/AIDS. As Tina observes, women dealing with HIV/AIDS can be given hope and support around taking medication and to survive stigma through digital story education.

Tina's response in the feedback session reveals how digital stories serve to educate and empower in multiple ways. The education is circular, fluid, and of movement. As an interview with Amy Hill attests, the participants in Silence Speaks and Sonke Gender Justice Network digital storytelling workshops hoped for more than to share a story. As one participant from Amy Hill's workshop shared: "(By watching my story), I hope people will learn not to judge others. They must know how to live life positively. They also must not isolate people infected with HIV/AIDS.

I need viewers to respect other people's rights and use condoms when they have sex" (Hill 2010).

Moreover, Silence Speaks' feminist, technological, and artistic methodologies and praxis, provides however, the participant's education is always centered:

> Our work at Silence Speaks always places storytellers front and center, prioritizing the need to ensure a meaningful process over organizational/ advocate agendas for developing "useful" content. This doesn't mean that a meaningful process can't yield useful content; it just means honoring women's experiences emphasizing the learning, leadership skills, technology/production skills, etc. so that they can gain through making digital stories in addition to emphasizing the potential use of stories as educational tools. (Ibid.)

Amy Hill's observations provide that centering the individual storytellers technological, storytelling, and HIV/AIDS education can also lead to creating "useful" content. Observations from both Tina from the feedback session and the South African participant who created the story illuminates the feminist pedagogical potential of technological and creative access. Digital stories – process, content, and product – can provide a vital intervention for education across media platforms, communities, and even, continents.

While the response to "From the Center" has been tremendous – from vital support from Jackie Gordon and SISTER, to FAP director Kate Monico Klein's unwavering belief in the project, commitment from Amy Hill and Silence Speaks, and perhaps most importantly, the tremendous inspiration and collaboration from and with formerly and currently incarcerated women – we've reached a critical point. To date, various attempts to seek funding have not been fruitful. As a result of its interdisciplinary and untraditional nature, it has been difficult to categorize "From the Center" within funding requirements and stipulations. And like many feminist based projects without institutional financial support, we struggle to prioritize the project with various contending constraints of limited time and resources. Additionally, collaboration with a diverse group of people, institutions, and networks remain challenging and not always encouraged. The worlds of academia and public health remain seemingly divided. However, we continue forward even with these difficulties in the belief it is necessary to create a bridge in order to create something wholly new and possible.[3]

From the Center: The Digital, Educational, and HIV Divide

In the process of writing our essay, we met weekly at the FAP office in down town San Francisco. On July 13, 2010, we sat in the FAP office – watching from a digital monitor – as President Obama's Administration announced the first-ever comprehensive National HIV/AIDS Strategy (NHAS). As a critical turning point in the nation's response to HIV/AIDS, the NHAS posits the possibility for change. As co-chair of San Francisco's HIV Prevention Planning Council and lead coordinator of FAP's prevention program, Isela had previously attended and participated in the White House's National HIV/AIDS Policy (ONAP). ONAP coordinated a dialogue on how to improve the role of public private partnerships in the era of NHAS. As NHAS was unveiled to the world that day, we were struck by Secretary of Health and Human Services Kathleen Sebelius's powerful remarks.

> ...we've been very successful at keeping HIV/AIDS incidence low for some populations. If you are a white heterosexual woman, like me, your chances of being infected by HIV and AIDS are very low, 1 in 50,000. But if you're a black female who's also an injection drug user, your chances of being infected are more than a thousand time higher than mine, 1 in 35. ("Announcing the National HIV/AIDS Strategy" 2010)

We felt Secretary Sebelius's observations to be poignant; structurally and systematically, HIV is not equal. Through identifying her own body as raced, classed, and gendered, Secretary Sebelius provides the urgency of the HIV divide that separates through racial and gendered lines. While the goals of HIV/AIDS prevention and education is not new, as Secretary Sebelius points out, the strategies must be innovative and resourceful. While technological access is not necessarily prioritized, we believe feminist new media education must be a part of this conversation. Recognizing the digital divide identifies populations in need, particularly those vulnerable to rates of incarceration (Davidson and Goldberg 2009, 21-22). "From the Center" illuminates how digital education is vital for those most marginalized and for women's studies, in particular, to address these disparaging statistics.

This divide in the space between life and death connects to the digital divide, one in which many incarcerated women may find themselves in. Shaped by increasing HIV infection rates, Black women's leading cause of death by AIDS, growth of the prison industrial complex, rising statistics of incarceration for women of color, and lack of access to technology and education – incarcerated women of color are oftentimes located within a "web" of social inequities. We utilize the term "web" purposefully, to emphasize how seemingly disparate social issues shape incarcerated women's lives and to make a pointed acknowledgement of the complexity of feminist cyberspaces. While the "web" is increasingly accessible in universities across the country for some women, much of technology is inaccessible to currently and formerly incarcerated women.

To understand the simultaneity of race, gender and other axes of difference, feminist scholars of color such as Kimberlee Crenshaw, Evelyn Nakano Glenn, and Patricia Hill Collins have utilized terms such as intersectional to describe how "race, class, gender, and sexuality" are "mutually constituted systems" and "intersecting oppressions" (Glenn 2002, 12; Collins 2000, 70). Here, intersectionality refers to particular forms of intersecting oppressions, for example, intersections of race and gender, or of sexuality and nation. Intersectional paradigms remind us that oppressions cannot be reduced to one fundamental type and that oppressions work together to producing injustice (Collins 2000, 18). To this end, we provide how technology and the digital divide may reproduce these inequalities as technology has largely not been apart of the dialogue to understand women's lives. Formerly and currently incarcerated women demonstrate issues of technological and educational access; the prison industrial complex, race, class, gender and HIV/AIDS are entangled, interlocking, connected, and intersectional.

Women of color, in particular, may find their lives structured by the "web" of inequalities, however, these axes of difference also may provide contours of resistance. At the same time, recognition of the digital divide can illuminate a possible avenue for social change. Feminist technological education, such as digital storytelling, may be one possible way to unbind heteronormative, patriarchal, and racialized hegemonic and structural constructions of difference. The ways women are marginalized through interlocking Oppressions signals the urgency to bridge these gaps. The digital divide then, "the systematic disparities in access to computers and the Internet" can and must be considered a feminist issue (Mossberger, Tolbert, and McNeal 2008, 8).

Technologically Entangled: Towards a Feminist Digital Resistance

...we have a situation that is much more complicated, yet far from disheartening.
—Lisa Nakamura (2009, 208)

As New Media and Asian American Studies scholar Lisa Nakamura articulates above, while the initial dream of the Internet as Utopian has been complicated, our predicament is "far from disheartening." Nakamura's point inspires and illuminates our interests, in the possibility of providing subjectivity, equity, and agency through media technologies and pedagogy. Our inquiries center on race and ethnicity with intersectional axes of difference, such as gender, sexuality, and class. Primarily located at the nexus of disciplines such as Ethnic, Women, and New Media studies, "From the Center" draws from diverse methodologies and theoretical alliances, bearing productive and fruitful bridges to address structural inequalities for all women.

The new media age, Obama Administration's new strategy on HIV/AIDS, and feminist interventions provide hope and movement. As Secretary Sebelius had announced on Whitehouse.gov, the Obama Administration's "ambitious vision:"

> That vision is that the United States should be a place where new HIV infections are rare. And when they do occur, every person regardless of age, gender, race, and ethnicity, sexual orientation, gender identity, or socio-economic circumstances, will have unfettered access to high quality life extending care, free from stigma and discrimination. ("Announcing the National HIV/AIDS Strategy" 2010)

While the goals may seem challenging, incarcerated women's voices are central to the strategy of combating HIV infection rates and HIV/AIDS stigma. Digital storytelling can be a possible intervention to the increasing divide(s). Breeyana Singletary's perspectives illuminate this potential, our hopes:

> The goal is for incarcerated/ HIV women and all types of women to feel and know that they are important and they do matter. And your goal should be to show the world that you are more than a HIV virus, more than a jail suit, more than a felony charge, show the world you can sell more than drugs or your body. Show the world that you are strong, you are talented and educated and that you do have the capacity to make a digital story and not just any digital story but (YOUR) digital story about your life and that's the best part about it.

"From the Center's" story is yet unfinished. However, we remain committed to this vision of change and will work to include the voices and lives of those most affected by these inequalities. We urge and imagine the feminist version of this vital vision, which can only be created together.[4]

Bibliography

"Announcing the National HIV/AIDS Strategy: National HIV/AIDS Strategy Video (NHAS)." 2010. *The White House.* July 13. Accessed August 25, 2010. http://www.whitehouse.gov/blog/2010/07/13/announcing-national-hivaids-strategy.

Banaszewski, Tom. 2002. "Digital Storytelling Finds Its Place in the Classroom." *Multimedia Schools.* January/February. Accessed January 2. http://www.infotoday.com/mmschools/jan02/banaszewski.htm.

Barbara Barry. 2010. Accessed August 10. http://alumni.media.mit.edu/~barbara/projects.html.

Boal, Augusto. 1979. *Theatre of the Oppressed.* New York: Theatre Communications Group.

Bransford, John, Ann L. Brown and Rodney R. Cocking. 2000. *How People Learn: Brain, Mind, Experience, and School.* Washington DC: National Academy Press.

Center for Digital Storytelling. 2010. Accessed August 25. http://www.storycenter.org.

Center for Disease Control and Prevention. 2010. "HIV/AIDS Among Women." *Department of Health and Human Services.* Accessed August 27. http://www.cdc.gov/hiv/topics/women/resources/factsheets/women.htm.

Collins, Patricia Hill. 2000. *Black Feminist Thought: Knowledge, Consciousness, and the Politics of Empowerment.* New York: Routledge.

Davidson, Cathy N. and David Theo Goldberg. 2009. *The Future of Learning Institutions in a Digital Age.* Cambridge: MIT Press.

Fields, Jessica, Isela González, Kathleen Hentz, Margaret Rhee and Catherine White. 2008. "Learning from and With Incarcerated Women: Emerging Lessons from a Participatory Action Study of Sexuality Education." *Sexuality Research and Social Policy: Journal of NSRC.* 5, no. 2: 71-84.

Fields, Jessica. 2010. "RISE Jailed Women and HIV Education: A Collaborative Investigation." *The Center for Research on Gender and Sexuality.* San Francisco State University. Accessed August 27. http://crgs.sfsu.edu.

—. 2008. *Risky Lessons: Sex Education and Social Inequality.* New York: Rutgers University Press.

Fraden, Rena. 2001. *Imagining Medea: Rhodessa Jones and Theatre for Incarcerated Women,* Chapel Hill: University of North Carolina Press.

Freire, Paulo. 2006. *Pedagogy of the Oppressed.* New York: Continuum.

Glenn, Evelyn Nakano. 2002. *Unequal Freedom: How Race and Gender Shaped American Freedom and Labor*. Cambridge: Harvard University Press, 2002.

"Going Digital with Personal Storytelling." 2010. *Planned Parenthood NYC*. August 25. http://www.plannedparenthood.org/nyc/doing-digital-personalstorytelling-15910.htm.

González, Isela. June 14, 2008. "Innovative HIV Testing Strategies in Correctional Settings," Presentation to HIV Prevention Leadership Summit participants, San Francisco, California.

—. July 19, 2010. Personal Conversation. In person.

Gordon, Jacqueline. July 17, 2010. Personal Interview. Telephone.

Hill, Amy. July 15, 2010. Personal Interview. E-mail.

hooks, bell. 1994. *Teaching to Transgress: Education as the Practice of Freedom*. New York: Routledge.

—. 1989. "Toward a Revolutionary Feminist Pedagogy." In *Talking Back: Thinking Feminist Thinking Black*, 24-49. Toronto: Between Lines.

—. 2000. *Feminism Is for Everybody: Passionate Politics*. New York: South End Press.

Jailed Women and HIV Education: Pedagogical Model and Curricular Notes. April 2009. Print.

Lambert, Joe. 2006. *The Digital Storytelling Cookbook*. Berkeley: Digital Diner Press.

Labonte, Ronald and Ann Robertson. 1996. "Health Promotion Research and Practice: The Case for the Constructivist Paradigm." *Health Education Quarterly* 23, no. 4: 431-47.

Mossberger, Karen, Caroline J. Tolbert and Ramona S. McNeal. 2008. *Digital Citizenship: The Internet, Society, and Participation*. Cambridge: The MIT Press.

Nakamura, Lisa. 2009. *Digitizing Race: Visual Cultures of the Internet*. Minneapolis: University of Minnesota Press.

Papert, Seymour. 1980. *Mindstorms: Children, Computers, and Powerful Ideas*. New York: Basic Books.

Resnick, Mitchel, Natalie Rusk and Stina Cooke. 1998. "The Computer Clubhouse: Technological Fluency in the Inner City." In *High Technology and Low-Income Communities,* edited by Donald A. Schön, Bish Sanyal and William J. Mitchell, 1-17. Cambridge: MIT Press. Accessed November 18, 2001. www.media.mit.edu/~mres/papers/clubhouse-chapter.pdf.

Reyes, Tina. October 26, 2009. Written Response from "FTC" CJ #2 Feedback Session. Print.

"Research on Inequality, Sexuality, and Education (RISE)." 2008. *The Center for Research on Gender and Sexuality*. Accessed August 25, 2010. http://crgs.sfsu.edu/research/rise.htm.

Rhee, Margaret. 2008. "By the Grace of God: Conference Presentation by Allyse Gray, Cat White and Isela González." *San Francisco Department of Public Health, HIV/AIDS Epidemiology Annual Report, HIV Epidemiology Section*. Accessed February 2, 2011. http://sfhiv.org/documents/AnnualReport2008.pdf.

San Francisco Sheriff's Department. 2008 Incarceration Rates. Internal and unpublished report.

Sibongile. *"Sibongile: My Life as A Widow Living With HIV" Responding to Violence and HIV/AIDS: Digital Stories From Southern Africa*. Video and Print. www.genderjustic.org.za/docman/digital-story-facilitators.../download.

Singletary, Breeyana. "My Face, My Voice, My Story." Unpublished Essay. Print.

"SISTER Program: Sisters in Sober Treatment Empowered in Recovery." 2010. *San Francisco Sheriff's Department*. Accessed August 30. http://www.sfsheriff.com/jailpgms.htm.

Silence Speaks. 2010. Accessed August 25. http://www.silencespeaks.org/.

"Digital Stories from South Africa: Responding to Violence and HIV/AIDS: Facilitation Guide." 2008. *Sonke Gender Justice Network and Silence Speaks*. Berkeley: Center for Digital Storytelling. 2008.

Sonke Gender Justice Network. 2010. Accessed August 25. http://www.genderjustice.org.za/projects/digital-stories.

Turkle, Sherry and Seymour Papert. 1990. "Epistemological Pluralism and the Revaluation of the Concrete." *SIGNS: Journal of Women in Culture and Society* 16, no. 1 (Autumn). Accessed August 22, 2010. http://www.papert.org/articles/EpistemologicalPluralism.html.

University of Houston. 2010. *Digital Storytelling*. Accessed August 25. http://digitalstorytelling.coe.uh.edu

Notes

[1] Breyanna Singletary's essay, "My Face, My Voice, My Story," emerged out of collaborative freewriting exercises FAP conducted as a team. "My Face, My Voice, My Story" is currently unpublished. For further information, or request for a copy, please email author at breeyanasingletary@gmail.com.

[2] Out of privacy considerations, all feedback materials written by women who participated in the October 26, 2009 feedback session will be referred by pseudonyms. Please note, Tina Reyes is pseudonym and indicated in this essay by

a *. For further information on feedback session materials, please contact the authors of this article. Isela González: Isela.Gonzalez@sfdph.org and Margaret Rhee: mrhee@berkeley.edu

[3] By the time of completion of revising this article, the pilot project of "From the Center" was granted funding by The Hospital Council of Northern and Central California: Africa American Health Disparity Project. "From The Center: A New Media Project For and By African American Women" was implemented in the San Francisco jails, December 2010.

[4] For support on "From the Center" and the writing of this article, we thank the following individuals: Kate Monico Klein, FAP Director; Breeyana Singletary, FAP Intern; Allyse Gray, RISE Co-Researcher; Michelle Pinkerton, FAP Volunteer and FTC participant; Jessica Fields, Ph.D. Professor of Sociology, SFSU; Amy Hill, The Center for Digital Storytelling and Silence Speaks; FTC Participants from feedback session; Jacqueline Gordon, SISTER Program Manager; JHWE, RISE Research team; Nicole Reed, FAP Administrative Assistant; HASTAC Scholars Program: Cathy Davidson and Fiona Barnett; Professor Kimiko Ryokai; Tai Cao; Caroline Rhee; Editor, Caroline Smith. Berkeley Center for New Media, Department of Ethnic Studies, University of California Berkeley, Center for Digital Storytelling: Gayle Nichols-Ali, and Bessie Dvora China Leipakumakaniokalani Ching (CDS).

CHAPTER FOUR

TEACHING WITH BLOGS
AND BLOGGING WHILE TEACHING:
USING BLOGS TO EXPAND ACCESS
TO FEMINIST (CYBER)SPACES

SARA L. PUOTINEN
AND KANDACE CREEL FALCÓN

The format of this essay is somewhat experimental. Drawing upon theories in feminist consciousness-raising, feminist pedagogy, and feminist technologies, we weave together critical reflections on our experiences with teaching with blogs and utilizing personal blog spaces while teaching. Our dialogues engage with accessibility in terms of expanding access to feminist (cyber)spaces with a focus on blogging. Specifically, we explore how we have found blogs to be useful within and beyond the classroom through a discussion of four key themes: visibility, training, engagement, and creating community. Throughout the many different forms in which we write, we firmly center our identities and research interests as a Chicana feminist and a white feminist troublemaker.

While our online and offline conversations cover a wide range of ideas about these four topics, we offer up the following tentative conclusions: blogs encourage us to make our thinking, writing and pedagogy processes as feminists visible to others (visibility); blogs enable us to learn how to experiment with new ways of sharing our stories and talking back to those who wish to marginalize us (training); they require that we rethink how we engage our readers through comments, as well as how we show students the importance of feedback over grading-as-evaluating (engagement); and they provide us with space for authentic expression and connections for engaging in shared knowledge production (creating community).

Because we believe that participating (reading, writing, and facilitating) in personal and course blogs make us more effective thinkers, writers, teachers, and feminists, and because we also like to practice what we teach, we decided to create a blog to document the writing and diabloging process that we engaged in as we collaborated on this chapter during the summer of 2010. We started writing and diabloging in *It's Diablogical! A Collaborative Diablog on Feminist Pedagogy* at the end of June and have used the blog to share our ideas and perspectives with each other, to post recorded dialogues, to give each other feedback on our work, to archive our notes from our weekly (offline) meetings, to expose our collaborative writing process for this chapter, and to document the development of our thoughts about feminist blogging.[1] Because we are aware that blogging requires a sharing of oneself in a public way, we choose to begin our piece by highlighting our specific feminist investments in situating ourselves within our scholarly work.

About Kandace Creel Falcón (KCF)

My life is about stories. I live to tell and listen to stories; I honor the value of stories, write stories, and would not be who I am without these many stories. To me, blogs are one of many ways that I share, collect, and disseminate these stories that hold so much meaning. Blogging allows my thoughts and stories access to new audiences in hopes that someone might stumble across them and feel a connection. This is true of both my personal blogging and my use of blogs in my feminist teaching. I have used my blog to counter what I see as a visible gap in diverse voices in the cooking blogosphere. I created my personal cooking blog (*La Kitchen Chicana*) in July of 2009 – purposefully blending storytelling with recipes and situating my experiences as a femme, lesbian, mestiza, Chicana feminist.

I use blogs to speak back to or against marginalization of Chicanas/Latinas.[2] In the fall of 2008, I created my first course blog for a course offered through the Department of Chicano Studies at the University of Minnesota. Part of the draw for this was my frustration with Googling "Chicana and gender/sexuality" and coming up with hardly any content of scholarly interest. Course blogging is about creating resources that serve my current students and others who may be interested in the topics after the course has ended. This is especially vital in the era of attacks on ethnic and women's studies disciplines. To me, this epitomizes the power and potential of using blogs in the feminist classroom.[3]

I have also relied on blogs as necessary and valuable creative writing outlets for my students and myself. I have worked on incorporating blogging as a means to increase students' confidence with writing. I enrich my courses through blogs that facilitate connections between examples from "daily life" and the feminist theories that I teach. I believe in the potential for transformative learning as a blogger, an avid reader of blogs, and as someone who loves to bring the joys of blogging to my many communities and my wonderful students.

About Sara L. Puotinen (SLP)

Last summer I fell in love with blogging. Sure, I had been using blogs in my classes since January 2007, but it wasn't until I started writing in my own blog in May 2009 that I realized what a powerful space for radical transformation, critical and creative expression, and community-building it is.[4] Now it is over a year later, and blogs play a central role in all aspects of my life as a thinker, learner, writer, teacher, and researcher. I write in three of my own blogs (*Trouble*, *It's Diablogical* and *Unchained*), and I make blogs a central part of all my classes.

I use my personal and course blogs to encourage myself and my students to archive our ideas, to document our research, to put seemingly disparate ideas or representations into conversation, to offer up various accounts of ourselves, to build relationships with visible and invisible/ known and unknown readers, to experiment with pedagogical techniques, to cultivate effective writing and thinking habits, to disrupt the rigid rules and disciplinary borders that discourage new ideas and unexpected connections, to lay bare our own thinking and writing process, to practice what we teach (and preach), to develop connections between our different selves, and to remind ourselves that being thinkers/learners/teachers can be energizing and fun.

In addition to all of these reasons, writing on my own blogs and using blogs in the classroom enables me to access my feminist troublemaking self. Through blogging, I reject rigid boundaries between disciplines, find creative ways to connect my research with my life, and infuse my ideas with a sense of humor. I play with what should count as rigorous scholarship or as proper objects of study. I cultivate a curiosity about the world that is motivated by a desire for engaging and experimenting with ideas as opposed to acquiring knowledge. And I invite my fellow bloggers (inside and outside of my classes) to join me at an experimental and unsettling space where we strive to remain open to new ideas and to critically exploring the limits of our own perspectives.

Part One: Some Definitions and Theoretical Considerations

Through the process of our online and offline dialogues about feminist pedagogy, blogging, and access, we found ourselves giving serious theoretical attention to a few key concepts: accessibility, virtual consciousness-raising, and "busting binaries." Before moving on to our dialogue, we want to provide a brief description of each of them.[5]

Accessibility[6]

When scholars think about "accessibility" in relation to the Internet, the discussion on who has (and who does not have) access to the Internet often emerges. While this is an important discussion in terms of who tends to gain access to the power of technology,[7] we choose to think of accessibility more broadly and to challenge the usual script about women's "access" to blogging/technology.[8]

As feminists, we see accessibility as a larger discussion in terms of how we purposefully choose to create avenues for access to be defined in relation to how we write, teach, and think. We see accessibility as connected to what we, as feminists, can gain access to through the use of blogging. For instance we see access in relation to accessing different parts of our self/selves. This means that blogging facilitates access to many different selves for both ourselves and our students – the writerly self/selves, the feminist self/selves, and the self/selves in community with others. Access to blogging in the feminist classroom means using blogs as a space where students can better access their own ideas and be accountable to them. We have discussed the idea that there is definite value in allowing students access to you as the instructor via blogging (either personally or in the conversations teachers and students have in an online forum like a blog). This, however, is a balancing act, for we do not wish to imply that the ability to access this online space necessarily means it is a "safe space"." Rather, it is a space where we encourage students to understand and value access in terms of accountability – being accountable to one's own ideas as well as being respectful of others.

While we conceive of access as a means to facilitate connections on many levels, we do not envision access as an "all access pass." In short, we do not suggest that accessibility to ideas, opinions, and different selves is an unfiltered process or one where someone gains unlimited access to others (their ideas, their private lives, etc.). Nor do we consider this to be necessarily an easy or uncritical task. However, as we consider blogging a

valuable feminist pedagogical tool and space for dialogue/conversation/
theorizing/reflection, we are committed to exploring how creating access
for these themes, ideas, and new political perspectives by using, writing,
and teaching blogging allows for our ideas on accessibility to emerge in
multifaceted ways while still requiring our students to engage with
learning in critically reflective ways.

Virtual Consciousness-Raising (VCR)[9]

Central to our arguments about accessibility and the transformative and
transgressive potential of blogging and feminist pedagogy is this belief:
blogging while teaching and teaching with blogs in the feminist classroom
allows us to engage in feminist consciousness-raising practices in online,
offline, and online/offline spaces.[10] Borrowing from Tracy L. M.
Kennedy's essay "The Personal is Political: Feminist Blogging and Virtual
Consciousness-Raising" (2007), we describe these practices as forms of
virtual consciousness-raising or VCR.

As we understand it, VCR is concerned with cultivating a feminist
self/selves. It can involve troubling the status quo by developing a critical
consciousness about the world, recognizing how the personal is political
and how our individual experiences and stories intersect in ways that we
might not always easily anticipate. It involves making deep and
meaningful connections with others through the sharing of stories and
focused critical reflection on oppression and promoting wide-spread
critical awareness and social transformation.

Using blogs enables our students to engage in these VCR practices in
exciting ways. Our course blogs provide students with a creative and
critical space for crafting, reflecting on, and expressing thoughts about
class discussion or readings, experiences and personal stories. They offer
students the means for sharing those expressions with a wide range of
others and for those others to share their expressions with them in
accessible and immediate ways. They present students with the
opportunity to collectively and critically reflect on their thoughts and
experiences and to expose the underlying structures that shape and
regulate those experiences. Our course blogs also provide students with
resources for developing the critical tools that they need in order to resist,
transgress, and transform oppressive power structures.

Our personal blogs also provide us with a space for accessing our
feminist self/selves and for engaging in some productive VCR practices.
For example, my (KCF) blog, *La Kitchen Chicana* (*LKC*), talks back to
the predominantly white and privileged foodie blog community and their

appropriation and uncritical consumption of the foods that ground my Chicana identity and that connect me to my familia. I (KCF) also use this blog as a space for spreading critical awareness about the significance of food for shaping culture, community, and our individual identities ("La Kitchen Chicana or Brown Hands"). I (SLP) use my blog, (making/being in/staying in) *Trouble*, to trouble the rigid restrictions that are often placed on what counts as academic research and writing and to inspire others to do the same. I (SLP) also use my blog to experiment with new ways of expressing and promoting feminist curiosity and of connecting my academic training with my life outside of the academy.

Busting Binaries[11]

Thinking/Feeling
Active Production/Passive Consumption
Public/Private
"Real" Life/Academic Life
I/You
Individual/Collective
Teacher/Student
Offline/Online
Academic Writing/Stories
Abstract Theory/Lived Reality

We are committed to blurring the lines and challenging the many binaries we often face when arguing for a feminist pedagogy (one that challenges the banking model of teaching) that includes blogging as one aspect of our teaching.[12] Drawing upon bell hooks and her promotion of cultivating engaged learning communities and Paulo Freire and his valuing of dialogue, problem posing, and asking questions, my feminist pedagogy requires a shift away from traditional models of teaching and learning in which the teacher-as-expert actively transmits knowledge to passive students. One of Freire's critical interventions in engaged pedagogy is that he requires teachers and students to be committed to a mutually informing system in which theory and practice and reflection are all necessary for critical thinking. For feminist scholars who have always connected the political (practice or action) with theory (scholarship or knowledge production), this key point of reflection can be cultivated through the use of blogs in the classroom. It a space where all three aspects of engaged pedagogy emerge – students and teachers make knowledge (theory), share knowledge broadly (practice), and reflect upon the ways we learn and share that knowledge.

For example the very premise of our dialogue emerges out of the connections we have observed between our research and writing in our personal blogs and our use of teaching with blogs such that neither is distinctly separate, thus we seek to bust that binary. In this way, we challenge oppositional thinking and argue the necessity for spaces (like blogs) to play with chronology and to engage with non-linear thinking. Our use of many different forms of writing (in personal blogs and our teaching blogs) allows us to confront the idea that there is distinction between proper academic writing and blog (or confessional) writing. This distinction does not allow for the complex relationships between all kinds of writing that we engage with and how we ask our students to do the same.

Busting binaries is not always about destroying a binary; SLP, as a feminist troublemaker, also likes to rework, distort, or invert them. In other words, she likes to play with binaries. For KCF, as a Chicana lesbian feminist, her identities are constantly challenging the notion that binaries hold the "last word." Because she so often navigates multiple binaries in her life, her commitment to busting binaries lies in teaching students to really think about how binaries/dichotomies do not allow for ideas that lie between them. Together, our goal in challenging, busting, or blurring binaries means a commitment to think about what lies before, between, and beyond the binaries that so often define our lives. Sometimes busting is just that, a need to destroy what often leaves our experiences out, other times it is about critically examining how those binaries come to be, who upholds these binaries, and creating strategies for deciding what we want to take away from these binaries.

For instance, we find that blogging allows us to challenge the binary between teacher and student as a means to establish authority in the classroom in non-hierarchical ways. We do not wish to totally dissolve the binary that exists between teacher and student, but we play with it through blogging by allowing multiple teachers in that space, through modeling assignments alongside our students on our teaching blogs and practicing what we teach on our personal blogs. This allows for both individual voices to emerge alongside practices of creating shared knowledges between or among class members and potentially beyond when a blog is in a public space. Further, we argue that blogging disrupts the binary between public/private exactly in this way; we challenge our students to engage in conversations in a public space that is no longer confined to the private realm of a closed classroom. Our article, dialogues, and diablogs engage with these processes through illuminating the complicated relationships between binaries in relation to pedagogy, technology, and authority in our feminist classrooms.

Part Two: The Dialogue/Diablog

Dialogue + blog = diablog (noun) A collaboration involving two (or more) people who exchange ideas with others via posts and comments on their shared blog. Our diablog involves a explicit commitment to engaging with each other through reading and commenting on our posts; referring to/incorporating ideas into our posts, and engaging in direct conversations with each other, both online via our blog and offline via our weekly meetings.
—Sara L. Puotinen and Kandace Creel Falcón, "What Is a Diablog?"

This particular collaborative project began at the end of June 2010 in a café in South Minneapolis.[13] Because we were writing about the importance of teaching with blogs and blogging while teaching, we felt compelled to engage in and document the process of our writing and collaborating on a blog. So we created one and named it, *It's Diablogical! A Collaborative Project in Feminist Pedagogy.* We then developed a plan for dialoguing and diabloging for eight weeks.[14] During that time, we posted writing assignments and comments for each other on the blog and met at each other's houses or at a local coffee shop every week to continue our conversations.

The following represents only a small portion of this very productive summer collaboration. Because we are invested in challenging traditional hierarchies of knowledge and because the dialoguing and writing process on our blog was never linear, we present our reflections on the four topics in a deliberately fragmented way. For each topic we offer a brief list of some points from our discussion and then describe our individual ideas about and practices of two of those points.

- Blogs make our thinking, writing, and pedagogy visible to others.
- Blogs make visible a wide range of models for how to think critically, express our voices and produce alternative forms of knowledge.
- They make the connections between ideas and different worlds visible.
- They enable us to express and connect multiple parts of our selves.
- They make us visible and accountable for our ideas.
- They make visible a wider, more diverse range of voices and ideas.

On Visibility[15]

How do blogs make our thinking, writing, and pedagogy visible to others?

SLP: As someone who likes to make trouble, I found myself wanting to use the term "exposure" instead of "visibility" in many of our dialogues/diablogs. To expose something is to lay bare the process of how ideas, knowledge, connections, or one's pedagogy are produced with the goal of critically exploring the limits and possibilities of those various productions. While exposing ourselves is risky and makes us vulnerable, it is an important part of critical self-reflection and coming-to-consciousness (and staying there, too). The course blog provides students with a dedicated and carefully crafted space for reflecting on and articulating their ideas and experiences.

Exposure is not only about exposing ourselves, however; it is also about being exposed to unfamiliar ways of thinking or feeling. In engaging with a course blog, students have access to other forms of knowledge. Not only can they reflect on different interpretations of the texts on their fellow students' (or my) posts, but they can also critically reflect on the new ideas being generated throughout the blogosphere in other course blogs, personal blogs, or news blogs, for example.

KCF: As I teach courses on Chicana feminism, I am often discouraged by the lack of information on Chicana feminisms (or gender/sexuality) online. So, part of my desire to create course blogs is to create a space where we (as a class) archive ideas, document discussions, and create knowledge related to a particular subject. This was the impetus for my first course blog when I taught Chicana/o-Latina Gender and Sexuality Studies. I see course blogs as making visible the very need to continue to ask students to engage with difficult dialogues on gender, race, sexuality, and class (among other identity categories). In having these difficult dialogues in the public space of the course blog, we make visible the relationships between teaching/learning and scholarship/practice. I see blogs as creating a space where feminists can engage with larger questions related to their scholarship (or the field – like Chicana feminisms, Chicana/o gender/sexuality) and how students (at many different levels) are engaging with it. As part of my pedagogy, I ask my students to think about their own identities in relation to what we read, discuss, and/or theorize.[16] Blogging enables me to facilitate this work on multiple levels, within the classroom in relation to texts and in cyberspace in relation to the many fields of Women's/Gender/Chicana feminisms. I facilitate this through the conception of assignments that require students to synthesize material that we read in class and applying those theories/concepts on their analysis of the themes through reflections on popular culture such as films, YouTube clips, or newspaper, magazine, and blog articles (Creel Falcón, *MSUM WS390 Chicana Gender and Sexuality Course Blog* 2010).

How do you choose to make your own processes visible to others?

SLP: I use my blogs to lay bare my own writing, thinking, and teaching process and to encourage others to do the same. I post ideas for academic articles ("My 100th Post"), musings on books that I am reading ("Category archive: Things I'm Reading"), reflections on what did and didn't work in my teaching ("A Blogging Breakthrough?"), preparatory notes for class ("What is queering theory, part 1"), fragments of autobiographical essays ("Category archive: Grief-writing-projects"), and questions about course readings ("Being in trouble vs. beings in trouble"). While exposing these processes makes me vulnerable to the critical scrutiny of my students and other readers of my/our blog, it also opens up the possibility for offering up more authentic expressions of my many selves – the teacher ("Category archive: Teaching with Blogs"), the student ("Teaching (and learning) how to question"), the curious feminist ("Why did we stop asking questions?"), the 1970s pop culture fan ("Tag: 1970s pop culture"), the grieving daughter ("Living and Grieving Beside J Butler") to the students. Plus, it enables me to engage in the same practices that I expect my students to do. After all, if I want them to be accountable for their ideas, I should be too.

KCF: When I was a graduate student, I used to not share my personal blog with my students until after the course has ended. While I regularly encourage my students to think about their own stories/how they hold value and my blog's goals engage with these ideas, I felt that, at the time, sharing my personal blogs gave my students too much access to me as their teacher. As a Chicana, I have also experienced students challenging my authority in the classroom. Because of this, I have been hesitant to share very personal, intimate, and vulnerable aspects of myself within the context of the classroom. While I am open about my queer sexuality in my classroom, allowing students access to my personal blog seems as if I may be allowing them to come into my home. As I have moved into teaching as faculty, I do not feel as vulnerable about sharing more about my investments in Chicana feminism and no longer feel as afraid to share my blog with my students. I see it as a further example of the ways that I engage with theory in my own life, and I like to model blogging as a positive site of knowledge production for my students.

As a Chicana I also am committed to being accessible for other women of color within the academy, and this places me in an uneasy balance between being too accessible or not accessible enough. Throughout the conversations we have had here on *It's Diablogical!* however, I have been opening up to the idea of sharing my course blog with my students in different ways. I think the actual process of diablogging with SLP has pushed me to consciously reflect on why I choose to blog and ask my students to blog in the ways that I do. Before this project I was not always so clear in articulating my choices in regards to how I choose to be accessible for my students. As a public scholar invested in accessible scholarship beyond the academy, I have realized that I want all of these sides of me to be acknowledged as equally valid for my life as a scholar. Also, in asking my students to be vulnerable as part of their transformative learning processes, I realize that I must also continue to push myself to model this for my students. These questions of intimacy, access, and the problem of dissolving binaries between teacher/student while retaining non-hierarchical authority shape my reflections on how my relationships with students shift and change and is very much related to my blogging practices.

On Training[17]

Why is instilling confidence and the desire to experiment with blogs important?

Training includes (but is not limited to) how to:

- Perform blog basics (posting entries, links, comments, etc.);
- Think differently about how to engage, how knowledge is or could be produced;
- Think critically about what we are reading, producing and sharing with others;
- Break bad habits of writing/thinking/sharing;
- Be confident and have a desire to experiment;
- Use links and tags subversively.

SLP: One slogan kept coming up in our discussions about training and blogging pedagogy: "This isn't a how-to manual; it's an invitation to engage." In fact, there can never be a comprehensive how-to manual for blogging while teaching and teaching with blogs in the feminist classroom because blogging technology is always changing and because blogging defies rigid rules. I can (and do) offer up strategies and suggestions to my students, but they can only ever scratch the surface of what is possible for blogs in the feminist classroom.

In my classes, I devote serious attention at the beginning of the semester to training students on some basic blogging skills. Then I spend the rest of the semester trying to instill in them an excitement about blogging and a willingness to try out new ways of expressing themselves. I focus considerable attention on the blogs and on discussions of the benefits of blogging. I participate on the blogs a lot and experiment with categories and ways of expressing myself. And I encourage students to be as creative as possible in their entries and comments.

KCF: Sometimes students can express trepidation over having to blog even though we often think of students who are entering college as being very familiar with the tools of "the digital age." However, if you spend time training students on the basics of how to use the blog it can actually become a space that is freeing for students. For instance, I have a former student who told me she was so happy that she had to blog because it helped her overcome her writing block. Not only did her knowledge of blogging increase, but so did her confidence in her writing (online and offline).

I also think that training students through getting them excited about blogging is valuable in allowing them to access different types of writing voices throughout the semester. If they are trained in terms of how to navigate blogs, post various content (written, pictures, embedding clips, etc.), commenting, and reflecting on their course blog, they can then begin to better access their own voice, the voice that we so often see students afraid to use. The blog also allows for creative reflection on topics that sometimes the space of a formal, academic paper might not.

Even though this essay is not intended as a "how-to manual," how have you managed the logistics of your course blogs? What training does the instructor need in order to manage course blogs?

SLP: I have used blogs in eighteen courses at the University of Minnesota. These courses have ranged in size from small seminars with eight graduate students (*Feminist/Queer/Troublemaking Course Blog*) to big introductory lecture courses with 120 undergraduate students (*politics of sex: spring 2011 course blog*). For all course blogs, I have used the official University of Minnesota blogging software, Moveable Type.

Because I partly use my course blogs to train students on how to negotiate their personal experiences in public spaces, I make sure that my blogs are all public. In order to get experience with producing blog content, all students registered for the class post (and edit) their own entries. Far more than extensive training on the technical aspects of blog posting, I think instructors need to have training in how to manage and maintain their course blogs; they need to develop tools for organizing the blog effectively and strategies for enabling students to keep track of their own blog participation.[18]

KCF: Teaching at two different institutions, I have experimented with multiple formats for blogging – Wordpress, Blogger, and Moveable Type blogs. Most of my facilitation of blogging has happened with small groups (five to twelve students) and medium size classes (twenty to thirty). For the small groups, I often find that I can manage reading through entries if I ask my students to all post to the blog for each assignment. For my medium size classes, I take an approach of asking them to post in smaller groups that I stagger for them throughout the semester. The use of group assignments can also be a way to manage a large number of students on a single blog. Because of the increasing use of technology in the classroom, most campuses have an instructional technology area giving assistance on setting up a course blog and learning how to use it. While learning to blog may present a challenge, the skills used are similar to those associated with using word processing software. I also recommend it to my students as another "tool" they have learned through taking/majoring in women's/gender studies.[19] Since it is a skill they are developing, I give all students access to the blog and teach them how to post themselves, but this also requires a discussion of what being in public means and recommendations on how to ethically engage with this type of social media.

On using technology to subvert, resist and talk back

SLP: I love how blogs provide us with many different ways in which to subvert dominant forms of knowledge and ways of knowing. For example, in our posts we can link to sources that are not usually read in the university classroom and that are frequently dismissed as not rigorous or serious enough. We can also deliberately use tags that drive traffic to our blog, potentially introducing a wide range of readers to feminism. And we can organize our blogs – through categories, tag clouds, archives, pages – in ways that allow for multiple layers and levels of thinking and knowing to exist beside each other. These various uses of blogging technology do not guarantee that we will engage in subversive and resistant practices. However, because they provide students with access both to a diverse range of sources of knowledge/knowing and to a variety of methods for engaging with those sources (and each other), links, tag clouds and other forms of organizing the blog have the potential to enable us (instructors, students, blog readers) to subvert dominant models of learning where knowledge, as a collection of facts/truths, is transmitted from instructor to student. All of these subversive/resistant practices require that we know enough about the technology and structure of blogs to discern some key features of the medium, features that distinguish blogging from other ways of communicating in the classroom.[20] In other words, we need to give serious attention to thinking and theorizing about why and how we blog and to sharing specific tips and strategies with each other.

KCF: I see knowing how to navigate and using blogs as a means to teaching students how to access new feminist studies resources (beyond the traditional text or course lecture) and create new collaborative resources on feminist topics within cyberspace. I always have a student ask when we discuss the course blog, "Why should we use a blog?" I have responded that blogs allow us new avenues to explore course material, feminist theory, and help to create communities (within and beyond the classroom). The great thing about blogging is that writing and learning is no longer simply linear. Through choosing strategic tags and categories for an entry a different means of organizing material can emerge.[21] I have always been intrigued with the ways that this breaking up of a linear narrative can lead readers, whether current students or the general public, to find out how they can connect and relate to the content that you produce. This is a process that we all enter together within the space of the course blog, which is not simply created by the instructor, but by students, who have a hand in shaping what gets highlighted, through the tagging of posts.

I also think that in challenging the usual format of a cooking blog (usually just a recipe or quick post about what happened in the kitchen that day) my use of storytelling and feminist theory helps me create subversive entries that challenge heteronormativity, white privilege, and negative cultural appropriation. For instance, I do not simply post a recipe; I interject my feminist ways of knowing and the importance of valuing my Chicanisma as a vital aspect of what readers must wade through in order to get to the recipe on enchiladas.[22] Tagging my posts or linking my entries to other blogs/content that engage in similar ways helps to encourage further thinking about feminist connections that my reader might not ordinarily access.

On Engagement[23]

What are the benefits and drawbacks of comments for engagement?

- Blogging provides access at any time, not just in the classroom, and allows students ample opportunities for out of class connections/ideas.
- Blogs enable students to engage with each other's writing through comments.
- Blogs provide many different ways to access ideas. This encourages students to actively engage as opposed to passively learn.
- Blogging facilitates multiple directions for evaluation: evaluation of students' work, evaluation of teachers' performance, evaluation of class exercises, evaluation of each other and our own ideas.
- The public nature of blogs demands that teachers rethink how they evaluate students' work and provides them with opportunities for developing new, potentially more feminist, methods for giving feedback.

SLP: Comments are great for engagement. While there are many reasons why this is the case, one key reason that resonates with my feminist troublemaking teaching philosophy is that, through comments, students get (and give) feedback to each other. This enables them to learn from each other, thereby assuming responsibility for shaping the class and inhabiting the role of teacher/mentor. As a result, they are able to trouble the usually rigid distinctions between the teacher and the student and to unsettle (at least a little) the typical distribution of power in which teachers have all the authority and students have none.

But comments don't always work, and they shouldn't be the only way in which students are expected to engage with each other. For example, some students are silent or invisible readers; they read everything on the blog, often getting much inspiration from it, but are never compelled to comment. In my course blogs, I try to encourage other ways to engage – like having students link to other students' blog posts or post an entry that discusses other posts or incorporates ideas/information from those posts.

KCF: The only drawback I can think of in terms of comments is that (undergraduate) students are not quite at the level of engaging in this process organically. In my first effort at a course blog, I realized that in not asking my students to comment on each others' work a certain number of times meant that they were less likely to do so. Not because they didn't want to, but as busy undergraduates who have plenty of other assignments to complete, they just didn't seem to have the time to go there after they made their post. Since then, I have always made each blog post they have to complete for credit in the course also have an attached assignment where they have to post a thoughtful comment on another peers' work. I am really interested in exploring how I might be able to continue to foster an engaged conversation on a course blog. I like the idea of now asking students not just to comment but also respond to comments they receive on their post as an effort to further conversation. I am invested in thinking through what engagement (with course material, with peers, with me as instructor) looks like in this online forum.

How do you evaluate students and give them public feedback?

SLP: I really don't like grades. It's not that I mind grading. I like reading students' essays; it helps me to develop a connection with them, especially the quiet ones. But, I don't like evaluating their assignment in terms of points or a letter grade. And I dislike how grades become the (almost) sole motivating factor for assignments. Evaluating blog assignments, especially ones in which the feedback is posted as comments online, require a shift in how and why we grade students. Sure, I still use points; they are a necessary part of ensuring that students actually do blog assignments. But, when I give feedback to students on their posts, it is not aimed at evaluating (judging) their performance. It isn't even solely aimed at them.[24] Instead, my feedback comments are intended to encourage all of the students to be curious about the readings/our discussion and to inspire them to keep pushing at their ideas. In this way, these comments become an essential part of the engaging and collaborating process, instead of individualized evaluations of (mostly) what students did wrong and (less frequently) what they did right.

KCF: I like to think about not just how I use or grade blog assignments to evaluate student learning but to also think about how students engage in evaluation in a blog space to reflect on their own learning. One valuable moment I had with blogging in the classroom occurred when I asked my senior GWSS students to reflect upon their writing process upon the completion of their senior projects.[25] I see this as a space for students to construct their own tools for evaluating their learning through actively reflecting on their work. In essence, challenging the notion that students are working toward a grade alone but rather moving throughout the semester to learn skills, tools, or ideas that they might take with them beyond the course. I also believe that there must always be this space for students to evaluate themselves (and the use of a course blog) at minimum during the end of the course, if not multiple times throughout the semester. This way, evaluating one's own learning encourages them to be accountable to their own learning practices as well as allowing them to publically evaluate where they are now and what they want to think about the future of their academic journeys. This reflection aspect is key.

Creating Community

How can we establish community through authenticity and accountability?

SLP: Writing in a public forum like a blog can help us to be more accountable to others for what we write. When you write something and post it on a blog, you are responsible for the claims you make, the critiques that you offer, and the stories that you tell. In other words, you are accountable to others. Being more accountable for the claims that we make helps us to be more careful and thoughtful about making them.

- Sharing on a blog creates avenues for collective consciousness-raising and for creating connections between one another's experiences.

- It enables us to connect with a wide range of communities inside and outside of the academy.
- Blogs provide us with a space for authentic expressions of our self/selves and encourages us to be accountable for our ideas and claims.
- Blogs also provide us with a space for engaging in shared knowledge production.

Of course there are many bloggers who do not act as if they are accountable to others; they write whatever they want. Rebecca Blood (*Rebecca's Pocket*) argues on her blog that the ability to abuse the blog process by not being accountable for our claims is built into the system when she writes: "Let me propose a radical notion: The weblog's greatest strength – its uncensored, unmediated, uncontrolled voice – is also its greatest weakness." This is one of the dangers of blogging. But, we can use the uncensored, unmediated, uncontrolled nature of the blog to produce insightful, creative, critical and authentic prose that moves (and provokes) others to think about the world differently and might enable us to create deeper connections that foster community.

KCF: Part of my pedagogical approaches in every course I teach involves the creation of some type of community within the classroom. In Women's/Gender Studies, it seems that this is an imperative for ensuring ample room for new ideas/different perspectives to emerge. Establishing and fostering a feminist community through blog space allows for more opportunities for virtual consciousness-raising to occur. In this way, students are able to access their feminist selves in multiple venues – in class, online, in the context of course work, and in connecting/applying coursework to their own lives. They might also be able to have a variety of venues within the context of the class to share different "selves" – their feminist self, their writerly self, their student self, their activist self (etc.) – in a more fluid and integrated ways, thus dissolving the borders between students' "real life" and their "school life." In terms of my own blog, I create the community in which I want to belong through the way that I write, what I write about, and how I choose to share that writing with others.

How do we engage in shared knowledge production?

SLP: Last fall, I tried an experiment with my Queering Theory students; I made almost all of their assignments directly connected to our course blog. At the end of the semester, I asked them to reflect on the process and what they did and didn't like about our blogging experiment. Many of them wrote about how sharing ideas online through entries and comments helped them to formulate (and/or reformulate) their understandings of the topic of our class: queer/ing. One student described how the blog allowed her to see other students as valuable resources for thinking about what queer could or should mean. Another student reflected on how much writing, reading, and commenting on the blog made her feel like she was contributing to a larger understanding of queer. And one other student suggested that the blog was a tremendously freeing space that enabled him and his fellow students to collectively shape their understandings of and engagements with "queer/ing" in the ways that they wanted and needed.

KCF: Blogging allows for students and teachers to create knowledge together. While posts may initially come from one writer, in engaging with a blog (through reading, writing posts/commenting), each author creates opportunities for new shared knowledges to emerge. I enjoy how blogging allows for multiple voices to be heard in conversation with one another and how the use of course blogging further facilitates dissolving the usual binary of theory-maker/theory-reader. While most of my blog assignments ask students to individually post and be in conversation with one another, I also see the potential in asking students to do group work together on blogs; this would instill a sense of communally-produced knowledge. I usually facilitate this on the blog itself through asking students to co-write posts or through a concerted effort to ensure that students are engaging in dialogue through their comments on each others' work. The great thing about blogging is that there are so many different ways to implement it within a course; the instructor can pick and choose what might be the best combination of assignments to encourage shared knowledge production in both explicit (group work/posts/comments) and implicit (reading, individual posts) ways. Producing knowledge together through course blogging also empowers students to create alternative (cyber) forms of community with their peers and instructor and within the greater interconnected webs of the Internet as well as valuing feminist principles of non-hierarchical knowledge production.

Part Three: Conclusion – A Beginning of a Collaboration

KCF: The process of writing this article has been a journey of collaboration on many levels. I have really responded to the process of working together and the use of different venues for conversation (blogging, writing together, conversing in person and online) have really allowed me to think about how ideas grow, evolve, and become shared. I have really appreciated how our conversations in all of these areas have helped me shape my ideas on the value of blogging in my personal life (which reminds me I need to attend to LKC more!) and the need for using blogs in our courses. In essence, this is the busting of many binaries but in particular the I/You binary, which so often seems to challenge non-collaborative or academic work.

SLP: I like your description of how we bust/challenge/play with the I/You binary. Through our collaborative process, we have been able to push at the borders of our own understandings and develop new, shared ideas as well. Our collaboration has not been one in which our ideas have been fused together, however. We have been able to hold on to our own unique positionalities, even while we engage in creating shared visions of VCR or accessibility.

KCF: I definitely agree with your assessment. I appreciate how you mentioned the structure of our chapter reflects different levels of collaboration and writing. Our first part emerges out of conversations that we engaged in together; the second part is fragmented in our dialogue that we wrote in response to our communally developed questions; and then this last part is a cyber/reality merging of ideas. Similar to the ways that we say we like to model blog use for our students by writing on our own blogs, *It's Diablogical!* has created multiple ways for us to also make visible our collaborative process and has busted (maybe redefined?) the cyberspace/reality binary.

SLP: Yes! Thanks for describing our structure. Something else I love about this collaborative project/process is how it enables us to experiment with news ways to express ourselves and to push at the limits of what counts as academic writing. Quite frequently I find that academic journal writing is not fun, just painful. I never found this process to be painful. In fact, it was often fun. And it still allowed us to be very critical, creative and productive.

KCF: Something that really strikes me about your response is the combination of the critical, creative, and productive. I like that idea; academic writing usually has to look a certain way. We challenged this from the beginning when we proposed in our abstract that we wanted to have a dialogue for our written chapter. I think we have also challenged this through the creative visual look of our blog and the creative approaches we have taken in producing our shared knowledges about blogging while teaching and teaching while blogging. I too agree; this has been fun, and it is necessary that this collaboration continues and hopefully inspires others to explore the power in collaboratively blogging/writing.

SLP: I definitely want to continue our collaboration. I am learning so much about my own pedagogy/teaching practices and how I want to continue to experiment with blogs. Our collaboration exceeds the boundaries of this particular writing project; in fact, we have already started working on another writing project. I have also been inspired to take ideas from our blog and incorporate them into both of my syllabi for the upcoming semester.

KCF: I think that is definitely a byproduct of doing collaborative work! While we have had many informal conversations about blogging (in multiple ways), this project has also helped me to make more concrete commitments to blogging in my life and through my course blog through having formal, structured dialogues/diablogs. We have created new assignments for course blogs, and our conversations have created new visions for my personal blog. I think this could only occur through our focused engagement on blogging in relation to feminist pedagogy. I also think in sharing our ideas with one another we have created a network, linking ourselves and other feminist colleagues, friends, and peers, who are also interested in these issues. I see the value in sharing our experiences on using blogs in these multiple ways to help further expand feminist commitment to these types of collaborations, shared knowledge productions, and interactions with technology.

SLP: Sharing and engaging are very important elements of blogging for me. Even though I didn't start my personal blog as a way to share with others (instead I just felt compelled to write, process, and document all of my ideas and research), the fact that you were a faithful reader and commenter encouraged me to keep writing. From that experience and from our collaboration this summer, I have become even more committed to blogging and to the belief that blogging demands that we share, connect, and engage with others.

KCF/SLP: Through our conversations on blogging, feminist pedagogy, accessibility, technology, virtual consciousness-raising, and busting binaries, we have exposed how the power of collaboration continues to shape our ideas on these topics. In many ways, this is not a how to guide but rather an invitation for others to engage and experiment with feminist blogging and an opportunity for us to continue accessing (and cultivating) our feminist selves. The experience of blogging while writing has further reinforced our belief in the transformative and transgressive potential of blogs for feminist educators inside and outside of the classroom. We invite anyone who is interested in these same ideas to join our conversation on *It's Diablogical! A Collaborative Diablog on Feminist Pedagogy.*

Appendix

How students use our blogs:
- Informal annotated bibliographies
- Media examples, artists, and ideas that were relevant to class
- Critical and creative engagements with the readings and key concepts
- Respectful, thoughtful, engaging comments on each other's blog posts
- Information about local events relevant to class
- Feedback about the course and the blog
- Summaries of their experiences on the blogs
- Wide range of examples of feminism and feminist issues
- Peer review feedback and status reports on paper revisions
- Tracking issues, providing more information for class on chosen topics

How we use our course blogs:
- Post announcement, handouts, revised syllabi
- Introductory thoughts on the discussion topics for week
- Links to and discussions of relevant blog entries from personal blogs
- A welcome to the blog and why it is important
- Media examples relevant to the class
- Questions about topics discussed in class
- Effective model for critically engaging with readings/the course
- Feedback on engaged readings and other posts
- Weekly questions related to the readings and the class
- Aid for in-class lectures/activities

Some Ideas on How We Use Different Blogs[26]

How we use our own blogs:
- Archive Ideas
- Document Research
- Offer up various accounts of our/selves
- Build relationships with visible/invisible readers
- Experiment with pedagogical techniques
- To have fun!
- Continue to challenge/bust binaries
- Put popular culture or current events in conversation with academic theory
- Disrupt the walls of the ivory tower by opening up conversations beyond our classrooms
- Foster creative outlets for our feminist theories/expressions

Bibliography

"Blogging Feminism: (Web)Sites of Resistance." 2007. *The Scholar & Feminist Online* 5, no. 2 (Spring). Accessed June 6, 2010. http://barnard.edu/sfonline/blogs/.

Blood, Rebecca. 2002. "Weblog Ethics." *Rebecca's Pocket.* Accessed January 30, 2011.
    http://www.rebeccablood.net/handbook/excerpts/weblog_ethics.html.

Creel Falcón, Kandace. 2008. *Chicana/o-Latina/o Gender and Sexuality Fall 2008 Course Blog.* University of Minnesota. Accessed January 30, 2011. http://blog.lib.umn.edu.floyd.lib.umn.edu/creel005courseblogs.

—. 2010. *GWSS 4108W Senior Seminar Course Blog.* University of Minnesota. Accessed January 30, 2011.
    http://blog.lib.umn.edu.floyd.lib.umn.edu/creel005/gwss4108.

—. 2011. *La Kitchen Chicana.* Accessed January 20.
    http://lakitchenchicana.blogspot.com.

—. 2011. *MSUM WS247 Perspectives and Intersections Course Blog.* Minnesota State University, Moorhead. Accessed January 30, 2011. http://collaborate.mnstate.edu/public/blogs/ws247kandacefalcon/assignments.

—. 2010. *MSUM WS390 Chicana Gender and Sexuality Course Blog.* Minnesota State University, Moorhead. Accessed January 30, 2011. http://chicanaws390.wordpress.com.

Freire, Paulo. 1993. *Pedagogy of the Oppressed.* 20th anniversary edition, New York: Continuum.

hooks, bell. 1989. *Talking Back: Thinking Feminist, Thinking Black.* Boston: South End Press.

Hurlburt, Sarah. 2008. "Defining Tools for a New Learning Space: Writing and Reading Class Blogs." *Journal of Online Learning and Teaching* 4, no. 2 (June). Accessed June 1, 2010.
    http://jolt.merlot.org/vol4no2/hurlburt0608.htm.

Hurtado, Aída. 2003. *Voicing Chicana Feminisms : Young Women Speak Out on Sexuality and Identity.* New York: New York University Press.

Kennedy, Tracy L. M. 2007. "The Personal Is Political: Feminist Blogging and Virtual Consciousness-Raising," in "Blogging Feminism: (Web)Sites of Resistance." *The Scholar & Feminist Online* 5, no. 2 (Spring). Accessed June 6, 2010.
    http://barnard.edu/sfonline/blogs/kennedy_01.htm.

McCulley, Lucretia and Patricia Patterson. 1997. "Feminist Empowerment Through the Internet." *Feminist Collections* 17, no. 2. Accessed July 8, 2010.

http://minds.wisconsin.edu/bitstream/handle/1793/21732/fcmccul.htm?
sequence=5.
Mitchell, Shireen. "Access to Technology: Race, Gender, Class Bias."
"Blogging Feminism: (Web)Sites of Resistance," in *The Scholar &
Feminist Online* 5, no. 2 (Spring). Accessed June 6, 2010.
http://barnard.edu/sfonline/blogs/mitchell_01.htm.
Puotinen, Sara L. 2010. *Feminist Debates: Spring 2010 Course Blog.*
University of Minnesota. Accessed January 30, 2011.
http://blog.lib.umn.edu/puot0002/3004.
—. 2010. *Feminist Pedagogies Course Blog Fall 2010.* University of
Minnesota. Accessed January 30, 2011.
http:/blog.lib.umn.edu/puot0002/femped2010.
—. 2010. *Feminist/Queer/Troublemaking Course Blog.* University of
Minnesota. Accessed January 30. 2011.
http://blog.lib.umn.edu/puot0002/8190.
—. 2010. *(Making/Being in/Staying in) Trouble.* Accessed June 9.
http://trouble.room34.com.
—. 2011. *politics of sex: spring 2011 course blog.* University of
Minnesota. Accessed November 10.
http://blog.lib.umn.edu/puot0002/politicsofsex/
—. 2009. *Queering Theory Fall 2009 Course Blog.* University of
Minnesota. Accessed June 9, 2010.
http://blog.lib.umn.edu/puot0002/glbt4403.
Puotinen, Sara L. and Scott Anderson. 2010. *Unchained: A Blog On
Breaking Bad Habits and Developing New Ones.* Accessed May 31.
http://unchained.room34.com.
Puotinen, Sara L. and Kandace Creel Falcón. 2010. *It's Diablogical! A
Collaborative Diablog on Feminist Pedagogy.* Accessed July 14.
http://teachingblogs.room34.com.
Solis, Brian. 2010. "Influence is Bliss: The Gender Divide of Influence on
Twitter." *Brian Solis*, August 4.
http://www.briansolis.com/2010/08/influence-is-bliss-the- gender-
divide-of-influence-on-twitter.

Notes

[1] To access our collaborative diablog, see http://teachingblogs.room34.com.
[2] Here, I draw on McCully and Patterson (1996) who begin their article "Feminist Empowerment through the Internet" by using bell hooks' quote from *Talking Back: Thinking Feminist, Thinking Black* (1989). Hooks states, "Moving from silence into speech is for the oppressed, the colonized, the exploited, and those

who stand and struggle side by side a gesture of defiance that heals, that makes life and new growth possible. It is that act of speech of 'talking back,' that is no mere gesture of empty words, that is the expression of our movement from object to subject – the liberated voice" (9). I see the connection between the goals of feminist consciousness-raising and how I access my feminist self/selves through my own blogging. This idea of speaking back also adds the political element so necessary in our teaching, as well as provides multiple/new spaces to share stories.

[3] See http://teachingblogs.room34.com/about-kcf for a list of my course blogs.

[4] See http://trouble.room34.com/archives/3237 for a list of my course blogs.

[5] We choose to use italics here in order to model the many voices one can use when working with blogs within the confines of this medium of writing. We find setting some writing apart like this can ask the reader to engage with multiple layers of writing and reflection as you might on a blog through the many different types of information you can access in the online space.

[6] We have created tags on our blog for many of the key terms that we discuss in this essay. For those who are unfamiliar with blog tags, this means that we have "tagged" (or marked) entries on our blog that address key terms. By visiting our blog and clicking on the tags found within the tag cloud, readers have access to even more of our reflections on key topics. Readers also have the opportunity to engage in dialogue with us by posting comments on any of our entries. To make it easier for readers to access these tags, we will provide links to the various tag archives throughout the essay. Here is the address for the tag for accessibility: http://teachingblogs.room34.com/archives/tag/accessibility

[7] Recently, discussions have emerged to challenge the notion that women do not use technology. For instance, in a recent study of women's use of the Internet, Brian Solis writes about the gender divide in social media ultimately concluding that "women rule" (2010). In particular, more women use social media than men in the following percentages based on his survey, Facebook 57%/43%, Myspace 64%/36%, and Twitter 57%/43%. While this is not specific to blogging, one can assume that more and more women are invested in accessing this type of social media on the Internet. See Solis's "Influence is Bliss: The Gender Divide of Influence on Twitter" for a fuller gendered breakdown on multiple sources of social media.

[8] Specifically, feminist bloggers have written about their investments with using this medium for their work ("Blogging Feminism: (Web)sites of Resistance" 2007). Furthermore, Shirleen Mitchell argues in her article, "Access to Technology: Race, Gender, Class Bias" (2007) that language about accessing the Internet as a scary space i.e. "The mainstream media continues to publicize every computer virus, Internet pedophile, online terrorist, and hate crime activity," can also serve to dissuade some women (in her case, single mothers of color) from accessing the positive aspects of technology.

[9] As indicated in footnote 6, we are providing addresses to various tags on our blog. This address is for VCR: http://teachingblogs.room34.com/archives/tag/feminist-cr

[10] For more information on entries with the tag, "offline/online," see

http://teachingblogs.room34.com/archives/tag/offlineonline

[11] For entries tagged with the key word, "busting binaries," see http://teachingblogs.room34.com/busting-binaries.

[12] (SLP) Drawing upon bell hooks and her promotion of cultivating engaged learning communities and Paulo Freire and his valuing of dialogue, problem posing, and asking questions, my feminist pedagogy requires a shift away from traditional models of teaching and learning in which the teacher-as-expert actively transmits knowledge to passive students. (KCF) One of Freire's critical interventions in engaged pedagogy is that he requires teachers and students to be committed to a mutually informing system in which theory and practice and reflection are all necessary for critical thinking. For feminist scholars who have always connected the political (practice or action) with theory (scholarship or knowledge production) this key point of reflection can be cultivated through the use of blogs in the classroom. It a space where all three aspects of engaged pedagogy emerge – students and teachers make knowledge (theory), share knowledge broadly (practice), and reflect upon the ways we learn and share that knowledge.

[13] While we started our diablog for this chapter in June 2010, we have been exchanging ideas about teaching and blogging and teaching with blogs for several years. As a result, our diablog about blogging, feminist pedagogy, and accessibility builds upon years (since 2006) of conversations and connections created through our shared commitment to engaged and relevant (that is, relevant to all of our communities and worlds) pedagogy.

[14] See "The Writing Project" (July 14, 2010) posted on *It's Diablogical.*

[15] For entries marked with the tag "visibility," see http://teachingblogs.room34.com/archives/tag/visibility.

[16] For instance, I will often ask my students to place themselves beside what we are reading. As I teach in Minnesota, most of my students tend to be white students – for me placing their experiences in conversation with Chicanas then is not about simply saying "oh, they're like me" but rather, how do we experience sexism or heteronormativity in similar and dissimilar ways. In this example http://blog.lib.umn.edu/creel005/courseblogs/2008/10/believers_workers_lovers_p ost.html, I asked my students to reflect on a section of Aída Hurtado's book, *Voicing Chicana Feminisms* (2003) while also acknowledging that their response should not rely on (re)centering whiteness.

[17] For tags marked with keyword "training," see http://teachingblogs.room34.com/archives/tags/training.

[18] For a good example of how I organize my blogs, see http://blog.lib.umn.edu/puot0002/fd2011.

[19] For some specific examples, please visit the assignments area of two of my course blogs. The first one was facilitated with five students (*Chicana Gender and Sexuality Course Blog*, 2010) the second one is a blog I have used with 20 students that asks them to stagger their posts (*Perspective and Intersections Course Blog*, 2011).

[20] In her essay, "Defining Tools for a New Learning Space: Writing and Reading Class Blogs" (2008), Sarah Hurlburt argues that many blog assignments fail because instructors are not employing a "pedagogy 2.0" or a pedagogy that takes into consideration the distinctive social and interactive (the 2.0) aspects of blogs. We have both found that this approach is not enough to fully integrate a course blog as a means to create new assignments; rather there also needs to be some training on the instructor's end on how to use a blog so as to move away from simply posting assignments on the Internet.

[21] For those unfamiliar with blog writing, categories and tagging are further ways you can characterize the content on your blog. When I teach I often create categories in order to label each assignment for easier evaluation of student work (when you click on the category all of the posts that have been categorized then are brought up in one timeline). For tags, I create some for the posts I put on the course websites, but students also add their own tags. You can click on any tag and all of the posts that have used that same tag will also come up. I see it as a new way for reading content within the context of the blog.

[22] Please read my September 14, 2009 entry, "La Kitchen Chicana or Brown Hands," as an example of how I try to subvert the cooking blog genre by theorizing through my relationship to my grandmother and familial traditions and the sharing of recipes with unknown audiences.

[23] For entries tagged with the key word "engagement," see http://teachingblogs.room34.com/archives/tag/engagement.

[24] Frequently I post entries in which I provide general feedback for the class. See http://blog.lib.umn.edu/puot0002/glbt4403/2009/10/some-thoughts-on-your-first-bl.html.

[25] See http://blog.lib.umn.edu/creel005/gwss4108/7-writing-process-reflection for my students' reflections on using the blog to help them write their final projects as well as http://blog.lib.umn.edu/creel005/gwss4108/2010/04/7-writing-process-reflection.html for the assignment parameters.

[26] These lists have been shortened for the purposes of this article. Please see http://teachingblogs.room34.com/ways-to-use-the-blog for a fuller list of the many ways we use, ask students to use, and collaboratively use blogs in our lives.

CHAPTER FIVE

CYBERQUILTING:
WEAVING OUR HERSTORIES
THROUGH ANTI-COLONIAL
FEMINIST RESEARCH

LISA CHILD, DEENA DADACHANJI,
SARA MOHAMMED AND DANIELLE SMITH

This paper is a sharing of the journeys that we, as peers, friends, and now co-authors, undertook, seemingly independent of each other but ultimately intersecting in multiple ways. It is a testament to the ways that we, as first and second generation women, are coupling indigenous research methodologies with modern technology to find new ways of knowing, creating, and disseminating information which ultimately informs how we come to know ourselves.

Throughout this process, we use gender analytically to address and evaluate the ways in which women's research methodologies differ from traditional research methodologies. Furthermore, we recognize the historically indigenous and auto-ethnographic research methodologies that have been delegitimized through colonial practices and policies and continue to do so within many institutions, including the one in which we met and started this journey, at the University of Toronto. Consequently, the utilization of these particular methodologies poses a challenge to hegemonic research methodologies, while simultaneously widening the space for women to gain agency in their own knowledge formation practices.

Our research and involvement with various research methodologies took place during an undergraduate course in which Dr. Jacqui M. Alexander led us to discover the depth of our own ancestral herstories. Through Dr. Alexander's teaching and guidance, we borrowed from indigenous and anti-colonial research methodologies to gather our data and stories, while simultaneously employing modern technology to help us in recording, conducting, and sharing this information. This initial process opened up a space for us to discover and discuss our ancestral stories, our own lineage, and our own legacies while simultaneously realizing the many connections that lay between these.

After our course was complete, we four shared our research through the Cyberquilting process. Using the Internet and video technology, we shared and disseminated our oral herstories with other women across geopolitical borders, thereby deepening and further strengthening the narratives that constructed our identity. In other words, by using technology in diverse ways to conduct, record, and share our oral herstories, we learned and re-membered our ancestral herstories, while simultaneously learning and re-membering who we are and where we are from.

Planting the Seeds

For the first time in 2008, Dr. Alexander offered *Migrations of the Sacred*, a fourth year undergraduate course, within the Women and Gender Studies Institute at University of Toronto. The final project for the course was to write a paper examining the lineage and migration of our ancestral and sacred traditions, knowledges, and practices by conducting an oral history with a family member. In other words, we interviewed our chosen family member in order to better understand how the sacred elements in and of our family have changed or been buried through migration to our various diasporic locations.

In order to prepare and understand this task, we read about the ethical issues surrounding interviewing and explored different methodologies for research. From here, we each decided what elements of our family's history we wanted to investigate, which family member would be the most appropriate to interview, what questions to ask, what technologies to use, and how to tie it all together. Next, each one of us employed multiple forms of technology, ranging from phone, Skype, and in-person interviews when available, employing notetaking, voice recording, and video recording. Once our interviews were complete and our stories became more complex and contextualized by sharing in the classroom, our final assignment was to compile our new knowledge into a written herstory.

We, the four authors of this essay, entered Dr. Alexander's course in different ways, each ultimately searching for new methods to identify and know ourselves. Lisa stumbled upon it by recommendation of the professor but was weary to enter this space, as the Sacred was a taboo subject in her family, and her suppressed resentments, coupled with the lingering unresolved effects of colonization, made the topic seem too complicated to deconstruct. The task of conducting an oral history of her family through examining the migration of the Sacred terrified her, to say the least. Despite her resistance, the personal growth that she was able to undergo and the new ways her self-identity was shaped made the course a transformational experience.

Years earlier, Sara had begun the process of reconciling the fractured histories and knowledges which have always been embodied within her identity as a woman of mixed-race heritage but had often been overlooked. Having previously taken a course with Dr. Alexander, Sara was drawn to this course but did not initially comprehend how deep this learning would go. She intuitively knew what needed healing but did not realize the extent to which silence had become a barrier to her own process of decolonizing and healing.

Deena's interest in the intersections of migration and spirituality, two major facets of her identity, brought her to Dr. Alexander's course. Though this was the last course credit for her Equity Studies major at University of Toronto, she soon discovered that it was, in fact, the first step towards a whole new way of living and being. This course ultimately led her to uncover the extraordinary parallels between her own journey of migrating from Pakistan to Canada and her maternal grandmother's journey of migrating from India to Pakistan. Additionally, the course enabled her to connect her family's experiences of migration with other South Asian women's families' experiences, ultimately discovering the recurring threads that run through seemingly disparate narratives.

Danielle had a journey that took a slightly different route, through an arts-based workshop called *The Personal Legacy Process*, a multi-faceted performance methodology aimed at ancestral reclamation as a source and inspiration for artistic creation work, as well as an anchor of sorts for ancestral identity within the challenging multicultural landscape of Canada. The workshop was a profound starting point and combined with enrollment in another of Dr. Alexander's courses. This experience led her to participate in *Migrations of the Sacred* as a route to continue to address her longing for the healing needed through ancestral reclamation and thus spirit reparation.

Research Methodologies and Frameworks

Throughout this course, there were many ethical issues we had to consider when planning and conducting our research. A particular question was how to consider research methodology and reclamation of ancestry as

an indigenizing and emancipatory process. Having been steeped in
Eurocentric histories and ideologies from the educational system and the
colonial society in which we live, reclamation of our herstories and stories
is central to decolonization and is thus emancipatory.

However, there is a tension that exists in research considering
historical methodologies embedded in a colonial educational system, and
this has historically delegitimized indigenous knowledges. In *Decolonizing
Methodologies*, Linda Tuhiwai Smith discusses imperialism as a discursive
field of knowledge that dictates educational systems and traditional
methods of research (2006, 21). Like talking back to colonial powers and
practices, and like writing back through literary terms, researching back
has been one of the focuses of both our individual and collective work as
writers, knowledge producers, and decolonizers. Western scientific models
of research are far from adequate for our purposes as it reinforces
disconnection since it prescribes objectivity, neutrality, and distance rather
than reconnection and subjectivity.

As a result, we not only had to maintain constant reflexivity but also
have to be ethical, respectful, critical, and humble in order for our elders to
trust us not simply as their inheritors but as students and researchers
(Smith 2006, 21). Depending on our skills to re-build colonial-based
fractured relationships with our family members and our ability to
introduce technology to record stories, we imagined that we could face
challenges which would prevent family members from revealing necessary
information and knowledge to use in our self-recovery. It may have been
difficult at times for them to provide this rich and important information,
because of painful experiences as subjects of the colonial project, wariness
of how they would be viewed within an academic context, or concern with
how the material they provided would be used.

According to Linda Tuhiwai Smith, historically, "academic writing has
taken the form of selecting, arranging and presenting knowledge. It
privileges sets of texts, views about the history of an idea [and] what
issues count as significant" (36). We have used both feminist and auto-
ethnographic frameworks in our writing as a way to shift the center from
an imperial one to one that tells a different narrative in the process of
decolonization for us as women. Carolyn Ellis, in her book *The
Ethnographic I, A Methodological Novel About AutoEthnography* (2004),
provides a model to address some of the issues Smith raises and describes
how auto-ethnography can be empowering by highlighting the personal
experiences of women and communities that experience marginalization.
Taking the personal experience as the primary site of "data collection"
turns traditional research on its head in that the personal experience is the

site of research and knowing the world, beyond what traditional research has typically discounted as illegitimate. We believe that the personal is political and is thus valid and vital for meaningful research. Ellis explains that:

> Autoethnography refers to writing about the personal and its relationship to culture. It is an autobiographical genre of writing and research that displays multiple layers of consciousness...Back and forth autoethnographers gaze...they look inward, exposing a vulnerable self that is moved by and may move through, refract, and resist cultural interpretations...Usually written in first-person voice, autoethnographic texts appear in a variety of forms...showcase(ing) concrete action, dialogue, emotion, embodiment, spirituality, and self-consciousness. (2004, 37)

Using indigenous and feminist frameworks of knowledge formation and research, we are not only centering our family, relatives, and ancestors but also ourselves as subjects of research for means of self-recovery and self-determination, conscious of the need for continuity from generation to generation in order to experience and nurture a cultural, familial, and ancestral sense of grounding, rootedness, and self. As Smith says, it is "a very powerful need to give testimony to and restore a spirit, to bring back into existence a world fragmented" (2006, 28).[1]

Integrating Technology

Further considerations included the relationship of our research and our re-membered stories within context of the Internet, since the World Wide Web has, for many, been seen as an extension of patriarchy into the age of technology and information.

Prior to the Internet, access to research, as well as the means of conducting it, was largely reserved for those with socioeconomic status; however, with the current norm of prevalent Internet usage and access, not only is research easily and readily accessible to more people, but researchers themselves no longer need to be confined to the Academy or be a person of privilege. Instead, the status of the researcher has evolved from an elite, privileged, or academic group to the more common layperson. While this is not the case for everyone, since Internet access continues to be determined and restricted by the race, class, gender, ability, and socioeconomic status of an individual, the Internet is nonetheless more accessible today than ever before. This is also true for many feminist organizations, some of whom employ community-based research methodologies by using online tools like surveys to gather data while also making research available online through open access websites. This has proven useful for increasing the sample size of women and their ability to voice their concerns and issues.

For many of us, however, a disconnection from technology was necessary to begin our research for this deeply personal project. We needed time, space, and silence to meditate on and think over our family stories. In this respect, the Internet and technology in general provided few, if any, tools to help us look within ourselves and at our family's past because our research for this project began primarily by looking inwards and reflecting upon our own family's stories and ancestral histories. We considered the lacunae in our pasts and determined appropriate and necessary questions to ask our family and ourselves about migration, ancestral histories, and the Sacred. This internally reflective starting point for our research project was by no means conventional, nor easy, and there was no previously determined formula for this methodology. We learned as we went along and are continuing to learn by developing and applying the skills suggested by Linda Tuhiwai Smith, as mentioned above.

In *Pedagogies of Crossing*, Dr. Alexander writes, "the details would daunt memory to produce a forgetting so deep, we had forgotten that we had forgotten. Missing memory. Who are my people? How will I come to know the stories and histories of my people?" (2005, 263). These are important questions that we struggled with throughout our work. If each cell in our body has the capacity to remember, how could there be so much about our ancestry that we still did not know? Many of us worked from the premise that our herstories were buried within us and we simply needed to locate that knowledge in its source. That, however, raised the question of whether there has been a process of conscious forgetting. To answer these questions and re-member those histories and connections dis-membered through colonization, we had to reach out to our family members and elders.

After considering the questions we wanted to ask our families and identifying the areas where gaps needed filling, we embarked on an interview process with the family member best suited to answer our questions. For some, this was as simple as going into the living room to ask our parents a few casual questions. For others, however, this process required much more planning and many more resources.

Given the spatial and temporal differences that physically separated many of us from our loved ones, we relied a great deal on technology to aid us in connecting with our families and those memories that had been forgotten. Various forms of technology were involved in our exchanges and experiences throughout this process. The Internet, combined with technological advances such as audio recorders, video cameras, and microphones made it possible for many of us to communicate with family across great distances and to document the conversations. Many of us used emails, telephone conversations, and/or video conferencing frequently to bridge the physical space between interviewer and interviewee.

The introduction of this technology made for an interesting change in the dynamics of the exchange. Even in the simplest of situations, tools like video cameras or voice recorders ended up complicating the exchange in multiple ways. For instance, after this new dynamic was introduced, many of our family members felt that they needed to be politically correct, or use sophisticated vocabulary, because they were being recorded for the purpose of academic research. In other instances, some members thought through their ideas and stories before verbalizing them, taking longer to formulate a structured response. Further still, some members omitted sharing information altogether because they did not necessarily feel that they wanted it shared verbatim (despite, perhaps, desiring to share their knowledge and history). Many of our family members felt that they had to be particularly careful with their words so that nothing could be used "against" them. Thus, it is clear that a tape recorder being present changed the dynamics of our conversations. While many eventually eased into the flow of the conversations, this piece of technology added an element of pressure that certainly, even if subtly, influenced the conversations. In some instances, much was shared after the recording devices were turned off and the formal interview was over. Conversely, a tape recorder proved useful in keeping a record of the narratives and knowledge shared and allowed us to refer back to this information to further deepen our understandings of ourselves.

Technology, and more specifically the Internet, has the potential to connect people of different backgrounds, experiences, and perspectives. Video conferencing online with one or more parties is not only possible but a common mode of communication for many people around the world who have access. It connects friends and family and allows us to make new friends. Many of us used video conversations to connect with loved ones and then connect with other women across the globe to share our findings and narratives, therefore further strengthening our connections and re-membering our herstories.

Cyberquilting

Although the course offered by Dr. Alexander ended in spring of 2008, many of us have maintained strong bonds and continue to connect, despite the temporal and spatial divides that come between us. We are also in contact with our professor, Dr. Alexander, who became the Cosby Endowed Chair at Spelman College in Atlanta, Georgia. In 2009, Dr. Alexander asked us to share our reflections on the experience and process of *Migrations of the Sacred* with her second set of students taking the same course in Atlanta. The sharing of these stories with women across the globe was nurtured amongst us through the use of technology and specifically through our introduction to a process called Cyberquilting, facilitated by Moya and Alexis Pauline Gumbs, both Spelman graduate students at the time. On their online community called *The Cyberquilting Experiment*, Cyberquilting is "designed to empower women of color...who are least represented within the mainstream media – to create their own means of information sharing and vision building" ("What is Cyberquilting?").

While our interaction with the students at Spelman College initially occurred via email, we later connected using software like Skype and ooVoo to form an online community through sharing our stories. Through Cyberquilting, the initial sharing of our stories in that small classroom at University of Toronto grew into an online sharing amongst women from Toronto, Ottawa, New York, Dubai, Atlanta and back, maintaining relationships as we moved away from Toronto with family across the globe. This process culminated in our presentation at Spelman's academic conference "Africa in the America's: Light, Movement, Sound, Water," where we, members of the Toronto course, participated live via cyberspace to Cyberquilt our stories and herstories with our colleagues at Spelman. We are grateful to Moya and Alexis, as well as the rest of the WebCT folks, for making the Cyberquilting session possible. As well, our colleague Tejpreet Saini provided ongoing support and reflection throughout the evolution of this work from Toronto and then New York. Our work has since developed into this final cumulative written document, which was woven together over Google docs, allowing us to write and shape this piece together, reflecting on our multiple and varied, yet similar, experiences.

Through the Internet, we were able to meet and create powerful connections and exchanges. It is through this experience of using cyber-technologies that we have come to support Boase's argument that the Internet "is enabling people to maintain existing ties, often to strengthen them, and at times to forge new ties. The time that most people spend online reduces the time they spend on the relatively unsocial activities [like] watching TV" (Boase et al. 2010, 16). Throughout the Cyberquilting process, technology facilitated collective connecting, sharing, discovering, deep learning, and re-membering with family members from all over the world, our colleagues at Spelman, and each other, which would not have been possible without it. Nevertheless, while technology afforded us many opportunities to connect and exchange in some ways, it also limited us in our ability to do so in others. In relying on technology as the primary medium of communication, it became difficult to be immersed in and feel the energy of the work that we were doing. For example, we could not reach out and hug each other in moments where it was necessary for human touch to bridge understandings. At other times during our own necessary self-reflection, technology simply was not useful or necessary, and at times it was even disruptive. Despite the varying advantages and limitations, technology has played a crucial and necessary role in shaping our experiences, exchanges, and identity formation through this process.

Cyberquilting with our sisters at Spelman allowed us to share our ancestral narratives with women who we would otherwise not have been able to connect with had the medium of the internet not made it possible. This process facilitated narrative-building and the sharing of collective discoveries and re-memories, which had long been lost to our conscious minds. Further, we were able to build upon one another's narratives and experiences, unlocking similarities and parallels through time and space. Cyberquilting revealed that our ancestral narratives are different, yet so similar, and we could not help but feel that we are shaped by multiple stories. These journeys and investigations have brought us full circle, making this process not only life-changing but also life-building. These exchanges were paramount in furthering our own individual journeys into our ancestry, as well as creating an understanding of the parallels between the process of migration and the spiritual connectedness of women across the globe.

While Cyberquilting cannot replace face-to-face interactions, it is the closest we can sometimes get to it. Cyberquiliting has its limits, often preventing the physical and spiritual interactions that you could have when you can physically share the same place. Additionally, we were unable to physically reach out to our families and to our sisters at Spelman during our conversations and let them know, with a simple touch, that we were there to support and reassure them on their personal journey. These were instances where it was clear that technology had failed us. The connecting between people, a two-dimensional image on a screen is different to the bonding and sharing of knowledge that happens in the same space. Much is lost in this interaction; however despite its weaknesses, the Internet has afforded us certain privileges. As described in the PEW Internet and American Life Project report, "as the internet has become a part of our everyday routine, it has changed our form of community and broadened our social networks" (Boase et al. 2010, 55). Consequently, these interactions in cyberspace allow us to share experiences with other women who we would not normally be able to have access to without this medium.

Our Processes of Decolonization, Reclamation and Healing: The Use of Memory and Re-memory in Research

Recovering our ancestral knowledges and making these the site of research and knowledge formation is one step in the larger process to decolonize and self-determine our own narratives. In part, this research was decolonizing, but mostly this research process grew out of a need to create a new language, tool, and conduit to research the silenced histories of our ancestors, elders, and immediate families. Reclamation of self and familial memories previously buried under layers of migratory scars was intuitively and holistically healing. Our thirst for memory, or rather the process of "re-memory," comes from identifying migratory scars that resulted in the silencing of our familial memories. The attempted colonial erasure of indigenous knowledges is what has connected us as a group in our collective longing for our herstories. In *Recovering the Sacred*, Winona LaDuke opens with this question: "how does a community heal itself from the ravages of the past?" She responds with: "the multifaceted process of recovering that which is 'sacred'" (2005, 11). This quote speaks volumes about the ways in which our research is intimately related to decolonization and healing from the scars that colonized communities carry both historically and still resonate into the present day.

In a fundamental and truly healing way, this research methodology grew out of a connected and reconnecting process of re-membering the sacred in our lives. We are decolonizing through a process of qualitative research that is inherently healing and intuitively based on the need to connect with our ancestors, dead and alive, through whatever medium available. In this context Cyberquilting and autoethnography, through gathering oral histories, proved to be the salve we needed to begin a collective journey of healing and reclaiming the histories and knowledges for which we yearned.

Linda Tuhiwai Smith in *Decolonizing Methodologies* argues that "self-determination in a research agenda becomes something more than a political goal. It becomes a goal of social justice, which is expressed through and across a wide range of psychological, social, cultural and economic terrains. It necessarily involves the processes of transformation, of decolonization, or healing and of mobilization as peoples" (2006, 116). In this way, research through a means that is self-determined and anti-colonial facilitates both the reclamation of ancestral and non-colonized histories and the mode through which our healing is shaped.

In *Processes of Decolonization* (2000), Poka Laenui identifies five stages: rediscovery and recovery of Indigenous history and culture, mourning, dreaming, commitment, and action. In the first of Laenui's stages, "rediscovery and recovery," the "phase of rediscovering one's history and recovering ones culture, language, and so on is fundamental to the movement for decolonizing" (2000, 153). In making claims to one's history and knowledges that were previously dis-membered and supplanted with colonial histories and knowledges, we can see how decolonization is synonymous with healing. To reclaim what was dismembered is inherently healing. Additionally, through Cyberquilting, we have created a community of women who have made similar investments in healing colonial scars. To employ a research methodology that is not only decolonizing in nature but employs a process of reclamation, healing is the necessary byproduct (and perhaps the desired outcome).

Now to take this one step further, in *This Bridge We Call Home: Radical Visions for Transformation*, Gloria Anzaldúa discusses how "by redeeming your most painful experiences you transform them into something valuable...[to] share with others so they may be empowered" (2002, 540). In sharing and connecting our processes of decolonization, we simultaneously collectively heal and empower, which is what makes this research process so unique. In embedding our collective experiences within a larger process of re-memory work, what manifests is our ability to realize how decolonization, reclamation, and healing also connect us with spirit. To decolonize is to reconnect with our capacity as spiritual beings in spirit outside of the colonial borders previously internalized. Thus Cyberquilting is a process that brings about healing, decolonization, and empowerment, ultimately strengthening the ways in which we come to know ourselves and our herstories.

Conclusion

A journey that started in the classroom has taken us beyond the borders of the university and into cyberspace, carefully bridging many of the limitations of time and space. Though we began with an academic assignment situating our lives and herstories as central, when the course was done, it was clear that our journey had only begun. Throughout this process, we challenged traditional Eurocentric academic frameworks by venturing into not only the personal but also the Sacred, to be re-affirmed that they are, again, political. Recovery, reclamation, and integration of our familial and ancestral herstories continue to be a process of decolonization and healing.

Through cyberspace we connected, shared, and continue our work. Much like quilting, traditionally a woman's craft, we are employing communication technologies to weave together multiple generations and legacies of herstories, thus bridging knowledges across international boundaries through Cyberquilting. Our journeys consisted, and still currently consist of, gathering stories, relationship-building, constant reflexivity, as well as utilizing technology as a means of coloring and breathing life back into the parts of our past that help us not only understand who we are today but also to direct us in how to live our lives with self-determination. Our pasts slowly remembered; our lives becoming fulfilled.

Appendix

Four Journeys

Note to reader: All four narratives are excerpts from our writings around our research and as such take on different voices and structures. We chose to include these so that you, the reader, can get a glimpse into our journeys of ancestral histories.

Lisa Child – This process of re-membering was a hard task because I have put in effort to avoid these conversations in the past. I purposely left the room or changed the subject of spirituality, religion, or the sacred whenever it came up. It is not that I did not have my own beliefs; it is that my beliefs are so vastly different from many members of my family, and I never wanted to stir the pot. My aunt, who lives in Barbados, has almost been the key to holding on to the memories of our ancestors. She has the memory of an elephant. She is the oldest of my mother's sisters and has taken the time to get to know many of our distant and not so distant relatives. She visits with all of our family members from around the world in an effort to keep us all connected through her memory. She is also identified as the most spiritual and the most religious member of our family. I chose to contact her to get to know more about my family and about her perspective on the sacred. It was interesting for me to find out how in one generation so much has changed. The journey that my parents took from the Caribbean to Canada was a brave one. They wanted something great for us, and they believed that to achieve greatness they had to move out of the Caribbean. I believe that there were elements of assimilation that they consciously took in order to "make it" in Canada. Through assimilating, I believe that much was lost. Spirituality took a backseat and became a distant memory. There was no church, and no praying in our house. But, whenever we went back to Barbados, we would go to church and were encouraged to pray before going to bed. It was like we were putting on an act for our family back home. Another element is that my maternal grandparents were the religious ones. But, they passed away when my mother was only 16 years old, and I never got the chance to meet them. Her performance of religiosity was paying homage to her parents.

I was not sure where I wanted to go with my conversations when we started the project, so my aunt and I just started talking. The conversation eventually led to my grandparents, and that is where I was most interested. As a child I always felt as if I was missing out on something really important because I never knew my grandparents. One of the most profound moments was when I learned that I already knew so much about my grandparents without ever meeting them; I just needed to re-member them. Through our conversations, I learned about who they were as people; I learned about what they did in their free time; I learned about how respected they were; and I learned how tall they were.

All that I knew of my grandparents was what everyone else thought was important for me to know. Before this project, I knew that my grandfather was in the police band and that my grandparents died in a Volkswagen Bug when my mom was sixteen, but through this process of re-membering, I came to learn that the most important bits of information for me to know were the things that everyone else took for granted, or thought was irrelevant, like their height and that my grandmother used to sew clothes for friends and family to make extra income for the family. I came to see how these "little" or "irrelevant" aspects of my ancestry play out in my life today. Instead of starting a lemonade stand to make some money, my sister and I used to sew hair scrunchies and pillows for our friends and sell them. I learned about myself as a woman by connecting with my aunt and by learning about my grandparents through her.

Since doing this project, I have continued my journey by going to Barbados and visiting with my auntie Candy. While in Barbados, she took me to the house where my grandparents raised their family. The following year, one of the women from the course also went to Barbados on her own journey and remembered my auntie Candy's house from my description and from our conversations. She sat with my aunt, and they shared stories together and realized that our families are connected. The many overlaps and parallels that have been discovered through sharing are profound.

Danielle Smith – The ancestor I decided to research was my grandfather. In saying that our stories need to be claimed/told/written, I mean any stories that have been silenced, in which I am acutely aware of racist heteropatriarchy playing a significant role. Something specific that I'm continuing to negotiate through this process of reclamation is working with so much male energy. My focus is on my grandfather, who was a teacher at an all-boys school. The women in my family, significantly those who carried family stories, have passed, so the majority of interviewees have been, and may continue to be, male – my grandfather's former students, my uncles, my father.

I began by interviewing different family members, and the mere interaction with them in this way was intense because this sort of formal inquiry was so rare. I mostly heard different versions of a similar story and re-learned that he was born in Jamaica in 1900 and was brought to Barbados at the age of five. As he grew up he went from student, to pupil teacher, to teacher and tutor, to headmaster of the same school, retiring only two years prior to his death, six years before I was born. He was a Scout Leader, and initiated the Literary and Sports Club and the Glee Club, was godfather to most of the boys in the district, and became the Sunday school superintendent. A year after his retirement, as a tribute to his community work he was made a Member of the British Empire.

Learning about all of his accomplishments actually left me with mixed feelings. Along with a deep respect for all that he had done and who he was, I was also strangely dissatisfied because I didn't get to understand who my grandfather was as a man, only as a legend in a colonial system, and, truth be told, I was suspicious of that. I was curious to know, with so many successes, did he have any regrets? At the same time, though, I was both grateful and overwhelmed simply with the transfer of information of one generation from its descendant to the next; so much so, that this first round of intense research, where my curiosity lied within the two years of his life between his retirement and his death, brought on not only profound emotional confusion in me but also symptoms which paralleled the illness he experience at the end of his life, throat cancer. I developed laryngitis and strep throat type symptoms during this research, which was in preparation for a focused ancestry workshop, unrelated to Dr. Alexander's *Migrations of the Sacred* but nonetheless which lead me to her class. All of my symptoms cleared up the day after the workshop and were replaced with a sense of belonging, connection, and strength to continue doing the sacred work of this type of self-discovery/recovery.

My focal points in the workshop ended up being two simple yet markedly profound pieces of information that one of my aunts provided for me – the ritual of the weekly Sunday night walk that he and my grandmother would go on to sort out how to make ends meet until the following Sunday. It was the first time that I learned from a family member how much of a financial struggle they went through. The other piece of information was an example my aunt gave of how he dealt with their financial struggle with so much grace and tenderness toward her after her request for a wristwatch, which he couldn't fulfill.

Digesting all this information, I continued my research, but only after some time had passed. Approximately a year later I began to interview non-family members, some of his students who are now in their 80s, and it was through them that I was able to contextualize more of who my grandfather was. I began to appreciate the impact that he had on those around him – one of his former students being brought to tears when talking about his kindness and the transformation of the community of which he was a part; another former student generously participating in several interviews with me, which usually lasted several hours each.

I was given a view of the time that he lived and worked and the Barbados he knew, one of intense violent systemic racism that maintained the plantocracy, an imprisonment for Blacks in impoverished hopelessness and despair with no economic or social mobility. I found out that it was his students who were the first in the district to break through the very low glass ceiling that Blacks faced in Barbados' labor force at that time, the first to gain schooling and employment as doctors, lawyers, teachers, etc., rather than butlers, drivers, field hands, or like most, unemployed.

Specifically with regards to my grandfather as I continue my research, I still wonder more about the intimate details of who he was and specifically how he was with his children, his son, my father. I wonder about the meaning of how he died. Throat cancer. What was he not allowed or able to say amongst all of his achievements? Also, as I continue to develop these relationships with his former students, I feel in a way that I am finally getting the chance to be grandfathered - an invaluable gift.

At times I feel as though I'm on a search for answers to which I sometimes do not yet know the questions; other ancestors' stories, which I carry with me, which have been passed silently or unconsciously through the generations. What I find so profound in this type of work is the self-discovery/recovery through those that have come before me, who are part of me, those that struggled, those that suffered sometimes to the point of unspeakable pain, those whose lives ended violently. Attempting to uncover what exists beneath and beyond the silences that can live in our stories, in our families, can feel threatening because of the reasons and the tightness in which they've been bound to that which they cloak. Despite the common purpose of these silences, pain remains; it lingers and continues sometimes through generations as an invisible weight, sometimes hovering, sometimes walking beside us or within us, a strange unrecognizable yet familiar pain manifesting in anxiety, anger, bodily ailments, confusion. Though in facing all of this, or at least as much as we can, the silences can get unbound, and what lies beneath can breathe, can have sound, can shift, be held and heal. We can know ourselves more thoroughly, write our own stories; we can be self-determined with the strength in the roots we've discovered. This may sound like inflated idealism, but my journey so far has been fueled with the hope to continue to discover this sort of love.

Sara Mohammed – My inheritances are as a daughter of immigrants whose stories vary yet converge in multiple instances and ways across time and through memories. This project started in search for the Sacred, yet it was my father's memories, both supposedly lost and others already known, that I craved. I conducted this interview with my father searching for my own inheritances as his daughter, my father, the only son of a family whose history can be traced back only as far as my father's memory will let me travel. The pains I have encountered are the stories and memories to which I do not yet have access. My father's first and second languages I regretfully do not speak. As a child I was taught both Swedish (my mother's first language) and English and only a few words from my father. The material items from my father's family are also few. I have two pictures of my grandfather and a few of my grandmother that only get brought out on rare occasions where it is my mother who is the one who holds them tight in a special photo album with other designated pictures and memories from Pakistan.

Much has transformed through migration. My father's family is from a town in Gujarat, India. This location has always been important in my memory. As a child, my father would talk about this place as if this is where he had grown up. Only as I got older would I learn that he has never been there. During Partition, my father's parents left with my father's older siblings and aunt. They fled in the middle of the night, took what they could carry, and walked to the water where they would be carried by boat to their newly designated homeland. What they left behind I do not know. My grandmother left at the age of 19, with her husband and 3 children to a new homeland that was carved out of a post colonial India, new borders drawn, and new memories to define a new life. My father was the first child and only son born in Pakistan in his family. My father has only told me his family's history of Partition once, and it was within the context of this oral history. As a child he did not hear these stories often. For his family, the stories were too painful to be recounted even to the children.

According to this story, our family was torn apart during Partition. Many of his mother's siblings were lost through migration and displacement, and it is in this way that their stories are not as easily accessible to me. After Partition, there was no communication or travel between the two newly formed nations. The borders were drawn, and families divided. In recounting his family's history, there was a tremendous wave of pain that collapsed over me as I sat listening. He did not cry. He used the stories of others to speak through and draw the picture for me. This drawing too fragile to be recounted of his inheritances required other's stories to explain the reality. Partition caused a dismembering of families, memories, and stories. These stories are fragile in the pain that surrounds them, yet powerful in their impact. During the interview I was overcome by emotions, yet the tears that needed to flow were not allowed at the time. My father kept his composure and continued, looking ahead and sitting in the silences as they came. Memories would flood in, and he would continue again and then recede back into silence. This moment would not allow tears; the tears that would later flow were almost uncontainable (I wonder if I inherited these tears that were not allowed when the pain was fresh). The moment was so delicate I was unable to keep composure or produce words; my cat was wailing unnaturally; my father un-noticing; the moment was still and thick with the emotions lining the stories of my family.

During this same interview I learned my father's family name – Andha. I wonder how it is I know certain names, yet the family name was not spoken around my brother and me. In migrating to the United States, my father's name was almost lost. The name Andha means blind. I wondered "why blind?" Why would a family be defined as "blind?" My father shrugged and responded that probably one of his ancestors was blind or had poor eyesight. This legacy of poor eyesight has been traced down through my father and now to me. Lucky for me to inherit my fathers' poor eyesight genes I always guessed. But not just poor genes, the legacy of poor eyesight comes down from my father and passed down to him from generations of people with poor eyesight and captured in the name "Andha." How much more is imprinted in my genes and in my memory that I have not yet uncovered?

In sharing these stories and experiences, we discovered the parallels between Deena's history and my own. Our families fled Gujarat in India to move to Karachi in Pakistan during Partition. Not only did Deena's experience and stories influence what I sought to uncover, it was through these stories that we discovered the connections we had in our histories. Our connections run deeper than this generation. We all came together with a similar interest in family, silence and migration to uncover how woven our histories were already.

Deena Dadachanji – It is an honor to be a part of this project and undertake this journey. I am deeply thankful to Professor Alexander, my sisters, and peers who walked this journey, and my beautiful maternal grandmother, my Nani, for watering the seeds planted so long ago. After many realizations on how little I knew about my own grandma, I began a series of telephone conversations (technically you could call these "interviews," but can one really interview their own grandmother?) which enabled me to scratch the surface of a history and a story that I did not realize I was a part of and, moreover, was a part of me.

My Nani was born and raised in Bombay (India) and moved to Karachi (Pakistan) upon marrying my grandfather. Since my grandparents were pen-pals and fell in love through letter-writing, they had never met each other until after they began "courting." My Nani only came to Pakistan upon marrying my Nana and moving there to live with him permanently.

My Nani spent a great deal of time and energy explaining her notions of a woman's duty and choice (or lack thereof) within migratory processes. Specifically, she explained how her decision to move to Pakistan was based on her husband's wishes. Within months of her move, my Nani wanted to return to India but could not because her father would not accept her back, especially since she was now pregnant with her first child. Thus, my Nani chose the next best thing, and visited India every year, and eventually bore three incredible children along the way, two in India and one in Pakistan.

It is within these reflections that I find an understanding of my own feelings surrounding family duty and obligation, within the journey of migration. Much like my Nani, I too migrated to Canada because it was my duty as the eldest child. While my Nani moved to be with her husband, I moved because my father had sought immigration for our family in Canada. Although my initial cries to move back would have been heard by my father, it was a sense of duty to my family that made me stick it out and remain in Canada. As women, my Nani explains, our decisions are never truly our own to make and are often influenced by the duty and obligations we have to our family and in particular to the men in our families.

Nevertheless, my Nani did negotiate agency and made her own choices, despite attempts to deny her the freedom to do so. After her children were grown, she denounced her Zoroastrian Parsee faith and began to follow Christian Science teachings. She proudly explains that she never fully understood the scriptures and teachings written in the Avesta and refused to simply follow these without question. Thus, she embarked on her own path of self-discovery and spiritual truth, much like her granddaughter would do generations later.

Throughout our conversations, my Nani clearly identified her feelings of uncertainty in belonging to either country – India or Pakistan. She explains that she travelled back to India annually, searching for herself in what she remembers, but never truly found where she belonged. Given the political struggles between India and Pakistan, she recollects feeling torn between her nationality (now Pakistani) and her birthplace and motherland (India). Having lived most of her adult life in Pakistan, she felt like a traitor to India. However, living in Karachi meant living without the independent life she had become accustomed to, living away from family, and being unable to relate to Pakistani culture. An outcast in Karachi and a traitor in India, my Nani is constantly, to this day, negotiating her identity across geopolitical boarders.

Learning about my Nani's issues surrounding belongingness, I have come to understand my own struggles of defining identity. While I was born in Karachi, lived in Dubai, and now live in Toronto, I continue to grapple with where I truly belong. In Karachi, where I lived until I was eight, I feel like a fraud with skin too fair to be South Asian, an accent too Canadian to be Pakistani, and a language too broken to be Urdu. On the other hand, in Canada, I feel like a stranger and a permanent foreigner by virtue of my skin, my accent, and my inability to follow Canadian cultural references. Through my oral conversations, I realized that my journey and my feelings of displacement are an echo of my Nani's journey several years ago. Much like her, my life is a legacy of negotiation and cultural compromise that is constant and ongoing.

Through the processes of unearthing the intricate life history of my Nani, I am better able to understand myself today. Not only have our conversations given me a glimpse into her life, but they have given me a deeper understanding of the historical, social, and political attitudes that shaped who she is and, thus, who I am. In learning about the empowering stories of this woman who came before me, I have been able to strengthen my own belief and trust in the Sacred in ways unimagined. Stumbling upon this course has not only changed the way that I view migration and feminist research methodologies, but it has changed how I view my own herstory and identity, therefore ultimately shaping my own spiritual relationships with the Sacred.

Bibliography

Alexander, M. Jacqui. 2005. *Pedagogies of Crossing: Meditations of Feminism, Sexual Politics, Memory, and the Sacred.* Durham, NC: Duke University Press.

Anzaldúa, Gloria. 2002. "Now Let Us Shift…The Path of Conocimiento…Inner Work, Public Acts." In *This Bridge We Call Home: Radical Visions for Transformation,* edited by Anzaldúa, Gloria and Ana Louise Keating, 540-578. New York, NY: Routledge.

Boase, Jeffrey, John B. Horrigan, Barry Wellman and Lee Rainie. 2006. "The Strength of Internet Ties: The Internet and Email Aid Users in Maintaining Their Social Networks and Provide Pathways to Help When People Face Big Decisions." *PEW Internet and American Life Project.* Accessed August 20, 2010. http://www.pewinternet.org/~/media//Files/Reports/2006/PIP_Internet_ties.pdf.pdf.

Ellis, Carolyn. 2004. *The Ethnographic I, A Methodological Novel About Autoethnography.* Walnut Creek, CA: Alta Mira Press.

LaDuke, Winona. 2005. *Recovering the Sacred: The Power of Naming and Claiming.* Toronto, Ontario: Between the Lines.

Laenui, Poka (Burgess, H.F.). 2000. "Process of Decolonization." In *Reclaiming Indigenous Voice and Vision,* edited by Marie Battiste, 150-160. Vancouver, BC: UBC Press.

Smith, Andrea. March 25, 2010. Blazing the Indigenous Feminist Trail. Keynote address presented at the Ontario Institute for Studies in Education, Toronto, Canada.

Tuhiwai Smith, Linda. 2006. *Decolonizing Methodologies: Research and Indigenous Peoples.* New York, NY: Zed Books.

"What is Cyberquilting?" 2010. *The Cyberquilting Experiment.* Accessed December 6. http://cyberquilt.wordpress.com/what-is-cyberquilting.

Notes

[1] See Appendix for our individual stories.

CHAPTER SIX

CLICKING IN A WOMEN'S STUDIES CLASSROOM: NEW INSTRUCTIONAL TECHNOLOGIES AND FEMINIST PEDAGOGIES

CHIKAKO TAKESHITA, JENNIFER KEYS AND CHRISTINE GAILEY

This paper draws on the experiences of using clickers by three seasoned instructors of a 300-student introductory course in women's studies, *Gender and Sexuality*, at the University of California, Riverside (UCR).[1] UCR is a Research One public university that is racially diverse and has a large proportion of students who are the first in their families to pursue higher education. The department faculty is also diverse in terms of nationality, ethnicity, and race. The introductory course in women's studies serves as a general requirement course and thus draws students from diverse majors. 10-20% students in each class are male. This course also serves as a recruiting gateway for women's studies majors and minors. Clickers, or classroom response systems, enable students to respond to multiple-choice or true-or-false questions using a wireless hand-held device. The signals from the remote-control-like devices are picked up by the receivers in the room, which instantly send the student responses to a computer. The clicker software generates a bar graph, which is immediately displayed on a screen in front of the class showing the distribution of student responses. UCR has made a major investment in the technology and has made it as inexpensive as possible for students and instructors. Many classrooms are already equipped with receivers and a computer loaded with the software that records student responses and generates the diagram. At other institutions, the instructor may have to purchase or bring equipment to class. Currently at UCR, students purchase their own clickers with unique clicker numbers for $50 (or less for a used device) at the campus store and register them under their individual student IDs. Clicker numbers are then linked to the class roster. The same clicker can be used in all UCR courses and there is no additional cost to the student. Students may sell their used clickers back to the campus store when they graduate. Some institutions require students to pay a clicker registration fee for each course or for each term.

Since student responses are not revealed to the class, clickers are a technology that allows anonymity, unlike a show of hands. The instructor can then use the "clicker responses" for various classroom pedagogical strategies, most importantly for us, to start a dialogue among students to encourage collaborative learning. She can also use the diagram on the spot to adjust classroom teaching based on what the responses tell about the students' attitudes toward an issue or their level of knowledge. She can, for instance, ask a follow-up clicker question by writing or typing it up on the board. The instructor can also use clicker information after class. Some software will let one see how long students took to respond to a question to gauge the level of complexity of the inquiry. In other words, the level of difficulty of a question can be gauged by the time it took for students to respond. If it is an attitudinal question, the response time gives an idea of how decided or undecided students might be about a certain issue. If desired, the system enables the instructor to trace the responses to specific students, although we do not regularly practice this ourselves.[2] The system can also tally up "clicker points" to be factored into the grading scheme. For example, each time a student responds to a clicker question, s/he may earn a point toward attendance or class participation. Clicker questions can also be set up as quizzes that earn extra points when students select the correct answer.

Classroom clickers have been around for over a decade and have become increasingly prominent as an instructional technology. A quick search on the *Chronicle of Higher Education* website yields several articles and a couple dozen blog entries on the subject, indicating the growing interest in this technology, pedagogical approaches around it, and the learning experiences of the students. A few "how to" books on teaching with clickers have also been published in recent years. Some institutions are going so far as to developing and experimenting with "super-clickers," or smart phones with applications that allow free-form responses in addition to performing the tasks of a regular clicker (Shieh 2009; Young 2008). Clicker technology is typically used (and a very efficient means) to record attendance, facilitate quizzes, check comprehension mid-lecture, and poll students. In short, the technology lends itself to factory-style standardized, large courses.[3] As education budgets shrink and class sizes increase, it comes as no surprise that a range of university administrators embrace this kind of technology as cost-effective. While some faculty testify that students' class engagement and learning experiences have been boosted by clickers, others view the encouragement of clickers as pressure to adopt a CEO mentality and as movement toward even greater alienation from their students. Some are reluctant to change their teaching style, but at the same time, fear that rejecting the clickers labels them as Luddites or as hopelessly behind the times. Others are suspicious that this is just another way that universities are accommodating accreditation boards that require easily quantifiable "results-oriented" outcomes for periodic reviews of departments and colleges.

Women's studies is no different in this respect from a number of disciplines but for different reasons. Faculty, who resist the use of clickers see the technology as inimical to feminist pedagogy because it seems to oversimplify complex issues by using a "multiple choice" or true-false format and in conflict with fostering critical analysis. At UCR, adoption of clickers in our large introductory courses is taking place at a time when accreditation agencies are insisting that public universities demonstrate "goals and leaning outcomes" for each of their courses and for departments and colleges. Hence, the instructional terrain for clicker technology is not without tension in our women's studies department. We were leery of what many faculty members perceived as an unsuccessful "No Child Left Behind" policy being shunted into the university level, which would be erosive of critical pedagogies in general. But we also recognized that because it makes quantification so easy, we might be able to use the technology to accommodate the requirements of the accreditation bodies, while at the same time facilitate our teaching goals. We decided to give it a try; we attended orientation and training sessions, sought individual tutorials from IT techs, and developed a range of questions alone and in consultation with other instructors.[4]

To a certain extent, the authors used the device in conventional ways for a more effective "classroom management," including taking attendance, discouraging students from walking in late or leaving early, giving in-class quizzes, measuring the level of understanding mid-lecture, and keeping students "engaged" in general. But we have also consciously repurposed the "master's tool" in accordance with feminist pedagogy. In short, instructors may use clicker technology as conventional instructional support, but feminist pedagogical strategies move this agenda in a very different direction. We will argue that feminist-embedded clicker technology creates a novel type of cyberspace namely, a safe, shared, peer-collaborative space within but beyond the confines of a lecture hall and the large classes imposed by university structures. The histogram representing the class response as a community generates a conceptual "space" that places students as producers of knowledge and sidelines the "omniscient expert" professor. The technology has potential that feminist pedagogical strategies can enable, and the technology enables feminist pedagogical goals in unique ways.

What Do We Mean by Feminist Pedagogies?

Feminist pedagogies draw on critical teaching theory developed originally by Paolo Freire, informed by his experience teaching in poor illiterate communities in Brazil. Among the central tenets that shape critical approaches are that the teacher is also a learner and that learners can be teachers; acknowledging experiences can be empowering for students; theory and practice are mutually dependent and mutually shaped; and teachers should use multiple techniques to reach the full range of students. Feminist scholar-activists, notably bell hooks in *Teaching to Transgress*, have extended this to emphasize what she terms "engaged teaching;" the teacher is accountable for her own practices in and outside the classroom; the goal is to produce in a collective manner the kinds of knowledge that students can deploy in emancipatory projects in society. These projects share a desire to transform institutions and practices that reproduce oppressions of race, gender, class, sexualities, nationality, and so on.

UCR has been ranked one of the most diverse campuses in the United States: nearly 40% of the student body is Asian/Asian Americans, nearly 30% is Hispanics, and about 30% is first-generation college students. Because of the intersectionality represented among the students, we are usually able to count on some of them to share their diverse experiential knowledges and positions that are relevant to the material we teach in our courses. We could also safely assume that student work would differ in approach, specific goals, definitions, and in the understanding of the meaning of gender equity. In short, we build on the diversity of our students to create discursive space for feminisms rather than feminism. We concur with Joan Scott (1991) that raw/remembered experience alone is not emancipatory knowledge but can be a step toward its production. The transformation of experience into knowledge requires reflection, problematizing memory, and sharing experiences with others in a collaborative manner.

This is easier said than done, particularly in a large lecture course, while the intimate atmosphere of a smaller class might more easily encourage students to vocalize their thoughts. Large lecture halls represent a "space" that is normally not very conducive to peer-to-peer learning. To begin, the setting itself is impersonal. The architecture and seating, direct students' attention to the front of the room, that is, to the instructor as the only comfortable line of sight. These conditions foster one-way communication. In our particular university, the student passivity that accompanies this creation of an "edutainment" space is compounded; demand exceeds the number of large lecture halls, so for some years the university has used a nearby commercial movie theater complex for morning classes. But even without this underscoring of "audience-ness," lecture halls in general discourage feedback from students, so instructors have difficulty gauging what students are thinking and how they are processing information. The expectation is that the students are receivers of knowledge, that they should be fed information. There is little opportunity for peer-to-peer communication beyond the immediate neighbor.

Our large introductory course, thus, is less than ideal. Yet it remains one of our most important courses because it serves as a gateway for future women's studies majors and minors, and, as a general education course, it introduces issues pertaining to gender and sexuality to a great number of students across campus (approximately 900 total in a year). Thus our faculty members have always taken great care in teaching this course. Before the adoption of clickers, instructors made the class as interactive as possible by soliciting student input with an extra hand-held microphone delivered to the audience around the classroom by a Teaching Assistant. We continue to use this modality of "shout outs" while using clickers to generate an environment that facilitates student participation and enhances peer-to-peer learning.

Bringing in clickers has not necessarily changed the content of the course, although it has affected the process. Widespread in feminist pedagogies is the awareness that the process of teaching matters as much as the outcome. For clickers, this means that we discussed the problematics of the technology with students at the same time as we deployed it. We explained to the students that while we do use clickers in conventional ways, namely to gauge comprehension, assumptions, and attitudes as well as to take attendance and give quizzes, we want clickers to facilitate collaborative learning, from each other as well as the instructor. We also pointed out that we shape our teaching by their responses, and so we learn from them as well. We emphasized that students had valuable information to share and that these may be initially solicited via the device but could then be elaborated verbally. We tried to give them a sense that they were producing, in concert with one another, useful knowledge.

Clickers in the Classroom: Starting with Instructional Support

Initially we adopted the clicker technology for more conventional instructional support. The transition from polling or checking understanding of concepts and issues to more collaborative learning developed as instructors became more aware of the potential for the clickers. Because we believe it would be useful to readers who have never used clickers, we will start our discussion with some examples of how we made use of the conveniences the technology offers. Usually, but not always, we asked three clicker questions per class period: toward the beginning, middle, and the end. In addition to supporting student learning, this format doubled up as an efficient way to take attendance and mitigate the lamentable tendency in large lecture-based classes for students to arrive late, leave early, or catch up on naptime during film screenings.[5] We also found it useful to ask an opening question at the beginning of an instructional unit on a specific topic, a "checking-in" question around the middle, and a closing question at the end. Furthermore, we used clickers to assist with the critical analysis essay assignments.

The opening questions were devised in such a way that they piqued the students' interest, gauged their preconceptions, or measured their knowledge on a subject. The instructor assured students that they would not be graded on their responses; it was not in that sense a "pre-test." For example, the following question was asked preceding the introduction of gender vis-à-vis sex differences and critique of gender binarism:

What is your gender?
1. woman
2. man
3. both
4. none of the above

This question that problematized the idea that there are only two genders gave the students a moment to contemplate the possibility of a non-binary system and stimulated students' own process of critical thinking.

"Checking-in" and closing questions may be similar as these are often used to get a feel for how students are processing information. For a teaching unit on sex differences versus gender and the multiplicity of gender systems, one of these questions looked like the following:

> Which of the following is TRUE?
> 1. Societies enforce beliefs about gender through such practices as allocation of space, rituals, and sexual norms.
> 2. Throughout the world, someone's sex determines the person's gender.
> 3. Cultural beliefs about gender never include being seen as the outcome of sex differences.

The overwhelming majority of students answered 1 by the end of the unit. For the few that responded 2 or 3, the instructor asked why someone might answer 2 or 3; other than not paying attention, what social and cultural forces might have people hold onto misinformation? This stimulated discussion of religious beliefs and community shaping of gender and sexualities as moral terrains. This dialogue among students led them to recognize the complex role of the public university and the separation of church and state. Even as we used clickers in a somewhat conventional way, namely to measure students' understanding of a basic concept in women's studies, the instant feedback from the histogram generated an opportunity for collaborative learning.

We also devised clicker questions that help students focus on the topic of the short analytical paper assignments and correct persistent misconceptions that lead to major errors in their essays. For example, the prompt for the first response essay for the unit on sex differences versus gender was:

> In many Western societies there is an expectation that a person's biological sex determines fixed, gendered behaviors. What is gender and how is it different form sex differences? What insights do we gain when we look beyond the binaries of female/male and women/men to consider the relationship between sex differences and gender as socially constructed cultural scripts?

Prior to students writing this essay, we asked clicker questions such as the following:

> Which of the following describe gender variations?
> 1. The Hua sense of gender as a process that changes through life and a person's experiences.
> 2. The Hijra view themselves as a third gender.

3. Societies where age and gender identities are closely linked, producing three or four genders.
4. Two-gender systems where no change or transgender is allowed.
5. All of the above.
6. 1, 2 and 3 only.

This question identified clusters of students who thought that two-gender systems are not social constructions. It also provided reminders of the readings that students could mine for examples in their essays. The clicker question was then followed by a class discussion, which provided a supportive environment for students to develop critical thinking and to become successful in their essays.

There were also instances when clicker questions helped draw the instructor's attention to areas that need further attention. For example, after screening the film *La Operación* on sterilization in Puerto Rico from the 1930s through the 1980s, students overlooked the way policies surrounding the sterilization of women in Puerto Rico had become institutionalized practices in a low-income community in New York. The following question encouraged students to think critically about some of the major points in the film:

> According to the film *La Operación*, which of the following statements is inaccurate?
> 1. U.S. goal was to sterilize 25% of the world's women, so there will not be an uprising that would jeopardize the interests of multi-national corporations.
> 2. The new economic model for Puerto Rico created employment opportunities – albeit limited – for women.
> 3. Two-child families, empty elementary schools, and men chatting in the streets exemplified "progress."
> 4. When Dr. Antonio Silva became the director at Lincoln Hospital (Bronx), there was a sharp drop in the number of sterilizations of low-income Puerto Rican women in the neighborhood.
> 5. Puerto Rican women were the first in the world to take oral contraceptives – at 20 times the dosage used today.

The correct answer is 4. More than half the students answered incorrectly, even though they were attentive during the film and in the discussion afterward. These results called for much more intensive exploration of student resistance to issues that involve discrimination "at home" and their hopes that "bad things decrease through time." The clickers did not ensure correct answers, but they did point out a useful arena for pedagogical work about intersectionality and discrimination. This example shows that without follow-up, the use of clickers would not facilitate feminist pedagogical goals, notably, encouraging students to think in terms of intersectional oppressions and the need for approaches that appreciate diversity wherever it occurs.

Clicker questions also presented situations in which the process of teaching came to matter just as much as the outcome. By the end of the initial unit on sex differences, students are expected to recognize that embryonic development of sex characteristics relies on more than the binary of XX or XY. The following question encouraged students to consider each option separately, followed by the correct answer "All of the above."

Primary and secondary sex characteristics can be affected by:
1. Chromosomes (X, Y, and/or the absence thereof)
2. Genes (DAX-1 or WNT-4)
3. The embryonic production of hormones (androgens or estrogens)
4. Proteins such as 5-alpha reductase
5. All of the above.

The instructor was concerned that the structure of the question was rather SAT-like in that students might be unsure of some of the examples, sure of others, and logically assume that it must be "all of the above." Fully 75% of the students responded with the correct answer, and she asked if they automatically assumed it must be 5. In part because of the classroom environment established in the beginning of the quarter regarding clicker usage, many students freely confirmed that this was the case. Subsequently, the instructor asked which options were confusing. Rather than reiterate the lecture material, she asked other students in the class to help flesh out the answers. Taking this approach enabled students to own their knowledge by providing support to their peers, and the instructor was able to gauge overall comprehension by their comments. Additionally, she was able to fine-tune the discussion by emphasizing key points that had been overlooked. The openness of the instructor to problematizing the question format itself demonstrated the transparency of feminist pedagogies.

We have come to value clickers for its tendency to generate spontaneous peer-to-peer instruction. We will thus end this section with another example. After discussing sexual violence and workplace harassment and defining types of sexual harassment, the instructor provided multiple examples, and the circumstances surrounding why some incidents could be prosecuted, while others could not. Then she gave a clicker question in which students considered several scenarios that could be identified as sexual harassment. The instructor anticipated that students would easily identify three of the scenarios as harassment but cast the second scenario as ambiguous. She hoped that students would debate it, and this would be one way to deepen their understanding around the issue.

Which of the following is not an example of sexual harassment?
1. A female executive tells her male assistant that he must perform sexual favors for her in order to keep his job.
2. An individual passes by her colleague's cubicle, sees offensive material on the computer screen, tells him that this makes her uncomfortable, and there is no repeat incident.
3. A female student continues to tell her female TA how "hot" she looks during class even after a private conversation in which the TA informed the student that this is unacceptable behavior.
4. An employee repeatedly witnesses his boss telling prospective employees they can get the job if they will "put out." The boss has never made gestures like this to the employee in question.

Overwhelmingly, students chose the second scenario (89%). However, as soon as the histogram appeared on the screen, they protested the options. Without any prompting from the instructor, they began to analyze the case. Some students defined harassment by whether or not a one-time incident could be prosecuted. Others emphasized the need to identify and report this incident as it could be repeated with others without any paper trail. Still others put themselves in the position of an employer, who wants to stop harassment but has no concrete evidence.

As we have illustrated, clicker questions can provoke curiosity, generate feedback, and foster a dialogue between the teacher and the group. They also help develop a collaborative thinking "space" in which students could look at alternative views of an issue. As an instructional support tool, clickers help feminist teachers overcome the rigid lecture hall structure. The great value in clickers, however, is in its ability to create feminist pedagogical spaces that are uniquely enabled by the technology.

Technologically Enabled Feminist Pedagogical Spaces

Clickers open up possibilities for invaluable learning experiences in a feminist classroom owing to the ways in which they are distinct from show-of-hands. First of all, clickers ensure anonymity, enabling students to take risks that they would not otherwise if their identity was readily revealed to their peers. Second, clicking requires the student to commit to one answer. When asked to participate in a show of hands, someone who feels unsure about where she stands on the issue may simply opt out or raise her hand multiple times. Having to select a single answer compels students to take a stronger stance, which also motivates them to engage. Third, because everyone must click simultaneously, it prevents "answer drift" whereby students' responses are influenced by seeing how other students responded to the question and feeling compelled to go along with the majority. Last, the technology provides an instant feedback of the precise breakdown of options chosen by the classroom community. Hand raising, gives a feel for the distribution of responses only to the instructor and students sitting in the back who can see the hands go up. The histogram provides this information to all students and readies them to analyze the results. These four features are in operation at the same time whenever clickers are used. While these characteristics may also be useful in non-feminist courses, they offer distinctive advantages for feminist teachers in creating a safe and empowering peer-collaborative learning space.[6]

Anonymity and Safe Space

Women's studies faculty must be aware of conditions that instructors in other fields may not necessarily have to take into account. For instance, while covering topics such as sexual violence, we are cognizant of the fact that many of the people in the classroom had most likely been subjected to or would be at high risk of battering, rape, or other forms of sexual assault and harassment. Non-anonymous or face-to-face conditions for explorations of highly contentious or upsetting issues are ethically troublesome for many feminist instructors. Especially in large courses, sharing deeply private information or a traumatic experience feels unsafe for the students. While feminist scholars know that one in four college women experience date rape before graduating, any decision to explore students' experiences of such trauma is an ethically charged one. Student input, however, is a vital component of collaborative learning, which we strive as feminist teachers to achieve. As such, whenever possible, we focus a great deal pedagogically on creating safe space in an intimate small class. The trust and safety needed for disclosure, however, is difficult to ensure in a classroom setting in general, and particularly so in a large class where students do not have a chance to build relationships with one another. Because responses are only presented anonymously to the class, clickers can be one "safe" way to respond to sensitive or unsafe questions such as "Have you ever experienced sexual assault?...date rape?...battering by an intimate partner?"

Unsafe questions that can be moderated by clicker usage are not limited to experiences of sexual violence. Discussing issues around sexuality may benefit from asking students to identify their sexual orientation, a question that LGBT students may not feel safe answering openly but may be willing to do so anonymously. The subject of reproductive health and sexual health may yield sensitive questions that are nonetheless useful for starting a dialogue such as "Have you had an abortion?" "Have you had a sexually transmitted infection?" "Do you know your HIV status?" and "Do you use a condom every time you have anal or vaginal intercourse?" Another delicate question that one of the authors has asked in class is about incarceration. After presenting material on criminalization of women and racial minorities, its impact on families and communities, and the overcrowding of the prison system in California, the instructor asked the students whether the issues discussed affected them personally in any way. Close to one third of the students felt that the problems of the current prison system had had an impact on their personal lives or the lives of those they knew. Given the demographics of our student body, this high number is believable. Clicking allowed students to contribute to the building of a communal knowledge with honest inputs without the fear of embarrassment or discrimination.

When asking these clicker questions, we are not simply polling the students but are reaching for further effects via the instant feedback of the histogram results. By seeing that multiple members in the room have experienced sexual assaults or identify as gay, lesbian, or bisexual, students come to recognize and acknowledge shared communities that may have not been apparent before. As a written portion of the course evaluation of one of the instructors indicated, the knowledge that others shared traumatic experiences instilled a sense of belonging. The bar graph serves as a visual representation of the group and helps the students understand the class as a community. It also brings the issue home when students realize that a significant proportion of women students have indeed been exposed to sexual violence.

This digitally constructed shared-yet-anonymous cyberspace thus provides a safe arena to explore controversial or highly sensitive issues and experiences that are nonetheless vital to feminist teaching goals. The effect of this may be that students who now feel that they are not alone in having certain experiences feel secure enough to verbally elaborate on them. For example, after the clicker question about personal experience with prisons, one student voluntarily talked about her drug-addicted father's experience of multiple incarcerations and offered her critique of the criminal justice system. Personal stories such as this one that represent the intersectional oppressions felt first-hand by members of our diverse student body create powerful moments of peer-to-peer learning. Whether it is truly "safe" for someone to reveal certain personal information, however, still remains a moral question for a feminist teacher to wrestle with and carefully evaluate every time she seeks student input on sensitive issues.

Simultaneous Response System and Student Empowerment

Clicker technology also enables students who are usually hesitant to speak up in class to take part in the collective knowledge making process. Typically students are uneasy to give input when they feel academically insecure and do not want to choose the "wrong" answer. Ungraded clicker questions that promises that they would not be judged create a condition that makes it easier for these students to contribute their input. Even when most students do get the answer "wrong," instructors can utilize the moment to facilitate the learning process. For instance, one instructor asked the following question prior to the instructional unit on sexualities:

Discrimination or violence against gays or lesbians would not happen if they would just "act straight."
1. True
2. False

Eighty-five percent of the students answered "true." Subsequent material on the LGBT community provided by the instructor included rates of assault, murders, and the less quantified forms of violence, such as familial abandonment, disowning, etc. as well as the rates of gay teen suicide. Students also contributed their knowledge of the climate in middle and high schools in the U.S. and how young people identified their peers relying on known information or beliefs about individuals' sexual orientations. At the end, the instructor asked a related question, which produced notably different results:

Which of the following is true?
1. Discrimination and violence against gays, lesbians, and queers is directly related to their becoming more visible in society.
2. Reporting about discrimination and violence by gays, lesbians, and queers is related to being more visible socially.
3. Violence has increased with visibility but discrimination has decreased.

The students answered 2 at a 93% level, and confusion regarding 1 and 2 cleared when peers pointed out that we actually do not know the rates of violence except through reporting and that discrimination is extremely difficult to prove. Clickers force students to participate in thinking, while allowing them to be "wrong." The anonymity frees students to subsequently change positions without appearing to others to "waffle," be confused, or be judged as weak.

Students who are reluctant to give their opinion in a women's studies class may be those who are worried that the instructor may not approve of, or their peers do not agree with, what they have to say. Those with less social power due to their gender, race, and/or class statuses may particularly feel this way. Especially if other students' positions became known prior to formulating one's own answer, marginalized students may feel the pressure to conform. Feminist scholars have long recognized detrimental effects of the inhibitions or performative scripts imposed by students' intersectional oppressions. In other words, in a face-to-face communication, students may feel pressure to conform to what they presume or perceived to be the instructor's or other students' gendered, racialized or ethnic, sexual, national, or religious expectations. The technology's requirement of simultaneous response mitigates this by soliciting answers that are not modified in relation to others' responses and perceived power differences. By ensuring anonymity and requiring all students to respond simultaneously, clickers equalize power relations among students and empower those in marginalized positions. The histogram may lead to further empowerment for students who had feared they might be alone, but realized that they are not. Clicker-enabled sense of sharedness, or having "allies," then can lead to students speaking up for the marginalized opinions and thus start a dialogue that engages and analyzes different positions in a supportive environment.

Peer-Collaborative Learning Space

Feminist teachers can take this further to equalize power between the instructor and the students in a couple of ways using clickers. One way is to ask provocative questions that elicit a wide variety of answers and create an environment where students become more invested in discussing a topic when they realize that other people hold beliefs that are strongly opposed to their own. One of our colleagues posed the following question and found that students enthusiastically engaged in a debate about the relationship between feminism and body image:[7]

A close female friend of yours asks: "Do I look fat in this shirt?" Which of the following is the best feminist response?
1. Gently suggest that the two of you start working out together at the gym
2. Tell her that fat is sexy and that it's normal for people to have fat on their bodies.
3. Say "No! Are you kidding? Of course you don't look fat! I am way fatter than you!"
4. Get mad and say, "I'm so tired of women asking that question! Get over it!"

For a similar question posed by one of the authors, the responses triggered an interesting discussion of body obsession versus health issues of obesity. In addition, men in the class offered the observation that it was a no-win question when posed by a woman and that they would avoid answering in real life. The class then discussed what additional responses might be more helpful: "Some fat is sexy, but if you're worried about becoming obese, we can talk about healthier life styles – and you are rocking that shirt!" A divisive and stimulating clicker question in this case fostered collaborative knowledge production among peers with little input from the instructor.

Another way to empower students in exchange of power held by the instructor is to allow students to select an answer, such as a statement that reflects common prejudices or misconceptions, which may not necessarily represent a "feminist" position. Again, because clickers protect the identity of the students, they do not have to feel that they have to get the answer "right" or select an option that will please their instructor. Clicker questions that fall under this category, but were not intended explicitly to hand over power to the students at the time they were asked, include the following:[8]

Which of the following statement best describes your relationship to feminism?
1. I don't identify as a feminist but I believe in gender equality.
2. I am a feminist.
3. Feminism is for angry, man-hating lesbians... and white women living in the 1970s.
4. I'm not sure what I think about feminism.
5. I don't like to single out the gender issue...I believe in equality for everyone.

How can we best explain the prevalence of rape in the United States?
1. Rape occurs because some men have no respect for women.
2. Rape occurs because some women say no when they mean yes.
3. Rape occurs because some men cannot control their sexual impulses.

4. Rape occurs because we live in a culture that encourages all men to view women as objectifiable and rapable.

As with the questions on "fat," these questions resulted in active dialogue, arguing various points. Some students' viewpoints would have been considered "problematic" from a feminist perspective. Fortunately, other students engaged them and called them into question. Some even eloquently made arguments that the instructor had hoped to make. Thus, while giving up power in this way can feel risky for instructors, it can also create a setting where an excellent message may emerge from one of the students in a peer-to-peer discussion, without having to impose a viewpoint from an authority position.

Besides empowering students by stepping aside and letting them be in charge of producing knowledge, this type of peer-to-peer interaction has another important implication for a feminist instructor. Teachers in women's studies, like those in ethnic studies, are targets of student accusations of bias to a degree not found in other disciplines. In our department, faculty have had to emphasize in introductory level courses that bias is not the same as perspective; one represents unexamined assumptions that are not shared with the audience, while perspective is accountable through reflection and sharing. By rendering the teaching process more transparent in a number of ways, including the clicker discussions that allow competing viewpoints to be considered, students gleaned a better sense of the distinction between bias and perspective. In constructing questions that permitted non-feminist students to respond and view how pro-feminist students responded – a jury of their peers – lifted the weight of "bias" somewhat from the shoulders of the instructor.

In sum, through the anonymity, simultaneous response, commitment, and instant histogram review facets of the technology, the clicker forges a peer-to-peer collaborative learning space. This peer collaboration transcends several of the most frustrating aspects of feminist pedagogy in large lecture course, namely, the fixed seating with its front-facing emphasis on the teacher as the sole producer of knowledge. Although limited in being multiple-choice or yes/no, the technology helps circumvent power differential among students as well as between students and instructors in a way show-of-hand format cannot and the follow-up histograms permit a sense of shared experience informing the subsequent peer-to-peer dialogue. The reentry of the instructor can be to emphasize the knowledge students have just created through their collaboration and to point out how that knowledge underscores the claims and arguments in readings or poses challenges to the literature. At several points in our courses, further discussion ensued about why the peer collaborative knowledge challenged the literature where it did; the feminist goal in this case was to have students gain first-hand experience as knowledge producers, to see knowledge production as a social activity, and to recognize that sharing and discussing diverse experiences leads to new knowledge. In short, clickers transform the physical limitations of the classroom and sheer size of the course to one of a shared space and shared experience enabled through technology.

Conclusions

Students have criticized clicker use in many classes as giving them an illusion of participating in their own education without really doing so. Students in our course have told us via comments on our teaching evaluations that our use of clickers diverges from this pattern. Because we use the responses displayed on the screen as a basis for discussion in the lecture hall and peer-to-peer communication and because we solicit student volunteers to explain their responses using microphones or "shout-outs," we have accomplished a kind of discussion format that students find engaging and useful even in a large lecture hall setting. It is not the same as the small section discussions that our teaching assistants create, but it is far less alienating than the physical environment and factory-style lecturing ordinarily produce.

At a time when institutional pressures are increasing to adopt instructional technologies for efficiency, clickers may seem like an extra burden that requires making changes to a well-practiced teaching style. Feminist instructors have developed a wide range of effective pedagogical strategies for various classroom settings. Hence we recognize that clickers may not be for everyone. Given our circumstances, we decided to adopt the "master's tool" and bent it to meet our needs and found that clickers are conducive to generating feminist pedagogical spaces. The anonymity the technology offers provided students a "safe" space in which they can respond to sensitive or challenging questions. The histograms represented the "shared" space where students found out that they were not alone in having had a certain experience or holding a certain opinion. These technologically enabled "spaces" can empower students and encourage them to engage in the peer-collaborative learning processes that are enhanced by follow-up discussion sessions.

The aspects of feminist pedagogies on which we have brought clicker technology to bear include theory/practice relationships, instructor accountability through making the technology transparent to the audience, and the redefinition of students from passive learners to knowledge producers. In developing feminist uses for clicker technologies, we also are collaborating with the people in our course to oppose re-inscription of hierarchical pedagogical models. Of course, this remains somewhat contradictory, since we faculty still must produce grades, but it does reduce the "omniscient expert" model of professorship. Our students retain the sense that in person interaction is crucial for education, remaining "real" rather than being pushed into a virtual realm of participation. The way we use the technologies both draws upon the diversity of people in our course and demonstrates to them how that diversity can produce novel and emancipatory knowledges.

In closing, we have found collaborative writing on this topic also is deeply resonant with feminist pedagogies. Working together and discussing what has happened in our "share" course has led to adopting our colleagues' ideas and techniques, problem-solving regarding knotty issues in the classroom, and breaking the assumption that large lecture halls breed passivity and are inherently inimical to feminist pedagogies. Clickers may click in a feminist classroom, but there are people pushing the buttons.

Bibliography

Banks, David A. 2006. *Audience Response Systems in Higher Education: Applications and Cases*. London: Information Science Publishing.

Bourgois, Philippe. 2003. *In Search of Respect: Selling Crack in El Barrio*. New York, NY: Cambridge University Press.

Bruff, Derek. 2000. *Teaching with Classroom Response Systems: Creating Active Learning Environments*. San Francisco: Jossey-Bass.

Deats, Sara Munson and Lagretta Talle, eds. 1994. *Gender and Academe: Feminist Pedagogy and Politics*. Lanham, MD: Rowman and Littlefield.

Duncan, Douglas. 2005. *Clickers in the Classroom*. San Francisco: Pearson-Addison Wesley.

Freire, Paolo. 1973. *Education for Critical Consciousness*. New York, NY: Seabury Press.

—. 1972. *Pedagogy of the Oppressed*. New York, NY: Herder and Herder.

Hawkesworth, Mary. 1989. "Knowers, Knowing, Known: Feminist Theory and Claims of Truth." *Signs* 14, no. 3: 533-557.

hooks, bell. 2010. *Teaching Critical Thinking: Practical Wisdom*. New York, NY: Routledge.

—. 1994. *Teaching To Transgress: Education As the Practice of Freedom*. New York, NY: Routledge.

Kirk, Gwen and Margo Okazawa-Rey, eds. 2007. *Women's Lives: Multicultural Perspectives.* 5th edition. Boston, MA: McGraw-Hill.

Patai, Daphne and Noretta Koe. 2003. *Professing Feminism: Education and Indoctrination in Women's Studies.* Lanham, MD: Lexington Books.

Scott, Joan. 1991. "The Evidence of Experience." *Critical Inquiry* 17: 773-797.

Shieh, David. 2009. "Going Beyond Classroom Clickers." *The Chronicle of Higher Education* 55, no. 27: A13.

Stephen, Lynn. 1995. "Women's Rights Are Human Rights: The Merging of Feminine and Feminist Interests among El Salvador's Mothers of the Disappeared (COMADRES)." *American Ethnologist* 22, no. 4: 807-827.

Young, Jeff. 2008. "Mobile College App: Turning iPhones into 'Super-Clickers' for Classroom Feedback." *The Chronicle of Higher Education*, December 15. http://chronicle.com/blogs/wiredcampus/mobile-college-app-turning-iphones-into-super-clickers-for-classroom-feedback/4434.

Notes

[1] We would like to thank Jane Ward for sharing teaching materials with us and Leo Schouest for helping us adopt and manage classroom technologies and for offering ideas on how to enhance students' learning experiences with them. We also thank the approximately 3,000 students in *Gender and Sexuality* over the past two years for their willingness to take intellectual risks, share sometimes difficult stories, and collaborate with others to make the course an ongoing success – one of the peer-recommended "You really have to take this" courses at the University of California, Riverside.

[2] Technically, clickers are not completely anonymous since instructors can see the results in more detail. If student anonymity is pedagogically important, the instructor can decide not to link the clickers with the roster. Alternatively, students can be told to trade clickers with a random neighbor for a given question so that the instructor cannot trace an answer to the individual.

[3] Smaller classrooms at UCR are also equipped with clicker receivers. Because we do not have experience using the technology in small to mid-size classes, we do not discuss these set-ups in this article.

[4] It is important to note that the authors' opinion toward clickers does not represent a unanimous view of all faculty members in our department. There are a variety of teaching strategies in a large lecture hall that our department faculty utilizes effectively, clickers being just one of them.

[5] Prior to clickers, attendance was taken by attendance slips or sign-in-sheets, which imposed a great deal of tedious work on the Teaching Assistants who had to

keep track of their students. Although we have seen no significant effect on overall attendance, "coming and going" during the lecture sessions have decreased when clicker points counted toward participation grade.

[6] For discussion on these characteristics of clicker technology, see the following blog entries on *The Chronicle of Higher Education* website – "Group Work that Works (Even in Large Classes!)" by Prof. Hacker (November 5, 2010); "How interactive Technology Can Help Minority Students Learn" by Mary Helen Miller (March 19, 2010); and "A 'Strong Case' Exists for Classroom Clickers" Letters to the Editor (January 30, 2009).

[7] This example was provided by one of our colleagues who also taught *Gender and Sexuality* using clickers.

[8] The following two examples were also provided by the aforementioned colleague.

CHAPTER SEVEN

DIGITAL GENDER STORY PROJECT: TEACHING GENDER IN THE DIGITAL AGE

L. AYU SARASWATI

The digital gender story project is a multi-media project (a 5-6 minute film consisting of images, audio narratives, music, and sometimes video footage) that pushes students to be active participants and creative knowledge producers in our digital age. I developed the digital gender story project for my honors class WGSS 202: *Introduction to Women, Gender, and Sexuality Studies* at the University of Kansas in the fall of 2008. There were seven students, all women, registered in this class. After teaching it in the fall semester, I made some changes, which I will discuss later, to improve the assignment. The discussion in this essay reflects the revised version that I taught in spring 2009.[1]

Digital storytelling projects were first popularized in San Francisco in the early 1990s with the original goal of giving voice to an oppressed population (High 2009, 26; Rossiter and Garcia 2010, 38; Fletcher and Cambre 2009, 113). This project stems from the assumption that telling one's story could function as a medium for social change. Indeed, some of the goals of the digital gender story project are: to distribute innovative research findings in creative ways beyond the classroom setting, to evoke certain emotional responses in the audience, to provide the audience with a space to relate to and reflect on these issues in their own lives, and to invite them to make some personal (and possibly social) changes in their lives.

Since then, they have been disseminated in higher education, K-12 education, and community activist groups, and acquired new goals and meanings (Rossiter and Garcia 2010, 37). As the name suggests, the digital *gender* story project focuses on personal stories about gender, as it intersects with other categories of identity such as race, sexuality, class, nationality, ability, and age. Although these stories are "personal," they are necessarily contextualized within larger institutional structures of sexism, racism, and heterosexism, thus enabling students to see themselves as active participants in the production of gender discourses and producers of feminist knowledges.

It is important that I clarify here, however, that, although this project may sound intimidating for students and teachers because of its digital form, this project is very doable. In assigning this project, teachers do not need to have an extensive knowledge in digital media. (I did not have formal training in digital media. I simply explored these software applications on my own and asked some experts, friends, colleagues, and family members who are digital media practitioners to provide me with some informal training.) If teachers opt to provide the explanations about how to make a movie themselves, they can simply learn from and show students the online tutorial of iMovie available online http://www.apple.com/ilife.video-showcase. Alternatively, teachers can ask someone from the "Instructional Development and Support" office or its equivalent on their campus to teach students how to use iMovie and Windows Movie Maker. Both programs are very easy to use, and students have fun exploring these applications.

Moreover, to manage the overwhelming feelings that students may have about the subject, I also divided the project into smaller steps so that students can work on their assignment for the entire semester. This is the only major project in the class and counts as 75% of the total grade. It is important to make the digital gender story project the only main project in the course because it would be impossible for students to devote such a large amount of time to producing a good digital gender story project when they also have to take exams, for example. The other components of the class are participation (15%) and "Bring Your Own Images" (10%) – students choose a day to bring and analyze an image related to the class reading materials and start our class discussion. Below, I will explain each of the five smaller steps, as well as how to prepare students to complete each step. Each step is weighed differently – I provide a grade percentage for each one as described below.

Step 1: Visual Narratives of Gender (20%)

From the very first day of class, I encouraged students to choose a topic that they felt most passionately about. I also gave them some creative examples of topics to further push them in thinking innovatively about their projects. These topics include how their fascinations with shoes or handbags are gendered and have economic, social, and global implications; how their choices of video games and the narratives in these video games are gendered, racialized, and hetero/sexualized; or how their experiences (or the lack thereof) with sex toys or sexualized Halloween costumes are implicated within and influenced by the gender, racial, heterosexual, abled-bodyism, ageism, and class structures in their lives.

In the weeks leading up to their submission of the first step, I spent about ten minutes before each class ended asking them about the status of their projects. When I observed that students were struggling with their topics or projects, I suggested that they meet with me individually to discuss their ideas. Some of the issues that students were working on included: the role of religion in formulating one's sexuality, romance ideology and a woman's choice to stay single, the benefits of all-girls education, and the most popular issue – gendered body image issues.

For the first step, students have to submit five images that comprise a coherent story about their topic. These images are not simply random images that are loosely related to their topic; these are the images that they will use for their final project. Together, the digital photographs tell a coherent story of how students learn and perform gender in the specific aspect of their lives (the topic) they choose to focus on. Each photograph has to be accompanied by one to two sentences that narrate a portion of the story represented in the photo. Students may submit images that they take with their digital camera or images of themselves that they have collected throughout the years. For example, a student who tells a story of how she learns gender at home submitted pictures from her private family photo album, such as the one in which she, as a young girl, was pushing a pink stroller with a doll in it.

Prior to having students submit these pictures, I had explained to them what this step entails and how to fulfill those requirements. This leads naturally to the second step.

Preparing students for this step:

For this assignment, students have to attend a visual literacy workshop that I teach. During this workshop, students learn how specific images convey meaning; they learn what visual metaphors are and how to read and write visual narratives. The particular reading methods that I work with use semiotic and discourse analyses. Moreover, I also find Lauren Greenfield's book *Girl Culture* very useful in providing students with specific examples for their first step (some parts are also available online at http://laurengreenfield.com.

Providing students with alternative learning modes through this step:

This step represents an alternative mode of engaging students in the knowledge building process in that they write a visual, rather than a textual, narrative of gender. Moreover, students have to compose this narrative digitally. Most students use a PowerPoint application to complete this stage of the project, but a few students might be more comfortable with using Microsoft Word. Some more technologically advanced students may use the iMovie application.

Step 2: Critical Narratives of Gender (20%)

For the second step, students submit a five- to seven-page paper that provides a critical analysis of the images submitted for step one. In its essence, step two functions as a research paper. This is because for this paper, students had to make an argument that is supported by convincing research materials and the images they submitted in step 1. To do so, they have to conduct a library research on the topic of their papers. In other words, in making their critical analysis about the images included in their paper, students have to also rely on thorough research.

Preparing students for this step:

For this assignment, students have to attend a library research workshop taught by Sherry Williams, our women's studies librarian at the university's Spencer Research Library. During the workshop, she shows students how to conduct library research and explains what resources are available for students. Additionally, students visited the Spencer library, where Williams introduced them to useful and relevant library materials. Finally, we have a class discussion about what makes a good argument and what counts as good evidence.

Providing students with alternative learning modes through this step:

The critical analysis is a research paper in the traditional sense. Students incorporate images and research materials to make a persuasive argument for their paper; however, students may elect to write their paper in the personal narrative form. I use articles from the text for this class, which incorporates personal narratives and research as good examples.

Moreover, by using personal narrative in their paper, students can use their paper as a blueprint for the narrative that they will tell in the final form (the movie) of the digital gender story project. In this step, students hone their writing and research skills.

Step 3: Meeting with the Professor (5%)

At this point in the project, I require that all students meet with me. During the meeting, students have to bring a storyboard that consists of a minimum of ten "panels" or "frames" to illustrate what the final project will look like. Students also have to present their timeline, indicating when each step of the project will be completed. For this step, students fine-tune their organization and management skills, both in terms of time and in terms of the project itself.

Step 4: The Gender Story Project – The Movie (20%)

For this step, students pull together everything that they have done from steps 1-3 to create the final form (the movie) of their digital gender story project. Students will reflect on how their project is related to class materials and various theories they have learned in class. Like their critical paper, this project requires that they articulate an argument and support it with theories they have read in class as well as additional theories they find through research. Moreover, in their project they need to tell a story about gender as it intersects with other categories of identity such as race, sexuality, nationality, and ability. Most importantly, this project has to be an embodiment of the notion that personal storytelling can be a medium for social change. In other words, in the telling of their stories, I do not encourage them to indulge in the grandiosity of the self. If not being directed carefully, students may tend to be self-centered and be over-excited about telling their own stories that they forget about the purpose of their story and how it relates to larger social issues. To avoid this pitfall, I ask them to be mindful about the ways in which they learn, perform, and socialize gender in their lives and how institutions help structure these processes. I also require that they clearly articulate the changes they propose in their digital gender story project. Students must explicitly state at least one specific recommendation for social change in their project.

Preparing students for this step:

I provide students with an iMovie (for Mac) workshop. (In other courses I have invited a guest speaker from the Instructional Development Support to teach students not only about iMovie but also Windows Movie Maker applications. An expert on iMovie and WMM who could explore more functions of these software applications worked better for the students.) During this workshop, students learn how to create a movie with the iMovie application. I also provide students with several examples they can follow:

- http://www.storycenter.org/stories
- http://www.thestoryproject.ca/women_support/videos/womensupport.mov
- http://www.thestoryproject.ca/Jen_Camille/Video/Camille_small.mov
- http://www.thestoryproject.ca/DWAVE/index.html

Providing students with alternative learning modes through this step:

This project incorporates various digital technologies. This allows students to feel comfortable with various computer applications and boosts their confidence in engaging with technology. Particularly because this class tends to be populated by women, it is even more empowering to have women learn and be comfortable with technology to close the gender gap in technology. This project embodies an alternative way to represent students' learning process on two levels: form and content. First, the form of this project, a digital movie, is certainly different from final exams or research papers that are usually due at the end of the semester. Because of its form, digital movie can be posted on public websites such as YouTube. Students can then invite their friends to view their projects. This process, as I will explain in the next section, functions to engage others beyond the classroom or academic circle. In addition, the content of this project provides an alternative way of representing the student's learning in that it considers one's personal lived experiences valuable while simultaneously articulating these stories through a visually engaging narrative that is interwoven with solid research materials. Its content also reflects the notion of personal storytelling as a form of social change. As such, I have thus incorporated activism in academia where it is not usually found. This is indeed an important feminist contribution to the project.

Step 5: The Presentation (10%)

Students have to present their digital movie project to the entire class. This step has three purposes. First, by showcasing their projects, students can take pride in their projects. Second, this step allows students to hone their presentation skills. Third, because students have to comment on each other's work, this step further builds the sense of collaboration and community that I have fostered in the classroom. By completing this stage of the project, students can then see how their project may provoke fascinating discussion and critical engagement rather than dispassionate or detached commentary.

Preparing students for this step:

Throughout the semester, students practice their communication skills by actively participating in class discussions. Earlier in the semester, students also have to do a class presentation, choosing and analyzing an image that is related to the reading material for the day of their choice. These activities nurture their presentation and public speaking skills.

Providing students with alternative learning modes through this step:

Unlike previous steps that focus on students' visual literacy, writing, research, and organization skills, this step hones their communication and presentation skills and thereby adds yet another different set of skills for students to master.

In this section, I have described the digital gender story project as an example of how I have incorporated technology in my classroom and accommodate the different ways in which students learn. Indeed, some students may be better writers than others, and some may be better at engaging visual materials and technology. It is therefore very important to acknowledge that a project such as this, featuring the use of new media technologies in an academic setting while also embracing many different modes of learning, may excite students but also may create a certain level of anxiety in students. This is a normal reaction when entering unknown territory. Nonetheless, if students are well prepared for each step, this move toward incorporating digital technology in the classroom is worthwhile if not inevitable in the digital age.

Feminist Pedagogy in the Digital Age

As English and women's studies scholars Nancy Chick and Holly Hassel have seen, feminist pedagogy strives to "revis[e] classroom spaces, learning activities and modes of communication and knowledge construction" (2009, 196). In this section I will discuss how digital technology informs and transforms feminist pedagogy. I will do so by using the example of the digital gender story project as it embodies and is shaped by my critical, engaged feminist pedagogy. There are three aspects of feminist pedagogy in the digital age that I will examine: a) envisioning new virtual subjectivities; b) facilitating engaged learning; and c) "teaching to transgress."

EnVisioning New Virtual Subjectivities

The virtual world necessitates that we formulate a way of seeing and teaching that extends, "occludes," and complicates our visual experiences offline (Mirzoeff 1999, 6; Bayne 2008, 395-396). The cyber "screen" is a visual field filled with interactive and structuring signs that requires a different mode of navigating this visual landscape and that limits what can be viewed/represented online. This new mode of seeing in the virtual world inevitably pushes us to think more creatively about our pedagogy (Fletcher and Cambre 2009, 111; Bayne 2008, 408). Being creative with our pedagogy in the digital age means that we stretch our teaching practices to allow for the formation of students' new virtual subjectivity, a subjectivity that is shaped by and found at "the intersection of the electronic image, popular culture, and a dire sense of indeterminacy" (Giroux 1999, 109). Indeed, I did not develop the digital gender story assignment as a project intended to fix or monumentalize student's subjectivity. Rather, I envision the project as nurturing the creation of a subjectivity that provides a rupture in the fluid formation of subjectivity in the digital age, a subjectivity that students can constantly create and recreate in the virtual world.

If the digital project fosters the formation of new virtual subjectivities, then it is necessary to first define what makes subjectivities "virtual." The term "virtual" evokes an understanding of occupying a space in between the real and the unreal. Virtual is understood as something that "is not real but appears to be" (Mirzoeff 1999, 91). Hence, virtual subjectivities are subjectivities that can only "appear" real but are not quite real. This is because in cyberspace (or, I may argue, even offline) there is no essence to one's subjectivity; in a virtual world there are "no *true* identities – because identities are constantly articulated and rearticulated" (McLaren 1995, 99). On one of the most popular social networking websites, Facebook, for example, a subject can "update" the narrative of their subjectivity every five seconds, quite literally.

Virtual subjectivities are subjectivities that involve "play" in their articulation. According to cyberspace scholar Daniel Downes, play is a mode of experimenting with identities (2005, 91). Hence, the digital project becomes another mode of play activity in the virtual world for students who engage in it. That is, in addition to their constructing their digital subjectivities through available sites such as MySpace or Facebook, students also have the chance to visually tinker with their subjectivity through the digital project, which will eventually be posted online as well. As such, the digital project functions as a site where students can articulate their "virtual" subjectivities specific to the digital age.

Play also helps shape the formation of virtual subjectivity because it functions as a system of knowing, an epistemology, so to speak. Philosopher James Hans argues that play is "a *structuring* activity, the activity out of which understanding comes. Play is at one and the same time the location where we question our structures of understanding and the location where we develop them" (1981). In this sense, play functions as an epistemological site because in order to play one must know the rules of the game and how to play – an intricate discourse in and of itself. As one immerses one's self in the game, one may even carry forward and improve the game. Play can therefore function as a mode of imagining a better future out of which "new patterns of reality emerge" (Hans 1981, 103, 106-110). In that sense, play is a productive activity because it can "provide impetus for change and defenses against repression" (Edwards 2008, 6). Hence, encouraging students to be playful as they craft the narrative of their new, fluid, and ruptured subjectivity is key to their creating solid, powerful, and emotionally engaging projects.

The digital gender story project affords students the space to playfully craft a new subjectivity by way of constructing specific narratives of themselves. Here, I purposefully employ and intersect both the theoretical trajectories of "play" and "narratives" together because narratives, like play activity, are also sites of knowledge production. Referencing Laurel Richardson (2005), sociologist Debbie Horsfall argued, "the act of writing itself is the method of both discovery and analysis. It is in and of itself, a way of knowing" (2008, 2). Hence, through writing a narrative for their digital story projects, students become immersed in the process of knowledge production. Ethnographer Dwight Conquergood stated:

> Narrative is a way of knowing, a search for meaning, that privileges
> experience, process, action, and peril. Knowledge is not stored in
> storytelling so much as it is enacted, reconfigured, tested, and engaged by
> imaginative summonings and interpretive replays of past events in the light
> of present situations and struggles. Active and emergent, instead of abstract
> and inert, narrative knowing recalls and recasts experience into meaningful
> signposts and supports for ongoing action. The recountal is always an
> encounter, often full of risk. (1993, 337)

In this sense, narrative thus functions as a mode of making sense of what
happens and of making meaning of one's life, that is, of constructing one's
subjectivity.

The subjectivities produced through the digital gender story project in
my women's studies class are, I argue, "new" and progressive. This is
because these narratives run counter to the "market" identity and "rupture
the dominant narratives of citizenship and destabilize the pretensions to
monologic identity that this narrative exhibits" (McLaren 1995,105). In
theorizing about a pedagogy that nurtures a formation of critical identity
against dominant "market identities," critical education theorist Peter
McLaren argues:

> …the classroom can be transformed into a hybrid pedagogical space where
> permission is not denied students who wish to narrate their own identities
> outside of marketplace identities and the politics of consumerism, a space
> where individual identities find meaning in collective expression and
> solidarity with cultural others, where mimetic, Eurocentric time recedes
> into the lived historical moment of contemporary struggles for identity.
> Here the imperatives of consumer culture and the hegemony of market
> identities are challenged by narratives of identity that are underwritten by a
> concern for liberation and social justice. (1995, 105)

A student, for instance, after being inspired by Mary Helen
Washington's article "Working at Single Bliss," produced a project that
embraced her single status in a society that devalues single women. This
story certainly ruptures the dominant narrative of the market identity that
subjects women to desiring white weddings in their lives as the ultimate
"happy" stories (Ingraham 1999). By telling her story and constructing her
single girl subjectivity, the student participates in creating a "narrative of
liberation [that] point[s] to the possibility of new, alternative identities
contemporaneous with modernity but not simply through inverting its
normative truths" (McLaren 1995, 221). After all, subjectivities only
appear in their ideological (and, in this project, visual) articulations.

In sum, the digital gender story project functions as the container and the playground of playful experimentation and articulation of subjectivity. It provides a learning environment that makes possible the formation of critical "agency" (Butler 1992, 13). It is an agentive subjectivity that may have the possibility of inviting others, through the digital gender story project, to rethink different ways of achieving social justice.

Engaged Learning and Learning to Engage Others

Feminist pedagogy operates as an "engaged pedagogy" when it values the process of learning from each other (hooks 1994, 158; Chick and Hassel 2009, 207). For Chick and Hassel, it is a pedagogy of exchange between equals:

> Feminist pedagogy produces a classroom environment of mutual respect where both teacher and all students take active, responsible, and shared roles in the learning process. This dynamic is achieved through classroom relationships that don't hide or gloss over the differences in experience and perspective within a community of learners. Within this community, students care about others' learning and well-being as well as their own, and they feel free to use their sites of authority – where they already stand and what they already know – to help contribute to the knowledge of the course. (2009, 199)

Here, engaged pedagogy is understood as a pedagogy that values every student's voice, strives toward productive collaboration, and emphasizes the "well-being" of one's self and others (hooks 1994, 15, 21). By way of hooks's and Chick and Hassel's notion of feminist pedagogy as engaged pedagogy, in this section I will lay out several ways in which the digital gender story project figures as the materialization or digitalization, if you will, of my engaged feminist pedagogy stance.

First, the digital gender story project embodies engaged feminist pedagogy in that it values *all* students' different expressions and allows for spaces of collaboration and contradiction. This atmosphere of respect toward each other's opinion does not, of course, appear magically. It requires thoughtful planning on the part of the professor – that professors are purposeful about how students relate to each other and to the professor is often a characteristic of feminist classrooms. Chick and Hassel have stated:

> Feminist pedagogy is deliberate about how students relate to each other. Do they communicate with each other regularly? What happens if someone

has a different opinion? Do they collaborate? Do they learn from each other and not just the instructor? How do the gender, race, and class of each student affect the class dynamic and learning? Feminist pedagogy is also deliberate about the student-instructor relationship. How does the instructor relate to the students? Through attention to these relationships and roles in the classroom, feminist pedagogy spotlights how power and authority are played out in the classroom. (2009, 198)

In being deliberate about how students relate to each other and to the professor through the digital gender story project, I rely heavily on cyberspace, specifically Blackboard (and then YouTube) to facilitate such connections. I require that students post their digital gender story project assignments on two different sections of Blackboard. The first section is the "assignment" section, where I post my comments and students' grades. (These grades are not viewable to other students.) The second section includes a "discussion" section where students are encouraged to inspire and give support to each other and make suggestions on each other's work. When a student criticizes another student's work without offering any suggestions, however, I always ask her/him to make specific recommendations to clarify their criticisms. On Blackboard, I also create a "HELP!" discussion forum where students may ask any questions they have about any of the assignments. I monitor these forums and respond to students' comments online and offline, even during class meeting time. When students learn that I read and comment on their online comments, they are more likely to participate in these discussions. Thus, it is through these simple online activities that I first build a sense of intellectual community among all members of the classroom. Indeed, this is what the digital world offers us: the ease of exchanging our works quickly and effortlessly and thereby allowing for a smoother process of collaboration (Mort and Horsley 2007, 518).

Collaboration, however, works better for some students than for others. Therefore, I prefer to provide as many venues as possible for students to work together with others, and I frame collaboration as enticing and as beneficial as possible. But, I do not force them to help or be helped by others when they choose not to. This is why I find assigning the digital gender story project as an individual rather than a group project works better for students; when assigned as a group project, students (and I) had to spend energy on negotiating group dynamics rather than perfecting their projects. Although being able to collaborate respectfully and productively is definitely a virtue I want to encourage in all of my students, I find "forced collaboration" – forcing first-year students to work together on a big class project with other new students while they are still figuring out how to navigate college classes – is unproductive for students at this stage. I also find assigning the digital gender story project as a group project less productive because the tone of the project then becomes less personal. The vibrant colors of their rich lived experiences cannot shine through in their project. Consequently, the project fails in serving its purpose of making visible the ways in which students are implicated in the gendered structure of power and how they exercise their agency in it. Hence, assigning the project as an individual project not only improves the quality of the overall projects but also enables students to reach the goal of learning how they produce, reproduce, perform, and even resist gender roles and expectations in their lives. When I teach this class in the future, I may combine this project with a service-learning program – asking students to volunteer at an organization of their choice – and implicate their stories within the stories of the organization they work at. As such, they will still focus on their own experiences but they will have to make even deeper connections between the self and others, the individual, organizational, and the structural.

Second, the digital gender story project reflects the values of engaged feminist pedagogy in that this project invites students to make connections with others. In engaged feminist classrooms, students are encouraged to make connections between the class reading materials and themselves, between themselves and the professors, among different thematic units of the syllabus, and among students and others beyond the classroom (Chick and Hassel 2009, 209). I purposefully design the digital gender story project to focus on an aspect of the students' lives so that they can establish what Freire called an "intimate connection"– connection between the knowledge students learn in classroom and the knowledge they learn from their own experiences (2009, 36). Throughout the semester, I foster this intimate connection by regularly asking students to share movies, songs, or other events they see or hear outside the classrooms that are related to the reading materials that we discuss in class and that may be useful for their digital gender story project. Through these processes students begin to bring the knowledge gained in the classroom to examine their lives while simultaneously enriching class discussions and enhancing their understanding of the reading materials by connecting them to their personal experiences. This process, which is undoubtedly embodied in the digital gender story project, is called "dialogic process"– "students mediate the texts through their own personal readings and understandings of the materials" (Lea 2004, 747). For example, through the digital gender story project, a student narrated how it was her *love* of dancing and being an active participant in the performing arts world that unfortunately caused her to be preoccupied with weight and body shape issues. She produced a powerful and emotional narrative that is different from the dominant narratives that we read in class in that she focuses on something that she enjoys doing such as dancing rather than the "evil" media as the cause for girls' obsession with their body size. It thus makes more sense to assign the project as an individual project because students can then focus on their personal lives and further learn about the process of identity and subjectivity formation as it is informed by popular culture, history, and the politics of everyday life (McLaren 1995, 21).

The digital format of their stories and hence the ability to post them online also affords students the opportunity to engage others outside the classroom (Généreux and Thompson 2008, 22). Moreover, because of this innovative digital format project, students in my class also had a more formal opportunity to present their works on campus when they were invited to present their projects at the Center for Teaching Excellence at the University of Kansas at the end of the semester. Faculty members across campus who were interested in hearing students' experiences in producing this project attended the event and were engaged in a lively discussion with the students.

Third, the digital gender story project is a manifestation of engaged feminist pedagogy in that it allows students to take on responsibility (or to "share" the authority) in making their own decisions about the specific knowledge they want to master and produce (Parr, Horssen, and van der Veen 2009, 35). To achieve this goal, professors cannot simply deliver knowledge "like a package" (Chick and Hassel 2009, 197). Rather, students, working together with the professor, produce specialized, or "situated," knowledge based on their research and learning processes. It is these tools that students learn in engaged feminist classrooms: to discover and identify *for themselves* the social problems they wish to examine and to position themselves within this hierarchical system of power (Blake and Ooten 2008, 66).

Finally, the digital gender story project is a project that is informed by engaged feminist pedagogy in that it focuses on the growth, empowerment, and well-being of the students (as well as the teacher) (hooks 1994, 15, 21). In other words, knowledge produced through the engaged learning process of creating the digital gender story project may have the capacity to heal. hooks shares this similar point on the relationship between theory and healing:

> I came to theory because I was hurting – the pain within me was so intense that I could not go on living. I came to theory desperate, wanting to comprehend – to grasp what was happening around and within me. Most

importantly, I wanted to make the hurt go away. I saw in theory then a location for healing. (1994, 59)

This notion of theory as a site for healing is very empowering. Indeed, it is one that I stress when I assign students this digital gender story project. Through the project, students may have the opportunity to articulate emotions that have not yet been addressed but may have spilled over to the public space of society. A student, for example, shared how the digital story project allowed her to retrace the painful memories of coming out and to reconfigure her relationships with her family and religious affiliations. For this student, the project ended up becoming a part of her healing journey, one that was long overdue. It is important to remember, however, that "theory is not inherently healing, liberatory, or revolutionary. It fulfills this function only when we ask that it do so and direct our theorizing towards this end" (hooks 1994, 61). In this sense, knowledge can engage the self and others when the producer and learner of knowledge embark on a healing journey and move forward to do something more with the knowledge and themselves after they produce such liberating knowledge.

Teaching to Transgress

At the heart of critical feminist pedagogy lies bell hooks's (1994) maxim of "teaching to transgress." She challenges the current educational system that values the banking of knowledge, which students can then "withdraw" during exams, for example. Instead, she proposes an engaged and liberatory pedagogy that takes into account emotions and feelings as well. In thinking through her call for an engaged and liberatory pedagogy and a way of teaching that transgresses, I see the ability of the digital gender story project to transgress several boundaries. First, the digital gender story project transgresses institutional disciplinary boundaries. I purposefully adopted Amy Kesselman, Lily McNair, and Nancy Schniedewind's (2008) book *Women: Images and Realities* for this class precisely for this reason; the book incorporates materials from different disciplines including English, Sociology, Anthropology, Health, and Law and is written in various forms, from poetry to short fiction to song lyrics and to traditional research papers. The book provides a myriad of excellent examples of writing students could use as models and invites them to think about some possible narrative forms, content, and tones of the knowledge they can produce. Having been exposed to these different forms of knowledge, students had an easier time synthesizing various forms of information in their digital gender story project; they combined personal narratives with grounded research and incorporated persuasive visual evidence and relevant music to help them set the tone of their story. Here, the digital story project functions as a site of "productive encounter" where tensions between the visual and the narrative are negotiated, where both reasons and emotions are embraced, and where sharing the story with others is expected (Fletcher and Cambre 2009, 120-2). Thus, because of its form, the digital gender story project necessarily forces students to traverse and transgress these disciplinary boundaries: mastering skills in visual, textual, digital, and narrative fields of knowledge.

Another boundary that is being transgressed through this project is the teacher-student boundary, in particular the border that sets apart the producer from consumer of knowledge. By way of the digital gender story project, students can nurture different relationships with knowledge because they are simultaneously the producer, distributor, and acquirer of knowledge. That is, the digital gender story project provides students with the hands-on experience needed to construct knowledge and understand the feminist notion of knowledge as "constructed" and "situated" (Fletcher and Cambre 2009, 202; Haraway 1988, 581). This knowledge is important because students can then better understand how education is always steeped in ideology and works to reproduce that ideology (Freire 1998, 91). Therefore, when students work on producing the digital gender story project, I tirelessly remind them to be mindful of the gender ideology they are challenging and reproducing as well as being complicit with, because as they are learning they are simultaneously producing new knowledges.

The digital gender story project also makes it possible to traverse he physical boundary of the classroom as the ultimate learning space. The project facilitates students' venturing outside the classroom to seek knowledge through several activities. First, I take students literally outside the classroom during class meeting times; students are required to attend workshops at two different libraries on campus and the Mac computer lab. Introducing students to these resources is particularly important for those who may not have computers with appropriate software applications; this allows them to produce digital movies at home, for example. Second, students also have to step outside the classroom to compile the five images they submit for the first step of the project. Some students may decide to go to specific places and take pictures related to their topic. For example, a student whose focus was on gender and religion went to some religious sites in town and took some pictures for her project. Alternatively, students may submit pictures from their own their photo albums or find images from their past, like the student who focused on gender and education who went to her high school to meet with her teachers and get copies of archived school photographs. She also contacted her high school friends to gather more images of their high school experiences. In pushing students to travel outside the classroom to produce/learn knowledge, the digital gender story project transgresses the very process of researching and producing knowledge itself (High 2009, 24).

The digital gender story project also breaks down the boundary that separates "emotion" from "reason" as legitimate sources of knowledge. For this project, I encourage students to rely on their "emotion" and "reason" – both are considered as "legitimate" sources of knowledge – thereby transgressing the troubling binary relationship between the two. In framing emotion as an epistemological tool, I reflect on Horsfall's questions: "How do I work with students who are researching heart-felt issues in an institutional environment which often denies feelings and emotions? How do I bear witness to oft-repeated narratives of abuse and oppression? How can I provide scholarly – rigorous – attention to the person-academic work that needs to be done?" (2008, 1). Being mindful about these questions while guiding students with their project is particularly important because the digital gender story project is, in some ways, an emotionally and passion-driven project. The digital gender story project indeed values highly this process of circulation of emotions and the powerful ways in which emotions may "move" us to act upon or because of these emotions so that social justice and change can be achieved.

Beyond the Victim Voice and Celebratory Praise

In this chapter, I have described the five steps through which I guide students in completing the digital gender story project and explained how the digital gender story project embodies feminist pedagogy in the digital age. This brief concluding section will simply touch upon a possible issue that may (and did) arise with an emotion-ridden project such as this digital storytelling project, the problem of students occupying a victim voice or articulating unproductive celebratory praise.

In *Feminist Theory: From Margin to Center*, bell hooks argues that "sexist ideology teaches women that to be female is to be a victim" (2000, 45). hooks then explains that this ideology has been adopted by women activists and therein lies its problem. Using victimhood as a ground for building feminist sisterhood is unproductive because women could then only position themselves as victims and not as agents of change (hooks 2000, 45-6). To stress this point, I begin very early in the semester with mini lectures on hooks's criticism against bonding based on victimhood.

Then, throughout the semester, I show how some reading materials we read in class take on a narrative voice of victimhood, emphasizing and how they are productive but limiting at the same time. I also encourage students who use this kind of victim's voice in their projects to move beyond it and to find more critical ways to use the "affective content" of their digital projects (Fletcher and Cambre 2009, 127). By "affective content," I am referring here to the ways in which they use certain emotions (i.e., sadness, happiness) in their digital projects as a mode of engaging the audience.

The digital gender story project is a visual, digital, and critical rewriting of narratives about gender as it intersects with other categories of identity. Specifically, I envision the digital gender story project as a project that refuses to accept the dominant gender narrative as a lens through which one makes meanings of one's life. Inevitably, there may also be a tone of celebratory praise lurking behind these empowering and empowered narratives as students feel and become more confident in rewriting their own narratives. There is certainly a danger in celebrating this newly articulated sense of the self because the goal of the digital project should not end there. That is, the digital gender story project should not simply be about unsilencing the oppressed group. Silence, as feminist scholars argue, is not simply a form of absence but it can (and I would argue it should) be a different form of engagement and resistance. Feminist scholar Trinh Minh-ha argues that silence is "a will not to say or a will to unsay and as a language of its own has barely been explored" (1997, 416). Working from the framework of silence as productive and as a survival mode of resistance (Bhattacharya 2009, 360), I contend that celebrating the new unsilenced subjectivity does not automatically count as a form of liberating knowledge that embodies critical engaged feminist pedagogy. In other words, the act of unsilencing alone may not be productive for social change unless the knowledges produced through these new unsilenced voices are ones that may lead us to social justice. It is therefore necessary that we perpetually seek new ways to articulate these critical voices as we continue to stride our way into the digital age.

In this essay I have shared the five steps through which I guided students in completing the digital gender story project that I designed for my introductory women's studies course. By doing so, I hope to encourage others and propose that we embrace the new media formats of the digital age that can provide us with a new mode of implementing feminist pedagogy in the virtual and digital environments. It is not only inevitable that we think and create new ways of teaching in the cyberspace, but it is also beneficial for students to learn new ways of being, navigating, and making changes in the digital world, as it is the world we currently live in. Cyberspace is indeed a space where gender, as it is racialized and hetero/sexualized, is articulated, and therefore we need to imagine a different and more progressive way of rearticulating these gender issues so that women do not become "othered" in this space. Rather, women, along with their male counterparts can become active producers of knowledge in this new mediated, digital space.

Bibliography

Bayne, Siân. 2008. "Higher Education as a Visual Practice: Seeing through the Virtual Learning Environment." *Teaching in Higher Education* 13, no. 4: 395-410.

Bhattacharya, Himika. 2009. "Performing Silence: Gender, Violence and Resistance in Women's Narratives from Lauhaul, India." *Qualitative Inquiry* 15, no. 2: 359-371.

Blake, Holly and Melissa Ooten. 2008. "Bridging the Divide: Connecting Feminist Histories and Activism in the Classroom." *Radical History Review* 102: 63-72.

Boulding, Elise. 1988. *Building a Global Civic Culture: Education for an Interdependent World.* New York: Teachers College.

Butler, Judith. 1992. "Contingent Foundations: Feminism and the Question of Postmodernism." In *Feminists Theorize the Political,* edited by Judith Butler and Joan W. Scott, 3-21. New York: Routledge.

Chick, Nancy and Holly Hassel. 2009. "'Don't Hate Me Because I'm Virtual: Feminist Pedagogy in the Online Classroom." *Feminist Teacher* 19, no. 3: 195-215.

Conquergood, Dwight. 1993. "Storied Worlds and the Work of Teaching." *Communication Education* 42: 337-348.

Downes, Daniel. 2005. *Interactive Realism: The Poetics of Cyberspace.* Montreal: McGill-Queen's University.

Edwards, Brian. 2008. *Theories of Play and Postmodern Fiction.* New York: Garland.

Fletcher, Christopher and Carolina Cambre. 2009. "Digital Storytelling and Implicated Scholarship in the Classroom." *Journal of Canadian Studies* 43, no. 1: 109-130.

Freire, Paulo. 1998. *Pedagogy of Freedom: Ethics, Democracy, and Civic Courage.* Translated by Patrick Clarke. Lanham: Rowman and Littlefield.

Généreux, Annie P. and William A. Thompson. "Light, Camera, Reflection! Digital Movies: A Tool for Reflective Learning." *Journal of College Science Teaching* 37, no. 6 (2008): 21-25.

Giroux, Henry. 1999. "Border Youth, Difference, and Postmodern Education." In *Critical Education in the New Information Age*, edited by Peter McLaren, 93-115. Lanham: Rowman and Littlefield.

Greenfield, Lauren. 2002. *Girl Culture*. San Francisco: Chronicle Books.

Hans, James. 1981. *The Play of the World*. Amherst: University of Massachusetts.

Haraway, Donna. 1988. "Situated Knowledges: The Science Question in Feminism and the Privilege of Partial Perspective." *Feminist Studies* 14, no. 3: 575-599.

High, Steven. 2009. "Sharing Authority: An Introduction." *Journal of Canadian Studies* 43, no. 1: 12-34.

hooks, bell. 1984. *Feminist Theory: From Margin to Center*. Reprint, London, U.K.: Pluto Press, 2000.

—. 1994. *Teaching to Transgress: Education as the Practice of Freedom*. New York: Routledge.

Horsfall, Debbie. 2008. "Bearing Witness: Toward a Pedagogical Practice of Love." *Reflective Practice* 9, no. 1: 1-10.

Ingraham, Chrys. 1999. *White Weddings: Romancing Heterosexuality in Popular Culture*. Reprint, New York: Routledge, 2008.

Kesselman, Amy, Lily McNair and Nancy Schniedewind, eds. 1994. *Women: Images and Realities*. Reprint, Boston: McGraw-Hill, 2008.

Lea, Mary. 2004. "Academic Literacies: A Pedagogy for Course Design." *Studies in Higher Education* 29, no. 6: 739-756.

McLaren, Peter. 1995. *Critical Pedagogy and Predatory Culture: Oppositional Politics in a Postmodern Era*. London, U.K.: Routledge.

Minh-ha, Trinh. 1997. "Not You/Like You: Postcolonial Women and the Interlocking Questions of Identity and Difference." In *Dangerous Liaisons: Gender, Nation, and Postcolonial Perspectives,* edited by Anne McClintock, Ammir Mufti and Ella Shohat, 415-444. Minneapolis: University of Minnesota.

Mirzoeff, Nicholas. 1999. *An Introduction to Visual Culture*. London: Routledge.

Mort, Graham and Lee Horsley. 2007. "In Virtuality Veritas." *Pedagogy* 7, no. 3: 513-525.

Parr, Joy, Jessica Van Horssen and Jon van der Veen. 2009. "The Practice of History Shared across Differences: Needs, Technologies, and Ways of Knowing in the Megaprojects New Media Project." *Journal of Canadian Studies* 43, no. 1: 35-58.

Richardson, Laurel and Elizabeth St. Pierre. 2005. "Writing: A Method of Inquiry." In *The Sage Handbook of Qualitative Research,* edited by Norman K. Denzin and Yvonna S Lincoln, 959-978. Thousand Oaks, CA: Sage.

Rossiter, Marsha and Penny A. Garcia. 2010. "Digital Storytelling: A New Player on the Narrative Field." *New Directions for Adult and Continuing Education* 126, no. 1: 37-48.

Notes

[1] The author sincerely thanks Dan Bernstein at the Center for Teaching Excellence (CTE) at the University of Kansas for being so encouraging about this project and giving her the permission to publish some portions of this essay that have appeared in various CTE publications including *Reflections, Teaching Matters,* and *Teaching Portfolio Gallery.* The author is also grateful for Kim Staking and the editors for their insightful feedback on this essay.

THE VIRTUAL CLASSROOM:

DISTANCE EDUCATION AND VIRTUAL WORLDS

Chapter Eight

Women's Studies and Cyberspace: Redesigning the Introduction to Women's Studies

Michelle McGibbney Vlahoulis and Marcella Gemelli

The proliferation of technology provides students in higher learning today unfounded capabilities for communicating, viewing visual images and gathering information to better understand their world. From using social networking sites to online job hunting and even in bill paying, students use technology in almost every aspect of their lives. Phone calls have been replaced by email, texting, and social networking sites, and newspapers and notebooks in the classroom have been replaced by laptops. In the educational setting, creative uses of the online environment can allow for a richer classroom experience, one where students use their technological abilities to better understand course content and material. Several studies indicate that technology and different approaches to online teaching can help students at all levels of education learn and excel in ways they never have been able to before (Schacter 1999, 3).

Creating a technologically rich classroom was one of the goals for the transformation of a traditional course into a hybrid for women and gender studies at Arizona State University (ASU). The Introduction to Women's Studies course, *Women, Gender and Society*, has been taught in the large classroom in the traditional manner, but now meets physically one day a week, with the additional class period taught online. Teaching the introductory course in hybrid format allows the faculty to be traditional yet current, linking class lectures with the increased use of technology. What we have found using this new approach is that we are able to increase student engagement, give students timely feedback, and educate a diverse student body all with a little help from technology. We have established an atmosphere conducive to critical and alternative thinking and developed a framework for analyzing gender, race, class, and sexuality in students' own lives. In familiarizing students with significant feminist contributions, we have helped them to analyze their lived experiences of gender. The hybrid format has also increased student enrollment with the ability to offer fewer sections, giving greater accessibility and continuing to serve as a recruiting ground for the program.

This hybrid serves as a gateway to other women's and gender studies classes. It is in this introductory course that students learn the importance of the field, the significant impact and contributions of feminist work, and the relevance of that work to their own lives, regardless of their major, gender, race, age or class. Getting students interested in women's studies and sustaining their attention hinges on the instructor's ability to stimulate student learning and to increase their desire to want learn more. Using technology is an excellent way to tie students to the content, engage them in critical discussions, and use current events to connect them no matter their social location, no matter the time of day.

Utilizing faculty-made podcasts on various topics titled "Women and Work in a Global Economy," "Global Barbie," and "Cautionary Tales," as well as YouTube clips on topics of race, class, gender, and sexual orientation, online discussion boards, short online quizzes and response papers, our introductory course is examining critical topics in an engaging way for the 21st century student. Using data collected since the initial pilot phase of the hybrid, we will show the success of using technology in the classroom, students' immediate connection to it, and its ability to help facilitate difficult dialogues that would prove impossible in person. Examples from the various technologies we employ, will demonstrate how the innovative hybrid format helps to further the goals of women's studies, engages students of various disciplines and creates lifelong learners who are able to connect important concepts and theories to their everyday lives.

Women, Gender and Society: **The Hybrid**

Our introductory course began as a traditional in-person large lecture class. In an attempt to meet the high demand for online and hybrid courses seen in many other fields and to respond to student interest, we began to think about the ways that students would be able to experience this class using media-rich technology. Using questions and exercises from the original course, we now complement our weekly lectures with exciting online content. Serving approximately 400 students per section and up to 3000 per year, this course is designed to introduce students to the field and allow for them to engage in more intimate discussions of critical issues than they are able to do in the large classroom setting.

Other educators have elaborated on their use of technology in courses with sensitive material; Shieh, Gummer and Niess (2008, 61) describe their findings on the quality of a web-based course from the perspectives of the students and the instructor by utilizing Chickering and Gamson's seven principles for quality undergraduate education practices (1987). They found in their course, "Women: Self and Society" that the principle of encouraging active learning among students was met in the online environment through weekly instructional activities such as discussions and journals (66). Additionally, they found in studies by Kiesler, Siegel and McGuire (1984) and Gunawadena (1995) that the online environment may provide a safe and comfortable place for shy or minority students to speak up more than they would in the traditional classroom due to their anonymity (62).

Using Blackboard, our university-provided virtual learning environment, we employ weekly instructional assignments such as discussion boards, response papers, and timed quizzes, as well as faculty-made podcasts and a variety of other activities that speak to different student learning styles to engage students with the available technology. The online portion of the course is available to students twenty-four hours a day, allowing them to work at their own pace and on their own time with pre-set deadlines. These deadlines provide a sense of routine and stability to the online portion of the course. Student athletes, working students who sometimes have full time jobs, and commuting students find the hybrid accommodating to their busy schedules.

Assignments: Linking Feminist Pedagogy with Technology

The hybrid course is designed for a 15-week semester, although it can easily be adapted for courses using less or more than 15 weeks. There are 12 weeks of content and related assignments posted on the Blackboard site. There is no assignment the first week to accommodate the fluctuating schedules of students, and two weeks are set aside for in-class exams. We use a variety of assignments to assess student capabilities and skills; short response papers to assess writing and applied skills, discussion boards to assess understanding of content and expression of informed opinion, and finally quizzes to test reading comprehension. Currently, there are three short papers, five discussion boards, and four quizzes spread throughout the course. Each of these assignments is discussed in further detail below.

Discussion Boards

One of the methods of assessment in the hybrid course is the discussion board. The discussion board can easily be created in the weekly unit housing the particular content and can be divided into smaller groups. For example, with classes of 200 students, discussion board groups are typically arranged into six to eight groups by student last name so that students are not responding to the entire class but to a smaller, more intimate, discussion group of about 25-35 students. Questions specifically related to the content for the week must be answered including a question for students to provide their own examples or experiences. To create the discussion and successfully complete the assignment, the student must also reply to another student's post. The discussion post as an assignment allows for opinion but one that is guided by specific questions and analysis of the material. Additionally, the discussion board is facilitates discussion among students creating a collaborative-based learning environment. The topics in discussion posts range from addressing representations of gays and lesbians in popular media, the difficulties for men and women to defy gendered expectations, and the current wage gap that exists between men and women.

Feminist teachers often utilize educational films and references to popular culture to illustrate course themes and concepts. Since moving to a hybrid format, we may not always have the classroom time to show a feature length film. Further, student feedback indicates an appreciation for shorter clips. These clips are easily embedded into the Blackboard site so that students may view them on their own time. For the weekly theme of "Women and Sexuality," we embedded an episode of *The Simpsons* titled, "There's Something About Marrying." This episode discusses the topic of gay marriage, while also illuminating related issues of sexuality, consumerism, and the construction of the white wedding in American culture. We see Homer Simpson performing gay marriages in his garage to make a profit, while Marge Simpson, originally a proponent of gay marriage, struggles with the issue when she discovers her sister wants to marry someone the audience is led to believe is a woman. Due to the way the messages are embedded throughout the episode, we find students can easily relate to the images, making it comfortable for them to converse about a heated topic such as gay marriage.

We also include a short introductory clip from the Media Education Foundation (MEF) film, "Further Off the Straight and Narrow: New Gay Visibility on TV." After viewing this and *The Simpsons* episode, students are required to provide their own example and explanation on the discussion board regarding stereotypes of gays and lesbians in the media. This assignment also provides an exercise for developing a critical framework around sexuality. Analyzing topics around sexuality as well as gender, race and class or around inequalities may be a new experience for the mostly freshman student population in the hybrid course. The balance of the comedic, yet thought provoking, clip from *The Simpsons* and the serious analysis of the portrayal of gays in the media in "Further Off the Straight and Narrow: New Gay Visibility on TV" provides an accessible point of entry into a controversial topic.

Although the discussion boards are graded and students are identifiable by name, these assignments allow students to remain somewhat anonymous in the virtual realm because they might not be known to other students. Students may feel more confident in expressing themselves online, particularly if they are divulging personal information, rather than face-to-face in a classroom of 200 or more students. Further, because the discussion board is graded according to a detailed rubric, based on inclusion of content and course material as well as a response to another student's post, students engage in the discussion in a serious manner. Discussion posts are graded for insight and originality, clear argumentation supported by class material, and in authentic responses to other students. We believe these criteria establish a respectful, engaging and safe environment to discuss sensitive topics.

The discussion board remains a favorite, according to student evaluations. One student responded, "I love to see how my peers approach these somewhat controversial issues and how these boards reflect our own lived experiences." Engaging in the discussion board allows students to hear how their peers interpret the issues, sometimes sharing similar ideas and concerns while learning to appreciate different life experiences. The structured environment permits a more open, honest, and complex approach to understanding diversity. These discussion boards accomplish several of our learning outcomes from establishing an atmosphere of critical and alternative thinking to assisting students in developing the tools of analysis to explain their everyday lived experiences within the virtual learning environment.

While new technology for our online course includes the options of blogs and journals, there is no straightforward grading option nor is there a straightforward way to structure or monitor the entries in Blackboard. The blog or journal without significant guidance may result in less than civil dialogue and may even be less engaging overall. However, these online tools may be useful for a less structured exploration of course content or they may be useful in a smaller online classroom environment. Because we teach such a large number of students per course, we feel that the guided and graded discussion board provides the structure necessary to keep the discussions healthy and engaging.

Short Response Papers

Another method of assessment in the hybrid course is the online short response paper. Similar to the discussion board, students are asked a number of questions to which they must reply based on the topic for the week. The topics include visiting a toy store to analyze gendered toys as they relate to the socialization of boys and girls, as well as identifying and analyzing an advertisement for gendered messages.

The short paper assignments are based on experiential learning; students learn through actively participating in an activity outside of class and then writing up careful reflection and insight into that experience. Under the introductory topic "What is Sex? What is Gender?" we introduce gender roles and the influence of something so seemingly innocent as toys upon gendered social scripts. Embedded in our site are a 1959 Barbie commercial and a 1960s commercial for G.I. Joe. Students are encouraged to watch the commercials, review the PowerPoint lecture, and are then prompted to visit a toy store in person or online to describe and analyze what they see in terms of gender for their assignment. They are asked to address class, status and race in their analysis and to reflect upon the toys they were given as a child or, if they are parents, what types of toys their children have.

The gender ad paper under the weekly topic, "Women and the Body," is another experiential learning assessment. After watching a small clip from Jean Kilbourne's *Killing Us Softly 3* and a short clip of the introduction to *Thin,* an HBO film about eating disorders, students are expected to find an advertisement to analyze for gendered messages. When they are asked to look at these representations with a critical eye, students are often shocked by the ads they find. This assignment encourages them to think about the images they see on a daily basis and what that means for their own body image or, for men, the images of women they see versus the real women in their lives.

Another exercise we have incorporated in this course uses *Ms.* online. Along with the textbook for the course, students are required to purchase the *Ms.* digital edition. For a small subscription price, students have access to four editions of the magazine. For this particular assignment, we allow students to pick any edition of *Ms.* and compare and contrast it with another popular magazine commonly found on store shelves, such as

Vogue or *Cosmopolitan*. The students analyze the content and messages inherent in these two different magazines and what they are conveying to young women today. This is a great exercise for students to see the difference in the types of portrayals of women and advertising. Students are able to see *Ms.* as a vehicle of social change and how advertising and magazines can indeed work to further the goals of advancing women's role in society.

These short paper assignments successfully combine feminist pedagogy with technology. The short papers rely on students' use of the Internet to search for appropriate ads, to look for alternative forms of media to serve as social change, or to find an online toy store, while also requiring their utilization of the Blackboard site. This online environment in effect creates the additional class period, or the virtual classroom, a classroom of new ideas and one available to students twenty-four hours a day. As one student remarked, "I really enjoyed the discussion boards and papers. They were extremely helpful as they helped me to delve further into what was covered in class. I learned more because of these exercises."

Quizzes

Students often struggle with trying to identify what course concepts are important and how to prepare for exams. With the redesign to a hybrid format, we developed a set of mandatory quizzes that match multiple units throughout the semester. These quizzes are timed and graded immediately through Blackboard allowing immediate feedback to students to help them assess their understanding of the course content and comprehension. The quizzes also help the instructor gage patterns of student difficulty. We include not only course reading and lecture in these quizzes but also the videos and podcasts found on our site, helping students connect with broader themes discussed during lecture. All of the online assignments created for the hybrid further students' knowledge while keeping them accountable to complete the online work in a timely manner.

Blackboard offers many features to help ensure academic honesty, a concern common among instructors teaching hybrid and online courses. As mentioned above, having the ability to time quizzes or even more tailored options such as randomizing questions or using Respondus Lockdown, a feature that prevents students from having other windows open on their computer while taking the quiz, are just a few examples. Other ways we have tried to ensure students are doing their own work in our own classroom is by reusing quiz questions on students' midterm and final exams. Students are informed at the beginning of the semester that random quiz questions will reappear on their exams. Not knowing what questions will be chosen, we hope to encourage them to understand all the material and content rather than memorizing or copying from their peers.

Podcasts: Using Technology to Facilitate Mini-Guest Lectures

Another use of the virtual learning environment to raise students' understanding of gender is through our faculty-made podcasts, which are produced in a studio. We received a grant for a large hybrid redesign as part of the Arizona Board of Regents (ABOR) Learner-Centered Education Course Redesign Initiative, a collaborative effort between ABOR and NCAT (2006-2009), and we used some of this funding to produce the podcasts, which range in price depending on many factors, including length of the podcasts, studio rental and time, and other miscellaneous expenses. We spent approximately five thousand dollars on a full day in the studio creating a total of eight podcasts. Various faculty in the program were recruited to record professionally shot and edited podcasts for the hybrid course. The faculty wrote and delivered their own scripts, and the studio provided assistance with recording, editing, and enhancing the visual productions. Since this course focuses mainly on issues regarding women and gender in the United States, the intention behind the podcasts was to introduce a global element to the mainly American based content. For example, in the "Eating Disorders" podcast under the weekly topic, "Women and the Body," Dr. Scheiner Gillis comments on the proliferation of eating disorders in Argentina, the strict standards of beauty Argentineans place upon women, and the popularity of beauty pageants. Students are often surprised to learn that there is a strong emphasis on beauty in other societies outside the U.S. Other podcast topics include mini-lectures on the sex trade and violence against women as well as the changing imagery and messages regarding women's sexuality in pop culture and representations of women of color in the popular media.

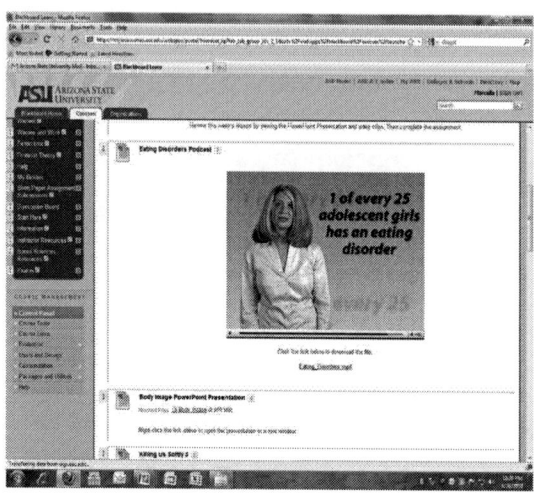

Figure 2: A paused clip of Dr. Scheiner Gills' podcast

Dr. Yasmina Katsulis' podcast "Cross-Cultural Comparisons of Gender" housed under the introductory topic, "What is Sex? What is Gender?" discusses the cultural constructions of gender and the many assumptions made about women's roles. She looks at different societies' expectations of women in regard to work, marriage, child-bearing, education and dress, and argues that these differences and inequalities allow us to see the full range of possibilities and that gender roles are not rigid but culturally constructed and malleable. In her podcast "The Sex Trade" she looks at the divergent feminist approaches to the sex industry. She informs students about the many dangers of the industry by discussing a range of complicated issues, from human trafficking, slave trading, and poverty to the AIDS epidemic, safety, violence, and even drug addiction. She also approaches the possibilities of improving workplace safety, as well as protection issues and problems of police insensitivity, as well as health and outreach issues. She really encourages students to think about the overwhelming nature of violence against women, women's struggles with poverty, and to consider workplace practices that would allow for a much safer industry.

These podcasts are a way to provide students with a guest lecture of sorts. Students learn from the expertise of different faculty members within the women and gender studies program, which may in turn encourage our hybrid students to take other classes offered by these same professors. The podcasts, like the videos on our site, provide part of the structure for the virtual classroom. Students spend time in this classroom to engage with the material and to complete assignments. The assignments and content in the online learning environment, as well as the material in the traditional classroom, assist students in further developing the tools of analysis needed to explain their lived experience of gender.

Feminist Teaching: Pedagogical Learning for Students, Pedagogical Opportunities for Teaching Assistants

A major goal of the redesign project was to increase active student learning. The required unit quizzes help students play a more active role in assessing whether or not they understand the material and encourages them to frame questions for a better discussion with the professor or the graduate teaching assistant. Rapid feedback is incredibly important to the student learning process. The required group discussion forums are designed to ask each student to put course concepts into their own words and to apply those concepts to real-life examples. Requiring participation helps to push students into an active learning mode, but based on previous experience, the liveliness and diversity of opinions can also pull students into the discussion. Here they learn in our class and in the field in general that every voice is valued. The short, faculty-made podcasts help to engage the students in the material and help them understand the kinds of research performed by feminist faculty.

Improving Student Engagement and Performance

A recent study shows how technology has improved student learning. A 1999 publication by John Schacter of the Milken Exchange on Education Technology synthesizes various studies regarding research on education technology's impact on student learning. One of the studies Schacter cites is a meta-analysis on over 500 individual research studies of computer-based instruction by James Kulik (1994). Schacter notes in his synthesis of Kulik's meta-analysis study, "Computer-based instruction individualizes the educational process to accommodate the needs, interests, proclivities, current knowledge, and learning styles of the student" (4). Schacter reports that Kulik found that students from elementary school to college learned more in less time and students liked their classes more with computer-based instruction (4).

In line with national studies showing greater student success and higher overall grades, our experience also reflects great learning outcomes with this course redesign that pairs the traditional in person women's studies class with cyberspace. The team of faculty who originally created this course completed several assessments comparing the traditional class with the new hybrid format. Our findings, using a t test, concluded for multiple semesters that both midterm and final exam grades were higher in the redesign across all faculty sections taught. We believe the use of quizzes to help students better prepare for the type of questions they would see on later exams had an immediate impact. We also believe that requiring students to do weekly assignments assisted them in keeping current with the materials and readings and gave them the ability to gage early on what concepts and ideas with which they were struggling. Using technology and its availability around the clock helped with different student learning styles, schedules, and comprehension skills.

Delivering the course more efficiently and consistently, we have guaranteed that students leave different faculty sections learning the same content and using the same student assessment tools. This makes it easy to assess student progress and areas of improvement both for faculty teaching and student learning. We have experienced positive student learning outcomes and improved the overall quality of student learning. Due to the implementation of multiple online exercises, we have actively engaged students in the material, have given them immediate feedback, and increased their chances for improvement on the next assignment. In the hybrid, we continue to offer in class, in person midterms and final exams so that students have the ability to ask about questions they might be struggling with; only our weekly assignments are offered online. As mentioned, our data show after the implementation of this hybrid course more students successfully completed the course and felt confident in their ability to achieve.

Further, our course evaluations, personal student conversations, and feedback, as well as hybrid students declaring women and gender studies as their major or minor after taking the course, communicate to us that our students are engaged in the material and want to pursue women's studies as a field of inquiry. Students tell us that they now view videos, movies, and commercials with a critical eye toward gender, race, and class. They report having lively discussions with friends and parents about concepts presented in class. The experiential short response papers and discussion boards alleviate a simple regurgitation of material. These assignments, along with the visually engaging Blackboard site, keeps students engaged and interested while also helping them succeed in the course.

Pedagogical Opportunities for Graduate Teaching Assistants and Undergraduate Learning Assistants

Other pedagogical improvement techniques used in the redesign was the implementation of undergraduate learning assistants (ULAs). Students enrolled in our courses now have the opportunity to not only interact with their instructors and graduate teaching assistants (TAs) but now also with peer teachers. The ULAs are students who successfully completed the introductory course and are recruited for their outstanding work from a prior semester. The role of the ULA in this course is to monitor, facilitate, and evaluate discussion board forums. In addition, the ULAs are required to participate in and complete an undergraduate pedagogy course. In this course, they learn how to assess student work and observe different faculty instruction, as well as help to develop new materials, both visual and experiential, and increase their technical expertise.

This class is a great pedagogical opportunity for undergraduate students interested in furthering their career in academia or simply to develop highly valued skills for the job market. Working with various faculty teaching the hybrid, these students observed different types of feminist instruction, particularly different approaches to sensitive issues and how to turn a particular issue into a teachable moment. The ULAs also work with finding new material and linking lectures to exciting content relevant to the field. They create various feminist activities to supplement the site including resources for body image, eating disorders, and domestic violence. Further, they incorporate clips from current films or TV shows popular amongst the college population focusing on issues of race, class, and gender and even locate supplemental online readings to support the text used. The work of the ULAs with the guidance of the faculty really creates a collaborative environment encouraging creativity and innovative strategies for feminist learning.

We worked with both ULAs and TAs to develop rubrics for the grading of the discussion boards and online response papers. TAs and ULAs use and appreciate these guidelines when evaluating student work. These detailed rubrics assure that the same expectations of quality are shared among the faculty while giving the teaching assistants the criteria to effectively and fairly grade student work.

The TA's role in this class takes many different forms. First, their main role is to support the online portion of this class. While the help desk on campus is able to troubleshoot any technical problems that may arise, the TA's job is to make sure all content is open and accessible, all assignments are functioning properly, and to communicate with students via email or announcements regarding the Blackboard site. TAs are also responsible for grading the short response papers. We also encourage TAs to attend all lectures and give mini-lectures of their own to help them prepare for teaching their own sections in the future.

The dynamic nature of inquiry in women's studies classes is full of variation based on background knowledge and lived experiences. Students are not judged for what opinion they have, but when making an argument in a class assignment, we evaluate how well they back up their argument through referencing course material. For example, if women use their sexuality to their advantage, is it powerful, or is it demonstrative of a larger patriarchal domination? While students have various responses to this, we require them to support their own argument using text and information given in the class, while also encouraging them to support those who do not share the same view. This same philosophy holds true for those grading. While the ULAs and TAs may not agree with the statements posted by students, they learn how to critically evaluate responses for well-defined arguments.

The pedagogy course well prepares ULAs to better understand the field of women's studies and how pedagogy and technology can connect in a feminist classroom. TAs, upon leaving graduate school, are now well trained to teach their own sections and have a better understanding of how a feminist classrooms operates from course development to implementation of activities and content.

The Challenges of Technology

Moving the traditional course online into the hybrid is not without its challenges. Students and faculty alike may fear the unknown. Do I want to take this class online? How will I learn online? Will the server have adequate space for use? Has my university made a strong commitment to the investment of technology? Will help be available? How can I best serve my students online?

While using new technology poses some small obstacles, a flexibility to change what doesn't work and sometimes just patience alone can help alleviate some of the issues. In the initial design of the site, there is an expectation that faculty, TAs and students will have a certain sophistication and level of knowledge with technology, as well as openness to the hybrid format. Sophistication with technology may impact faculty engagement; not all faculty have worked with more advanced computer-based instructional tools, and many still hold the opinion that women's studies is not a suitable discipline for online learning. Getting faculty buy-in may present a challenge as women's studies courses are thought to be more personable and engaging of personal matters. However, we find that feminist pedagogy is not lost in the online environment. Careful planning and development of course material and exercises can prove to encourage positive communication among faculty and students as well as with peer-to-peer interaction.

We were able to make the transition from the traditional classroom to the hybrid format smoother by making our site as user friendly as possible. A development shell was created that can be imported across faculty sections. This development shell served as a template whereby the structure of the online portion stayed consistent but also allowed faculty to include their own PowerPoints or other links to individualize the site. The development shell was first piloted in just one faculty member's section to evaluate what exercises and assignments best complemented the material being taught, what technological problems arose, and how students ultimately learned from the Blackboard site. Once the pilot phase was over and some of these problems were addressed, we then imported the shell across multiple faculty sections. This allowed consistency and the ability to assess student comprehension among the various faculty teaching the course.

The hybrid design keeps all weekly materials under one assessable tab with each weekly unit opening one week at a time. Information on technology trainings and tutorials available for students on campus and the link to contact information for the university help desk are posted in several areas on the Blackboard site. We find it imperative to carefully and methodically explain the hybrid format to students and to go through the syllabus and other materials on the site in the first class period. Further, we also anticipate that the first discussion board, quiz, or paper submission may not run smoothly, so we introduce one of each during the first three weeks to troubleshoot any problems that may occur later on in the semester. The detailed syllabus highlights the importance of attending both the face-to-face and asynchronous online meetings. We do not feel that our hybrid course is exclusionary; students may access the online portion of the course through their own computer or use one of the many computing commons on campus if they do not have their own computer. Again, the flexibility of the hybrid allows students to complete the online portion at their convenience.

In 2010, the National Federation for the Blind (NFB) certified Blackboard Learn as being the most accessible learning platform they had tested, the first and only to date ("Blackboard Learn is First Learning Management System to Achieve Certification" 2010). Along with the

NFB's findings, we to see our hybrid course as easily accessible for students with disabilities, helping to break the barriers they are often faced with in the classroom. The already established site allows a working relationship between the student and his/her on campus accommodations. It also allows easy conversion of the materials and is easily adaptable to any special software that may be needed. The virtual classroom also helps with the problem of time constraints. For example, student assignments are open for 3-4 days, which gives the student the ability to work at their own pace and the option to easily extend the time allotted for quizzes and tests.

Designing a hybrid course with online content has many issues to consider, including the design of a user-friendly format that will not frustrate students or faculty. We have found that the benefits of creating and teaching the hybrid course has outweighed the challenges and that, in the long run, the redesign has improved student learning and the effectiveness of the way the course is delivered. In the end technology triumphed over traditional, and we are pleased with all the possibilities it presents. We are encouraged to know that many educators now believe that women's studies and online learning are not only feasible but indeed a wonderful match.

Conclusion

The hybrid course has been a work in progress. When the online portion of the hybrid was first launched, we relied on the visual learning environment of Blackboard, which was limited to the very basic organizational structure of the environment. With the help from an instructional designer, we were able to make the online site more aesthetically pleasing. Undoubtedly, we live in a time of the visual image, and we understand that students have a heightened visual awareness in their personal lives. The visual is also becoming increasingly prominent in classes in higher education through online and hybrid offerings. Bayne elaborates on this point in his analysis of the virtual learning environment, "As the practices of higher education shift online, the work of learners, teachers and scholars increasingly takes place within the domain of the image" (2008, 395).

High demand for women's studies classes and now hybrid and online classes has kept us competitive, open-minded, and creative. We are able to provide students with a media-rich environment and challenging material with help from technology. This redesign shows feminism and cyberspace can connect and make for a richer classroom experience.

Marrying feminist pedagogy and the virtual learning environment, the hybrid format has allowed consistency, creativity, and the ability for faculty, graduate teaching assistants, and undergraduate learning assistants to assess feminist pedagogy and student success. This course is sustainable and replicable so new faculty can easily transition to teaching the course while bringing their own research interests and teaching style. Students tell us that they enjoy the flexibility, the way the online activities reinforce what is learned in lecture, and the benefit of these various exercises playing to different learning styles. Upon finishing this course, students have a better understanding of what feminism means and how it is relevant today, which sometimes results in students taking more women's studies classes and even declaring majors or minors. To be sure, our use of technology proves that we are current, thinking outside the box, and able to keep up with the demands of the time. Students acknowledge this through the consistently high enrollments in the course, making it one of the more popular courses on campus.

In order to stay connected and relevant women's studies programs must remain at the digital forefront. Using technology in the classroom as a way of learning not only engages the student in familiar territory but complements the field in many amazing and exciting ways, expanding the opportunity of learning and allowing students to participate and to have a voice. This is especially critical on campuses nationwide where large classrooms are becoming the norm.

Bibliography

Bayne, Siân. 2008. "Higher Education as a Visual Practice: Seeing Through the Virtual Learning Environment." *Teaching in Higher Education* 13, no. 4: 395-410.

"Blackboard Learn Is First Learning Management System to Achieve Certification." 2010. *Disabled World*, August 12. Accessed May 31, 2011.
http://www.disabled-world.com/disability/accessibility/blackboard-learning.php#ixzz1IOijnqoG.

Schacter, John. 1999. "The Impact of Education Technology on Student Achievement: What the Most Current Research Has to Say." *Milken Exchange on Education Technology*, Feb. 1. Accessed November 13, 2011. http://www.mff.org/publications/publications.taf?page=161.

Shieh, Ruey S., Edith Gummer and Maggie Niess. 2008. "The Quality of a Web-Based Course: Perspectives of the Instructor and the Students." *TechTrends* 52, no. 6: 61-68.

Chapter Nine

A European E-Learning Program on Gendered and Sexualized Violence: Developing a Feminist Pedagogy of Non-Violence

Mervi Heikkinen, Suvi Pihkala and Vappu Sunnari

A need for concerted worldwide action to defend human rights and eliminate violence has long been recognized at different levels and in different ways.[1] Public awareness of gendered and sexualized violence has also increased during the last decade. Violence prevention and the provision of aid for the victims of violence remain acute issues, however. According to European Commission (EC) estimations, every year in Europe around 3,500 children under the age of fifteen will die as a result of physical assault and neglect. Ten percent of schoolchildren face violence at school, states the EC; some of that violence is so traumatic that suicide seems the only way out. Vappu Sunnari (*"I cannot speak about it": Physical Sexual Harassment as Experienced by Children at School in Northern Finland and Northwest Russia* 2010) reports the figure at twenty to twenty-five percent of 11 to 12 years old girls in Northern Finland and Northwest Russia had experienced physical sexual harassment at school or on the way to school. A smaller percent of boys had corresponding experiences. Moreover, according to EC; recent studies on gender-based violence suggest that an estimated twenty to twenty-five percent of all women in Europe have experienced the physical acts of violence at least once during their adult lives and that over ten percent have suffered sexual violence involving the use of force. One particularly serious form of violence, also in the European Union, is human trafficking: an estimated 100,000 victims of trafficking per year, eighty percent of whom are women and girls (*Daphne – Prevent and Combat Violence against*

Children, Young People and Women and to Protect Victims and Groups at Risk 2010).

Studies have identified gender and sexual violence as one of the most considerable obstacles to the establishment of gender equality and human rights (Garcia-Moreno et al. 2010; Hageman-White and Bohne 2010; Hageman-White, et al. 2008; Huuki 2010; Kelly 2005; Manninen 2010; Sunnari 2010; Sunnari, Kangasvuo, and Heikkinen 2003; Walby 2005). On global or EU levels, no easy access exists to systematic multisectoral and multidisciplinary education specializing in examining violence and abuse and their prevention. Professionals in various fields should know about the multiple forms of violence and their consequences and how to effectively intervene to prevent violence or its escalation in their professions and in multisectoral collaboration. A clear need exists to increase professional competence regarding these issues in institutions including medicine, social work, education, law, media, and economics. Towards that end, numerous feminist researchers and activists worldwide have been working for decades to develop professional education to promote non-violence and gender equality.

Global work carried out against gendered and sexualized violence has formed a basis for European and national action and for action on local levels. The European Commission's community-based action to combat violence against children, youth, and women – entitled Daphne I,[2] II,[3] and III[4] – has provided necessary funding and allowed development work to be done in various projects[5] over the past decade, resulting in a network of NGOs and public authorities for action in Europe. The Women's and Gender Studies at the University of Oulu has developed a multisectoral, multidisciplinary 25 ECTS minor study program, based on e-learning. The development work has been done over the past decade, six Daphne-funded projects,[6] and international collaboration. The minor study program, coordinated by the Women's and Gender Studies, is now included in the curriculum of the Faculty of Education at the University of Oulu.[7] The program is offered regularly and biannually in Finnish and English, and updated versions of the study program entitled "From Violence to Caring"[8] were realized in the academic years of 2009 to 2010 and 2010 to 2011.

The University of Oulu study program is suitable for Bachelor's, Master's, and Doctoral students in various fields as well as for working professionals. The studies combine numerous experiences and backgrounds and provide fresh insights into interdisciplinary research on violence and non-violence. The program also aims to increase student awareness of the multiple forms of gendered and sexualized violence and to offer measures for students to recognize forms of violence, to help victims of violence, and to prevent violence in their future professional environments and in various sectors of society and across the globe – encouraging to multiagent collaboration.

As researchers on gendered and sexualized violence, VAW activists, and online course instructors, we recognize the prevalence of violence and the probability that our students have witnessed violence, if not experienced some form of violence personally; therefore, we consider that the study program should recognize both the individual and collective learning process, which mutually constitute each other. The theoretical work of Morwenna Griffiths, Susan Kappeler, Myra Hird, Jane Parpart, and Janet Townsend has inspired us in explicating a *pedagogy of non-violence*. The ideas central to our approach include *empowerment*, *responsibility*, and *human agency*, the latter encompassing the important dimensions of self. Kappeler stresses that the most crucial element to preventing violence is the building of non-violent structures to promote action and support the growth of non-violent selves and agencies. Violence as a structure for action is a continuum, she argues; violence either *is* or *is not*. Accordingly, the key to prevention is not permitting certain forms of violence while attempting to prevent others but developing non-violent agencies and non-violent structures for action. The quality of social relations and the orientation of the individual to those social relations is vital. We must consider the spectrum of emotions in human relations and refuse to deny the existence of part of that spectrum.

Human beings are configured through social, political, and cultural spheres of life, and – as Hird in particular emphasizes – serious consideration is needed on the meaning of discourses regarding violence and on the political character of violence and its prevention. In a non-violent pedagogy, it is important to support the development of individual and collective conscientization and the ability to work collectively, which aids the discovery of opportunities to bring about change and encourages people to use their own voices, share their experiences, discuss their dreams and needs, and construct their political visions of non-violence. We contend that a caring, empowered self is central in pedagogy and the foremost aim to developing the quality of learning from a perspective of non-violence, of human agency, and of equity or equality.

In this article, we will reflect on the meaningfulness of an Information and Communication Technology (ICT) based learning environment for studying gendered and sexualized violence, a demanding topic. We analyze what students wrote about their feelings and examine the implications for student self-empowerment. Our data comprises the course assignments students produced during their studies, including study journals and feedback forms written by three-hundred students from fifteen European countries, collected between 2006 and 2010. Qualitative data analysis was carried out on student writing on themes derived from the theoretical development of non-violent pedagogy; this research is therefore deductive in nature.

The Design of the Minor Study Program

Our starting point in using ICT in teaching and learning was practical: to overcome the challenges presented by the geographical distance between participants interested in studying gendered and sexualized violence and its prevention. We have gradually extended our teaching and learning towards new spheres, from the very basics – course material available on-line for students – to more sophisticated online minor studies involving synchronous and asynchronous teaching and collaboration between students. The current realization of the program employs a traditional e-learning platform (Discendum Optima), combining that platform with externally-available ICT tools to support student interaction and intellectual development.

The curricular structure of the program, five consecutive courses, aims to create a full learning cycle for participants. The aim is to offer a comprehensive overview of violence and an extensive understanding of non-violence and the possibilities for caring on individual, societal, and global levels, both practically and politically. The program begins with the orientation and conceptualization of gendered and sexualized violence during a person's lifespan and continues through global contexts of violence and sexual exploitation to an examination of the possibilities of work against violence in practice; it closes with visions of non-violence and equality, bringing the instructed learning process to an end for the moment but to be continued in the personal and professional lives of participants. We approached the task of creating the program not only by leaning towards knowledge and information but by constructing multidisciplinary, multisectoral professional studies whose philosophical foundations are in a feminist pedagogy of non-violence.

The curriculum[9] was planned so that, while the pedagogical principles in relation to a caring, empowered self are clear during the entire program, each of the five courses focuses on a particular pedagogical principle. Course I (Gendered and Sexualized Violence in Schools, Work Places and Home – Multidisciplinary and Multiprofessional Introduction) aims to break the silence around violence and provide space and safety for students to share individual experiences and feelings; Course II (Multiple Forms of Violence in a Global Context) focuses on the politics of personal behavior and therefore on belonging and being are examined; Course III (Sexual Exploitation and Trafficking) challenges students to overcome collective irresponsibility and challenges to take a critical but active stance; Course IV (Measures for Intervening in Violent Situations, Supporting Victims, Preventing Violence and Creating Caring Atmosphere) provides practical online tools for individual empowerment and agency, embracing authenticity; and Course V (Human Rights, Legislation and Policies in Constructing Gender Equality and Non-Violent Environments) concludes the program with texts about non-violent culture and about gender equality as a human rights issue, providing a perspective on the interdependency of the topics discussed throughout the whole program. The duration of each course is between six and eight weeks; the overall study program occupies students for a whole academic year, with both desired and undesired consequences. A lengthy program results in some drop-outs but also in an intensive learning experience for those persisting. The attending students come from various backgrounds, and some have no previous experience of e-learning – in which case developing fluent e-learning skills requires additional time.

The program employs a variety of activities for inspiration and variation, requiring diverse skills; academic articles are at the core of the study material. Animations, document extracts, movies, music, and information searches are used to obtain shared ground for discussing a topic – asynchronously in a group space or synchronously in a chat room. These are different tasks with different cognitive loads, besides the emotional load that studying violence may incur. According to a careful estimation of the workload, an academic year is sufficient to complete the study program. Some students also continue their studies by writing a thesis relating to the topic area.

A caring atmosphere in the e-learning environment is supported and maintained by encouraging learners to verbalize their feelings and needs, which helps foster compassionate connections between participants. In the web environment, the majority of communication is in written form, requiring clarity and reflexivity of texts. An ethical code of conduct is also introduced and emphasized at the beginning of the course; students are asked to attend to their manner of interaction online and to the challenges that mediated communication might entail, such as the dangers of – for instance – misinterpretation, irony, and humor. In addition to being directed to follow so-called "netiquette," students are challenged to consider how openly they would like to share their experiences: an important consideration, particularly concerning violence as a theme. Ethical guidelines form the ground for a caring learning culture, leaving room for personal experience and for each participant to make individual, conscious choice of what feelings and experiences to share and how to share them.

The course is structured around work performed in groups and individually, in a shared, user-restricted learning environment guided and evaluated by mentors. This core program forms the basis for new ideas and awareness, for sharing information, and for constructing new knowledge in a mentally safe, secure virtual setting. All the course materials, instructions, and interactive forums are available to students via the e-learning platform, and the courses are built to support the learners' sense of belonging and presence through assignments that offer opportunities to write about feelings and experiences. Asynchronous communication leaves room for flexibility and for distancing oneself from the often-distressing study contents, before returning to materials and discussions for support. Progression in the program is regulated and restricted; the entire class follows the same schedule, and a new topic is opened every other week. Regular feedback from mentors and peer support from the learning community offer tools for emotional and intellectual learning.

A large part of the work online is carried out in groups and stands on peer support. Students receive written instructions on an online message board requiring them to participate in online discussions that are usually asynchronous; however, live internet chat, which is more socializing for students, is also the subject of experiment and usually produces some puzzlement. Whatever the method, discussion obliges students to reflect on assignments for a greater length of time than they would otherwise, making the completion of those assignments more accurate. Activities such as "wiki-writing" are also employed as a group activity to support the learning process and the production of common knowledge. Constant requirement to learn new technological applications may easily cause excessive cognitive overload for students previously unfamiliar with those applications. Tools should be relevant, for instance, from a productivity perspective, assisting in the completion of collective course assignments.

A group composition in which students with advanced ICT skills help the group to begin their studies may ease anxiety at a critical phase of an assignment. Students are instructed to use the materials to discuss a weekly topic in group message boards; group exercises encourage interaction, including the sharing of practical experiences and discussion of theoretical viewpoints. Discussion groups are arranged differently in each course and group sizes vary from groups of three to groups of forty, depending on the goal of a particular discussion. Access to other groups' discussion also varies. In the beginning of the program, groups are "closed" so as to support the group grounding process; later, students can view the discussions of other groups for learning purposes or even participate in multisectoral discussion.[10]

Besides group work, students on the study program reflect on their learning and experiences course-by-course in a study journal. The journals are strictly private between student and mentor and are submitted after each course – in other words, after six to eight weeks. Each student completing the entire program submits five study journals in total. The study journals afford room for intellectual pondering and for reflection on one's own life history and experience of violence. Discussion and group tasks alone cannot cater to all the emotional and theoretical needs of the students. This, in turn, emphasizes the role of the study journal in the program. For example, a mismatch between expectations and presence in a discussion board may be compensated for by continuing the discussion more privately within study journals – with room for more personal reflection. Course mentors review the journals after each course and provide written questions, comments, and individual feedback to each student; therefore, a journal is perhaps the most important form of guidance for a student, a regular channel of communication between student and mentor throughout the entire program.

Our experience of the study program has established that violence is an issue of sensitivity to students and that this presupposed sensitivity should not be overlooked. The emotional burden of the themes – closely tied to all the feedback and commentary the course evokes – can be read in student journals and encountered in the direct and spontaneous responses of students. The learning materials and sometimes the discussions include stories, facts, voices, and images very emotional to the students. Encountering various forms of violence through text, image, and sound is strenuous. We feel for others; we feel empathy. Studying violence can also raise memories of personal experiences. For an individual student, the study program may offer the possibility for a meaningful learning journey. One student expressed a reaction as follows "I got the feeling that we started with our own circles, did one round on the globe, and returned to our own subjective sphere of experience; I do not know if that was the plan but it works for me."

Challenges for Becoming a Caring Empowered Self in an E-Learning Setting

"I have been a victim of sexual harassment twice in university, once abroad while being an exchange student and once in Finland."

This quote from a study journal marks the beginning of a description of two sexual harassment "cases" encountered by a student during her academic studies. While the student was abroad, a sociable, friendly professor reportedly presented visual material of a highly sexual nature in his lectures. Towards the end of his course, the professor then approached the student with a postcard bearing the text, "Missing the daily miracle of your presence." The student heard later that the professor in question had been reprimanded for sexual harassment at an earlier time, and was perhaps acting more carefully with her, "but" – she wrote – "he evidently continued harassment in spite of the reprimands."

The same student experienced harassment in a Finnish university; harassment that was also careful and insidious. A teacher, liked by students, used to have long discussions with them; the student had considered his behavior normal, but the interactions began to change to include uncomfortable, intrusive gazes and comments. In both situations, the student felt acutely uncomfortable and wrote in her journal of the difficulty of seeking intervention, "In both cases, the authorship position of the harasser and my unpreparedness for the harassment lead to the fact that I never reported either of the harassment cases…I preferred to let them pass and forget them rather than undergo a stressful reporting procedure in which I might have suffered myself. Also, both of these male teachers were so careful in their harassment (perhaps intentionally) that it seemed I did not have any waterproof evidence."

According to various studies (Heikkinen and Sunnari 2010), experiences of mundane forms of sexual harassment, such as innuendo or unwanted attention, are common in higher education. Naming these phenomena sexual harassment is important in limiting the oppressive and ethically incorrect behavior of teachers attempting to disempower students (Wise and Stanley 1989). Changing the climate or culture that objectifies young female students in higher education and belittles their academic aspirations or attempts to tune them to a sexual purpose seems particularly difficult.

Experiences of our own surroundings are an important source of knowledge in aiming to learn more about gendered and sexualized violence and its prevention and to help victims of violence. Sexual harassment – alongside workplace bullying and hidden forms of discrimination such as racism, ageism, and ablebodienism – is among the most prevailing forms of gendered and sexual violence in academia. We use sexual harassment in this article as an example of violence likely to define the collective group experience of students today in their academic life (Collins 1999).

We will in this article explore the interconnectedness and outcome of ICT and pedagogy in the minor study program designed and arranged by the Women's and Gender Studies at the University of Oulu. Principles of a feminist non-violent pedagogical approach suitable to e-learning are applied, developed, described, and elaborated on in the following sub-chapters, which focus on feeling, belonging, authenticity, interdependency, and on how those dimensions are applied practically into our own practice in the e-learning program.

Feelings in Knowledge Construction Online

Feelings may be involved in academic studies in various ways and a feeling of *fear* clearly influences learning in a negative fashion. Moreover, feelings are essential to human understanding. However, a person's feelings are not simply private and individual; they are social. We consider like Griffths in "Feminism, Feelings and Philosophy" (1988, 148); feelings and emotions must be understood, therefore, in terms of the history of an individual's life and of the social context in which that life is lived. Feelings are consequently a source of knowledge and should be treated seriously as such.

In the previous example of sexual harassment in institutions of higher education, an uncomfortable feeling and repulsiveness were mentioned in relation to sexually-harassing teachers, resulting in the student avoiding those teachers. The relationship between feelings and knowledge should also be recognized, or, as Griffiths puts it, feeling as knowledge. Some students are privy to sexual harassment in their educational institution and, like the student quoted in the beginning of the previous chapter, write of their experiences of sexual harassment in a study journal. An online course offers an easily accessible platform to share privy information. The act of passing on personal accounts – for instance – of sexual harassment in an educational institution so that other students might become aware that it exists and build knowledge of it can be understood as a strategy, a subtle means of resistance.

A question of ethical responsibilities also exists and of the ethics of official intervention in particular. When a student shares an experience of sexual harassment, course mentors may guide the student, referring him or her to the appropriate authority in that organization. When knowledge is shared with other students, staff, and an entire institution, those parties would be able to take interventive and preventive measures, meaning that continuation of the harassers' harmful practices might be prevented. We suggest that matters of this type – namely, voicing and sharing personal experiences, aiming collectively to effect change, and learning about collective responsibly – are central feminist pedagogical, epistemological, and political concerns that may be traced and elaborated on particularly in and regarding virtual spaces. Often students do not share their "insider knowledge" publicly but write it in a study journal, which is the first step towards recognition of the phenomenon as problem that is wider than just a private matter.

Students in the study program shared their experiences of violence in various forms, including domestic violence, child physical punishment and suicides in the family, violence between intimate partners, violence in school, and encounters with sexual harassment. Some experiences had been discussed openly in their past, while others had been acknowledged only "silently," such as when students wrote of their experiences in study journals and the group mentor was the only person in the course who read and knew about the encounter with violence. A student discussing an experience in the message board of the e-learning environment may be breaking that silence, coming out – speaking of it for the first time openly.

One factor influencing the student's decision to speak openly of an experience of violence may be that the easy, open atmosphere in an asynchronous e-learning environment provides space sufficient to reflect on one's experiences. Personal life histories were permitted as part of the study process, and students reflected on their histories particularly in study journals; trust and sensitivity towards personal experience were therefore very important. One student wrote, "I could start the study journal by explaining how violence and bullying are connected to my life already, because personal encounters do exist." The study journal was a regular communication channel between student and mentors, and some mentors reported acting as "online counselors" at times. Students reported finding the feedback mentors gave them in response to the journals extremely important, not only personally but in theoretical terms, assisting them further in learning.

Written asynchronous communication allowed participants to manage or control their psychosocial distance in the e-learning environment. As described, the program included several organized structures for support, and students used the available individual "vents" to deal with emotional load, retreating for a time or deciding not to "dig so deep." One student put it as follows, "because some things felt repulsive at times it was good that one was able to be flexible in familiarizing oneself with the contents: you could have a break if it felt like it and choose to spend more time on other content if you wanted to."

Belonging to a Virtual Learning Community

Discussing self and self-esteem, Griffiths ("Learning to Learn: Action Research from an Equal Opportunities Perspective in a Junior School," 1993) stresses the importance of *belonging*. Griffiths contends that belonging in its various forms is more fundamental to the formation of self than achievement. She also emphasizes *becoming* as central to self and self-esteem, as well as *practice* or specifically being part of a practice and belonging to a location identified with that practice. However, communities of practice are also marked by embodiment, diversity, and systematic, structural power (Griffiths, "A Feminist Perspective on Communities of Practice" 2005). Moreover, on an individual level, the possibilities for and quality of participation are marked by how a community handles embodiment, diversity, and power.

Access to the learning community in an institution of higher education may be determined by one's gendered body; alternatively, belonging to the community may be restricted to certain levels of that community: a form of hidden discrimination. Sexual harassment has been thought as form of gender discrimination preventing the equal access of women to institutions of higher education. ICT may result in new forms of access and belonging to communities of learning, teaching and knowledge production in such institutions. Feminist pedagogy as a more general approach would actually improve e-learning as a tool for knowledge production and social change.

Strategies for embodiment in an online community differ necessarily from strategies in a "real life" situation. As Donna Haraway[11] and Karen Barad[12] have seen, technology is already in us or defining what we are – there is no escape. Therefore one should attend to technologically mediated e-learning setting in quest of embodiment, in which competence and skill in technology use define participation. Learning has become integrated with technology in a network in which students, teachers, hardware, software, knowledge, and skills "intra-act" (Kirkup et al. 2010). Becoming "cyborg" offers each learner different challenges.

Trust is often seen as a key to meeting the pitfalls of mediated communication. In a group context, revealing one's personal experiences requires sensitivity from others, requires group members to listen and participate in a dialogue and be valued, accepted, and respected. This listening and participating in turn emphasizes the need for structures such as ethical guidelines to ensure safety – whether one chooses to reveal or to hide one's emotions – and for pedagogical choices guiding students to "*move on from being horrified*" with the support of the learning community or more privately such as in a study journal. These issues are closely related also to the politics of personal behavior and to the challenges such politics present in an online community.

Belonging to a learning community and the ability to be involved in that community were meaningful for students both emotionally and professionally. One student describes the goals she had set for herself in the following terms: "I would like to be involved in identifying new means to prevent violence, to intervene in violence, and to recover from violence. I would also like to be involved in developing something new."

Students valued the opportunity to share and take part in a multisectoral e-learning community bringing together experiences from theory and practice and in which participation felt easy and safe. A type of professional identification or even self empowerment may also have developed during the studies, evident in the phrase, extracted from a student's text, "as we are the instruments of the work in this field." The virtual learning community connected people with similar experiences of gendered and sexualized violence and its prevention and common challenges. Even close friendships between persons with similar experiences and more long-lasting contacts were possible.

The closeness of the groups and of the students in the program – many from very different backgrounds – was strong for some but not for others. Not all students tackled personal issues with the same intensity, a fact that may have caused a mismatch in expectations: where one student in a group waited to discuss concepts of sexual exploitation, others were dealing with the emotions the materials had evoked. When planning and supervising the study program, attending to the various and diverse background of the participants was crucial. For example, diverse ideas of humanity, differing world views, and other epistemic differences occasionally caused open conflict and sometimes a desire to withdraw from, rather than participate in, the learning community. Differences in expressed opinions or values could also cause heated discussion and expressions of frustration, both of which influenced the learning atmosphere. Some participants felt they had nothing to contribute due to a lack of work experience. For the instructors of the program, a clear challenge exists to consider the composition of groups thoroughly from the perspective of students' ability to *be* and *feel* accepted and valued as participants belonging to a learning community.

The openness of the groups may have also had its effect. Belonging to a smaller sub-group clearly added to a feeling of belonging and of safety; whereas participants in groups and discussions available for viewing by all seventy students may have experienced pressure. While a restricted e-learning platform provides comparative safety, a student might ask consciously how much she or he can share if seen by the others in a learning community.

Authenticity as a Challenge for Learning in Cyberspace

Closely related to self and belonging is the theme of *authenticity*. In "Learning to Learn," Griffiths argues that self-identity is formed by both avowing one's history and transforming it. For groups of people who are not part of the establishment,[13] this gives a notable, political importance to the experience of exclusion in relation to authenticity. Trying to "pass" means devaluing oneself. On the other hand, a refusal or inability to "pass" can also lead to inauthenticity because the very fact of exclusion prevents the self from being what it wants. Unlike resistance, rejection often appears so painful that a person may – inauthentically – avoid facing it altogether, pretending that one's wants are different, or even that one's abilities are less. Such a presence will inevitably mean a devaluation of the self. Individuals often believe they must leave parts of the self "at the door" as also Griffiths considers.

Authenticity as an ability and a permission to share one's life history must be given a caring context that offers room and enables vulnerability. Being able to relate to and rename one's own encounters involves an aspect of empowerment. Voicing one's experiences – perhaps for the first time and in a context in which they are relevant – generates a process of reconceptualizing one's past, or as one student put it, "Topics on the course made me think about my own life." What had been encountered and passed by silently now had the space to be voiced, named, and felt. The student continued, "In my experience, what touches you is important to you." Such vulnerability sets challenges for the entire learning community. For the instructors of a program, the challenge is to maintain a caring dialogue that does not violently discriminate against individual processes and that simultaneously guides learning forward.

According to the students on the study program, the distance often perceived and described by the students as "anonymity" and "facelessness" offered a safe setting in which to share and reveal personal experiences authentically. Page et al. (2007, 147) discuss this phenomenon in terms of an extended openness and of an "ease of collaboration" on a level of feelings in relation to mediated communication. Our student feedback indicated a fluctuating movement between *being there* – belonging – and enjoying the benefits of distance. That fluctuation was especially clear when online communication was discussed in relation to a need for face-to-face meetings: "From time to time it would have been nice to talk face-to-face about the emotions the course materials brought up. However, I thought our mutual 'anonymity' quite pleasant; bringing up one's own point of view was more free and easy than face-to-face interaction." When discussing anonymity, we contend that the above student was correct to put the word "anonymity" in quotes, as participants did in fact use their own names – some even their own pictures – and that ultimately it might be more reasonable to talk about *perceived anonymity* than anonymity. The learning context afforded the students the space to discuss the topic, but the technology itself offered specific possibilities for openness with regard to experience and feelings. One student wrote, "When we aren't face-to-face, it's possible to share even painful things more easily." However, this experience of ease is inevitably problematic. One can never control how the message will be received by others. Thoughts should be shared with the understanding that they may also be discussed from opposing perspectives and by participants who do not share the same world views. An emphasis on conscious choices and sensitivity in all phases of discussion – including writing, reading, and responding – is one way to support the individual safety.

While students valued the opportunities presented by the technology to share experiences easily, sharing constitutes a choice of what to share and with whom and always requires a level of trust, which was not easy for some online. In e-learning, students face the task of drawing boundaries. "I've written about private issues that I don't want made public to others," stated a student. To a certain extent, anonymity and facelessness could have produced loneliness and anxiety in the midst of heavy issues, although students were given the possibility to share and talk about their feelings and encouraged to do so.

The study journals ensured a safe place for participants to reflect on and share their experiences and feelings. On the other hand, participants felt they had sufficient support, and many reported having discussed themes at home and at work. E-learning affords students the possibility to expand their personal learning environments into unique combinations of co-presences and co-locations. Home as a location or a close friend to co-view a video recording are among the multiplicity of choices available to the learning process. At home, with family, some students are in a safe setting in which emotions are easily reflected upon. Similarly, people are often comfortable talking to co-workers with whom thoughts provoked by the studies can be dealt with in a professional setting.

Interdependency in a Web-Based Learning

Liberation – and equal opportunities in education – consists in the acquisition of confidence in one's right, whoever and whatever one is or does, to take up space in the world and create one's own identity. However, it also affirms that the creation of identity is a collective affair in which each has a valuable contribution to make. Liberation is therefore highly individual in the sense that it values the person who does not believe that some are dispensable or that some are more dispensable than others and highly communal in the sense that it believes the individual can only exist through the community and that the community is diminished by the diminution of an individual (Griffiths, "Learning to Learn: Action Research from an Equal Opportunities Perspective in a Junior School" 1993, 6). Properly conceived, education should preserve and develop aspects of dependence and independence. That independence is often automatically regarded as more desirable than dependence has much to do with a natural human dislike of risk and vulnerability (Griffiths and Smith 1989, 283, 289). Much of the problem in thinking about dependence and independence is caused by the propensity to think in terms of a binary system in which everything is characterized as on or off; for example, an attribute is there or is not, or "he or she who is not with us is against us." The whole of experience is often reduced to the binary, as if experience could be encompassed by just two possibilities in a zero-sum game played with a digital counter (Griffiths and Smith 1989, 291). One solution to these problems would be to find another word – "interdependent" is the obvious candidate – that does not suffer from the pejorative connotations of dependence, in order to express the kind of values in education and aspects of personal relationships we alluded to above (Griffiths and Smith 1989, 292).

For the students participating in the study program, collaborative learning opened a new perspective on equality and caring. Sharing information is crucial to web-based learning.

> It is comparatively difficult to come up with a practical means of how to prevent sexual and gendered violence, especially as an individual and alone. Through this course, my belief in the possibility for a change got a little bit bigger. It is comforting to acknowledge that this course exists, and that so many people attended it, and that so many of them are working with children and are therefore able to influence matters on a grass roots level. I

am convinced that during the course, many noticed that knowledge, learning, and teaching are the key to solving equality-related problems.

In an online course, a student's capability to intervene in workplace violence he or she has just encountered may emerge. "I was being subjected to workplace bullying by my boss while the course was going on. I found the last two courses really helpful; they helped me in a practical sense to try to put some actions into place instantaneously," wrote a student.

The use of information and communications technology (ICT) offered the students the possibility to enroll and take part in multidisciplinary discussions in an international context. Students and in-service trainers from various mainly European countries provided knowledge and resources that were country-specific, but in sharing and comparing experiences, more extensive, in-depth and critical views were produced than a solely country-specific view could provide. National contexts such as legislation on violence, general awareness, attitudes regarding gendered and sexual violence, and services for victims of violence differed. The international program, networking, and the sharing of local perspectives and personal accounts contributed to the personal and societal empowerment of those involved. One student wrote as follows: "It was nice to meet persons from Germany, England, Finland, and Italy; even if we didn't meet personally, we shared a lot and in a deep way. I'm still in contact with some of those persons, and perhaps one day we will meet, and hopefully do something together to put in practice what was learnt." E-learning is and has been an important development issue for the European Union; ICT infrastructures and easy internet access exists across diverse European countries, despite differences in e-learning cultures and native language.[14]

An international study program with no regular face-to-face meetings or general orientation sessions presents a challenge for organizers to ensure easy access, the development of trust, and a safe learning community. In particular, the sensitivity of violence as a theme for study had to be considered thoroughly when planning the courses. For the participants, handling the emotional issues through and with the collective proved rehabilitative. One student remarked as follows: "[The program was]...difficult and amazing, but to my mind rehabilitative. Studying the whole program perhaps resulted in professionalism such that one got the entire picture and was not just horrified at the phenomenon, and that one saw the connections in the bigger picture."

How Does Technology Affect a Feminist Pedagogy of Non-Violence?

Based on our research and experiences over an entire academic year on the on-going development of an entire academic year long comprehensive minor e-learning study program on gendered and sexualized violence, we found that technology presents a feminist non-violent pedagogy with certain individual and collective advantages. The ICT-based distance e-learning environment proved meaningful to the study of violence and discrimination in its various forms and to the study of the themes of equality and equity. ICT-mediated communication offered psychosocial distance, giving each student left room to build a personal, unique space for learning, thereby enabling personal growth. The environment also offered the ability to control the intensity of learning, allowing students to distance themselves from the topic, group, or supervisor at will. Other advantages included the ability to freely manage learning through ownership of time and space and that the virtual community serves as a think tank for elaborating on various everyday situations, offering room to learn collectively and to construct practical measures for intervention.

The study program constructs a critical, reflective learning environment that respects the individual dignities of students and the shared learning process, and we contend ensures equal relationships among the participants and treats the topic with the sensitivity it deserves. The program platform offers participants an opportunity not only for possible self-empowerment in their contemporary work or in their future career but to combat gendered and sexualized violence collectively in their everyday lives.

Offering students the possibility to belong to a learning community in which experiences are valued can be empowering. Indeed, the construction of structures to support the growth of an international, multidisciplinary network of personal and professional relationships should receive increasing attention. Numerous examples exist of how ICT can provide an effective means of information delivery and of assembling people with similar interests. While little gender-sensitive education is available on violence, a minor study program with a seemingly "marginal" topic offered via a learning community over the Internet can bring together a geographically distant population. The challenge is also to consider ways in which *belonging* to such networks might continue after the program itself ends. For this purpose – for example – the use of social media tools might be explored.

Even given the advantages of e-learning, studying a theme as potentially personal and emotional as violence is not easy. Instructors must constantly offer support while allowing students to work independently and taking into account the various backgrounds of the students. *Time* and *space* are particularly essential; the time and space accorded by e-studies offer the possibility to examine a topic from different angles without hurry or the requirement for immediate interaction with other students or teachers, who are nonetheless available for support if necessary. Balancing the *emotional* and *intellectual* is also challenging. Feelings, essential to human understanding, are social and therefore shared in a large part with groups of others. More might be done to attend to and reflect on feelings collectively, and the e-learning platform would provide a possible space for such attention and reflection, since articulations of feelings are recorded in the space as written text. On the other hand, the question, "What is the optimal setting to embrace a caring empowered self?" is becoming increasingly relevant as learning spaces expand into the realm of social media and online social presence is enhanced with avatars and virtual, game-like worlds.

Does an e-learning setting create an optimal space for a caring, empowered self? Although it is possible to enable other people to do something, it is not possible to empower them, to *give power to*, Janet Townsend and her co-researchers (*Women and Power*, 1999) argue. Empowerment must be understood as including both individual conscientization (*power within*) *as well as* social components. Institutional, material, and discursive contexts must be taken seriously when attempting to support the development of self-empowerment, which can lead to politicized power with others, which provides the power to bring about change.

We conclude here with a case in which a student writes about her experience of sexual harassment during her academic studies, both abroad and in her home country. This case exemplifies per se how feelings are a source of knowledge in terms of the history of an individual's life and the social context in which that life is lived. The student wrote about her knowledge of the sexual harassment in a study journal that related closely to course content. She learned that the question was not just about individual harm; sharing one's experiences of gender and sexual harassment required complex processes and increasing awareness, characterized by cognitive and conceptual stages as follows: through *definition*, a person must define the encountered harassment as exceptional behavior; *recognition* allows the behavior to be named gender and sexual harassment; and through *discrimination*, the person admits that sexual harassment is a problem on at least some level and takes action to seek "justice." Systemic discrimination such as tolerance to sexist behavior or to sexist atmosphere discourages the reporting of harassment, negatively influencing the agency of an individual (Cairns 1997; Ramazanoglu 1987). In a virtual environment, an individual has a space to get in touch with his or her feelings related to that experience and to elaborate alternative possibilities for actions and think through of their consequences. The student in question did not make an official report, preferring to write about the behavior in her journal.

Agency is central to a pedagogy aiming at a caring, empowered self. As we have described, the learning process is interdependent and interactional on a personal and social level. A "collective group experience" – for instance – sexual harassment is a classic example of the rise of feminist agency and knowledge construction. Individuals in such groups may lead the group to knowledge or to a standpoint that may in turn influence the group's political action (Frankenberg 2000; Collins 1999). Can we share, receive, and respond to personal accounts in feminist cyberspace on a level and emotional intensity enabling the formation of a collective group experience across borders, languages, genders, sexualities, ethnicities, abilities, ages, beliefs, and worldviews? The challenge of how to take collective responsibility for appropriate intervention on a local level also remains unanswered.

Sexual harassment in European higher education institutions has been dealt with in various ways, depending on national legislation and university-level policies. Prevention of sexual harassment and gender discrimination has been addressed in the EC recommendations,[15] but legally binding and more precise definitions do exist in some European countries – including Finland – in national legislation (i.e. Act For Equality Between Women and Men, 2005). Collective feminist efforts, networks, and research collaboration on the issue have been sustained over the past two decades in European educational institutions. Interestingly, students themselves have been active in taking actions to prevent sexual harassment.[16] Sometimes parallel intervention seems necessary to effect social change, and ICT may be useful in achieving that intervention. Comprehensive European sexual harassment policy for higher education is still to emerge.[17]

Realizing and developing an entire online minor study program on gendered and sexualized violence and its prevention was a rewarding challenge. The task now is to keep that program interesting, inspiring, and varied without making it too technical, theoretical, practical, or narrowly serving certain professionals while excluding others – rather, to maintain a wider, multi-professional approach. In addition to practice-oriented development, the inclusion of a theoretical and conceptual orientation is crucial due to cross-cutting in academic study. It is also important to make the program available to professionals who are already in their field or in initial training. New, practical solutions are being searched for and their potential explored. Recent innovations include the use of Second Life or blended learning with practice-oriented internships for students. Differentiation is also an important issue concerning the entire student group. Online distance education provides possibilities for those doing the minor study while in full-time employment and may offer a solution towards the reconciliation of family life, work, and studies. We are also currently working towards a joint international Master's program utilizing e-learning and various ICT tools, based on our experience, knowledge of research on the topic, and on a societal and individual need for more competence in the area.

Bibliography

"Act on Equality Between Women and Men (Finland)." 1987. *UNHRC: The UN Refugee Agency*, January 1.
    http://www.unhcr.org/refworld/docid/3ae6b51c0.html.
Barad, Karen. 2007. *Meeting the Universe Halfway: Quantum Physics and the Entanglement of Matter and Meaning*. Durham, NC: Duke University Press.
"Best Practices Against Sexual Harassment and Violence at European Institutions of Higher Education." 1998. Publication of a project: *No Means No The Hidden Agenda – Sexual Violence at the Universities*, edited by Kathrine Vangen and Rosi Posnik, 1-84. ESIB: The National Unions of Students in Europe.
Cairns, Kathleen, V. 1997. "'Femininity and Women's Silence in Response to Sexual Harassment and Coercion." In *Sexual Harassment: Contemporary Feminist Perspectives,* edited by Alison M. Thomas and Celia Kitzinger, 91-111. Buckingham: Open University Press.
Collins, Patricia Hill. 1999. "Some Group Matters: Moving Beyond Gender. Intersectionality, Situated Standpoints and Black Feminist Thought." In *Fighting Words: Black Women and the Search for Justice*, edited by Patricia Hill Collins, 201-228. Minneapolis: Univeresity of Minnesota Press.
European Commission. 2011. "Daphne II Programme 2004-2008 to Combat Violence Against Children, Young People, and Women." *Europa*. Accessed February 11.

http://collections.europarchive.org/dnb/20070702132831/ec.europa.eu/
justice_home/funding/2004_2007/daphne/funding_daphne_en.htm.
—. 2011. "Daphne III Funding Programme." *Europa*. Accessed October
30.
http://ec.europa.eu/justice/grants/programmes/daphne/index_en.htm.
—. 2011. "The Daphne-Toolkit: An Active Resource from the Daphne
Programme." *Europa*. Accessed October 30.
http://ec.europa.eu/justice_home/daphnetoolkit/html/welcome/dpt_wel
come_en.html.
—. 2005. *The Daphne Experience 1997-2003 - Europe Against Violence
Against Women and Children*. Luxembourg: Office for Official
Publications of the European Communities. Accessed October 30,
2011.
http://ec.europa.eu/home-
affairs/funding/2004_2007/daphne/docs/daphne_experience/daphne_ex
perience_en.pdf.
Eyre, Linda. 2000. "The Discursive Framing of Sexual Harassment in a
University Community." *Gender and Education* 12, no. 3: 217-234.
Frankenberg, Ruth. 2000. "White Women, Race Matters." In *Theories of
Race and Racism. A Reader,* edited by Les Back and John Solomos,
447-461. London: Routledge.
Garcia-Moreno, Claudia, Henrica A.F.M. Jansen, Mary Ellsberg, Lori
Heise and Charlotte Watts. 2005. "Multi-Country Study on Women's
Health and Domestic Violence Against Women: Initial Results on
Prevalence, Health Outcomes and Women's Responses." *World Health
Organization*. Accessed October 30, 2011.
http://www.who.int/gender/violence/who_multicountry_study/en/.
Griffiths, Morwenna. 1988. "Feminism, Feelings and Philosophy." In
Feminist Perspectives in Philosophy, edited by Morwenna Griffiths
and Margaret Whitford, 131-151. London: Macmillan.
—. 2005. "On Feminism and Gender: A Feminist Perspective on
Communities of Practice." *The University of Edinburgh: The Moray
House School of Education*. Accessed October 30, 2011.
http://www.morwennagriffiths.pwp.blueyounder.co.uk/Feminism.htm.
—. 1993. "Learning to Learn: Action Research from an Equal
Opportunities Perspective in a Junior School." *British Educational
Research Journal* 19, no. 1: 43-58.
—. 1998. "Self-Determination and Learning to be Cruel." *The European
Journal of Women's Studies* 5: 217-232.

Griffiths, Morwenna and Richard Smith. 1989. "Standing Alone: Dependence, Independence and Interdependence in the Practice of Education." *Journal of Philosophy of Education* 23, no. 2: 283-294.

Hagemann-White, Carol, Judith Katenbrink and Heike Rabe. 2006. *Combating Violence Against Women – Stocktaking Study on the Measures and Actions Taken in Council of Europe Member States.* Strasbourg: Equality Division, Directorate General of Human Rights, Council of Europe. Accessed October 30, 2011. http://www.coe.int/t/dghl/standardsetting/equality/03themes/violence-against-women/CDEG%282006%293_en.pdf.

Hagemann-White,Carol and Sabine Bohne. 2007. *Protecting Women against Violence. Analytical Study on the Effective Implementation of Recommendation Rec(2002)5 on the Protection of Women against Violence in Council of Europe Member States.* Strasbourg: Council of Europe, Directorate General of Human Rights and Legal Affairs. Accessed October 30, 2011. http://www.coe.int/t/dghl/standardsetting/equality/03themes/violence-against-women/CDEG%282007%293_en.pdf.

Haraway, Donna. 1985. "A Manifesto for Cyborgs: Science, Technology, and Social Feminism in the 1980's." *Socialist Review* 15, no. 80: 65-107.

Heikkinen, Mervi, Suvi Pihkala and Vappu Sunnari. 2008. "Constructing a Pedagogical approach for an E-learning Programme on Gender and Sexual Violence." In *Conference Proceedings: From Violence to Caring – Gendered and Sexualized Violence as the Challenge on the Life-Span,* edited by Vappu Sunnari, Mervi Heikkinen, Tuija Huuki and Sari Manninen, 203-216. Oulu: University of Oulu. http://herkules.oulu.fi/isbn9789514290084.

Heikkinen, Mervi and Vappu Sunnari. 2010. Developing Gender Equality Policy in Finnish Higher Education: Sexual Harassment at a Focal Point. Paper presented at the International Conference Mapping the Gender Equality: Research and Practices – The National and International Perspectives, University of Cyprus, October 22-23, 2010. http://www.ucy.ac.cy/goto/unesco/en-US/publications.aspx.

Hird, Myra. 2002. *Engendering Violence. Heterosexual Interpersonal Violence from Childhood to Adulthood.* Chippenham, Wiltshire: Antony Rowe Ltd.

Huuki, Tuija. 2010. "Koulupoikien Statustavoittelu Väkivallan Ja Välittämisen Valokiilassa (The Status Work of School Boys in the Light of Violence and Caring.)" PhD diss., University of Oulu.

Kappeler, Susanne. 1995. *The Will to Violence. The Politics of Personal Behaviour.* Padstow, Cornwall: T.J. Press Ltd.

Kelly, Liz. 2005. "Inside Outsiders: Mainstreaming Violence against Women into Human Rights Discourse and Practise." *International Feminist Journal of Politics* 7, no. 4: 471-495.

Kirkup, Gill, Sigrid Schmitz, Erna Kotkamp, Els Rommes and Aino-Maija Hiltunen. 2010. "Towards a Feminist Manifesto for E-learning: Principles to Inform Practices." In *Gender Issues in Learning and Working With Information Technology: Social Constructs and Cultural Contexts*, edited by Shirley Booth, Sara Goodman and Gill Kirkup, 255-274. New York: Information Science Reference.

Manninen, Sari. 2010. "'Iso, Vahva, Rohkee – Kaikenlaista': Maskuliinisuudet, Poikien Valtahierarkiat Ja Väkivalta Koulussa (Big, Strong, Brave – All Kinds of Stuff: Masculinities, Power hierarchies, and Violence in School.)" PhD diss., University of Oulu.

Page, Tom, Marian Hepburn, Miika Lehtonen, Gisli Thorsteinsson and Subramanian Arunachalam. 2007. "Emotional and Aesthetic factors in Virtual Mobile Learning Environments." *International Journal of Mobile Learning and Organisation* 1, no. 2: 140-158.

Parpart Jane, Shirin Rai and Kathleen Staudt. 2002. "Rethinking Em(power)ment, Gender and Development: An Introduction." In *Rethinking Em(power)ment: Gender and Development in a Global/Local World*, edited by Jan Parpart, Shirin Rai and Kathleen Staudt, 3-21. New York: Routledge.

Ramazanoglu, Caroline. 1987. "Sex and Violence in Academic Life: Or You Can Keep a Good Woman Down." In *Women, Violence and Social Control*, edited by Jalna Hanmer and Mary Maynard, 87-95. London: Macmillan.

"Recommendation Rec(2002)5 of the Committee of Ministers to Member States on the Protection of Women Against Violence." 2002. *Council of Europe*, April 30.
https://wcd.coe.int/wed/ViewDoc.jsp?Ref=Rec295&Language=lanEnglish&Site=CM&BackColorInternet=9999CC&BackColorIntranet=FFBB55&BackColorLogged=FFAC75.

"Recommendation CM/Rec(2007)13 of the Committee of Ministers to Member States on Gender Mainstreaming in Education." 2007. *Council of Europe*, Oct. 10.
https://wcd.coe.int/wcd/ViewDoc.jsp?id=1194631&Site=CM.

"Recommendation CM/Rec(2007)17 of the Committee of Ministers to Member States on Gender Equality Standards and Mechanisms." 2007. *Council of Europe*, Nov. 21.

https://wcd.coe.int/wcd/ViewDoc.jsp?id=1215219&Site=CM&BackCo
lorInternet=9999CC&BackColorIntranet=FFBB55&BackColorLogged
=FFAC75.

Sagay, Abigail C. 2004. *What Is Sexual Harassment? From Capitol Hill to the Sorbonne.* Berkeley: University of California Press.

Sunnari, Vappu. 2010. *"I Cannot Speak About It": Physical Sexual Harassment as Experienced by Children at School in Northern Finland and Northwest Russia.* Saarbrücken: VDM Verlag.

Sunnari, Vappu, Jenny Kangasvuo, and Mervi Heikkinen, eds. 2003. *Gendered and Sexualized Violence in Educational Environments.* 2nd revised edition. Oulu: University of Oulu.
http://jultika.oulu.fi/Record/isbn951-42-7150-5.

Townsend, Janet, Pilar Alberti, Marta Mercado, Jo Rowlands and Zapata Rowlands. 1999. *Women and Power.* New York: Zed Books.

Walby, Sylvia. 2005. "Introduction: Comparative Gender Mainstreaming in a Global Era." *International Feminist Journal of Politics* 7, no. 4: 453-470.

Wise, Sue and Liz Stanley. 1989. *Georgie Porgie: Sexual Harassment in Everyday Life.* London: Pandora.

"Women's and Gender Studies: From Violence to Caring." 2010. *University of Oulu.* Accessed October 30, 2011.
http://www.oulu.fi/naistutkimus/english/studies/FVC_study_programm
e.htm.

"Women's and Gender Studies: Projects." 2010. *University of Oulu.* Accessed October 30, 2011.
http://www.oulu.fi/naistutkimus/english/projects/index.html.

Notes

[1] Global milestones in this work have been the 1979 Convention on the Elimination of All Forms of Discrimination against Women, the 1989 Convention on the Rights of the Child, the platform for action of the 1995 Beijing Conference, and the 1996 Stockholm Declaration and Agenda for Action at the first World Congress against the Commercial Sexual Exploitation of Children, as well as various national implementations along those lines.

[2] The first Daphne initiative was in 1997. A brief history of Daphne (*The Daphne Experience 1997-2003 – Europe Against Violence Against Women and Children* 2005) is available online.

[3] The Daphne II Programme to Combat Violence Against Children, Young People and Women ran from 2004-2008 ("Daphne II Programme 2004-2008 to Combat Violence Against Children, Young People, and Women"). For more information please see the website.

[4] On June 20, 2007 the European Parliament and the Council adopted Decision No 779/2007/EC establishing, for the period 2007-2013, the specific program Daphne III as part of the General Program "Fundamental Rights and Justice." The general objective of Daphne III will be to contribute to the protection of children, young people and women against all forms of violence and to attain a high level of health protection, well-being and social cohesion. The program will achieve its objectives by means of transnational actions (grant funding), which aims will be to e.g. setting up and supporting multidisciplinary networks; expansion of the knowledge base and exchange, identification and dissemination of information and good practice; designing and testing awareness-raising and educational materials ("Daphne III Funding Programme").

[5] The work of those previous projects is available for viewing online through "The Daphne-Toolkit," which is both an archive of the results of those projects and a resource for future projects.

[6] These projects are Aware 2000-01, Aware II 2003-04, Work, Safe Place 2005-06, GVEI 2007-09, APROPOS 2007-09, and ALLIES 2010-12 ("Women's and Gender Studies: Projects" 2010).

[7] Institutions of teacher education are in a unique position to influence violence and achieve its prevention by educating future teachers to be agents of change in schools, working towards the non-violent construction of school culture, educating pupils, and – intermediately – educating the parents of pupils.

[8] See "From Violence to Caring."

[9] Please see Heikkinen, Mervi, Pihkala, Suvi, and Sunnari, Vappu's "Constructing a Pedagogical Approach for an E-Learning Programme on Gender and Sexual Violence" (2008).

[10] The following are theses for web discussion closing Course I (Gendered and Sexualised Violence in Schools, Work Places, and at Home: A Multidisciplinary and Multiprofessional Introduction).

a) Those group members who have worked with violence voluntarily or by profession could start the group discussion by sharing their experiences of multisectoral collaboration. What collaboration would you conceive as important in supporting the victims of violence and violence prevention? What works and what doesn't?

b) When examining violence and the continuum of violence from the perspective of a person's life span, one may identify critical junctures at which it might be possible to intervene. In your opinion, in what situations should one intervene? What persons would be key to intervening in violence? How do you see your possibilities to intervene in violence in your current or future job?

[11] In "A Manifesto for Cyborgs: Science, Technology, and Social Feminism in the 1980's" (1985), Donna Haraway argues that we are all "cyborgs," a hybrid of machine and organism.

[12] Karen Barad states that organic and technical mutually constitute each other – "intra-acting" (2007).

[13] The term establishment is used here to refer to a dominant group or elite who holds power or authority in a society, to a closed social group that selects its own

members and excludes "others" based on, for example, gender, sexual orientation, ethnicity, age, disability, beliefs, or world views.

[14] By November 24, 2010, the EU had twenty-three official languages, and the number will increase as new countries join. Europe has more than sixty indigenous regional and minority languages, some of which have official status locally. Examples include Sami in northern Europe, Sorbian towards the east, Sardinian in the south, and Basque in the west. Also, immigrant communities continue to bring new languages with them (*EU Languages and Language Policy* 2010). The challenge of multilingualism is clear for e-learning, particularly for those that aspire to European coverage and do not want to support English language hegemony.

[15] Recommendation Rec(2002)5 of the Committee of Ministers to member states on the protection of women against violence; Recommendation CM/Rec(2007)13 of the Committee of Ministers to member states on gender mainstreaming in education; and Recommendation CM/Rec(2007)17 of the Committee of Ministers to member states on gender equality standards and mechanisms.

[16] Student organizations ESIB: The National Unions of Students in Europe ("Best Practices against Sexual Harassment and Violence at European Institutions of Higher Education" 1998) and CLASHES: Collectif de Lutte Anti-Sexiste Contre le Harcèlement dans l'Education Supérieur (The Collective for the anti-sexist fight against harassment in higher education in English) (Sagay 2004) have been actively combating sexual harassment in European Higher Education.

[17] Please see Heikkinen and Sunnari's "Developing Gender Equality Policy in Finnish Higher Education: Sexual harassment at a Focal Point" (2010).

CHAPTER TEN

ASSISTIVE TECHNOLOGIES: ACCESSING VOICE AND SELFHOOD IN AN AGE OF DIGITAL TECHNOLOGIES

SUSAN SMITH NASH

Online learning and assistive technologies have increased access to education and have enriched the lives of many people, often in unexpected ways and places. Individuals with special needs who were once isolated and had limited choices can take courses toward a degree for lifelong learning or for personal and professional development. In doing so, special needs students contribute to a larger learning community which benefits from their fresh ideas, knowledge, and new perspectives.

New doors to online learning have opened for all students, including those with special needs, due to a combination of factors. These include new assistive technologies that make content available in ways that allow people with special needs to interact with it. Assistive technologies in online courses include many tools to help students see, hear, and interact with the instructional materials, including easy-to-read closed captioning for audio, screen readers that convert text to audio, special keyboard and mouse designs, large-icon touch screens, specially equipped tablets, breath-activated controllers, and more.

New instructional design approaches have also opened doors because they help find the best ways to bring together the assistive technologies and the wide array of new media (videos, voice recordings, texts, maps, virtual worlds, and simulations) that can make learning come alive in new ways for people who may have felt excluded.

Reconnections: Assistive Technologies in Assisted Living

Entire communities can benefit from seemingly minor changes of focus, and there are many cases that show just how powerful the impact can be when individuals are given access. The case of introducing online courses with assistive technologies in an assisted living center is a good example.

For 78-year-old Myra Selfridge (not her real name), assisted living provided a lifeline no one in her family expected when they reluctantly faced the fact that their bright, vibrant grandmother could no longer live alone, due in part to her lack of mobility and macular degeneration, which led to low vision that glasses and surgery could not correct.

The assisted living center had a full array of assistive technologies in the cheerful computer center, along with an arrangement with a local professor who agreed to facilitate online courses offered by a local university's open courseware project. Myra, who had always had an interest in exploring the cultural history of her hometown and who was also interested in studying comparative religions, was delighted when she found that she could use the specially equipped computers which had easy-to-use keyboards, large font display, and a touch screen for navigation. In addition, the computer had a screen-reading program that converted the text to audio that one of the lab assistants would download to an mp3 player. She liked to listen to the lectures on the sacred texts of different religions as she sat in her garden-side room in the evenings, which helped her deal with thoughts of the people she had loved and lost.

Three weeks after the assisted living center opened their new computer center and launched the guided open courseware project, the management started to see significant changes with their residents. They first noticed that the people who were taking the courses took far shorter afternoon naps. Requests for pain relief and anti-anxiety medication dropped. Residents started writing more, and they began asking the center to purchase additional printers so they would not have to wait to print out the papers and journals they were writing.

The management of the assisted living center also noticed an uptick in the number of outside visitors to the center. For the first time, people who were not relatives were starting to visit with frequency. Most were student interns who were earning college credit in the local university that hosted the open courseware. The student interns decided to offer a few face-to-face lectures and to facilitate discussions because they felt a need to visit the people they were getting to know through the Open Courseware project.

Like Myra, the other residents liked to take courses. Some of the residents were even able to help write the courses; two professors emeriti in history helped work on courses in their area of expertise: *Heroes of Ancient Greece* and *Red Scares and Red Dreams: The Early Promises and*

Betrayals of Communist Europe. The topics were popular with the residents; many had always wanted to delve into the classics but had never had the time. Others could relate to the *Red Scares and Red Dreams* course because they remembered living through those times during the Cold War.

The residents also liked the 24-7 access they had to the new online Open Courseware courses, and they enjoyed the media assets that came with it. They could listen to podcasts and watch videos that were included in the instructional content. In addition to having screen readers and other assistive technologies, they also had access to large displays, thanks to a 60-inch monitor that had been purchased by the center and placed in one of the lounges.

One evening, just after dinner, one of the nurse's aides encountered Myra in the garden room. Myra was wiping tears from her eyes and looking out into the garden, where a hummingbird flitted around a glass feeder.

"Are you all right, Myra?" asked the aide.

"Thank you, Sylvia. It's all right. It's just the first time in a long time I've felt anything at all. Do you know what it's like to be a cold, sad, stone inside? To feel nothing? To spend all your time trying not to feel, but then, realizing that not feeling is not survivable, but then realizing that you've lost the ability to feel?"

"I don't know," said Sylvia. "I guess so."

"Believe me, it's better to hurt with sadness and passion than to feel nothing at all." Myra paused. "Let me let you read what I've written for my Open Courseware class. For the first time since Elmer died, I feel a heartbeat inside me."

The Open Courseware project was something very special. That was immediately apparent to the management and staff of the assisted living center. Residents were coming together to discuss the lessons and to watch the instructional materials. They would work alone and with each other.

The project provoked many questions among the observers. Could this be applied everywhere – to everyone? To all those who had previously felt themselves marginalized, neutralized, and unworthy of having a voice or their own thoughts or opinions?

Myra Selfridge is a non-traditional online student in the sense that she is not working toward a degree or certificate, and the learning process could be characterized as tending more toward the informal rather than formal. Yet, it demonstrates the potential for assistive technologies to materially impact the lives of life-long learners as well as those who are in primary, secondary, and post-secondary institutions of learning.

Myra and her fellow residents became resources for several different communities. First, they helped their neighbors find meaningful outlets by taking courses and helping write them. Second, they interacted with their learning communities in ways that helped bring together many different views of the world from people with very diverse backgrounds. Finally, many communities benefited from the preservation of intellectual and cultural histories. Older students can record, share, and preserve their memories and add to the richness of collective knowledge.

Getting Started

Myra is able to achieve her dreams largely because of online learning and assistive technologies, which have transformed the lives of people who may not seem to be likely candidates and who are often overlooked.

We can't really blame Myra and her family if they did not recognize the possibilities. After all, we often see online learning as something that young adults and individuals in the middle of the careers might do. We don't often think of seniors as online students. Further, if we think of assistive technologies for seniors, we often think of end-of-life types of issues. We're not used to thinking of seniors as people with a future, although, truth be told, many people live a good twenty or thirty years after their official retirement, and they are very motivated to continue to be productive and feel as though they are contributing to society.

Although we see assistive technologies in operation in many places, there is still broad confusion when it comes to defining and identifying both assistive technologies and the applications they produce. Assistive technology is, broadly speaking, any technology that facilitates the performance of an individual. The term is usually used to denote technologies covered by statute to enable equal access, which is required by law in the U.S. by the Americans with Disabilities Act (ADA), revised in 1994 (http://www.ada.gov/) and contains the legal standards for accessible design. While most educators on a traditional campus may have a good idea of how the law requires accommodations to be made, they may not know how the idea of access has expanded over the years, particularly after the Individuals with Disabilities Act (IDEA) was passed in 2004.

The law calls for colleges and universities to make sure that all students have access to educational courses, programs, and services. It has not been as easy to implement as some would like, mainly because of a lack of funding or an understanding of how to gain access to the funds that are earmarked for facilitating access. While programs have been in place for K-12 schools to provide assistive technology to students with a defined need, the story has been different for post-secondary education. Funds have been available, but the means of distribution have been less clearly defined.

Because assistive technology has had a positive impact on students' learning (Sze 2009, 420) the potential for its adoption in e-learning is very positive. However, what is the best way to implement it? What is the best approach in, for example, a women's studies course? Perhaps the first thing to recognize is that teachers/instructors need to have freedom to incorporate assistive technology in a way that meets the individuals' needs and which fits the particular circumstances of instruction. It's important to keep in mind that the main thing to focus on is what you'd like to get from the course. What are your learning outcomes? They should be more important than the technology of the device you'd like to incorporate. For example, it's not unusual to hear of schools or programs that receive different types of devices – tablets (iPads, for example) or mp3 players, but how many are sitting around after a year gathering dust – either underutilized or not used at all? It's not an unusual situation because it's "how teachers adapt and utilize the technology that makes a difference and not the technology itself" (Sze 2009, 420); instructional design concerns are paramount.

Because disabilities are highly personal and individual, the assistive technology must, by extension, be equally personal/ personalized. So, the initial challenge of assessing the need for assistive technologies is not as easy to quantify as it may have first seemed.

Let's take the case of a person who has a disability that makes it difficult for them to type on a keyboard. A tablet would be a very good option because it has a touch screen, and it would allow her to touch icons in order to access the instructional materials – the websites, readings, graphics, maps, etc. – that comprise the course. It would also be a good option if she has a good headphone with microphone and can record her responses to questions. She can record them, save them, and then send them to the instructor or post them on the discussion board. For example, Wimba is a program that can be incorporated in the learning management system, and it can allow students to record their responses to each other by means of their threaded voice boards and voice-enabled email. For schools that can't afford Wimba, it's often easy for students to sign up for a free podcast hosting service where they can make a recording, publish it, and then provide a link to it very easily. Students can also post their work to VoiceThread, a free online collaborative tool that permits contributions by telephone as well as by computer.

However, this can't happen in a vacuum, and the student will need someone who can help her configure her tablet so that with a single click or touch she can go directly to the places she needs to in order to access her course materials. Also, someone will need to help her by setting up her iPad so that she can easily make recordings and then send them or post them by using the touch screen rather than having to type on a keyboard.

How do you know what to do to help your students? How do you match technologies with needs? It can be a complicated process and needs a methodological approach (King 1999). As you prepare to help develop a good pathway that brings students along the way to their learning goals, it's a good idea to follow the following steps:

- First, find a way to assess your student to pinpoint just where assistance is needed. What are her capabilities? What are her special talents, and where does she have unique knowledge? What are her interests and enthusiasms? What are her limitations? It might be a fairly simple process – you may just need to ask your student to identify their needs. On the other hand, it could be a bit complicated if the needs are subtle. If your student has attention deficit disorder, or is cognitively impaired due to a stroke, it might be necessary to have her do a few exercises and to fill out a questionnaire.

- Second, what kinds of assistive technologies are available to you? Your student might benefit from 3D visualization in a specially designed room or an immersive simulation using augmented reality. But, those particular solutions may be out of reach financially or physically. So, look at what you have and try to find a way to work with your existing inventories of assistive technologies. If you or the student has a budget and can afford to purchase or lease technology, find out what's available and how much it costs. In many cases, there are programs that can help provide support. For example, if your student is a veteran or receiving social security benefits, there may be funds to purchase equipment. There could be Medicaid funding as well. Further, many private sector entities do have programs to provide discounts. If one is a member of a Native American nation, there is often funding. Private sector sources include companies such as Apple, IBM, churches, community service organizations (United Way agencies, for example), and foundations.

- Third, after you've identified the technologies that are out there, and decided on the ones that are affordable and available, it's

important to consider the level of complexity of the tool. What will
it take for the student to learn how to use them? What will it take
for you, or the staff, to set up the equipment so that it can be used?

- Finally, make sure that you are carefully matching the tool with the
person. Make sure that the devices aren't out of line with the
student's learning preferences; for example, students who are visual
learners should not be matched with devices that are highly
auditory dependent.

Look Within Yourself: What's Your Attitude to Disability?

You may be surprised at your own attitudes to disability. Do you think
of disabilities in a social context, or as a medical situation? There are
basically two different competing models: the social and the medical. It is
useful to note that the social model of disability is generally conceded to
be more inclusion and access-oriented than the medical model announced
by the World Health Organization (1980), which focused on terms such as
"impairment," "disability," and "handicap" that prevent a person from
functioning in a "normal" way. Thus, by extension, a person with a
disability is "abnormal," which may lead to compartmentalization,
segregation, and "Otherness."

In contrast, the social model, which was first developed by the Union
of the Physically Impaired Against Segregation (*Fundamental Principles
of Disability* 1976), looks at impairment as the "functional limitation
caused by physical, sensory, or mental impairments" (Hersh and Johnson
2008, 194) and seems to be a somewhat kinder, gentler idea of disability.
It does not focus on "normal" vs. "abnormal," as does the early medical
model and because "disability" is defined as the "loss or reduction of
opportunities to take part in the normal life of the community on an equal
level with others due to physical, environmental, or social barriers" (Hersh
and Johnson 2008, 194), then it suggests looking at ways to help level the
playing field and to open up opportunities for those who have had reduced
or limited access.

Later, it became clear that a definition based on functionality rather
than participation in the world was too limited, and thus the World Health
Organization updated their definition of disablement to state that it is a
condition that results from "the interaction between an individual's health
and contextual factors" (Hersh and Johnson 2008, 194). That said, the
medical model, even updated, still focuses on the body of the individual,
while the social model takes a larger view and ascribes the problem to that

of the society, rather than the individual. The core idea is that society has in place certain physical and social barriers which can make it difficult for certain individuals to have access.

Consequently, the two competing models tend to inspire completely different solutions to the problem of access. For the medical model, the emphasis is more on creating devices for the body, while the social model looks at the interaction between devices, the environment, and individuals. Hersh and Johnson have described the way that engineers and designers approach the challenge:

1. Design for all; that is designing and constructing devices and environments to be accessible and useable by as wide a range of the population as possible, including disabled people.
2. Design of assistive technology systems, for example, the design of devices to overcome existing environmental and social barriers thereby extending the opportunities and options open to disabled people. (Hersh and Johnson 2008, 194)

Which approach resonates with your own beliefs and attitudes? For example, if you look at a person who is low-hearing, do you think of ways to improve her hearing? Do you immediately think of implants? Or, do you think of how to make her environment such that she does not really need to hear everything? For example, do you think of including closed captioning? Do you provide a script if you're asking people to watch a video of a play?

What Can Technology Do? An Overview

When Mary Kate came back to school a year after the devastating motorcycle accident that left her with traumatic brain injury and chronic pain from a crushed pelvis and spinal nerve damage, she felt fortunate to be alive and to have the chance to study courses. Her interest was in counseling, especially those who had experienced severe injuries.

One of the first things that her advisor did was to schedule an appointment with the office where she would be assessed and recommendations made to help her obtain the technology she might need.

"You'll get more time on tests," said her advisor. "Also, you can borrow equipment from the Technology Office. We recommend screen readers so that you can listen to your assignments when if reading them gives you a headache."

"It was all a blur," said Mary Kate to her friend, Marquisha, who was a professor at the same university. "I answered five different questionnaires, and they gave me rules and regulations to read and to sign. I felt more confused than ever."

Mary Kate was happy to have the equipment and also the special dispensation on exams. But, instead of making her feel as though she had been given a helping hand, she felt as though someone had put a big label on her.

"I feel even more ashamed than ever that I'm different and that I have issues," she told Marquisha as tears welled up. "I am just so embarrassed. There's no way I'll ask my professors to give me more time. They'll just think I'm working the system."

"Don't worry," said Marquisha. "I think it's normal for you to feel uncomfortable, but the key is to find out how to use the technology. And, well – when it comes to your professors and needing more time – don't worry about that, either. Just take it slowly and work with the technology to help you."

Marquisha went on to explain to Mary Kate that, in an ideal world, assistive technology gives individuals who have considered themselves marginalized or relegated to Otherness, an opportunity to express themselves in new ways, new terms. They can make connections that may have felt lost or unavailable to them.

For example, said Marquisha, for individuals who have low vision, low hearing, restricted mobility, or cognitive impairments, assistive technologies can mean not just empowerment but an opportunity to reconstruct one's self and sense of identity. Instead of defining oneself by one's perceived limitations, one can begin to redefine oneself by one's potential transformation.

Here are some of the areas where technologies can be of real help for students in online courses as well as in the traditional face-to-face class:

Low Vision

Assistive technologies include screen readers that convert text to audio so that the learners can listen (rather than read) lectures.

Being able to listen to your text is a great advance, said Marquisha. In the past students with low vision were not able to work without an assistant, or they were put in a different group (isolated) – the performance expectations were normalized downward so that the lack of sight became the new norm, and the materials / ideas available were limited to audio books, audio lectures, and voice conversations

Assistive technologies allow the non-sighted student to produce materials that the sighted students can interact with and relate to. One could say they expand options and open new communities for the non-sighted students.

In addition, if you need to communicate with other students and you have difficulty reading the screen, you can use web conferencing with programs such as Skype and GoToMeeting, which allow individuals to interact by having conversations with each other.

By converting audio to visual, one can liberate the non-sighted people from an overdependence on audio that is prerecorded, making it possible to generate one's own audio/materials and to combine media forms or mash up and mix up rather than simply copying and conforming.

Low Hearing

The challenges here are a bit different than in the case of low vision. For example, a video may be played: the low-vision person can hear the audio and get a sense of what is going on. In the case of low hearing, one would turn to closed captioning to read what people are saying. For recorded interviews, it is possible to get transcripts.

> "What about lectures that my professor might record?" asked Mary Kate.
>
> "In that case, in contrast to the solutions for low vision, audio is turned into text. Voice recognition software makes this possible. It is interesting to see people with disabilities helping each other, and contributing to the community as they create a full loop. It goes from individuals with low-vision who use voice recognition to convert their speech to text, which is then, in turn, converted back to audio by individuals with low hearing. In many cases, the best solution is to make content available in multiple formats and delivery modes," said Marquisha.

Marquisha continued explaining the benefits of assistive technology to Mary Kate.

> "There's a great opportunity for students to start shaping a new sense of self, particularly since visual identities can be very important in the online environment, particularly for the low-hearing student. Collages are important because you can put together collections of related audio and graphics that are interactive. You can mouse over them, and they'll have a closed-captioned label, and an audio file. The discussion board starts to

take on new importance. Text and closed-captioned videos really help as well."

Mary Kate was very interested and couldn't help expressing her thoughts to Marquisha.

"It would be interesting to caption a video based on the students' own videos. Essentially, these would be expressive forms and the closed-captioning would allow own to connect thoughts with images. The students could be encouraged to try for the poetic in terms of text that moves/pushes identity. In the end, the approach would encourage spontaneous performance (fluxus)," she said.

Low Mobility

Difficulty typing, manipulating a touchpad, and using a small mouse are alleviated by means of technologies that accommodate individuals who may have difficult using their hands, fingers, or arms. There are even breath-activated technologies that are ideal for individuals who are paralyzed.

Cognitive Issues

Simple design, the avoidance of distractors (which include animated gifs and pop-ups) can help individuals who suffer from what may manifest as attention deficits or even seizure disorder.

Helping Out: The Design Side

The best solutions combine design and technology, they focus on all users, and they focus on achieving a goal. The best solutions are also inclusive; they do not exclude able-bodied individuals, or those who have not identified special needs. Perhaps the most powerful example is that of universal design.

Universal Design for Learning is an approach that takes an integrated, inclusive approach to making sure that assistive technologies benefit all people, not just those with specific disabilities. Developed by the Center for Applied Special Technology (http://www.design.ncsu.edu/cud/), universal design's key characteristics include incorporating multiple options for access, respecting diverse learning styles of learners. An item or product with universal design is one that can be used by individual who may or may not have disabilities, and it is not necessary to adapt or modify the item. Examples include curb cuts, automatic doors, ramps, etc.

Everyone benefits from attention to design. When you go to the library and the door automatically opens, you benefit regardless of whether or not you have a disability. The advantages of universal design is that it focuses on providing a benefit to all users, being flexible, having a simple and intuitive design, requiring little physical effort, and having a wide tolerance for error.

Universal design principles are often underutilized or simply overlooked in e-learning programs. Here are a few universal design ideas that could be implemented in online courses and which would benefit all users:

- Make sure that there are audio lectures as well as text versions.
- Put together a very clear color-coded design.
- Simplify navigation and provide a link to a site map that includes all links on a single screen.
- Make sure that users can enlarge the view to make the text and the graphics as large as they need.
- If you're using an e-textbook, be sure to provide links that go directly to the readings required for the specific units. Don't make the student search through the entire text.
- Present all core concepts in at least three different ways: text, video, and audio.
- Incorporate easy-to-use internal players to avoid the necessity of lengthy and complicated downloads of plug-ins. For example, if you want to show a video, and you have a choice between having a student download the video, or going to YouTube, it would be better to use YouTube. YouTube has a "click and play" interface that is in the browser, and you can embed it so that all the student has to do is click (rather than download and play through special software).
- Build in an easy-to-use text-to-speech converter. For example, one of the easiest and most affordable is vozMe.com, which allows you to copy and paste text into a textbox and then it creates a male or female voice audio file. It plays right in your browser. Granted, the voice is clearly computer generated, but the pronunciation is clear. You can even add the text-to-speech converter box to your website, which is a bit more complicated but very convenient.
- Create a clean, clear, cheerful interface which is both easy to navigate and free of clutter and distractors.

- Encourage each learning module to include material that accommodates all learning modalities and preferences (audio, visual, kinaesthetic – include text, audio files, videos, interactive). That means including relevant activities, such as interactive maps, as well as audio and video where available.
- Rehumanize with scenario- and case-based problems, which can be accessed through text links and also illustrative graphics links. For example, you might put an image of Zora Neale Hurston, along with text to questions about *Their Eyes Were Watching God*. Then, make sure you can click it and hear the questions. You could also include a brief biography of Zora, with maps and a description of life in all-black communities such as Eatonville, Florida.
- Make sure that students can download key items and play them on their smartphones, tablets, or other portable devices. For example, if you want students to read a text, make it available in pdf format, since most smartphones and tablets can display it, but they may not be able to display a Word document.

Making Sure Your Online Courses Build In Both Approaches: Design and Technology

The instructor can add a few additional design elements to help make the course easier to follow. Any assistive technologies that are being used will be even more effective if the following guidelines are followed:

- *Simplify the presentation.* Make sure that the instructions are clear and that they appear in more than one place.
- *Bundle units/content.* Make sure that the contents are easily accessed together and that the student is not forced to go through a virtual labyrinth to find the content/activities.
- *Use situated learning strategies where possible.* Situated learning focuses the individual learner on a concretely defined task and involves bringing in other individuals in a learning community. Introducing abstract concepts by anchoring the student in a concrete example requiring hands-on collaborative interaction will result in a better sense of support and mastery.
- *Incorporate social learning.* The use of discussion groups is both a barrier and an opportunity in most e-learning programs. Discussion boards are quite limited in the nature of interaction, and many learning management systems are inflexible in the way that the threads are arranged. Alternative, yet non-distracting, collaborative

tools can be used to good effect. Wikis are perhaps the easiest to implement. Sharing images and videos for collaboration can be easily incorporated using a Flickr or YouTube type utility.

- *Consider portfolios.* As you start to design assignments that assess the student, it's a good idea to focus on portfolios rather than skills-based tests and quizzes. A portfolio approach encourages individuals to present knowledge and demonstrate the ability to achieve learning objectives.

Cultural perspectives should be kept in mind. Because performance norms are culturally mediated/determined, what is "good" performance in skill may privilege males of a certain demographic or may privilege certain cultural backgrounds.

In general, it is important to find approaches that encourage collaboration between all students. Ideally, in an online environment, fellow students do not know if/when assistive technologies are being used. Assessment of student performance relates to how knowledge acquisition is seen to be taking place. The feminist classroom, with its emphasis on social justice, deep communication between class members, and a profound level of trust, may take as its primary challenge the exploration of how best to demonstrate that learning objectives have been met and how the learning has been communal/community-oriented. Ultimately, institutions of higher education prepare their students to have an impact on society. An impact is not possible without a learning community of sorts, which gives all the more validation to the notion that the best kind of assessment in the feminist classroom is that which is collaborative.

The Big Picture: What Institutions Are Doing To Accommodate E-Learners with Special Needs

How many of the approximately five million learners who take at least one online course from a U.S. institution have special needs? For the past several years, online enrollments have been growing, with spikes in growth in 2006 and 2008 due to high cost of transportation and the demand for education due to economic downturns (Allen and Seaman 2010, 5). Growth has continued, and enrollment grew by almost a million students, with students in 2,500 colleges and universities enrolled in at least one online course in fall 2009 .

It follows by extension that the growth rate of e-learners with special needs would be high, but whether or not the growth is disproportionate to the overall growth is difficult to determine. Public institutions have reported the highest level of increased demand for online courses, which they attribute to the economic downturn (Allen and Seaman 2010, 1-2).

Paradoxically, public institutions have had the hardest time retaining online students (Allen and Seaman 2010, 14), which certainly bears investigation. It could be that better accommodations in e-learning for special needs students could have a positive impact on retention. Further, low-cost and easy-to-implement assistive technology solutions could have a high positive impact as well.

It's hard to obtain an accurate number for the number of learners in online programs who would need assistive technology under current legislative guidelines established by the Americans with Disabilities Act (ADA) and the Individuals with Disabilities Education Act (IDEA) because the same structure, reporting requirements, and programs are not "mainstreamed" in the colleges in the same way that they are in K-12. Students must self-identify, usually by contacting the office that handles ADA accommodations or by contacting their professor. Further, even though colleges and universities offer accommodations in accordance with ADA and IDEA, the issue becomes complicated with respect to identifying and providing technology.

ADA requirements are currently followed by providing more time on assignments, providing different kinds of assessments or more time for completion of assessments, and providing other simple solutions using easy-to-acquire accommodating technologies (larger controllers, mouse, etc.).

Many potential accommodating efforts by the instructor are often inhibited by the notion that one might run afoul of health related privacy regulations (HIPPA), which creates a rather paradoxical situation where efforts to identify existing needs are thwarted. It is also rare for the courses themselves to be innovative in terms of building in accommodating AT software (mouse-over pronunciation, text-to-voice software, icon – rather than color – coding/differentiation, scalable text, a "go-to" vertical navigation page – course map) that avoids nested links.

It is very likely that the most effective accommodations are not made simply due to structural and logistical realities within the college. The situation could be vastly improved by creating better channels of communication, with more options, by establishing more universal surveys/questionnaires to assess needs, by setting out smoother referral services, and by mandating more accommodations involving AT, which could range from a software download to actual equipment. Cost-effective AT could mean better accommodations for students in the distributed classroom that often involves students across multiple countries and time zones, who frequently change locations.

Competing Approaches: Which Do You Choose?

Organizations and institutions that seek to make sure students have assistive technology may chose from a number of frameworks as they plan to meet the needs of students. It is good to keep in mind that some of the frameworks may be more effective in the online environment than others.

Here are four frameworks which will give a good overview of how most institutions currently approach getting the right technology to the users who can benefit from them.

Hersh and Johnson (Hersh and Johnson 2008) proposed a new comprehensive modeling framework, Comprehensive Assistive Technology (CAT), which allows educators, educational institutions, end-users, medical and clinical rehabilitation practitioners, social support staff, and the engineering community to communicate in an integrated manner to achieve overall goals of inclusion, access, and improved education/social environment. The CAT model takes a social view of disability rather than a medical one, which means that the basic steps for identifying needs and delivering the service to the learner would focus on modifying the environment and educating people in the community, not just "fixing" the individual's body through technology.

In order to assure that everyone has an equal chance at obtaining the technology they need, it is very important to have a standardized process or procedure in place which includes the following steps: obtaining referrals, setting goals, conducting evaluations, selecting devices, identifying funding sources, determining training needs, following up on the effects of assistive technologies, and modifying goals.

SETT (Student, Environment, Tasks, Tools) Framework (Zabala et al. 2004) is an approach that relies on a team to help identify the student's needs and then to find the appropriate tool, given the environment and the tasks that the students need to accomplish.

Tech Points (Bowser and Reed 1995) is a framework that focuses on planning by developing a specialized referral and assessment process and the utilization of clinical settings where the special needs of assistive technology users are addressed. Colleges or universities would need to direct the student in need to a clinic where the assessments would take place. This approach is relatively expensive and may not be the best fit for institutions that are located at a long distance from clinics.

Chambers Model (Chambers 1997) encourages an ongoing evaluation to make sure that the tools fit the task while the Unifying Functional Model (Melichar and Blackhurst 1993) emphasizes the way in which assistive technologies affect the learner's situation with respect to resources, goals, and even perceptions. The bulk of the work takes place at the beginning during the initial assessment. Once every six months or so, the student provides an update. It's a good idea to follow the Chambers model when technology changes quickly and also when the courses change delivery methods. For example, the technology a student uses with an online course that uses regular textbooks may be different the course that uses e-textbooks. The Chambers approach reveals the relationships between the technology and one's view of oneself in society while one takes courses.

Is Technology More Than Mere Tools?: Technology as Unveiling/Revelation

Britta was one of the first to buy an iPad, and she quickly made sure that all her courses had texts that could be accessed online as well as in traditional paper.

> "I love it – it's so convenient and interactive!" she said. "I have low vision, and I really like the fact that I can zoom in and blow up the text and the graphics. For the first time, I'm not straining to see things, and I don't feel tense! I know my students will feel the same way."

Britta was largely right – the students who could afford a tablet did like the new approach. There were a few concerns that the e-textbooks she had selected could not be downloaded and stored – they were only available if you were online and hooked in via high-speed connection to the textbook publisher's website in "the cloud."

> "Using the iPad makes me see things that I would not have seen before," said Britta. "I'm even starting to see myself in a new way."

It's always worthwhile to ask ourselves what we're doing, especially when there's a lot of buzz and/or enthusiasm about a new process, procedure, or technology. In certain ways, that's the nature of our interaction with technology – while we're creating our latest and greatest new thing and while we're using it. It is interesting to see that others have looked at that relationship and have had a number of observations.

For example, the philosopher Martin Heidegger wrote in 1954 in *A Question Concerning Technology (Die Frage nach der Technik in Vorträge und Aufsätze)* that technology is much more than simple enhanced functionality. According to Heidegger, technology is more about the person who has designed or who is using the technology than the technology itself. Behind the technology is the need or the desire to use it, and, more to the point, the idea of what the technology can do for the individual or group. Technology is not an end in itself.

What informs technology and technological innovation is the understanding of what the technology will do for the individual, the transformative capabilities, and the underlying notions of the ideal. This may seem self-evident but is one goes through the steps of examining Heidegger's notions and then applying them to assistive technologies, a number of insights – some which may even seem startling – manifest themselves. If we accept the basic premise that technology involves a basic unveiling or revealing process, how do we learn about ourselves in e-learning? What does an iPad reveal about us?

In the following passages, Heidegger suggests that technology has to do with a "bringing-forth" that has a strong relationship to the notion of poiesis. In other words, technology carries with it not just its denotative meanings and its literal functionality but also its metonymic/metaphoric element. Technology is symbolic of something deeper, and assistive technology, by extension, is the same, representing not only the literal functionality of the technology but also what it represents in the human spirit – which can't be easily distilled to a single meaning but should be considered to be an ongoing process, as Heidegger points out, a "bringing-forth":

> It is of utmost importance that we think bringing-forth in its full scope and at the same time in the sense in which the Greeks thought it. Not only handicraft manufacture, not only artistic and poetical bringing into appearance and concrete imagery, is a bringing-forth, poiesis. (1954)

Heidegger follows his first points that technology brings forth a metaphorical or metonymic meaning by pointing out that the core of the word, technology is the Greek word "techne" which indicates revealing and unconcealing. The passage in which Heidegger discusses precisely how/where technology starts to do its work of unveiling or revealing the underlying core values, beliefs, and ideas that precipitated the human activity of invention in the first place.

> Thus the clue to what the word *techne* means and to how the Greeks defined it leads us into the same context that opened itself to us when we pursued the question of what instrumentality as such in truth might be. Technology is a mode of revealing. Technology comes to presence in the realm where revealing and unconcealment take place, where *aletheia*, truth, happens.

For the purposes put forth here, technology – specifically assistive technology – reveals an underlying truth. "Truth" could be a constructed notion – an amalgam of beliefs, desires, ideas, goals, and idealized images that one holds in one's mind and which has been socially crafted and/or mediated. We often like to observe that truth (along with reality) is socially constructed (Berger 1964).

In the case of the iPad and smartphones, the way we use social networking lets us understand our relationship with ourselves and our need for contact. How inclusive are our social networks? Perhaps the way that the iPad and smartphones facilitate the formation of groups can let us see how oppression can occur and how communication can remove oppressive attitudes and values.

So, in this case, technology reveals something about the fabric of a society and its values. The values of the society are what drive the change, and yet the focus is on the technology itself, which results in an inability of a society to be introspective and understand itself through technology. Instead, it may become obsessed with the mechanics of the technology.

> And yet, the revealing that holds sway throughout modem technology does not unfold into a bringing-forth in the sense of poiesis. The revealing that rules in modern technology is a challenging [Herausfordern], which puts to nature the unreasonable demand that it supply energy which can be extracted and stored as such. But does this not hold true for the old windmill as well? No. Its sails do indeed turn in the wind; they are left entirely to the wind's blowing. But the windmill does not unlock energy from the air currents in order to store it. (Heidegger 1954)

In the case of assistive technology in e-learning, the individual may become focused on buying bigger and better screen readers and keyboards, rather than on what motivated her/him in the first place – the desire to engage in a learning process that involves contact with the outside world.

Technology Revitalizes, Reinforces the Feminist Core Perspective

In order to gain an appreciation of precisely how assistive technologies can help accomplish the goals of access and social justice that may inform the feminist classroom, it's useful to take a close look at the different way in which revelations and unveilings take place.

The fact that assistive technology exists at all reveals something about the function of the technologies themselves – that they are bringing in a focus on certain human functions, isolating them, and clarifying their core purpose and/or function. For a technology to "assist," we have to establish a norm or baseline of what that function is in the first place.

For Britta, who loved the iPad because it helped her access information and read it, her baseline norm had to do with an expectation of being able to read a text easily and without a struggle. Her iPad was the technology that eliminated the gap.

This presupposes that meeting the gap is desirable. For Britta, that was obviously the case. The technology helped her achieve the level of vision she wanted to have. However, there may be cases when performing up to the norm is not really relevant. For example, the new technology may help a person read an exam, but if the exam or assessment is biased or culturally skewed, then the technology did not really do anything to fix the underlying problem with the exam itself.

At any rate, from a Heideggerian perspective, the promise of technology to be a "gap-filler" reveals assumptions about what people are supposed to be able to do or, better yet, what the dominant group has decided that they should be able to do.

A Future Today? A Vision of Community-Based E-Learning for All Ages: Concluding Thoughts

Assistive technologies are in place to help bring voice to those who formerly did not have an opportunity to be heard and to let individuals have more freedom as they shape a sense of self and identity. While it may be easy to focus on the technologies themselves and say that they are the vectors of transformation and change, it is useful to take a look at how design concepts/processes flow into the making and implementing of assistive technologies. The idea of universal design has made it conceivable for all individuals to fully take part in learning. Further, the transition from a medical notion of disability which focuses on how an individual deviates from a set norm, to a social view of disability, which focuses on how environmental issues prevent a person from participating in an activity or community, are reflective of the feminist theories that have been in place since the 1970s.

Assistive technologies and "assistive pedagogies" can be drivers of change, first in an individual sense, as the individual learner uses technology to feel a higher level of participation and self-efficacy/mastery. At a second level, however, the social elements of assistive technologies will encourage the development of communities that are uniquely flexible and responsive to changing needs and times. Rather than emphasizing performance and linear skills, the new communities forged from people who now have access due to assistive technologies, may begin to privilege the creative combining of knowledge, skills, and facts, rather than simply looking at the performance of an individual body as the metric that determines an individual's value. A learning community that values creativity with disjunctive combinations and at-will participation can build confidence and sustainable energies for the future. Assistive technologies and universal design, along with e-learning, can help make it a reality.

Appendix

CATCHING THE DRAGON: TECHNOLOGY YOU CAN USE

http://adarocks.wikispaces.com/X+Resources+Susan+Smith+Nash

Ability	Skills / Tasks	Types of Devices	Examples of Products
Low Vision	Memory	Mobile recording / playback devices	Numerous
	Reading	Video magnifiers	Numerous
			Biggy: Provides large cursors http://rjcooper.com/biggy/
	Reading	Scanner / OCR devices	Acapela Group: Text to speech solutions http://www.acapela-group.com/
	Reading	Text to Voice	Claro Software: speech technology, image technology and touch technology. http://www.clarosoftware.com/
	Reading	Text to Voice	vozMe: easy to use translater from text to voice that is completely web-based http://www.vozm.com
	Reading	Braille translation software	Dolphin screen-reader with Braille and speech support: http://www.yourdolphin.com/products.asp?cat=1
	Reading	Braille embossers	Enabling Technologies, Inc.: Braille embossers / printers http://www.brailler.com/
	Reading	Screen readers	JAWS® screen reading software - - Freedom Scientific Products http://www.freedomscientific.com /product-portal.asp
	Computer access	Screen magnification	Numerous
	Mobility	Touch screen navigation	Numerous

Ability	Skills / Tasks	Types of Devices	Examples of Products
Low Hearing	Videos	Close-captioning	Numerous
	Recorded interviews	Voice recognition – create text transcripts	Dragon speech recognition http://www.nuance.com/dragon/index.htm
	Interviews / computer sounds	Assistive listening devices / amplification / hearing aids	Numerous
Low Mobility	Computer access	Keyboard modification	Numerous
	Computer access	Alternative mouse / pointing	Tobii Technology: Tobii Technology specializes in eye tracking and eye control. This technology makes it possible for computers to know exactly where users are looking. http://www.tobii.com/corporate/start.aspx
	Computer access	Alternative keyboards	Madentec Ltd.: New keyboards and joysticks http://www.madentec.com/intro/
	Computer access	Alternative mouse / pointing	Origin Instruments: The HeadMouse Extreme replaces the standard computer mouse for people who cannot use or have limited use of their hands. http://orin.com/
	Computer access	Screen keyboard / touchpad	Applied Human Factors: screen keyboard computer access http://ahf-net.com/
	Computer access	Commands via speech recognition	

Ability	Skills / Tasks	Types of Devices	Examples of Products
Cognitive Disability	Reading	Mouse-over speech / pronunciation	Numerous
	Reading	Portable digital dictionaries	A number of these download to mobile devices; standalones include Ectaco's digital readers and dictionaries http://www.nuance.com/dragon/index.htm
	Reading	Developmental reading software / comprehension / note-taking	textHelp Browsealoud is designed to improve website accessibility for those who struggle to read content online. It works by reading website content aloud in a high quality, human-sounding voice at no cost to the end user and zero implementation for the web owner. http://www.browsealoud.com http://www.texthelp.com/
	Note-taking	Recording pens	Livescribe
	Math	Talking calculators	Metroplex Voice Computing, Inc.: Speech-recognition mathematics http://metroplexvoice.com/
	Writing	Grammar, spelling, style-check software	Numerous
	Math	Modeling / graphic software	Numerous / Texas Instruments has several handheld graphic calculators

Bibliography

Allen, I. Elaine and Jeff Seaman. 2010. *Class Differences. Online Education in the United States, 2010.* Accessed April 8, 2011. http://sloanconsortium.org/sites/default/files/class_differences.pdf.

"Americans with Disabilities Act 1990." 2009. *ADA Home Page.* March. http://www.ada.gov/pubs/ada.html.

"Assistive Technology Act 1998." 2009. *National Dissemination Center for Children with Disabilities.* December. http://www.nichcy.org/laws/ata.

Berger, P. L. and Luckmann, T. 1966. *The Social Construction of Reality: A Treatise in the Sociology of Knowledge.* Garden City, NJ: Anchor Books.

Campbell, Diane M. 2004. "Assistive Technology and Universal Instructional Design: A Postsecondary Perspective." *Equity and Excellence in Education* 37, no. 2: 167-173.

Chambers, A.C. 1997. *Has Technology Been Considered? A Guide for IEP Teams.* Reston, VA: CASE/TAM.

Elyburn, Dave. 2009. "Instructional Design Advances in Special Education Technology." *Exceptionality* 17, no. 2: 63-65.

Fundamental Principles of Disability. 1976. London: UP-IAS. Accessed June 1, 2011. http://www.leeds.ac.uk/disability-studies/archiveuk/UPIAS/fundamental%20principles.pdf.

Gibson, B., Upshur, R., Young, N. and P. McKeever. 2007. "Disability, Technology, and Place: Social and Ethical Implications of Long-Term Dependency on Medical Devices." *Ethics, Place, and Environment* 10, no. 1: 7-28.

Hasselbring, T.S. and M. E. Bausch. 2006. "Assistive Technologies for Reading." *Educational Leadership* December 2005/January 2006: 72-75.

Heidegger, Martin. 1954. *A Question Concerning Technology (Die Frage nach der Technik in Vorträge und Aufsätze).* Accessed October 4, 2010. http://www.wright.edu/cola/Dept/PHL/Class/P.Internet/PITexts/QCT.html.

Hersh, M. A. and Johnson, M. 2008. "On Modelling Assistive Technology Systems – Part 1: Modelling Framework" *Technology and Disability* 20: 193-215.

Hersh, M. A. and Johnson, M. 2008. "On Modelling Assistive Technology Systems – Part 2: Applications of the Comprehensive Assistive Technology Model." *Technology and Disability* 20: 251-270.

Judge, S., Floyd, K. and Jeffs, T. 2008. "Using an Assistive Technology Toolkit to Promote Inclusion" *Early Childhood Education J.* 36: 121-126.

King, T. W. 1999. *Assistive Technology: Essential Human Factors.* Boston: Allyn and Bacon.

Kuczewski, M. 2001. "Disability: An Agenda for Bioethics." *The American Journal of Bioethics* 1, no. 3: 36-44.

Lee, H., Templeton, R. 2008. "Ensuring Equal Access to Technology: Providing Assistive Technology for Students with Disabilities." *Theory into Practice* 47: 212-219.

Marshall, M. 1999. "Technology to Help People with Dementia Remain in their Own Homes." *State of the Art for Practice in Dementia* Fall: 85-87.

Melichar, J.F. and Blackhurst, A. E. 1993. "Introduction to a Functional Approach to Assistive Technology." Accessed November 13, 2011. http://www.texasat.net/docs/Eval.Supp.Lit.pdf.

Nash, S. "Assistive Technologies." *E-Learning Queen.* http://www.elearningqueen.com, last modified 2010.

"Principles of Universal Design." 1997. *NC State University.* Accessed October 5, 2010. http://www.design.ncsu.edu/cud/about_ud/udprinciplestext.htm.

Raskind, M.H. and Higgins, E. 1995. "Reflections on Ethics, Technology, and Learning Disabilities: Avoiding the Consequences of Ill-Considered Action." *Journal of Learning Disabilities* 28, no. 7: 425-438.

Riley, D., Pawley, A. and J. Tucker. 2009. "Feminisms in Engineering Education: Transformative Possibilities." *Feminist Formations* 21, no. 2: 21-40.

Rose, D. H. and Meyer, A. 2002. *Teaching Every Student in the Digital Age: Universal Design for Learning.* Alexandria, VA: ASCD Books.

Sloan Consortium and the Babson Research Group. 2009. "Learning on Demand: Online Learners in the United States." *SLOAN-C.* Accessed October 4, 2010. http://sloanconsortium.org/publications/survey/pdf/learningondemand.pdf.

Sze, Susan. 2008. "The Effects of Assistive Technology on Students with Disabilities." *Journal of Educational Technology Systems* 37, no. 4: 419-429.

Tourigny, A., Durand, P. and L. Bonin. 2004. "Quasi-Experimental Study of the Effectiveness of an Integrated Service Delivery Network for the Frail Elderly." *Canadian Journal on Aging* 23, no. 3: 231-246.

World Health Organization. 1980. *International Statistical Classification of Impairments, Disabilities and Handicaps.* Accessed November 13, 2011. http://www.who.int/classifications/icd/en/HistoryOfICD.pdf.
Zabala, J., Bowser, G. and Korsten, J. 2004. "SETT and ReSETT: Concepts for AT Implementation." *Closing the Gap* 23, no. 5: 10-11.

CHAPTER ELEVEN

WOMEN'S HEALTH AND WELL-BEING: A TRANSCULTURAL/TRANSNATIONAL TEACHING AND LEARNING COLLABORATION

KIMBERLEE STAKING

This essay reports on an e-learning course in which participants explored women's health and well-being from a transcultural/transnational perspective. It does so by describing and re/presenting the experience from the multiple and diverse points of view of members of this virtual learning community. Ford Foundation funding earmarked for internationalizing web-based teaching tools brought together feminist academics and their students from five geographically dispersed universities in Africa, the Caribbean, the Middle East, and North America to collaborate on this project. In documenting *Women's Health and Well-Being: Transcultural Perspectives*, taught cross-institutionally in 2005 and 2007, this essay contributes materially to literature chronicling the pedagogically and technologically innovative projects constituting feminist-constructed cyberspaces (McShane 2004; Moore 2008; Tisdell 1998).

As one of the five teacher/scholars who designed this e-learning course (or *module* as those outside the U.S. context referred to it), I share stories of our cross-cultural and trans-national cyberspace interactions from my point of view – as an extremely fruitful collaboration that was both joyously rewarding and highly labor intensive. However, the voices of *others* who participated with me in this virtual classroom – co-designers and students – are equally critical to the meaning-making processes by which this narrative becomes constituted as feminist pedagogical knowledge. Important as it is to engage all participant perspectives in any learning collaboration, it is perhaps even more critical to do so in transcultural/transnational contexts given the additional markers of socio-cultural-political difference and the relational exercise of power with which such transactions are inscribed (Subedi 2008; Staking 2010). Thus, with their consent, participant narratives form a significant part of this analysis.

In writing about the course not as *my* story but as *our* story, I make explicit my investment in self-reflexive collaboration with others. In this, I am joined by pedagogues across disciplines in asserting that such engagements facilitate deep learning and are crucial to our ability to construct trangressive knowledge (Buchanan, Wilson, and Gopal 2008; Lave and Wenger, 1991; Rohleder et al. 2008; Staking 2010). In re/presenting the voices of students alongside my own, I assert their value to the knowledge building transactions of the entire learning community, in which I include the reader. I anticipate that readers engaging these multiple and occasionally contradictory voices will experience the dialogic process of our course interactions. By intentionally constructing a multi-voiced narrative without attempting to reconcile inevitable differences in perspective, I enact collaborative process as one path available to feminists seeking to deploy ICT tools, and I affirm that such engagements are the very stuff out of which knowledge building in feminist cyberspaces can and should be constructed.

One of the central questions this anthology explores is that of the potential of new media technologies to promote student engagement with feminist knowledge frameworks in the women's studies classroom. In directly re/producing student narratives constructed in response to course assignments, I allow students the power of voicing for themselves how they engaged these knowledge frameworks as they interacted virtually with transnational peers. Participant voices re/produced below reflect cogently upon the benefits and barriers to successful engagement in the virtual classroom as they experienced them. While barriers identified focus chiefly on technological challenges, benefits described center on the co-construction of knowledges that challenged, modified, and altered previous assumptions about women's health through virtual transcultural/transnational interactions with peers.

After describing how our teaching collaboration was initiated, this essay focuses on the voices of students from the 2007 course. As their narratives amply demonstrate and attest, participants found that their virtual interactions permitted them to explore women's health and well-being from a range of interdisciplinary and transcultural perspectives, which in turn prompted them to interrogate the diverse socio-cultural, geographic, and historical contexts that gave shape to their real worlds. Their sustained dialogic interactions with one another trace the emergence of transgressive new knowledges that are global in scope.

Their narratives also challenge the definition of who can be a digital native, introducing critical questions of resource availability and access. Although Buchanan and Subedi have recently grappled with these questions, in general, they have often remained obscured when the situation is neither constituted through cross-cultural interactions nor contexualized (as was our course) by the still deeply persistent nature of the north/south digital divide. Participant narratives also document the ways in which learners discovered the utility of social-constructivist pedagogies in navigating the often challenging journey to building an effective sense of community in cyberspace across their psychic barriers and physical borders of difference. These narratives of student interactions with one another and with feminist literature on women's health and well-being overwhelmingly indicate that despite often severe resource constraints, participants discovered enormous benefits from participating in the course.

Background: Course Design

I have elsewhere described how I became involved with this transnational teaching partnership only indirectly through my dissertation research at the University of Maryland, which explores the potential of new media technologies in facilitating high-quality peer-to-peer collaborations (Staking 2010). My interest in web-based pedagogies led to this opportunity to expand my interest in teaching transnationally by participating in a summer institute in which academics from the University of Maryland were joined by colleagues from the *International Consortium for Graduate Studies in Women and Gender* to co-construct online curricula. The Consortium was somewhat serendipitously launched five years earlier following the seventh Women's Worlds Conference in Tromso, Norway. Subsequent to that meeting and under the aegis of the University of Maryland's *Curriculum Transformation Project*, women's studies scholars from institutions in Asia, Africa, Europe, and the Caribbean gathered for a series of institutes intended both to "internationalize curriculums" and "to facilitate the transnational exchange of ideas and knowledge, and contribute to the evolutions of women's and gender studies, especially at the graduate level" (Staking 2010).

Prior to our coming together at the Consortium's 2004 summer institute, neither I nor my colleagues envisioned ourselves forming a transnational teaching collaboration to explore women's health and well-being. However, we each came to the institute deeply invested in the project of creating curricula that would mobilize bodies of knowledge across institutional borders, thus serving our students more effectively than could be done within our local contexts. The potential benefits of a transnational collaboration convinced us that the project would be worth the effort and commitment it would require of us (Staking 2010).

My work deploying technology-based constructivist teaching practices in student exploration of visual media complemented the expertise of my four colleagues, each of whom came from a different consortium affiliated institution: Grace Bantebya-Kyomuhendo of Makerere University, Uganda (a social anthropologist applying IT to her work on HIV/Aids, and maternal and reproductive health); Vivienne Bozalek of the University of the Western Cape, South Africa (a social work scholar with emphases on family studies, and women and social policy who was already partnering with colleagues at local institutions through IT); Rivka Tuval-Mashiach of Bar-Ilan University, Israel (a clinical psychologist specializing in women, trauma, and mental health); and Yasmeen Yusuf-Khalil of the University of the West Indies, Jamaica (a distance learning curriculum specialist focused on gender, educations, and economic development).

Because we each focus on some aspect of women's gendered identities, we chose to design our course as an exploration of women's health and well-being, a topic broad enough to encompass each of our special interests and training, and to take advantage of the experiences, both pedagogical and technological, that we each brought to the table. Despite the challenges of international teaching collaborations reported in the literature (Fung 2004; McAlpine 2002; Volet and Wosnitza 2004), we were persuaded to undertake this project because of the importance of the topic and the potential for new knowledge construction and acquisition for teachers and students alike. Although most of us were relatively inexperienced in using online teaching platforms, we shared an enthusiasm for using social-constructivist methods of inquiry in our teaching practices. In retrospect, it was this combination of factors – our initial willingness to experiment with technological innovation, along with our similar pedagogical commitments – that kept us working together through the challenges that lay ahead (socio-cultural distinctions, resource constraints, time zones, time commitments, etc.). Institutional support was limited to the external funding grant from the Ford Foundation, but the generously unstinting step-by-step guidance from the University of Maryland ICT staff supported our fledging efforts.

Each of the modes of engagement that we designed for the course drew upon relational interactions. Learner tasks were socio-constructivist in nature, requiring students to engage one another in the knowledge building process. Hoping to create an engaged and interactive virtual learning community, we chose a range of communication technologies (both synchronous and asynchronous) from the university's web-based course management system (WebCT). Our design thus foregrounded joint knowledge construction across geographical contexts, utilizing ICT tools to promote the social aspects of learning (Jefferies 2003; Lewis and Allan 2005; Littlefield and Roberson 2005).

Fostering collaborative knowledge building through tasks that would be shared and peer reviewed, we placed a high value on critical reflection, respecting student views and perceptions in the knowledge building process (Vygotsky 1978; Wenger 2000). The questions we posed about women's health and well-being were ones that really puzzled us and to which there was no right or wrong response. In this context, students' interactive participation in the co-construction of knowledge was explicitly regarded as valuable (Lave 1991). In scaffolding tasks that were both manageable across a range of institutional ICT capabilities and engaging for students in diverse disciplines and locations, our intention was that the module would build the capacity of students at each of the institutions to engage productively in distance learning. We further anticipated that participation in the module would assist students to develop deepened understandings of transcultural realities with respect to women's health and well-being (Yusuf-Khalil et al. 2007, 55). We also hoped that as our students engaged virtually with one another across interdisciplinary, transnational frameworks, they would be better enabled to co-construct enhanced and deepened understandings of women's health needs globally (Staking 2010).

Course Implementation

Our first opportunity to implement the course was as a three-week pilot integrated into our existing courses in the spring of 2005. Graduate students from all institutions except the University of Maryland (where my undergraduate students served as external reviewers for the final projects) participated in cross-institutional work groups of five to nine members each. Each group produced a project posted to our e-learning platform; group collaboration was facilitated by one of the five course designers. As facilitators we mediated virtual group discussions, marked and provided feedback on assignments, and guided technology resource usage and content exploration; we envisioned ourselves as "more knowledgeable peers" rather than as "experts in the field" (Lave 1991, 35). Topics addressed through group projects were Bodily Integrity, HIV/Aids, Mental Health, Reproductive Health, and Social Well-Being.

Additional Ford Foundation funding enabled us to report on the pilot at
the Seoul 2005 Women's Worlds Conference and to reconvene at the
University of Maryland in July 2006 to expand the pilot into a semester-
long course. However, the expense and technological challenges of hosting
an entire semester course on UM's WebCT platform with the bulk of
participations coming from other institutions necessitated our moving its
home to an open source platform (KEWL) hosted at the University of the
Western Cape (UWC). As had been the case at University of Maryland,
we found the ICT staff at UWC to be both capable and generous in their
assistance; additionally, Bar-Ilan University funded a technology aide to
work online with the ICT staff at UWC to upload the revised course to its
new platform in time for our spring 2007 course. Students from the
University of the West Indies (UWI) were unfortunately unable to
participate because of budgetary constraints.

We recruited forty students, the maximum the four of us were able to
facilitate without the participation of our colleague from UWI. Once again,
students were placed in transnational cross-institutional work groups to
explore the topics of Bodily Integrity, HIV/Aids and Reproductive Health,
Mental Health, and Social Well-Being. With our remaining funds, we
added an online video conference feature that virtually convened
participants from all sites to present their research findings. This video
conference, which allowed students to communicate visually with their
collaborative peers, became a centerpiece of the course, one that students
universally expressed enthusiasm for (Staking 2010). Our funding having
expired, our e-learning course is currently approved only at the University
of the Western Cape. Notwithstanding the greatly lessened costs of such a
course relative both to traditional face-to-face courses and in comparison
to other options for translational learning at the undergraduate level,
funding participation from other institutions remains problematic – this
despite our course location on UWC's open-source e-learning platform. It
is our hope that as more academics become aware of the course and of its
transnational learning potential for their students, they will secure funding
from their home institutions.

As we worked fiercely together to hammer out the details of the full-
length course in 2006, the five of us recognized, both from the intensely
productive nature of our collaboration and from analysis of the data
generated by the pilot, that participatory engagement in the e-learning
course had exceeded our expectations. In subsequently analyzing the data
from the 2007 course, we noted that benefits to participants in this regard
were more than realized. As my colleague Vivienne Bozalek writes,
"What we could not have anticipated was the extent to which the module

that we designed would provide all students multiple affordances to develop new skills, talents, abilities and knowledge. Nor could we have predicted the striking degree of authenticity which would characterize their virtual exchanges with one another, or their ability to both dialogue and contest new understandings of women's health and well-being with each other" (Bozalek and Staking 2008, 3).

Virtual Dialogues Exploring Women's Health and Well-Being

Participants engaged one another in productive conversations from their first virtual exchanges. The first task was to write a 350 word introductory e-journal that included their own definition of what constituted health and well-being with relevant illustrations or personal examples. Learners next responded to the postings of at least three students not from their own university. While detailed rubrics were provided, participants were advised: "There is no right or wrong answer so feel free to express yourself according to your own understanding. Please note that both your e-journal and your responses to your virtual classmates will be in a public discussion space available to all members of our course. Also, note that during the period of this course you will have the opportunity to change or modify your views" ("Women's Health and Well-Being: Transcultural Perspectives" 2011).

Notable in all postings was the sense of intense anticipation and pleasure with which participants engaged virtually in these transcultural interactions. Equally notable was the degree to which knowledge construction was observed to be participatory and collaborative. Excerpts that follow originate from the course archive on the KEWL e-learning platform at the University of the Western Cape; in consideration of space, all are abbreviated ("Women's Health and Well-Being: Transcultural Perspectives" 2011). Emphases added are my own and are made with the sole intention of underscoring the rich dialogic conversations and contestations about women's health and well-being that occurred.

Hallo from a rather hot South Africa! I am a single 27 year old female living in Cape Town. I was born and bred in South Africa and moved quite a bit during childhood. We are very close knit family and I believe that families can have a positive effect on your health and well-being. I am currently doing my Masters in Women and Gender Studies at the University of the Western Cape. I am aiming to do my thesis next year in the area of women and technology...To answer the question posed, women's health and well-being is different but closely connected.

Women's health refers to one's physical and mental state while well-being would refer to one's financial and mental health. I believe that women's health and well-being has an interconnected relationship as without the other, one's life becomes complicated...various conditions affecting women's health and well-being. For example, war would affect women's health and in turn affect their well-being as the country they find themselves in are politically not stable and women are affected the most during these pressing times...Thus I would say the two terms are separate but connected. I am looking forward to your responses!

The openly collaborative attitude towards her virtual classmates in the richly detailed excerpt above is characteristic of students in this and all subsequent assignment. In responding to this introduction, a virtual classmate, below, asserts the socio-cultural component of women's experiences of health and well-being.

Hey, this is S. from Uganda. It's a pleasure to participate in such a great course that is helping us to get to interact with different people from different localities. It's good to understand different cultures since this widens your understanding...and can also help us to know how different cultures impact on women's health and well-being. Your post is interesting and I do agree with you on the fact that women's health and well-being are connected because a popular use of the term well-being usually relates to health. However when you say health refers to ones physical or mental state only, you are leaving out the social well-being. So please to define health, let us consider it as "a state of complete physical, mental, and social well-being and not merely the absence of disease or infirmity" (United Nations 2010).

The posting above generated general agreement and extensive commentary as students participated in the give and take process of collaborative knowledge building. The comment below focuses not only on the inter-connectedness of the two concepts but on the impact of socially constructed frameworks such patriarchy and gender to both.

I am a female Ugandan married with three children. Am a social worker by profession with a 25-year work experience as a welfare officer with the Uganda police force –Ministry of Internal Affairs. Am a third year evening student...in the final semester, pursuing a bachelor's degree...Gender and development studies is my major course emphasis and psychology is the minor...The terms "women's health" and "women's well-being," in my understanding refer to conditions of good and comfortable living of women in all aspects of their lives; emotionally, spiritually, physically, psychologically, socially, culturally and politically...it is hard to differentiate one from the other because they overlap each other, they are complimentary to each other...In my view women's health is relating more to biology, bodily integrity, reproduction, and child- birth. In this case I look at health in the absence of disease as a major aspect of women's living. Well-being has to do more with women's ability to think clearly, be able to understand what goes on in their societies and the ability to judge what is best for them in terms of culture and other norms that subject them to the second class position. Women must have the ability to embrace the efforts being taken by others to emancipate them. For example a woman may be very healthy physically, emotionally, and the rest of the conditions mentioned above but then she may not have good interpersonal relationships with the social networks like the husband, relatives, friends...This will make the woman's well-being not good...

The social component of well-being continued to be extensively dialogued and contested in this set of exchanges below as students focused on tensions between individual and collective well-being:

Greetings to everyone, I am a 22 year old Ugandan male, the only child of my beloved mother, and the first born of my father's five children. Currently, am a full time student at the university of Makerere...Am a major of social administration, and a minor of gender and development studies. Health in my understanding covers the physical, mental, sexual, psychological, and spiritual well-being in totality. It is not necessarily the absence of disease, but rather...constitutes aspects like good feeding, having access to foods with all nutrients necessary for good health, access to routine medical examination, being genuine to one's self through life style, getting enough sleep, or relaxing after a stressful day. On the other hand, well-being, an important concern, involves access to resources and services, freedom, and happiness. Our well-being is shaped by our upbringing, personal circumstances or choices, and the social condition in which we live. Collective well-being is improved if we live in a peaceful, flourishing and supportive society. This explains the fact that it flows from individuals to society. Health is one of the aspects that determine well-being.

Note that this student has differentiated very clearly between the two terms, indicating his sense that well-being depends on one's socio-political location. As expressed by the University of Maryland student below, the posting above caused her to re-consider her understanding of how women respond to their differently positioned circumstances.

I really enjoyed your description of health. I found that it showed me what my own definition – and even understanding – of women's health is missing. This is because a lot of the examples you gave – "good feeding," "getting enough sleep," "relaxing after a stressful day" – depict women as agents in regard to their health. It wasn't until I read these examples that I realized that the definition I gave lacks any acknowledgment of this agency. By failing to mention this agency...I portrayed women's health as conditions to which women and their bodies were defenseless. Thus, I really like that you made me realize that women's health isn't just medicine and science – it's action, and women have the power to act.

Another respondent below both validates and contests the original posting.

I completely agree with your definition of health, it is not just the absence of disease and illness...However I believe that well-being is more than just material and mental things; my opinion of well-being is that it's a goal that we try to strive for. Well-being deals with realms that impact us spiritually, physically and psychologically. V. from the U.S.

The original respondent's counter-reply below demonstrates the kinds of dialogic relationship-building that marked interactions between peers as they included references to their own health and well-being; such exchanges personalized and made relevant the work of virtual knowledge building across the potential barriers of transnational difference. This aspect of their virtual experience was noted by many students as being effective preparation for their subsequent small group collaborations.

Hi V! Am so happy that you are in agreement with me. Did you have a nice weekend? How was it like? Mine was full of fun. I joined friends at the beach. We played volleyball (do you like it?), and fed ourselves to the fullest. You should join me (us) next time. Thanks for your knowledge of the fact that well-being is just more than material, and mental things. Please believe with me the aspects of political, economic and socio-cultural concerns around us. We strive to get employed, and work with well paying companies, which will easily give us the base to set up our own. In this we seek to be economically upright. We also strive to exist in politically sound environments where all institutions that influence well-being of individuals are active without any instability, or even to participate in politics, where it will be possible to influence decision making, to positively represent the vulnerable groups for the betterment of their well-being and ours as well. We also strive to break patriarchal sentiments in our socio-cultural settings in order to pave way for women to enjoy the benefits of the public sphere. All this considered impacts our lives for the better...I wish you the best of today, B!

Virtual peers were not unwilling to ask for clarification and/or to pointedly contest their understandings of health and well-being as the example below illustrates.

> Hello S (from Israel). I do not agree with what you said about health and well-being. I feel like the terms are inter-changeable and identical. Health does describe the general condition of the mind and body, but that refers to a person's well-being! In fact health encompasses well-being. When I think of well-being I think of the "welfare" or *health* of a person and happiness. A person is happy if they are healthy, prosperous, and free! Do you see how easy it is to use the two interchangeably? J. Univ. of Maryland

***

> Thank you for your reply. I still do not agree with you and think that "well-being" is a broader term than health. My friend does not strike me as "unhealthy," although I definitely feel her overall welfare/well-being is severely damaged from her depression. S.

As will be noted from excerpts of essays students wrote at the conclusion of the course, most participants experienced some modification in their original notions of women's health and well-being. Students such as the one above who asserted the inter-changeability of the terms health and well-being were the most likely to re-construct their notions in dialogic engagements with their transnational peers. New understandings were theorized in reflective response to these engagements and the ways in which they highlighted lived experience as well as academic studies. For example, the respondent below highlights the impact of historical events in her geographic location.

> I am a Kenyan lady residing in South Africa with my family and studying at the University of Western Cape, doing a Masters in Advanced Midwifery and Neonatology. I previously worked in intensive care unit and currently working with high care neonates and maternal units. My interest is in gender and reproductive health. My thesis will be based on HIV positive mothers and their neonates...In the past women's health was focused on reproductive health issues such as maternal care and family planning...It did not put into account the fact that this was just a part of the woman and she is encompassed by more than just the need to space children...as a mother and wife. Well-being in my view is encompassed as the core of her functioning, the woman being able to realize that she always should have her "cup full" before she can take care of the rest of the society especially in the African setup where the woman puts herself last and the needs of everyone else before hers...The woman needs to be part of

the decisions and policies made for her. Doesn't always happen in practice for most of the population in Africa that I know of; does it in your populations? Your responses please!!!!!

This posting initiated a vigorous discussion about the impact of societal practices equating and/or reducing women's bodies to their reproductive capacities. The posting below simultaneously validated the journal above in seeing women construct their own well-being as a secondary concern while simultaneously demonstrating how her own culturally informed ideas about women's health conditions in Africa had been challenged.

> I'm a Israeli woman and an expert in psychotherapy with women. It was very interesting to read what you wrote about women in Africa. It seems that they really suffer from oppression and they can't choose about their life?...I strongly agree with you about the idea that a woman must take care of herself in order to take care for all the others. And I'm working with my clients about this point. It's amazing to look at the very common idea that women should take care and nurture the "whole world," as you wrote, without being nurturance [sic] for themselves. It is impossible to do it, and I agree with you that it is not a realistic expectation, and its hurts the women's well-being because they feel that something is wrong with them. I also agree with you about the idea that women "need to be part of the decisions and policies" in order to improve well-being – and as a result from improving the women's well-being, their health will improve.

Another respondent underscores the ways in which political, social, and environmental conditions inform women's abilities to make reproductive choices.

> Am glad to know that I have someone from my country Kenya taking the program with me. Let me take this chance to appreciate what you have been doing and what you are still doing for the good health of women and their well-being...I want to concur with you in your definition of health in relation to women that it entails the physical, mental and the psychological as well as their spiritual soundness. It's true that in the recent past women's health was only looked at from the reproductive side. Such has caused a lot of sufferings and even death to many women due to the neglect of the **social environment in** which women live and its impact in their health...I look at women's social well being as having all the important human values that would help one to be able to attain a good standard of living free from discrimination, coercion, isolation, and all forms of inequalities.

The posting below generated deeply empathetic responses from virtual peers.

> Society is responsible to keep its members healthy. Israel is very developed country in terms of health system. Giving birth to my baby was safe and good...Giving birth to *motherhood* was much more difficult because of the same society, its expectations of women, values, and beliefs that left me very lonely, healthy (thank God) but my being wasn't well. I'm religious and it is very central in my life and I'm a committed feminist, struggling in conflicts between the two identities...I've started a journey to PhD in gender studies, because I hope it will deepen my understanding in both worlds Jewish and feminist. I wish to contribute something to the dialog between the two. Well-being enables good health and vice versa. When my first son was born I was depressed...It took few weeks until I was healthy again, but my well-being was threatened, and it took me three years to really overcome this crisis. I felt I'm losing everything that made my life worth living: my brain, my body, my sexuality, intellectual interests, vitality. I felt angry at myself, my husband and above all- my baby. I was disappointing everyone; this is not what motherhood meant to be.

The dialogue that ensued from the frankness with which this participant described knowledge constructed out of her lived experienced served as the impetus for a final group project that superbly explored the transcultural dimensions of maternal mental well-being.

Engagement with Relevant Literatures

Building upon the new understandings generated through these introductory dialogues, learners next read critical feminist literatures. This was another layer of preparation for their upcoming assignment to conduct a face-to-face interview with a woman informant about health and well-being. All students read an essay about Martha Nussbaum's human capabilities approach, selecting additional readings according to their own research interests. The resulting postings demonstrated that introductory dialogues contributed to many students' abilities to construct more complex and nuanced theoretical frameworks by which to engage the literature. A University of Maryland student found Nussbaum's essay useful in critiquing her national health care options.

> ...Martha Nussbaum's formulation of "capabilities" seemed to me very salient to issues of women's health and well-being. In particular, this can be seen...by considering the crucial differences between rights and capabilities with respect to how women are actually doing. In the United

States, many people do not have adequate access to health care; the state is hesitant even to fund health insurance for the children of working poor through the Children's Health Insurance Program. While health care could be considered a "right," there is a fundamental difference in the state's role in terms of rights and capabilities: a woman here has the right to purchase health insurance for herself, but in reality she can only do so if she can afford it. Other nations such as the United Kingdom, have interpreted health more in terms of capability...In my mind, Nussbaum's "capabilities" framework could provide an excellent way to look at this issue in the United States, because it would mandate working towards conditions that were actually conducive to women's health.

An Israeli student demonstrates an equally widened understanding of health and well-being, highlighting in her excerpt below how differently experienced socio-geographic contexts influence differing perceptions of health and well-being.

In particular, I have a greater understanding of how health and well-being are viewed differently in other countries. In Africa, health and well-being is viewed from a survival standpoint as opposed to the U.S., where women are more concerned with self determination. In general, women's health and well-being is enhanced when their basic human needs are met and only then can they consider striving for internal self-determination, knowledge, and empowerment. Women's health and well-being is generally compromised by relative positions of power and subordination. These social and cultural barriers impede women's opportunities and progress towards self-determination.

These are just two of many compelling illustrations of transnational knowledge building that emerged from the collaborative and negotiated sense-making interactions between virtual peers and in conversation with critical literatures. These meaning-making engagements were facilitated by our scaffolding assignments that allowed learners to tap into prior learning and experience and to build upon it.

Interviews and Final Projects

After reading protocols about qualitative interviews, students posted potential interview questions for peer and facilitators feedback. Participants then conducted a face-to-face interview with a woman of their choice (most of who were mothers, sisters, friends or professional colleagues). Each student posted an edited transcript of his/her interview along with a guided reflection about the experience. As reflected in their final course narratives, the interview was a powerful learning experience for many students. Threaded consistently through their comments is the perspective that previous tasks had prepared them well for the interview.

Having been placed in small-team work groups, students then culled interview transcripts for data to be used as resource material for their final group projects in conjunction with that derived from previous tasks. Working collaboratively in both synchronous and asynchronous modes, with instructor facilitation as needed, students developed a project outline, conducted necessary research, compiled results, wrote reports, and provided peer review to one another. Findings were posted to a class wiki along with introductions to each of the team members, descriptions of the interview informants, and contextual background explaining both the local and global situation for women with respect to their research topic.

Projects explored an aspect of one of several themes identified by Nussbaum as having daily impact on women's health and well-being globally: bodily integrity, mental health, reproductive health and HIV/Aids, and social well-being. Projects concluded with analyses of existing policies with respect to their topic and recommended future policies that if implemented locally or globally would have a positive impact on women's health and well-being. Each project demonstrated both a thorough engagement with existing theoretical frameworks and deepened understandings on the research topic as it connected to women's individual and collective health and well-being. Each project also provided acutely incisive recommendations for policy and practice changes at levels both local and global. Final projects remain archived online but a more complete analysis of their content is regrettably outside the scope of this essay.

Each student presented a portion of his/her project findings at the course videoconference. Following the videoconference, students wrote reflective essays evaluating their project experience and their overall degree of engagement with the entire course. They also provided feedback on the projects produced by the other teams. As chronicled below, student reflections demonstrate that they acquired paradigm-changing insights as they interrogated dimensions of women's health and well-being in an online transnational feminist learning community.

Participant Reflections: Technology Challenges and Constraints

Student narratives reflected frustration with the technological challenges that impacted the virtual learning environment. Two of these were particularly acute: the lack of adequate technology resources for many of the students and the lack of institutional ICT support. These challenges remain problematic, particularly at institutions in the global south. In the summer of 2010, I again co-facilitated this course for students enrolled at two universities in Africa. Despite familiarity with the most up-to-date new media, yet unable to afford such resources on their own, participants were severely hampered by the lack of sufficient technology resources and institutional support at their respective campuses. As was the case in 2010, all participants in the 2007 course had nominal access to comparable tools and technologies. However, many of the students outside of the U.S., and particularly those in the southern context, had to rely exclusively on university computer labs and internet cafes. Externally produced aggravations including governmental budget shortfalls, frequent power interruptions and outages, university labor strikes, and local political unrest often impeded even this access.

These technology exacerbations complicated the already heavy and multi-faceted epistemological challenges that students encounter in learning to communicate and collaborate effectively with peers across diverse geographic and cultural contexts. Similar constraints are noted by other academics implementing e-learning across transcultural contexts (Fung 2004; Jonsson et al. 2001). While many scholars grapple as we did continually with a digital divide that manifests itself in terms of both physical access and epistemological uptake, we noted in our data analysis that many students self-reported their growth in online learning skills to be one of the most satisfying aspects of the course.

Participants simultaneously expressed appreciation for the opportunity made available through technology to participate in a transnational exchange of this type and challenged the variety of institutional limitations that short-changed their ability to fully experience the virtual capacity of the course. While time constraints are always a notable source of frustration for students, the ways in which technological access was unnecessarily curtailed by institutional inadequacies often cost students additional precious time as they sought other avenues of online access. As is evident in the comments reproduced below, students were perhaps most troubled by the ways in which issues of access interfered with their ability to collaborate with peers.

> The use of e-learning is superb despite its challenges but efforts should continue to be made to accommodate those with limited access.

***

I did not enjoy as much to work in the final group assignment because it was very difficult to get hold of my other classmates even though I was using e-mail.

***

The chat room experience was good, although it was difficult to try and coordinate chat times because of time zone differences between all of the participants. I was a bit annoyed with the response time – I kept on getting logged off. As a result, I lost the data and information that I was trying to discuss with my colleagues.

***

There were many challenges; a major one was access to a fast and reliable internet facility. Living in a small city that has only two internet cafes which break down frequently, are overcrowd and sometimes fail to connect to the ISP is highly problematic for this module. This needs stressing to new students from resource-poor countries.

Participant Reflections: Transcultural Collaborations

Students' final narratives reflect not only changed and deepened understandings about women's health and well-being but also their perception that the module's feminist, social-constructivist orientation, as well as its transcultural learning environment provided an efficacious approach by which to engage the topic. Their narratives, as excerpted below, assert that these elements of the virtual classroom facilitated their ability to nourish virtual collaborations, even in challenging circumstances. In many cases learners also self-report that these interactions assisted them to acquire a greater awareness of themselves as *g/local* citizens.

One of the most illuminating experiences was reading the interviews that were conducted in Africa because they used such candor in describing the daily interactions that affect gender issues.

***

I thought it was great to begin with the main topic, which is women's health and well-being, but then go deeper into health and well-being areas that we find more interesting such as the reproductive health, bodily integrity, etc. It was also pleasant to read about all of those topics at the end of the course and be able to extend my knowledge of women's health in other locations as well.

***

One of the most unique aspects of this course was the opportunity to gain an international perspective from our group members. This...integration of viewpoints allowed a comprehensive analysis of the topic in relation to the challenges that women face globally and would not have been possible in any other course format.

***

It was not a textbook version of women's health and well-being, but, focused more on the practicality and reality of how women actually feel. The interviews, for instance, provided an awareness of women's health and well-being that, perhaps a regular classroom setting of learning cannot provide.

***

I really enjoyed that some of the assignments were to give comments regarding our virtual classmates work and that I was also given comments from them. This motivated me and made the work very interesting... furthermore the learning was more enjoyable and I think I got a lot out of the course without even realizing that I was learning so much.

***

I think the way the assignments were thought through made it very easy to learn and to try to be open minded about other points of view regarding the same topics. I liked that we were able to assess and be assessed by our own class members. I really enjoyed doing the interview since it was the first interview that I did in my life using tape recording and doing it formally.

***

Through the thoughtful assessment and feedback in this course, I was able to continually modify the development of my research by incorporating different perspectives and analysis.

***

Hitherto, my notion about women's health and well-being was biomedical and culturally defined, despite encounters with situations of power and gender disparity. The contribution of my colleagues and facilitator and the general content of the course have changed all that. Community participation is now considered the most effective approach to achieving the "health for all" goal particularly in resource poor countries. Unfortunately, women's role in health is limited to compliance with decisions made by the male members of the community. Community participation is meaningless unless women have capability to influence the decision-making machinery in the home, community, and local government.

Conclusions

As demonstrated in the voices of participants narratively inserted throughout this essay, teachers and students alike engaged this challenging virtual collaboration in the anticipation that it would offer rewarding learning interactions and a unique opportunity to interrogate the dimensions of women's health and well-being from a transnational/transcultural perspective. And while we have all benefitted beyond our expectations in acquiring these deepened and transculturally informed perspectives, our collaborations have also made many of us more keenly aware of the wide range of pre-existing structural conditions that inevitably create situational inequalities in any international collaboration. Social, political, economic, and developmental factors have material and virtual consequences for academics as well as their students that we cannot and should not minimize or ignore.

While these pre-existing factors have complicated our collaborations, they have also enhanced the opportunities for both teaching and learning. Many of us experienced, as has been previously reported in the literature, that the social dimensions of our collaborations with others as equally knowledgeable peers across difference have sharpened our virtual encounters (Kamugisha 2007; Tisdell 1998). In our course, this aspect of our collaboration served to foster an increased and deepened awareness that differential access to resources significantly affects women's health. Our collective virtual exploration of women's health and well-being assisted many of us to gain a clearer perspective of women's health needs transnationally and to better understand the complexities of global resource allocation with respect to women's health.

My colleagues and I initially envisioned our collaboration as an opportunity to discover "whether it is possible to successfully provide access and support to implement a web-based course on women and gender across borders given the geographical, cultural, economic, social, and interdisciplinary differences that students would encounter" (Yusuf-Khalil et al. 2007, 54). In sharing the insights drawn from members of our onlinetransnational feminist learning community, this analysis makes a valuable contribution to the "growing literature on collaboration among academics in higher education across borders, and the role of new media technologies in facilitating team teaching and social-constructivist learning as a means of exploring issues of women and gender" (Yusuf-Khalil et al. 2007, 64). As is evident in this analysis, narrative reflections strongly reflect the perception that participants' experience in the course perceptibly enhanced their ability to engage feminist frameworks interrogating and theorizing dimensions of difference (race, class, gender, nationality, etc.).

In reflecting upon our collaboration on the *Women's Health and Well-Being* course, I and my colleagues have concluded that virtual collaborations of this sort have enormous potential to benefit all learners; however, we also caution that they require serious effort and time commitment from all participants. Despite this and the other not inconsiderable obstacles we encountered (including socio-cultural differences, uneven dispersal of institutional and technological knowledge, resources, support, access, and capabilities), I assert that virtual collaborations across borders offer feminist pedagogues substantive possibilities for meaningfully internationalizing their teaching and learning experiences within the expansively interdisciplinary but as yet too infrequently *g/localized* spaces of women's studies. It is my anticipation that feminist pedagogues reflecting on our experiences will be enabled to consider more accurately both the risks and the benefits of seizing opportunities as they spontaneously arise to work collaboratively on projects that will support and expand feminist cyberspaces.

Engaging the perspectives of student participants as they have reflected on the opportunities to collaboratively e-construct new understandings about women's health and well-being transnationally, I recognize that through these transactions I, too, have experienced a transforming awareness of myself as a *g/local* citizen. My dissertation and subsequent work as a feminist pedagogue and women's studies scholar have been re-envisioned as I have participated in the virtual collaborations of this transnational feminist learning community.

Bibliography

Bates, A.W. and Gary Poole. 2003. *Effective Teaching with Technology in Higher-Education*. San Francisco: Jossey-Bass.

Bozalek, Vivienne and Kimberlee Staking. Oct 18, 2008. Cross-Continental Transdisciplinary Conceptions of Women's Health and Well-Being: Growth of Learners in an Online Constructivist Learning Environment. Paper presented at the International Society for the Scholarship of Teaching and Learning, Edmonton, Alberta, Canada.

—. 2009. "'Not a Textbook Version of Women's Health and Well-Being': Enhanced Student Engagement Online." Faculty Working Paper.

Buchanan, Julian, Stephen T. Wilson and Nirmala Gopal. 2008. "A Cross Cultural Virtual Learning Environment for Students to Explore the Issue of Racism: A Case Study involving the UK, USA and SA." *Social Work Education* 27, no. 6: 671-682.

Fung, Yvonne Y. H. 2004. "Collaborative Online Learning: Interaction Patterns and Limiting Factors." *Open Learning: The Journal of Open and Distance Learning* 19, no. 2: 135-149.

Jefferies, Pat. 2003. "ICT in Supporting Collaborative Learning: Pedagogy and Practice." *Learning, Media and Technology* 28, no. 1: 35-48.

Jonsson, Lars-Erik, Sylvi Vigmo, Louise Peterson and Annika Bergviken-Rensfeldt. 2001. "Sharing Thoughts in Computer Mediated Communication." *Journal for Asynchronous Learning* 12, no. 1: 1-11.

Kamugisha, Joseph. 2007. "ICT Education Key to Women Empowerment in Rwanda." *The New Times,* Feb. 15. Accessed Feb. 15, 2008. http://allafrica.com/stories/200702150828.html.

Lave, Jean and Etienne Wenger. 1991. *Situated Learning: Legitimate Peripheral Participation.* Cambridge: Cambridge University Press.

Lewis, Dina and Barbara Allan. 2005. *Virtual Learning Communities: A Guide for Practitioners.* Maidenhead: Open University Press in association with The Society for Research into Higher Education.

Littlefield, Melissa B. and Kendra C. Roberson. 2005. "Computer Technology for the Feminist Classroom." *Affilia* 20, no. 2: 186-202.

McAlpine, Iain. 2002. "Collaborative Learning Online." *Distance Education* 21, no. 1: 66-80.

McShane, Kim. 2004. "Integrating Face-to-Face and Online Teaching: Academics' Role Conception and Teaching Choices." *Teaching in Higher Education* 9, no. 1: 135-149.

Moore, Brenda. 2008. "Using Technology to Promote Communities of Practice (CoP) in Social Work Education." *Social Work Education* 27, no. 6: 592-600.

Nussbaum, Martha. 2000. *Women and Human Development: The Capabilities Approach.* Cambridge: Cambridge University Press.

Öberg, Gunilla. 2009. "Facilitating Interdisciplinary Work: Using Quality Assessment to Create Common Ground." *Higher Education* 57, no. 4: 405-415.

Pritchard, Alan. 2007. *Effective Teaching with Internet Technologies, Pedagogy and Practice.* London: Paul Chapman Publishing.

Rohleder, Poul, Vivienne Bozalek, Ronelle Carolissen, Brenda Leibowitz and Leslie Swartz. 2008. "Students' Evaluations of the Use of E-Learning in a Collaborative Project Between Two South African Universities." *Higher Education* 56, no. 1: 95-107.

Rosenfelt, Deborah. 2005. "International Consortium for Graduate Studies in Women and Gender." *Curriculum Transformation Project*. Accessed July 20, 2010. http://umd.edu.

Staking, Kimberlee. 2008. "Women's Health and Well-Being: An International Teaching Collaboration." *On Campus with Women*. Accessed July 20, 2010. http://www.aacu.org/ocww/volume36_3/fromwhereisit.cfm?section=2.

Subedi, Binaya and Jeong-eun Rhee. 2008. "Negotiating Collaboration Across Differences." *Qualitative Inquiry* 14: 1070-1092.

Tisdell, Elizabeth J. 1998. "Poststructural Feminist Pedagogies: The Possibilities and Limitation of Feminist Emancipatory Adult Learning Theory and Practice." *Adult Education Quarterly* 48, no. 3: 139-56.

United Nations. 2010. "Health Topics." *World Health Organization*. Accessed July 20. http://www.who.int/topics/en/.

Yusuf-Khalil, Yasmeen, Vivienne Bozalek, Kimberlee Staking, Rivka Tuval-Mashiach and Grace Bantebya-Kyomuhendo. 2007. "Reflections on a Collaborative Experience: Using ICT in a Transcultural Women's Health Module." *Agenda- Empowering Women for Gender Equity* 71: 54-65.

Volet, Simone and Marold Wosnitza. 2004. "Social Affordances and Students' Engagement in Cross-International Online Learning: An Exploratory Study." *Journal of Research in International Education* 3, no. 1 (2004): 5-29.

Vygotsky, Lev S. 1978. *Mind and Society*. Cambridge: Harvard University Press.

Wegmann, Susan and Joyce McAuley. 2009. "Going Fully Online: Reflections on Creating an Engaging Environment for Online Learning." *International Society for the Scholarship of Teaching and Learning* 3, no. 1. Accessed July 10, 2010. http://academics.georgiasouthern.edu/ijsotl/v3n1/essays_about_sotl/_WegmannMcCauley/index.htm.

Wenger, Etienne. 2000. "Communities of Practice and Social Learning Systems." *Organisation* 7: 225-246.

"Women's Health and Well-Being: Transcultural Perspectives." 2011. *E-Learning at the University of the Western Cape*. Accessed January 30. http://kewl.uwc.ac.za.

Chapter Twelve

Feminist Web 2.0 Pedagogy: Collaborations that Sustain Difference

Karen Keifer-Boyd

In 2010, for five weeks, I lived at the Human Rights and Peace Center in Kampala, the capital city of Uganda, to launch the Transcultural Dialogue project. I worked face to face with a focus group of faculty and students at Makerere University in Kampala, Uganda and at a distance with art education students at The Pennsylvania State University in piloting the transcultural critical dialogue project. I have received Penn State Institutional Review Board approval and participant consent to write for publication about the Transcultural Dialogue project, their artwork, and their participation.

The focus of this project is to facilitate transcultural dialogues about contemporary visual culture, including art, in U.S. and Ugandan contexts to erode assumptions, ignorance, and misunderstandings about each other's lives, beliefs, and values. The geographical contexts are in themselves sites of assumptions, epistemologies of ignorance, and misunderstandings. The Penn State group of eleven participants was comprised of four undergraduate and five graduate art education students, one doctoral alumnus, and myself, a professor of art education and women's studies. There was one male and ten female participants in the U.S. group. All had lived in the U.S. for many years, and eight for all of their lives, although two were Taiwanese citizens and one a Canadian citizen. The U.S. citizens included two of African descent and six of White European descent.

The twenty-one Ugandan participants assumed that the U.S. participants would all be White and affluent (group meeting, March 11, 2010). Most of the U.S. participants did not know where Uganda was located other than on the African continent. Ugandan students have been socialized with the global reach of television, movies, and other U.S. visual culture mass marketed representations of life in the U.S., and many perceived the U.S. as individualistic, greedy, and violent (Professor Kabiito, pers. comm., April 2009). Penn State undergraduate art education students, who are primarily from rural areas of Pennsylvania, come into the art education program with more than eighteen years of socialization to have anxiety about those who look different from them as evident in their distress in teaching in the urban environments of diverse student populations in the Pittsburgh public schools, which is the site of practicum placements in the Penn State's art education program. Students, who will be K-12 art teachers, need to explore their own lives and contemporary times within the context of a transnational world to diminish fears and stereotypes of people of color. This project aligns with the Penn State Art Education Program's Strategic Plan 2008-2013; Goal II: Prepare students to thrive in a global environment; Strategy 3: Make international experiences a hallmark of every academic unit; and specifically with Section A: Develop a faculty and student exchange program with at least one university located outside of North America and Europe. This goal and specific strategy is based in the art education program's vision that education will contribute to a more just society and world. In the same way, the proposal aligns with Margaret Trowell School of Industrial and Fine Arts (MTSIFA)'s Strategic Plan 2007-2018, which aims to "improve and consolidate the School's pedagogical strategy in view of the changing needs and demands of the art and design profession."

The Ugandan group was comprised of thirteen male and four female graduate students and/or studio art faculty members. The MTSIFA faculty members and I wanted to try the process as a pilot project with the intention to incorporate Transcultural Dialogue in our courses in future semesters, which we did in fall 2010. We expect to continue, each time learning and revising from prior experience. The greatest obstacle has been the unreliability of electricity and weak broadband of under 48K (less than dial-up, phone line connection in the U.S.) in Uganda. Although two of the U.S. participants were in Taiwan, time zone difference was not a problem, as the project was designed to be asynchronistic with deadlines for the different steps translated into the time zones for each group. However, with daily electrical outages of varied duration, and sometimes several days without internet availability for the Ugandan participants and myself while living in Kampala, flexibility with deadlines and extensions of time between stages of the project was expected and respected. I observed patience from my Ugandan colleagues who were relaxed and talkative while waiting for the slow processing between an action of clicking a link and the effect of the action.

The critical action research project discussed in this essay involved collaboratively building an online architecture for participation in transcultural critical dialogue about visual culture. Web architecture concerns the navigation and connectivity of cyberspaces. Participatory architecture in the online environment is the designed functionality of what is referred to as Web 2.0, which is an architecture or structure that enables all who can access a particular website to build and change it. In many cases the website is built by its use. There are varied ways to design participatory architecture. For example, cyberfeminist artists, such as Margaret Lovejoy in *Turns* or Natalie Bookchin in *MetaPets*, program specific websites so that the artwork is created by the responses from the interactivity of viewers. In what follows, I present a theory of feminist Web 2.0 pedagogy from a specific example of its application in the Transcultural Dialogue project.

As critical methodology, the purpose of transcultural dialogue is for "a reflexive discourse constantly in search of an open-ended, subversive, multivoiced, participatory epistemology" (Denzin and Lincoln, 2008). In order to develop a pedagogical process to engage reflexive dialogue, the cultural knowledge and experiences of diverse students is validated in the learning environment (Gay 2000). Instead of a bell curve view of learners, a multifaceted crystal is a more appropriate analogy of the varied strengths and richness that teachers can mine from individual difference. In sharing one's experience and perspectives through dialogic activities and art creation, reflection on experience is given tangible form. Moreover, there is potential for transformative learning and empowerment in the collaborative and reflective process of the Transcultural Dialogue project. Empowerment emerges from a sense of self-worth and opportunities to be heard and to choose (Buskens and Webb 2009). Patricia Cranton's writing on transformative learning defines emancipatory knowledge as self-awareness through critical self-reflection that frees us from constraints of others' representations of us. She believes that "the acquisition of emancipatory knowledge is transformative" (2002, 64). Working with these theoretical understandings of transformative learning and empowerment as curricular goals, I designed the Transcultural Dialogue project to elicit self-awareness from the process of challenging others' representations of how participants in the project see themselves.

How can we enact feminist pedagogy in the online environment? Resistance to feminist pedagogy in the online environment includes expectations by students of teachers to deliver content, i.e., to dispatch a hierarchy of expert knowledge to students. A feminist pedagogue asks students to bring their metaphors, experiences, and ideas to the group as content from which to question assumptions of the neutrality of knowledge. A feminist pedagogical process challenges a hierarchy of knowledge by situating all knowledge claims in histories of knowledge formation.[1] In the Transcultural Dialogue project, the participants in the project are the experts about who they are. The feminist pedagogical architecture as a Web and curricular structure provides the strategies by which participants challenge others' representations of them. The curriculum goal is to shake the tree of expert knowledge and learn from the lived experiences of people situated in different contexts.

Feminist Pedagogy, Transformative Learning Theory [2] and Web 2.0 Participatory Architecture

The goal of feminist pedagogy is transformative learning and empowerment of all people. Feminist pedagogy makes transparent the production of knowledge and how it is transformed in interactions involved in learning and teaching. All forms of pedagogy concern *content and methods* of teaching and learning and, more broadly, the nature of knowledge and learning. A goal of feminist pedagogy is to make explicit the social nature of knowledge and learning in terms of issues of power and privilege. Revealing and critiquing the power of specific discourses, people, and ideas over others – in a given context – is part of the work of feminist pedagogy. In seeking to bring a feminist pedagogy into the online learning environment of the Transcultural Dialogues project, I developed a participatory architecture for the social network that would facilitate critique of beliefs and assumptions, while also rendering personal narratives within larger socio-political issues. Using the term *transcultural* does not imply that the goal is to reach a unified understanding, or that cultures are similar, but rather difference can be *sustained* in dialogue and through collaborative artmaking. In asking the ontological question, *what is real*, the position here is that reality is transformed in the sharing and in the exchanges with others different from oneself. Feminist pedagogy enacted in the Transcultural Dialogue project involved critical self-reflection as transformative emancipatory knowledge.

The participatory online architecture of the Transcultural Dialogue project is situated in transformative learning theory. The body is a point of departure in art creation, making tangible the interdependency of self and the world. Fischer argues "that a feminist-pragmatist understanding of transformation is conducive not only to the project of personal transformation, but also to social and political change more generally" (2010, 67). Embodied and relational art makes privilege visible by reframing and, thereby, transforming what seems normal in our daily lives. Transformative learning involves an activating event that exposes a discrepancy between what a person has assumed to be true and what has been experienced (Cranton 2002). The design, facilitation, strategies, and activities of the participants in the Transcultural Dialogue project, discussed throughout this essay, are outlined below with Cranton's summary of facets of transformative learning theory:

- An activating event that typically exposes a discrepancy between what a person has always assumed to be true and what has just been experienced, heard, or read
- Articulating assumptions, that is, recognizing underlying assumptions that have been uncritically assimilated and are largely unconscious
- Critical self-reflection, that is, questioning and examining assumptions in terms of where they came from, the consequences of holding them, and why they are important
- Being open to alternative viewpoints
- Engaging in discourse, where evidence is weighed, arguments assessed, alternative perspectives explored, and knowledge constructed by consensus
- Revising assumptions and perspectives to make them more open and better justified
- Acting on revisions, behaving, talking, and thinking in a way that is congruent with transformed assumptions or perspectives. (2002, 66)

In what I call Web 2.0 pedagogy – such as the use of Wikipedia for collaborative knowledge construction and blogs for journalistic reporting of first-person eye-witnessing – is the generation and publication of content that can be commented on, disputed, and extended. In this way, knowledge is transformed by the interactions enabled by the participatory architecture of social networking programs with their built-in functions enabling all who have internet access and who have joined particular online communities to tag images that seem to relate to a specific concept; hyperlink definitions, examples, or viewpoints; and collaboratively build references with bookmarked websites to substantiate claims (Alexander 2006). Web 2.0 technologies can be used to facilitate feminist pedagogy through multimodal and multimedia communication among many people at diverse locations and is interactive beyond linking and clicking (Delacruz 2008; O'Reilly 2005). It is a pedagogy of creating and sharing (Buffington 2008). Web 2.0 pedagogy "involves increased learner control and accountability for learning. Learning occurs as a process of recording thoughts and actions, revisiting thoughts and actions, and engaging in dialogue with self and others about their own learning practices" (Sharma 2007, 20). Such learning processes are referred to as *self-organized learning*, in which "the learning process is structured around conversations, specifically termed as learning conversation" (Sharma 2007, 5).

At the heart of Web 2.0 is tagging, which refers to agency in naming, with a signifier, that which is posted or bookmarked on the Internet. These signifiers can then be used to collect all other instances in which that same construct has been used. Feminists have known the value of naming "the problem that has no name," since the consciousness-raising groups of the 1960s in the United States. For positions on the value of naming one's world and concerns, see Betty Friedan's 1963 book, *Feminine Mystique*, which led to critical discussion and consciousness-raising among middle-class White women in the United States in the 1960s and 70s, and see Paulo Freire's *Pedagogy of the Oppressed* (1968), which was important for social change in the conditions of lower-class men in Brazil. Zhang Wei and Chéris Kramarae's (2008) discussion on feminist collaborative work for social change in the digital era of Web 2.0 multilogues also involves naming topics that are taboo within local epistemologies. Tagging in Web 2.0 communication protocols can be considered an extension of this *tagging as naming* strategy in that these are cultural productions rather than "mute 'cultural objects' that invite the postmortem gaze of dissection" (Parameswaran 2008, 416). See Figure 1 for an example of how tags are added by a group to create a vocabulary of significations.

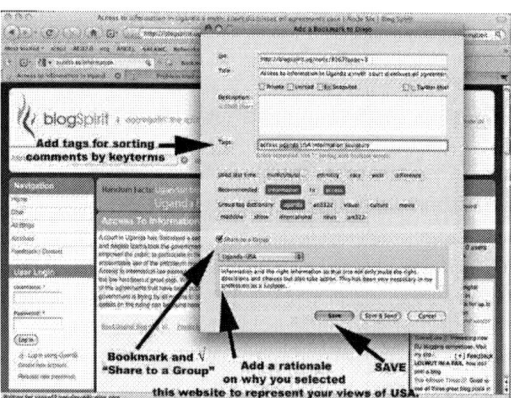

Figure 3: This screen capture of the Diigo interface shows how tagging is integral to building a vocabulary of significant concepts to and by a specific group.

Architectures of participation is a term that Tim O'Reilly created to refer to the "nature of systems that are designed for user contribution" (2005, 1). The notion of architectures of participation challenges the monolithic and hierarchical architecture of institutional formal sites of learning, which are designed in a vertical scaffold offering the explicit goal of reaching the topmost rung of the ladder of knowledge. The activity of many people participating in creating, sharing, responding, hyperlinking, and tagging content on the World Wide Web decentralizes knowledge. Feminist postcolonial practice involves disrupting hegemonic socio-political systems and sustaining difference. Feminist Web 2.0 pedagogy utilizes participatory architecture of social networking tools that enable tagging (naming), hyperlinking (intertextual referencing), and commenting to create counter-narratives.

For the Transcultural Dialogues, I designed a system for participation and collaborative artmaking with Web 2.0 free applications, using the social networking tools Diigo and VoiceThread, as well as e-mail. Diigo is a free internet application that expands the functionality of Web browsers; it enables a group to share bookmarked websites and to post notes or to annotate and highlight text on any website, simulating how one might use a physical highlighting marker on printed text in which each person uses a different color highlighter on the same text. Diigo also provides a forum, for invited members to a group, to initiate new topics. We bookmarked websites with Diigo and saved the Web bookmarks to our Diigo group forum. Diigo enables the layering of virtual post-it or sticky notes on a website, allowing users to comment on each other's entries, much like the comments section of a blog. When closed, the "floating sticky notes" look like a cartoon speech-bubble with a number inside indicating how many people have commented on that particular note. Double-clicking on the speech bubble icon opens a window of comments with the option to add a comment that is visible privately to the poster, or publicly to all those registered with Diigo, or to be seen only by a specified group.

The purpose of the architecture of participation that I designed for the Transcultural Dialogue process is to facilitate a postcolonial feminist critique that maps "the nuances of hegemony and resistance in visual texts that are embedded in larger systems of representation" (Parameswaran 2008, 418). The Ugandan participants selected websites that each saw as representing the visual culture of the United States, while the United States participants selected websites that they believed represented the visual culture of Uganda. We looked at what was bookmarked to represent each group's country, read the rationales for the selected representations, and responded whether, how, and to what extent these representations related to individuals' lives. We used email to send images to each other during the visual art-making stage of the Transcultural Dialogue process. After the artwork was created individually and then synthesized by group members as a single artwork, we published each group's artwork online using the online application VoiceThread. VoiceThread enabled us to display the artwork and to audio-record responses to two questions; the first asks about subjective relationships to the image, and the second encourages the student to think about what knowledge is needed to understand the artwork.

The participants collaborated on the creation of visual art from the content of their dialogue. Nussbaum (2010) makes the case for the arts as crucial to the "health of any democracy internally, and to the creation of a decent world culture capable of constructively addressing the world's most pressing problems" (7). Naples posits that "a reflective dialogic process can offer a context in which conflicts in interpretation are revealed and, more importantly, renegotiated in a more egalitarian fashion than is found in traditional social science methodology or in other approaches to activist research" (2003, 201). A conversational performative text is a form of cultural critique in that more than one perspective in included, often as counterpoints, and readers are invited to participate in the dialogue (Conquergood 1998; Parameswaran 2008).

Two excerpts from the dialogue provide an example of how the dialogue itself functioned to make transparent and to question beliefs and assumptions. The use of terms *Ugandan* and *United States* are oversimplifications of the subjectivity of each participant but is used here to emphasize dialogue about perceptions of two countries by those who had not traveled or lived in the other country and in some cases had not previously had a conversation with anyone from the nation not a resident.

Ugandan participant: I always had two impressions of the USA: My first impression of the USA was a place dogged with violence, shootings, and intolerance towards minorities. ... the other side was an ideal place to live, where by everyone seemed well off ... PARADOX indeed. I have always tore myself between what impression to go by and which one to discard.

United States participant: I too find myself making certain assumptions of places i have never been. For some reason i always seem [to] put the united states above everyone else but i know this is wrong of me to do because i do not have the experiences to do so. ... I hope that some day i will be able to rid my views of other countries and get the chance to travel and experience a different culture.

This content of website selections and commentary generated the content for collaborative artworks in which we planned to use Dabbleboard, a free online program useful for combining digital and non-digital art making process. Dabbleboard permits those with a fast enough internet connection to draw with all others who are at the same webpage. All who click on the link to the drawing area can see and draw in the same space as well as upload images into the drawing space for others to see and even modify. However, the broadband was too weak in Uganda to work in Dabbleboard on a collaborative artwork. Instead we used email attachments to exchange images among groups of approximately three participants from Uganda and a similar number from the United States. This participatory form of visual production has the potential to address the complexities of diverse cultures through the collective enterprise of sustaining difference (Parameswaran 2008). I present an artwork and its surrounding discourse from the March 2010 Transcultural Dialogue project in the next section of this essay as an example of feminist Web 2.0 pedagogy that sustains difference.

The Penn State students uploaded the collaborative artworks into VoiceThread since they had stronger broadband. We discussed the artworks by recording, either directly with the record function of VoiceThread or by speaking into an iPod voice recorder. I transferred the audio files to VoiceThread after I returned to the U.S. where the broadband was strong enough for the record function of VoiceThread to work. While there is an option for text comments, hearing each others' voices enhanced the sensory presence of each member. Difference in dialect and ways of speaking became more apparent than in the written responses to each other.

We specifically responded to these two questions:

- How is subjectivity constructed in the image, and whose subjectivity is constructed?
- What prior knowledge is assumed?

The question on subjectivity concerns looking at oneself in relation to the image and recognizing that a position of subjectivity is constructed in the relational spaces between viewer, image, maker, and context. The feminist epistemological quest is to stimulate difference in interpretations and to situate knowledge within specific contexts from which meanings or significations reside (Haraway 1991). This is demonstrated in the final section of the essay. Next, I contextualize my own agency and critical awareness as situated knowledge in relationship to the Transcultural Dialogue project.

Pedagogies of Postcolonial Feminism: Cultural Identity and Local and Global Injustices

Transcultural dialogues are ways to investigate the semiotic spaces of global and local culture. The Transcultural Dialogue in Diigo topical threads provided a place of learning, a place to lay bare (mis)understandings. The physical and cultural distance between student groups combined with the sense of safety students felt in remaining in their own familiar environment generated dialogue that is more candid and bold than is typical in face-to-face teaching environments of diverse people. For example:

Ugandan Participant: Many Americans, I believe, do have an ignorant approach to the way they perceive Africa. Most Americans feel that Africa is a dark continent, but those who get an opportunity to come to Africa – their lives change for good. They begin to view things differently.

Ugandan Participant: To experience it is crucial. Friends of mine attended a week-long yoga training on inner engineering here in Kampala, and one of the ideas i picked from what they said, was that experience has no equal in one being able to comprehend a situation. However, sharing experiences is very valid and valuable to me, since experience is sometimes unattainable.

The selected quotes above align with a view long held by anthropologists that immersion in an unfamiliar socio-cultural context brings an awareness and often challenges one's beliefs about others. Moreover, what is known as normal practices and ways of knowing the world is decentered, in that normalcy requires a center from which all else is judged.

Reflection on my five weeks of immersion in Ugandan culture at Makerere University and at the homes of some of the participants informs my efforts to make visible the power dynamics of the research, teaching, and narrative accounts selected as examples for this essay. My process of framing this analysis is as an active participant in the Transcultural Dialogues project. In other words, I not only developed the pedagogical architecture using Web 2.0 tools, I contributed to and shaped the dialogue. The experiences I had in Uganda during the first iteration of the Transcultural Dialogue project entered into the online discourse. A glimpse into my situated knowledge at the time supports the view expressed by a Ugandan participant that those who come to African "begin to view things differently." The following is an illustration of an eye-opening experience in the everydayness of my life in Uganda.

* * *

You are welcome. This is the greeting upon entering a home in Uganda. At first, the phrase confused me, as it seemed like a response or answer to something that I thought I had missed. From my cultural perspective and practice, having been raised in the United States, "you are welcome" typically follows "thank you." I point this out because even when we think we know a language thoroughly, we learn that cultural context can alter the meaning of even familiar phrases. While in Uganda, I did not know what was normal or unusual, which is a state of unknowing that initiates the erosion of epistemologies of ignorance. For example, to show respect for the death of two students and for the loss of a cultural heritage site, I wore black for several days. I noticed being stared at more than usual. Having red hair and being the only White person on the Makerere University campus or at the nearby market where I shopped, I stood out as different. By the fourth day after these tragic events, I wore a pink salmon colored suit. I was worried that the bright color might offend during this time of grieving. However, the MTSIFA dean greeted me with the comment that I fit in wearing the brown colors of mourning. Later, I learned that in the native Luganda language that there is no word for pink and that brown is the primary color. The names of colors are the same names as elements in the natural environment.

Keeping in mind my state of unknowing and growing awareness of my ignorance, I share with you my perceptions into Ugandan cultural contexts from my experiences. In visiting a friend's family in southern Uganda, I was clearly marked as White (muzungu), but for the first time in my life my gender was not marked. I was outside the gender constructions and treated as androgynous because as a foreigner I could not be situated within the traditional gender roles in this cultural context. Placing myself in an unfamiliar cultural context challenged my familiar self-knowing. Similarly, conversational learning with those from different cultural contexts, even when it seems all are using the same language (i.e., English), begins to call attention to what is familiar through the difference made apparent. In this way, feminist pedagogy sustains difference.

My gendered experience was completely unlike that of my friend's wife, whose gender role literally forced her to go into hiding. Since cultural customs in southern Uganda necessitated that the father-in-law should not lay eyes on his daughter-in-law, she kept out of his sight. Her daughters and their nanny were free to be seen and heard; however, these privileges were denied the daughter-in-law. This 300-year-old custom was not part of her cultural traditions in northern Uganda.

I asked the father to describe the belief behind this tradition, which he did. The tradition is based on potential lust for a young woman by an elder man who is in a position of power within their relationship. He was talkative and spoke about himself and his role in the community and family. He discussed his beliefs and questioned mine. He ended his response regarding the tradition that the father is never to see or hear his daughter-in-law – stating "traditions change." I asked if he thought change was good. He responded he thought it was. Later, I shared his responses with the daughter-in-law who showed surprise that he said change is good. Her husband said that the elders would not allow his father to change.

My unknowing was further challenged when I visited the Kasubi Tombs four days prior to the arson that burnt this important cultural site. Kasubi Tombs in Kampala, Uganda, is the burial grounds for four previous Kabakas (Kings of Buganda Kingdom). It was designated a World Heritage Site. The royal enclosure at Kasubi Hill was first built in 1881. This tragic event occurred during the Transcultural Dialogue project in March 2010. It was global news. My friends and students emailed me concerned for my safety, and some advised me to leave Uganda. The Transcultural Dialogue project provided a site and way to pay homage to the tragedy by those from afar, who might not have paid attention to this news if it was not for their emphasis in the project on a particular place and time in the lives of participants in Kampala, Uganda. Moreover, the event was discussed in the dialogue, which is an example of situated knowledge.

One Ugandan woman said of its destruction: "The kasubi tombs incident is sad indeed. I guess the whole country has to learn to live with the loss, pick up the pieces and move on." This exemplifies the resiliency among the Ugandan people I observed. The mass grieving, which involved barefoot pilgrimages wearing bark cloth from distant villages to the UNESCO World Heritage site, indicated what a loss it was to many Ugandans. Ugandan participants shared with me their distrust of government and reverence for indigenous culture symbolized by royalty.

During the Transcultural Dialogue project, I wrote in my journal about what I learned, experienced, and observed. I include two entries below to provide a glimpse into the campus climate at Makerere University during the launch of the Transcultural Dialogue project. Uganda project participants ventured to the computer lab on campus to learn how to use Diigo with me as their guide. They were in a state of grieving, proud of their cultural heritage, and resilient to change their future through education and self-representation in global media.

March 12, 2010 journal entry

Today, Richard took me to the Kasubi Tombs, traditionally known as Muzibu-Azaala-Mpanga, which is situated on a hill within Kampala-Uganda. The tombs are a burial place for the previous Kings of Buganda known traditionally as Kabakas.

The first king to build the residence had 84 wives. There are houses for each wife and her children. The roof of the king's residence is thatched every other year. Women are not to go in while it is thatched or the belief is it will leak. However, foreign women can go in without such power to make the roof leak. The thatching stopped while we went in and the thatcher told our woman tour guide to only take five minutes for the inside portion of the tour. Instead, she said she would need to take 20 minutes, as there is much to share. No woman could go into the Royal drum hut. Richard could and did. The drummer, in which the tradition continues, is to be celibate. A woman entering his drum hut might disturb this tradition. Kabaka Kintu, the first king is said not to have died but to have disappeared into a forest at Magonga. So when a king dies they say he has disappeared in a forest. The guide referred to the thatched roof hut, where the tombs were, as the forest.

I learned further that if one who is not of royalty passes a threshold of hay in the residence, the belief is that the person would disappear. I did not dare to pass over it.

March 17, 2010 journal entry

Two students were shot and killed the night before last, and the Kasubi Tombs, a historical cultural religion site, burned last night. There are protests and mourning. I took safe shelter at a studio faculty member's apartment until the tensions eased. Since the two students killed were Faculty of Law students, there was a concern that the protests "no more violence, we want justice" might be infiltrated by outsiders and turn violent in my area of campus. We had gone up the hill for a meeting with the director of gender studies but when we arrived, we noticed parking lots closed and a bonfire in the road. We were told by someone at the entrance to the building that all had left for safety reasons, and things were being locked up. Students were demanding the bodies be brought to the hill for mourning; there were fears that the bonfires and excitement could turn to violence and looting. We went one way and could not pass, then we drove around the smoldering bonfire in the road to another part of campus that was calmer. The police were drawn away from campus as they were dealing with the tragedy of the arson of the Kasubi Tombs.

* * *

My experiences documented in my journal are insular reflections not yet exposed to critical reflection that occurs through dialogue with those who witnessed the same events from different perspectives. Transcultural dialogue challenges the cultural centrism of internal reflections similar to how experiences outside of one's own cultural zones of familiarity make the familiar unfamiliar. The work and words of another help individuals to see something differently in their own life. I select three fragments from the Transcultural Dialogue as example:

U.S. Participant: Thank you so much for sharing your poem. I am very moved and have now been inspired to create my artwork around the visuals your words induce in my being. Here are some lyrics to a song I also wrote in 1992...

***

Uganda Participant: Do the Americans still have a right to privacy?

U.S. Participant: You ask a very good question. It actually has become so rare to find a store or even an area without surveillance that it doesn't seem to bother people. Personally, I don't feel differently if there are security cameras around or not.

These three fragments from two different topical threads initiated by participants are examples of two different forms of exchange. The first is as inspiration through association. The last two excerpts are the more common form of question-and-answer. Both forms stimulate self-reflection.

Critical Reflections for Cultural and Individual Differences Nurtured and Sustained

Cranton's research on transformative learning found that "student autobiographies can be a powerful technique for unearthing assumptions" (2002, 67). The participatory architecture of the Transcultural Dialogues project engaged a feminist pedagogy strategy of politicizing the personal.

The prompt to read the rationales for the selected representations and comment in response regarding whether, how, and to what extent the representation relates to the participants' lives resulted in autobiographical material as dialogue content. A third form of exchange was elicited by the participatory architecture when participants wrote autobiographical stories in response to each other. For example:

Male Ugandan Participant: My mother once told me that my childhood was so unique. Unique in a sense that had she not gone to the hospital may be she and myself would have died in labour because I was so big and worse more with a rectangular head. I actually grew with a nickname of "Wanganga," which is a bird with an unproportional head. My father who actually died at 39 years of age when I was 8 years used to call me a doctor. His reasoning was to console me that each part of my head was a bank of wisdom and knowledge. My speech was also not clear because I could not pronounce the letter "r" and I cannot even now. To him it was a basis of speaking good English, incidentally it would be a shame if he came back because up to now I am not a good English speaker. He wanted me to become a medical doctor. Why? I do not know. I wish he could tell me. After the death of my father that dream was never pursued. Uganda was in turmoil and my mother could not send me in schools that offer sciences because she was not empowered. The other unique part of my life was that I collected so many junk materials and put them under my bed. Whenever I would go grazing cows I would collect many roots, stones of different shapes and trunks of trees that were eaten by termites. To me they looked nice and every time I would see something nice. The most disappointing thing is that many of them I never put them to use and my mother would throw them out and clean under my bed. I would add more or re-enter the ones she threw out. ... When did I start to become an artist? Many of us have similar stories but how often do we reflect on them and see how they have shaped our destiny. ...

Female U.S. Participant: You pose a very difficult question that is very hard to answer. Sometimes I also wonder when I started becoming an artist. I believe that everyone starts young. There may be some people that influence us to do art or maybe we just had that talent in us all along until someone in our life pointed out our skill. I too was kind of supposed to be the scientist in the family, you know, working in hospitals in such, but I just couldn't do it. I couldn't motivate myself to study all the facts. I'm just not that "text book" learner. I think we use art to figure out who we are and what we should do in life. Of course it's a skill and a talent, but also an autobiography or a poem without words. Every artwork has some kind of story or history to it, and I'm sure that your artworks show your interest in fulfilling your father's wishes. Perhaps one way to find out when you started is to look back at your earlier artworks (and your first drawing ever) and see what it's about. Even if it's a portrait of yourself that you did at the age of 3, it may explain how and why you became an artist.

The U.S. participant can relate to not following the dream of a parent for a career. However, an epistemology of ignorance is expressed in the assumption that the Ugandan participant would have access to drawing materials and that there were conditions for preserving drawings from childhood. The architecture of Web 2.0 pedagogy in the Transcultural Dialogue project needed to have participants reflect on the dialogue to see similarities and differences, to see their own lives through the ignorance revealed in relating to another and making the unfamiliar familiar. The creation of artwork from the contents of the dialogue was one approach to facilitate reflection.

From a Lacanian psychoanalytic perspective "discourse operates upon the subject and the subject upon discourse" (Walker 2009, 81). When discourse is the content of collaborative artworks by those generating the discourse, how would they see their subjectivity in the artwork they produced in negotiation with each other in the artmaking process and its signification? From an in-depth look at one of the five collaboratively created artworks from the Transcultural Dialogues and the discourse surrounding it (see Figure 2), I present a multi-voiced interpretation that begins to show how a layered process of reflection is made visible.

I have selected some excerpts from interpretations recorded using VoiceThread available for listening at http://explorations.sva.psu.edu /uganda-usa/critiques.html. Listen to or read the following to discern shared cultural meanings with individual difference and divergences, as well as the importance of considering our subjectivity and assumptions in creating and seeing the world.

Female U.S. Participant 1: I created several images that represent my view on our transcutural dialogue on Diigo. In all of the images, I have a bottle filled with newspaper clipping. This represents the collection of information that we have shared with one another. In one image, the bottle tilts over spilling various curvy lines, which symbolizes our interaction. Surrounding these lines and bottles are jewelry, magazine clippings of a doll, hat, and keys, and a fortune from a fortune cookie that says, "What is hidden in an empty box?" All of these things just seem like random items that don't really fit together. However, we have opened up and created intriguing conversations. Before we started communicating on Diigo, we really didn't know each. We set up a group on Diigo not knowing what the communication would be like. It was as if Diigo was our "empty box" that hid all of this information, facts and our voices (which is the bottle).

Figure 4: Collaborative Transcultural Dialogue Artwork by LaMonique Adom, Karen Keifer-Boyd, Muwonge Kyazze, Kanuge John Bosco, Banaddo Godfrey, Nakisanze Sarah (March 2010)

In another image, I have the bottle facing upward with yet another fortune that says: "Listening well is as essential to all true conversation as talking well." I believe that we have shared so many interesting facts about the news but also about ourselves. We provided feedback to each other and inspired others to think. For instance, M. asked everyone "when do we start?" So many people responded back with their stories of how they started. It's amazing how one question leads to many different answers. And it's just great how we can come together through the Internet and communicate.

Male Ugandan Participant 2: The Marabou Stork is like it is misplaced, or it is possibly representing the type of person who puts these clothes on the line. Possibly that is what is hidden in the empty box.

Male Ugandan Participant 3: So the prior knowledge, that assumption of the one that is going to view this image knows about the dialogue, the transcultural dialogue, what has been taking place in the transcultural dialogue. Also the assumption that the viewer is familiar with the images and the background on which these images are designed.

Female U.S. Participant 4: We are quick to say there is nothing in an empty box but this dialogue. I thought, well, we are having a communication, that's all. But there is so much more to it than that. There are hidden secrets being exposed and emotional responses being shared. We just need to know that things are not what they seem. Instead they can have an impact on you.

Female Ugandan Participant 5: How is subjectivity constructed in this image? Clothesline communication. The "supertaster." Things are not what they seem. Oh what a story. The network. The network of communication. And to me it is quite amazing the relationship. The story told by the hanging clothes. The charcoal stove. Time to eat. The seemingly thread twirly, whirly, drive around like. ... Oh the Marabou Stork. What a menace. Dust to life. It is actually organic. What a challenge it is. How toxic. Natural toxicity, that bad dust. With the rain or dry, whatever, it is just a menace. ... What prior knowledge is assumed for my inner thoughts to be constructed. It is an assumption that one should know about this charcoal stove, the need for me to eat. It is an assumption that this part is widely advertised...It is an assumption that human beings should wear clothes, should have your skin under some new fabric. It is an assumption that you have to get into the box and discover what's there. Venture very far, and you know, keep moving to get what is there. It is an assumption that you can know more – that you can understand.

Female (me) U.S. Participant 6: Wow – a car rim transformed into a stove! I love the addition and the meaning it brings to our group's visualization of transcultural dialogues. I have selected a photograph that I took this week to contribute to our collaborative art regarding the transcultural dialogue. It is of a huge Marabou Stork co-existing with humans on the Makerere University campus. The large birds are everywhere on campus. I am told that few Ugandan artists include the bird in their artwork. I have taken many photos of them and watch their behavior like this one gathering sticks for the huge nests they build at the top of trees. I see the laundry hanging on the clothesline symbolic of the threads of dialogue that have different lengths and depth. I think about the space between the clothes like the silence about some of the topics brought out and not engaged with by the 28 participants in this Transcultural Dialogue project.

Male Ugandan Participant 7: [The rim of the car wheel] is showing that nothing is ever complete. Everything is raw material to another area. This is a complete kind of work to a car-maker but to the person who made the charcoal stove, it is a raw material. The rim is a raw material and is making a charcoal stove, which is very common with us here in Uganda. When the wheel is discarded, people turn it into charcoal stoves. So to me, that is what I get. Nothing in this world is complete. It is a process that is ongoing and it can serve as a raw material.

The Marabou Stork is a bird that is very common here. Very huge. Very big. You would think that it is a chicken, that is big, and something good to eat, but people bypass it. It is believed to be poisonous. Despite the fact that it is a big bird, it is not good when it comes to eating. People even know that. The word "supertaster" fits it very well. It eats anything that it comes across. At times it eats poisonous papers once it suspects there is something to eat there. ... It will try to taste it first before it confirms that it is not good to eat.

The discourse surrounding this one artwork begins to uncover a palimpsest of densely intertextual meanings. What are the particular discourses of gender, nation, race, creed, or class in this image and surrounding critical reflections?

In these interpretations, the Marabou Stork in the artwork became symbolic of perceptions expressed in the dialogue of the United States as a superpower. The analogy is that the U.S. consumes, like the Marabou Stork, and then discards what is not useful. Unintentionally, yet due to the United States' size and appetite, the lack of discernment poisons the earth and relationships with others.

Analyzing the discourse in terms of class, I notice the different ways the car rim stove was interpreted. The U.S. participants did not know how to make a stove from a car rim, nor had they heard of such a practice, nor had they thought of a car rim as an important "raw material." I expressed surprise, while others from the U.S. did not mention the car rim stove, which is an element in the group's collaborative artwork. Much can be learned by what is not attended to in interpretations. The Ugandan participant refers to the car rim as symbolic of ingenuity and resourcefulness of the Ugandan people, who see potential in discarded items. In Uganda, vehicles are often repaired with used parts since industrial manufactured items are not easily available and beyond the economic means of most Ugandans.

The women participants in both countries refer to the clothesline as symbolic of communication and of topics that were absent or avoided in the dialogue. Several mentioned the empty box, but it held different meaning for each. The U.S. participants 1 and 4 thought of emptiness as an opening for communication and that they had agency to fill the emptiness. The Ugandan participant 2 interpreted the box with the surrounding images as an emptiness representing misplaced indigenous knowledge after generations of colonialism.

Seeking to Understand

To conclude, I invite readers to consider the value of Transcultural Dialogue for eliciting micro cultural views that are specific and unique (i.e., they sustain difference) yet also are shared within or part of macro-cultural knowledge. The act of meaning-making from micro-cultural practices sustains as well as changes the macro-cultural. For example, the Marabou Stork is misplaced (like the clothes on the clothesline), a menace with its natural process of creating toxicity, a supertaster, that co-exists.[3] The car rim turned to a charcoal stove symbolizes that nothing is complete; meaning is in *the process* of meaning making. The empty box conveys communication in which nothing is as it appears, yet, we keep trying – assuming that we can understand. Perhaps this last point about the empty box in the image developed in the process of creating the collaborative artwork, as well as in the interpretations of the image, sums up nicely that it is best to acknowledge that we don't understand: the process of seeking to understand is what is meaningful.

Bibliography

Alexander, Bryan. 2006. "Web 2.0: A New Wave of Innovation for Teaching and Learning?" *EDUCAUSE Review* 41, no. 2: 32-44. Print.

Buffington, Melanie. 2008. "What is Web 2.0 and How Can it Further Art Education?" *Art Education* 61, no. 3:36-42.

Buskens, Ineke and Anne Webb, eds. 2009. *African Women and ICTs: Investigating Technology, Gender and Empowerment.* London and New York: Zed Books.

Conquergood, Dwight. 1998. "Beyond the Text: Toward a Performative Cultural Politics." *The Future of Performance Studies,* edited by Sharon Dailey, 25-46. Annandale, VA: National Communication Association.

Cranton, Patricia. 2002. "Teaching for Transformation." *New Directions for Adult and Continuing Education* 93, no. 2:63-71.

Delacruz, Elizabeth M. 2008. "Visual Arts: Technology Pedagogy as Cultural Citizenship." *Ubiquitous Learning,* edited by Bill Cope and Mary Kalantzis, 216-226. Urbana, IL: University of Illinois Press.

Denzin, Norman K. and Lincoln, Yvonne S. 2008. "Introduction: Critical Methodologies and Indigenous Inquiry." *Handbook of Critical and Indigenous Methodologies,* edited by Norman K. Denzin, Yvonne S. Lincoln and Linda Tuhiwai Smith, ix-xii. Thousand Oaks, CA: SAGE.

Fischer, Clara. 2010. "Consciousness and Conscience: Feminism, Pragmatism and the Potential for Radical Change." *Studies in Social Justice* 4, no. 1:67-85. Accessed November 17, 2011. http://ojs.uwindsor.ca/ojs/leddy/index.php/ssj.

Freire, Paulo. 1968. *Pedagogy of the Oppressed.* Translated by Myra Bergman Ramos. New York: Seabury Press.

Friedan, Betty. 1963. *Feminine Mystique.* New York: Norton.

Gay, Geneva. 2000. *Culturally Responsive Teaching: Theory, Research, and Practice.* New York: Teachers College Press.

Haraway, Donna. 1991. *Simians, Cyborgs and Women: The Reinvention of Nature.* New York; Routledge.

Naples, Nancy. A. 2003. *Feminism and Method: Ethnography, Discourse Analysis, and Activist Research.* New York: Routledge.

Nussbaum, Martha C. 2010. *Not for Profit: Why Democracy Needs the Humanities.* Princeton: Princeton University Press.

O'Reilly, Timothy. 2005. "What Is Web 2.0." *O'Reilly Media*, September 30. http://www.oreillynet.com/pub/a/oreilly/tim/news/2005/09/30/what-is-web-20.html.

Parameswaran, Radhika. 2008. "Reading the Visual, Tracking the Global: Postcolonial Feminist Methodology and the Chameleon Codes of Resistance." *Handbook of Critical and Indigenous Methodologies.* Edited by Norman K. Denzin, Yvonne S. Lincoln and Linda Tuhiwai Smith, 407-428. Thousand Oaks, CA: SAGE.

Sharma, Priya. 2007. "Supporting Self-Organized Learning with Personal Web Publishing Technologies and Practices." *Journal of Computing in Higher Education* 18, no. 22: 3-24.

Walker, Sydney. 2009. "Artmaking, Subjectivity, and Signification." *Studies in Art Education* 51, no. 1:77-91.

Zhang Wei and Chéris Kramarae. 2008. "Feminist invitational collaboration in a digital age: Looking over disciplinary and national borders." *Women and Language* 31, no. 2. Accessed November 17, 2011. http://en.wikibooks.org/wiki/Gender,_Communication,_and_Technology/Feminist_Invitational_Collaboration_in_a_Digital_Age:_Looking_over_Disciplinary_and_National_Borders.

Notes

[1] See Donna Haraway's *Simians, Cyborgs and Women: The Reinvention of Nature* (1991), especially Chapter 9, "Situated Knowledges: The Science Question in Feminism and the Privilege of Partial Perspective."

[2] Two useful websites to locate and learn about Web 2.0 tools are Marzano's list at *Web2ThatWorks Wiki!* at

http://www.web2thatworks.com/index.php?title=Web_2.0_Tools and *Go2Web20 Web Applications Index* at http://www.go2web20.net/.

[3] One Ugandan participant bookmarked with a hyperlink to the term "superpower" because that is how he perceives the United States. Another from Uganda comments, "I take this superpower word very lightly ever since i hear a song by *They Might Be Giants* called Supertasters. [Listen to or see

http://www.metrolyrics.com/john-lee-supertaster-lyrics-they-might-be-giants.html]

I cannot take the word seriously anymore. It makes me smile. But on a serious note, I think power is getting fragmented and is shifting to other parts of the world especially economic." I asked about and photographed the Marabou Stork, a huge bird that can fly and builds large nests all over campus. Their droppings are poisonous to humans and burns the skin if one is unfortunately is hit by the bird droppings. It was hard to find shade on campus that was not a danger zone of Marabou Stork droppings.

CHAPTER THIRTEEN

FEMINIST TEACHING IN VIRTUAL WORLDS: DEVELOPMENT OF A PEDAGOGY

SHARON COLLINGWOOD

A virtual world is an online 3D space that can be shared by many participants. Accessed through a browser-like program, these worlds are usually free to enter, although fees are charged for reserving an area for personal or institutional use. Participation in a virtual world is made possible by the "avatar," a digital persona that can be modified according to the user's wishes; users may prefer to appear in a form that approximates their real-life appearance, or they may choose something far-fetched, like an animal, or even an object. Operated through simple keyboard commands, the avatar moves in a persistent online space where virtual models of anything that exists in the actual world can be created, as well as many things that are impossible in real life.

For the past five years, The Department of Women's Gender and Sexuality Studies at The Ohio State University[1] has been developing materials for virtual worlds instruction through our entry-level distance course, WGSS110. To access the virtual classroom, students must first sign up for a free account, choose a username, and download the program, which continues to reside on their computer; when opened, it requests the student username and password, and when these are supplied, students see a 3D representation of themselves, an "avatar" that is controlled through the keyboard. The avatar is situated within a virtual space, where it enables to student to walk around and explore, meet other avatars, join a class, organize a study group, work on a project, or review work posted from previous classes.

Figure 5: A discussion group of avatars can be held in text chat or voice, and this can be supplemented by private instant message to individuals or to the group as a whole.

A virtual educational space can be of any size, depending on the institution's budget. The largest discrete unit of size is the island, an area replicating 65,546 square meters of land surrounded by a glistening ocean. The program provides simple tools for content creation; many educators design virtual spaces that are a reassuring replication of their own campus, building classrooms and discussion areas with access to text-based assignments, posted videos and podcasts, and examples of student work. Others try to stretch the student's imagination through challenging 3D recreations.

Virtual Macbeth, created by Angela Thomas of the University of Tasmania, demonstrates the power of a virtual environment for students of Shakespearean theater. A model of the fortress of Dunsinane, this simulation has been used by students as a backdrop for avatar performances, but it is also an intriguing site to visit. Music and extracts from the play float in the air as you explore, ghosts walk to and fro, and the general atmosphere is one of menace. A video fly-through of the site gives some idea of the experience (Hayes 2008). There are many examples of this approach being used in the sciences as well; *OSU Medicine,* a virtual campus designed by Dr. Douglas Danforth of the School of Obstetrics and Gynecology at Ohio State University, is designed to give a microbe's-eye view of the human reproductive system. Avatars explore this site as part of their coursework, riding round the builds in flying cars to gather information for assignments. A video fly-through of part of this site is posted on YouTube (Danforth 2009). OSU Medicine also has a hospital with "robot" avatars controlled by artificial intelligence programs; students interview robots and are judged on their diagnoses.[2]

Each of the above approaches to the virtual classroom is adapted to the needs of the instructor. A virtual space modeled on an actual campus is very useful in helping students find their way around, especially when they do a great deal of independent work. A provocative build like *Virtual MacBeth* can be useful in encouraging student engagement and spurring their creativity. Immersive experiences like *OSU Medicine* help students visualize difficult concepts, and the innovative roleplay aspects of the virtual hospital add another dimension to learning. Educators in virtual worlds are usually self-taught; not everyone is capable of building complicated sites like these, but most of us can make simple classroom tools, and we are constantly finding new ways to use virtual worlds technology.

Minerva, the virtual classroom for Women's Gender and Sexuality Studies, occupies the middle ground between simple replication of the campus and dramatic content creation. We have a natural space with many plants and trees and few buildings. Our island has discussion areas of a variety of sizes, usually defined by a simple circle of seats. Class discussion and group work are what we do most, with some small attempts at co-creation of content, so what is needed is a calm and relaxing space with room for breakout groups.

The virtual classroom is tied to a course management system (Desire2Learn), where readings and podcasts are posted for each class. The course management system also contains tutorials and other orientation material to help students learn about the virtual classroom before they begin, and a short video introduces them to classroom work (http://bit.ly/minerva_introduction). The system is set up to encourage students to be prepared for class work; for example, students take self-paced automated quizzes on the factual content of readings, and once this first level of understanding has been established, they can then use the virtual classroom to discuss their own interpretation of what they have read, expand on their knowledge through classroom presentations, or begin research in the virtual world itself.

Discussions in the virtual classroom are held in both voice and in text chat. Once the browser-like client is downloaded and the login has been completed, a user's avatar will be seen by all participants in the immediate area and can see and interact with others, much as students do in a traditional classroom space. Like the traditional classroom, this is a collaborative space that enables students to form relationships as they work together. Although at first some students may be disoriented by the cartoonish nature of the avatar, this is soon forgotten in the give-and-take of classroom discussion, and by the end of term, a genuine social environment has been established.

Most activities of the actual classroom can be replicated in the virtual one; most educators are capable of making a simple screen and entering a URL that calls up a lecture or podcast for viewing, but if not, a URL can be pasted into text chat, and everyone can watch in a separate window. In addition to class discussion, students can give presentations, using PowerPoint, Flickr, SlideShare, VoiceThread, or many other free online tools that can either be connected to the virtual classroom or viewed in a separate window. Students can use a screen to study web material together, they can write collaboratively on a Google whiteboard, and they can even decide to work in smaller breakout groups as the need presents itself. However, the virtual classroom also offers a range of possibilities that would be hard to duplicate in an actual classroom.

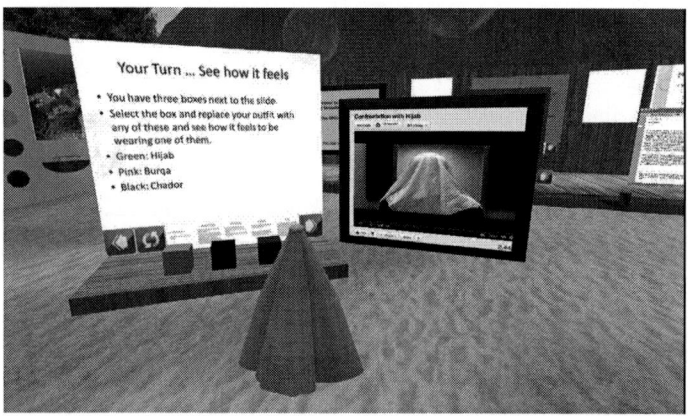

Figure 6: Students can easily upload PowerPoints to structure their in-class presentations. In this example, the avatar wears a gift of clothing provided by the student presenter to underscore points about Western attitudes to Muslim dress.

Distance becomes irrelevant in a virtual world. Field trips to other educational sites are accomplished with a click of a button, classes from opposite sides of the country can meet and exchange ideas, and invited speakers need only have access to a broadband connection to participate with students in real time. The virtual nature of our online course has allowed me to arrange many positive experiences for my students. Some examples of the use of virtual sites for situated learning include a field trip to a midwifery clinic in New Zealand where students could learn about the philosophy of natural childbirth while standing in a reproduction of a birthing room. We have also collaborated on an information-gathering session at the Afghanistan Museum, situated in a high mountain setting where students learned about the many cultures of that country. One class was lucky enough to participate in a real-time project with students at Dubai Women's College, in which students shared experiences of home, work, and family. As the resources of virtual worlds grow, experiences like these are becoming easier to facilitate, increasing opportunities for feminist transnational work.

Distance is only one of the limitations that can be overcome through the virtual classroom. A virtual world is more than software; it is a social environment. Students have the opportunity to meet members of the general public or collaborate with communities of practice. They also have the option of displaying their work in a public 3D space; an "open house" is a common way to conclude a term taught in a virtual world, allowing students to see the effects of their work within a social context. This is not to say that the classroom must always be open; spaces can be locked to ensure privacy, privacy settings can be toggled on or off, and private virtual worlds can also be created on a university server and made accessible only to students.[3]

For online courses like ours, the richest educational resource is a public virtual world, and understanding the revolutionary nature of these immersive and persistent spaces is crucial in the development of a feminist pedagogy of virtual worlds. In the pages that follow I would like to sketch out the most important aspects of these 3D spaces for feminist teaching and research; I am particularly interested in illustrating the ability of these worlds to replicate existing social structures while at the same time offering powerful tools for social critique and personal transformation.

A few elements of virtual worlds are supplied by the platforms that support them (trees and plants, water, clouds and a few basic personal possessions); however, as mentioned above, most objects are created by the users themselves, through building tools included in the software. Residents of virtual worlds can learn to make furniture, clothing, buildings, and many other things in a relatively short time, but it takes practice and skill to make the most prized objects, and in some worlds users sell their creations. At its worst, the virtual economy that results is based on consumerism and a class system that values expertise or the ability to buy it. At its best, this economy encourages a respect for creativity, supports intellectual property rights, and fosters a shared art and cultural space.

The economic structure of virtual worlds provides a framework for the societies that grow within them; societies that are neither a direct replica of the actual world nor an inversion of it. Students soon learn to identify virtual world behaviors that are closely connected to the actual world, particularly those associated with education, business, and social activism, and they can distinguish these from behaviors that reveal a desire to evade, for a certain space of time, the demands of the everyday, as seen in the many roleplay communities found in virtual worlds. However, whether or not the activity is connected to the actual world, the society created by these avatars reveals existing social attitudes and cultural patterns, and students interested in social analysis find a rich body of material to study.

An essential characteristic of a virtual world is the sense of "being there;" although the avatar and its surroundings may look cartoonish, the social exchange that takes place can have a deep psychological reality, and many of the created environments have a strong immersive quality. Virtual worlds are community spaces and, like other social media, use a variety of networking tools to facilitate communication. Avatars can interact through voice and text chat as well as through individual or group instant messaging. The avatar itself is often modified by its owner to express a personal preference or an aspect of personality and gives many social cues, marking a user's identity in a community that relies on reputation. It is considered impolite to ask about the true identity of avatars, and it is acknowledged that a user may have more than one avatar; this is seen as normal in the context of a virtual world. However, reactions to newcomers remain reserved until the avatar builds friendships and is judged trustworthy. The resulting social ethos is characterized by a concern for reputation, a high tolerance for identity play, and an acknowledgement of the multifaceted nature of personality.

Feminists working in virtual worlds communities are particularly interested in the social attitudes ingrained in the computer programs that bring these worlds into existence; these attitudes are exemplified by the avatar and can be useful for study. Participants begin their virtual world experience by using a stock avatar provided for them by the program. These avatars are predominantly young, beautiful, and hypersexualized, and although the user can change their appearance quite easily, because of restrictions of the software, it is difficult to model all kinds of human appearance; for example, the avatar skeletons available through the program do not adapt well to modeling a truly representational full-figured persona. Students can use the avatar to question the role of physical beauty in our society and in virtual worlds; they can fashion unconventional images of beauty and study the reactions of other avatars, or they can ask themselves questions about their own attitudes to beauty and the body, seen in their self-portrayal as an avatar. A less often asked, but equally important question is whether beauty has any value at all when it can be chosen like a pair of shoes; students may then go on to ask whether a different standard of beauty is developing in virtual worlds.

Many other questions of identity and representation are open to student exploration. Race is a serious issue for virtual worlds, which are seen as the preserve of the white middle class. This accusation is in some respects unfair, as virtual world societies are made up of a number of communities, some of which rarely intersect. However, it cannot be denied that up to the present time whiteness is a dominant feature of the virtual worlds experience, and observation of this social fact can be of great use in studying oppression.

Issues of language, culture, age, and other social variables can also be studied in virtual worlds, and although sexism and homophobia are as prevalent there as they are in the actual world, so, too, is social activism and a strong sense of a community bond, seen in annual events like Second Pride, a popular event in Second Life, the most populous of the virtual worlds. Like many charity events in Second Life, Second Pride raises thousands of actual dollars for charity. Another charity event, Relay for Life, is an annual fundraiser for the American Cancer Society; in 2011 the campaign raised US $375,341 in donations, an increase of US $150,000 over the previous year's campaign (American Cancer Society). Feminist efforts in Second Life include the Sixteen Days of Activism Against Gender Violence, a series of lectures, concerts, and art events in November and December, which brings together many different social activist groups. The American Association of University Women[4] Virtual Community Project, housed in my own university's space in Second Life, sponsors monthly social and educational gatherings. Students can easily attend events like these; they can gain valuable knowledge and experience through volunteering and even make contacts with actual world organizations through virtual worlds communities of practice.

The presence of charitable and activist groups in virtual worlds demonstrates the possibilities of modeling actual world problems and situations for study. Paradoxically, however, we also have the opportunity to break away from physical reality in order to become someone radically different from ourselves or to exist in an environment completely at odds with anything we have ever seen before. These two aspects of the virtual world experience are extremely valuable to the classroom, not only for the exploration of self but for understanding others, particularly in the case of disability.

In a world where avatars have a wide variety of choices in representing themselves and where there are few physical restrictions (avatars can fly, "teleport," and breathe underwater), many people with disabilities choose to represent themselves as they appear in the actual world. Avatars operated by those without a disability often fail to understand why anyone would do such a thing, and this presents opportunities for learning and growth. A discussion sponsored by Gimp Girl, an association of women with disabilities in Second Life, indicates some useful approaches to identity and self-representation in virtual worlds disability communities.

Gimp Girl is a very strong and active Second Life group, holding weekly discussions and workshops. In 2008, Rivka Rau (the avatar identity of Dr. Cary Costello, Department of Sociology, University of Wisconsin-Milwaukee) led a workshop on body image with a group of approximately 50 avatars, some present in the group's 3D site and some who were present at the meeting through IRC chat (Costello 2008). In the transcript of this workshop, Rau introduces the terms "realforming" and "dreamforming" to describe different attitudes to self-representation and gives different examples from her own research to support these descriptions. The ensuing discussion shows not only what our students can learn about gender and identity in this new medium but also how the community itself is developing a new ethic of self-representation.

Rau begins the discussion by quoting a previous conversation with an avatar (noted here as "Avatar A"), whose operator deals with autism spectrum disorder. Avatar A replicates her actual self as closely as possible within the virtual world, but she has difficulty with the built-in animations (programs for movement that are coded into avatars):

> Basically I got the avatar to look like me physically in almost all other ways...But then it looked, [without the animation] like me only like I was possessed or something by some other person, I didn't move at all like me, so I created animations to make it feel less like I had this possessed version of me walking around.

By programming her virtual self to exhibit the movements of a person with a disability, Avatar A demonstrates kinship between her actual self and her digital representation; she replicates her disability because she sees it as part of her identity. For Avatar A, "realforming" has a strong psychological dimension; it is important how others perceive her in this social space, and it is important for her to feel connected to the space.

Rau brings another dimension to the discussion by quoting a conversation she has had with another avatar, "Avatar S." Like many people who use wheelchairs in their actual lives, Avatar S uses a virtual wheelchair in Second Life. She explains why the chair is important to her:

> I started my avatar off on her feet, because that is how avatars come in SL. That simply did not feel comfortable, too distant. I needed an avatar I was in touch with, that – indeed – did mirror me because there are aspects of me I want to play with.

Like Avatar A, Avatar S is looking for comfort in the alignment of her physical and virtual bodies. However, she also expresses the idea that although she wants to represent herself authentically in virtual society, she also sees self-replication as an opportunity to view herself from another perspective, perhaps using the avatar to tinker with aspects of her actual identity. This process of visualization is common in virtual world environments, where the avatar can be used as a tool for reflection, for self-understanding, or even for facilitating personal change.

Many theorists have commented on the therapeutic use of virtual worlds.[5] It is not difficult to see how virtual embodiment, as described above, could be used in a women's studies course to promote an experiential understanding of gender and identity. However, there are hurdles to overcome in this kind of teaching; Sherry Turkle (2011) reminds that if the materials of online life can be used to confront the problems of the actual world, they can also be used to enclose us in an endless loop of reenactment, with little possibility for growth (157). A pedagogy of virtual worlds must not only acknowledge this effect, but must also suggest ways of overcoming the psychological limitations inherent in virtual worlds.

There are also some unsettling possibilities for social control in virtual worlds. A recent study at Stanford's virtual reality laboratory showed that subjects on an exercise program exercised much harder, and lost weight faster, when they watched their avatar exercising at the same time; subjects seemed to be encouraged by their avatar's weight loss (Fox and Bailenson, 2009). While this demonstrates positive uses for the avatar, it is also important to reflect on the powerful influence of this new medium. If virtual worlds and related multiplayer online environments like World of Warcraft are to become more central in our society, our students need to understand how they are affected by this new technology, and studies like Rau's are a first step toward such an understanding.

In discussing her efforts at self-portrayal, Avatar S indicates another aspect of identity in virtual worlds. She chafes at the restrictions of 3D self-portrayal but is very aware of the wheelchair as a symbol:

> Could I make my avatar be a paraplegic...No. Not really. The chair
> then...The chair defines [my] identity, and that frustrates me. I am in touch
> with my body in RL [real life] – very much so – and I have a strong...urge
> to have an avatar in SL [Second Life] that shows [my] body logic as I do in
> SL. I do want to show my disability in my avatar, not primarily through a
> chair. Well, that requires a lot of sculpting and a whole toolbox of poses
> and animations. No time for that.

Avatar S. hints at a political motive in self-portrayal that has been widely
discussed in the disability community. Portraying oneself realistically in
virtual worlds may lead to better self-expression and self-understanding,
but it also scores a political point, making the community itself more
visible. This kind of social activism is not unknown in virtual worlds,
particularly in Second Life, where avatars have participated in political
protests and where the semi-derisory term "SLacktivism" indicates the
ambivalence of residents to this activity. While it is true that virtual
activism lacks the force of physically participating in a social movement, it
is, for some people with disabilities, one of the few ways to "stand up and
be counted." If virtual worlds become a mainstream medium for social
exchange, this kind of representation will become increasingly important,
and will offer our students a unique opportunity to participate in virtual
communities of interest.

Rau leads the conversation on to a more problematic discussion of the
intersection of disability and sexual identity, taking up the topic of "Avatar
T," whose operator is described by Rau as "malebodied, white and
physically limited." Avatar T's operator has polysthemia and grand mal
seizures, but this has not prevented him from exploring other identities. He
has a Second Life identity as a graceful, sexually active Japanese woman
and is open about his actual sexual identity.

Avatars can be used to simulate sexual activity in virtual worlds,
although, as Tom Boellstorff (2008) reminds us, it is primarily the words
that count (160). Virtual worlds are only the most recent iteration of
internet culture; given the immersive nature of a 3D space, it is not
surprising that activities seen elsewhere on the web appear there. In
Second Life regions are coded according to the activities that are
permitted; a "mature" area does not admit users who have not identified
themselves with payment information, and inappropriate behavior in areas
that are coded "G" (general) can cause offenders to lose their account. In
addition, managers have the ability to eject visitors who do not conform to
the code of conduct in their region. Still, it is important to inform students
at the beginning of term that, as elsewhere on the Internet, they may come
across sexually-oriented material.

Rau asks the group what they think of the idea that some people would be disgusted at the idea of cross-gender sexual roleplay. Reactions are mixed:

– but why
– nobody else's business.
– yes why
– a different race?
– but if she is sexually active people could have very emotional responses
     to that...
– lol
– lol
– so
– hehe
– grins
– must admit that she finds "raceplay" problematic

The group's reaction reveals a relaxed attitude to avatar sexual activity, one that is fairly widespread in virtual world societies, where gender play is a common activity that may or may not have a sexual nature. Rau responds that, for her, Avatar T is not a man pretending to be a woman for duplicitous sex; "she's a transgendered person who's unlikely to be able to transition in [real life], living as a transgendered woman in [Second Life], able to live the life of which she dreams." Her response to the off-topic remarks on "raceplay" is a somewhat somewhat elliptical reply that Avatar T is "very knowledgeable about Japanese culture, and feels she's learned a lot by exploring racial embodiment here." This comment does not really engage with the implied criticism.

Conversations like the above are very common in virtual worlds societies, as ordinary people try to grasp the nature of this new environment. Rau shows a nuanced understanding of individual explorations of disability and gender and an acceptance of the humanity of gender play, but in this discussion, there is no time to deal additionally with the controversial topic of "race play" and no opportunity to question the use of simplistic stereotypical representations of race and gender. However, the discomfort felt by participants suggests that there is fertile ground for exploration in the feminist classroom, particularly after students have gained a full understanding of virtual embodiment.

The issue of race is complex in virtual worlds. A virtual world is really just a 3D website, a part of the Internet, and attitudes and behaviors seen on the Internet in general are also found there. Some of my students have elected to use avatars of another race and have generally met with favorable experiences, although a minority have been surprised or even shocked at reactions to the racial group they choose to portray. The anonymity of a virtual world makes class discussion of race much more relaxed and open, and one of our most heated topics is the ethics of "wearing someone else's skin." Much work is still to be done on the meaning of race in virtual worlds and on how we can use the portrayal of race appropriately with our students.

Race, gender, and disability are important aspects of virtual embodiment, but many other facets of human experience are open to exploration in virtual worlds. The deeply social nature of an environment produced by avatar interaction fosters replicated communities with great educational potential, particularly for survey courses like my own. I have led "field trips" in virtual worlds to a wide variety of sites that connect to the interests of my students; nursing students were particularly interested in the American Cancer Society's island in Second Life; those interested in African American studies have benefitted from a trip to the Yoruba Light Project, an African exhibit hosted by Cleveland State University and Virtual Harlem, hosted by the University of Central Missouri, as well as from our visit to St Isabella's Isle, a privately-funded site that replicates the Gullah culture of the Georgia Sea Islands (now closed). Virtual Ability Island, a gathering place for people with disabilities, holds much information for students in disability studies and provides links to the virtual world disability community as well. Given the plastic nature of virtual worlds, these sites develop and mutate quickly; they often consolidate with other projects, may even move from one virtual world to another, and sometimes disappear altogether. There is no one group that coordinates cultural and educational sites in virtual worlds, although the Second Life Educators mailing list (SLed) and the Virtual Words Education Roundtable (VWER) are valuable resources for finding sites like these.[6]

In their investigation of gender and identity in virtual worlds, students learn to see the sites we visit as the creations of individuals or groups who have a specific purpose in building them and in making them available to the public. Instead of looking at the topic through a linear book or two-dimensional web page (although both of these are valuable ways to acquire knowledge), students walk in a simulated living landscape, one that not only reflects the personality and consciousness of its creator but also indicates the community of experience from which that landscape was created. For example, a visit to the Texas State University Virtual Field School allows our students to think about the importance of place for a critical understanding of society. Students have the opportunity to critique the visibility of gender in a recreated village that was built to teach geography; they may also think about how the learning process varies from discipline to discipline. However, the brown hills and adobe houses of the village that has been created there shows, in a very visceral way, that the creators of this project have a background and perspective that differs from our own.

The Virtual Native Lands is a site that also owes a great deal to the origins of its creators. Built by aboriginal people, it has exhibits on the economy, history, and traditions of the Native peoples of the Americas. As they wander at will through the site, students experience the natural landscapes and listen to the Native music that is streamed in the background; they develop a reflective, holistic appreciation of what is being presented to them. They can stop and discuss what they have seen or recommend a particular display to a companion through text chat. The program allows them to take pictures and download them free to their hard drive. These pictures are the student's intellectual property and are often used in class assignments, usually accompanied by descriptions that underscore the immersive nature of the experience. This material could be presented through a video, but a video would not have the same immersive effect; students are truly implicated in the scene and record their own presence. Although the Virtual Native Lands, like all virtual worlds sites, is still at a very primitive stage, wandering in these woods already has a strong influence on our students. In the near future, the technology for creating experiences like this will by much more advanced. What landscapes could feminists fashion to make their concerns more understandable and accessible?

My own experience of content creation began in 2006, when I made a classroom display called "Much to Be Done." It consisted of a washline with clothing that flapped in the wind; each article of washing, when clicked, gave printed statistics on women's work and quotes from international sources on the condition of women around the world. I found that creating this display caused me to think very deeply about my subject material. As a scholar, I had no difficulties in finding moving quotes that neatly encapsulated meaning in the fewest possible number of words, but I also had to learn some simple skills of the graphic artist and computer programmer. This had the effect of making my creation much more real to me; worrying about color, scale, format, and ease of use made me think about my work from perspectives to which I had been unaccustomed.

The act of replication also made me concentrate on my topic. Was a lace tablecloth appropriate? What kind of people are represented by the clothing itself? How many diapers should be on the line? This project made me think deeply about the people who would experience my exhibit.

Was my symbolism clear? How would it be received? Nothing is as ephemeral as artwork made of pixels, but this washline was and is very real for me; because of my own investment of time and thought, my reaction to the resulting display had surprising emotional depth and complexity. I believe that this kind of content creation has an important role in the virtual classroom, allowing students a deep connection with their work and with those who will view it. However, because of the nature of my class, the relative inexperience of my students, and the time limitations we face, content creation plays a small role in our class work. Hopefully, when virtual worlds teaching becomes more common and students are more used to the virtual classroom, they will have the time, confidence, and support to create presentations that really push them to look at their subject material from many perspectives.

Students do create projects in my class, but they are very basic, usually a PowerPoint presentation, plus a prefabricated object to attract visitors (a table with tea and cookies is very popular). Student blogs and wikis often form the basis of a collective class project, and these are set out at the end of term, when we usually invite the general public to view our work. In collaborating on these projects, students become aware that they are contributing to the culture of our virtual world, and the feedback they receive from the general public is very important to their learning.

The virtual classroom allows students to be co-present; they see and hear each other, and each can observe the process of the other's work. It also permits collaborative co-construction of projects, and this social aspect of the 3D classroom has tremendous potential for learning. For example, students working on the Triangle Factory fire could easily replicate a courtroom and roleplay the trial of Isaac Harris and Max Blank, the owners of the Triangle Factory; they might even invite students from other universities to be on the jury. An advanced class could build a replica of the factory, complete with displays of the historical documents and a streamed background of songs and oral histories of the fire. Students could write blogs about the fire and have their blog pages mounted within the project; they could collect online references through Twitter or Del.icio.us and archive their contributions at the site; they could hold dramatic recitations and invite the general public or collaborate on a display with students in unrelated disciplines like architecture, music, medicine, or law.

A project of such a scope would cost a great deal of money in the actual world, and it would take an enormous amount of time and effort to coordinate. In a virtual world, many of these problems are greatly reduced. The instructor has control of the virtual classroom, and students can only create objects with permission; access can be revoked at any time, and inappropriate content can be removed quickly. This makes it easier to give students more responsibility by allowing them to coordinate the project themselves. Basic content creation is learned fairly quickly, and communication tools can be set up to facilitate group work. If the institution requires faculty approval for student work that is to be presented to the public, privacy can be ensured during preparation of the project by closing the area to the public; privacy settings can easily be toggled on or off.

Relaxing control over the project not only lightens the instructor's workload, it also makes for a more committed, immersive, and collaborative experience for the student. The cost is negligible, as online blogs and wikis are free, and the virtual classroom can be used for the project. With the students' permission, projects could be archived. All that is really required for such a project would be a well-defined set of objectives and regular support and oversight

The above example gives some ideas of how dispersed individuals and groups could use a virtual environment to focus their efforts. A project like this could be used as in a traditional classroom, particularly one that emphasizes outreach to the community. It could also be used as a complement to a hybrid online/face-to-face class, and it would be of immense value for a synchronous or asynchronous online class.

An early example of the possibilities of distributed learning in the virtual classroom was seen in the fall of 2006, when Charles and Rebecca Nesson and Gene Koos collaborated on a three-tier course for the Harvard Law School. The course, titled *Cyberone: Law in the Court of Public Opinion*, dealt with three different constituencies. Charles Nesson's lectures were delivered to students in a face-to-face class at the Ames Courtroom at Harvard (tier 1). These lectures were recorded and used in an extension course though Harvard (tier 2), and a third component was held in a replica of the Ames Courtroom in Second Life; it was open to the general public and was structured around discussions of the recorded lectures (tier 3). Students from all tiers could meet in the Second Life discussion space to exchange ideas (Nesson, 2011)

My first thoughts on teaching in virtual worlds were formed through participating as a member of the general public in this early attempt at a multilayered hybrid class. I learned a great deal from my participation, and I think the format itself has great potential for feminist teaching. For example, a course could be adapted along these lines to deal with antiviolence issues. There are a number of possible combinations for such a course; students in a traditional or online classroom could have the opportunity to be introduced to communities of practice through virtual meetings with workers from a local shelter. Students at differing levels of expertise could collaborate on different aspects of a problem, even if they were not in the same class. Students whose interests were very narrow could work with like-minded students from another university, or even from another country. Members of activist groups and others interested in the topic could also contribute, and all in a safe space, where identities can be registered while at the same time protecting the identities of those who wished to remain anonymous through avatar usernames. At the same time, the immersive and engaging nature of the virtual classroom would provide a welcoming space for collaboration, encouraging social cohesion and promoting the easy exchange of ideas. This is the kind of teaching that would allow our students to see the interdisciplinary and transformational nature of women's and gender studies.

The possibilities of virtual worlds teaching for feminists have yet to be fully explored; however, there are obstacles. Students are unfamiliar with it, and few institutions offer support services. In my experience, fewer students every year have technical problems or broadband limitations that make the course difficult for them, but this can still be a concern. The software itself is only a little more difficult to learn than some programs they are already using, like Facebook, but for many of them it is radically different from anything they have done before. Some students are drawn to the course because they are excited by the possibilities of a virtual environment, but others are uncomfortable at the idea of learning in a "video game." Overcoming these prejudices takes time; at the beginning of term I typically spend one hour for every four or five students, taking small groups through scheduled orientation sessions. It is a lot of time to spend, but I do this because it is the most gratifying teaching I have ever done.

Unlike my face-to-face classes, in the virtual classroom I am no longer the center of attention; the very nature of the program means I am unable to "shout down" or dominate a class. A successful class in a virtual world does not come from a brilliant lecture, it comes from careful preparation; activities must be varied, materials must be well chosen and interactive, and goals must be clearly stated. Students must be encouraged to take control of their learning, through leading discussions, collaborative writing, or group assessment of information. In this classroom, I am a facilitator and a guide; I believe that because my class is less hierarchical I have a more honest and open relationship with my students.

I often have the experience of "watching myself teach" in my virtual classroom. I observe my avatar as she is busy entering information in the chat window, calling up material for students to view, answering questions in private group chat, facilitating discussions, or leading students on field trips. I see her make mistakes in her teaching, and I learn from those mistakes, but I am far less likely to be upset by them than I would be in an actual classroom. My students report similar reactions; they are more willing to participate in class discussions and are less likely to take offense at what others say. I believe that this is because we are in an environment that allows us to feel safe while we interrogate our own actions as well as the social structure that constrains us. We can see ourselves from a different perspective and think about change.

One of the most important texts in my course is Suzanne Pharr's classic *Homophobia: A Weapon of Sexism*. Students learn to see the intersectional nature of oppression through this text, but what is most important to me about Pharr's article is its positive and hopeful approach. Rather than despair over the inequities in our society or rail against those we feel are responsible for oppression, Pharr encourages us to "vision" a new and better future, as it is through the vision of the possible that we gain the courage to achieve it. Pharr acknowledges that it may not be easy: "It is sometimes difficult to create a vision of a world we have never experienced, but without such a vision, we cannot know clearly what we are working toward in our social change work" (1988, 6).

Virtual worlds may offer us tools for the development of such a vision; they demonstrate a remarkable plasticity in their responsiveness to the human imagination, and they can be safe spaces to create alternate or fictive societies where mutual trust, collaborative effort, and personal creativity can replace old models of competition, hierarchy, and conformity, giving our students an inkling of "what might be." Although virtual worlds pedagogy is now in its infancy, there is a lively and growing virtual worlds educational community, and many opportunities to become involved with this new teaching medium. I hope that more feminist teachers will see the value of this innovative tool and bring their own perspectives on teaching gender and identity to virtual worlds.

Appendix

The following listing of groups and sites was made in the spring of 2011. Sites referred to are all in Second Life, the oldest of the virtual worlds, although at the time of writing, educational projects are rapidly expanding into other worlds. Unlike Second Life, which remains a stand-alone product, these worlds are forging connections with each other ("the metaverse"). Change happens quickly in virtual worlds, and some of the landmarks to Second Life sites may become outdated; a current hyperlinked version of this appendix will be maintained on my website at http://www.elliebrewster.com.

Locations: The locations listed below that are open to the public end with a link to the site. To access these sites you must sign up for a free membership; the Second Life viewer is available here: http://secondlife.com/support.downloads.

Afghanistan Museum

This interactive site is a showpiece museum in Second Life, rich in cultural and historical information about the people of Afghanistan.
http://slurl.com/secondlife/Four%20Bridges%20Exhibit/39/80/70

Connected to the Afghanistan Museum is the exhibit for RAWA, the Revolutionary Army of the Women of Afghanistan. Both sites are maintained by activists, and supported by donations. Students should be cautioned to look at this site critically.
http://slurl.com/secondlife/Four%20Bridges%20Exhibit/64/82/641

Contact in Second Life: Trill Zapatero

American Cancer Society

The ACS has a beautiful island in Second Life, staffed by volunteers who help direct visitors to health resources and in-world survivor support groups.
http://slurl.com/secondlife/American%20Cancer%20Society/128/158/21

Dubai Women's College

In the spring of 2008 my Ohio State class collaborated with Jumana Samara's class at Dubai Women's College. In spite of time zone difficulties, both classes were able to host meetings where students could discuss their differing cultural perspectives in real time. As interest in virtual worlds teaching increases, a network of instructors interested in collaborating on related topics is developing; hopefully this kind of exchange will become more common. Note: Dubai Women's College is a private site.

Minerva

The Department of Women's, Gender and Sexuality Studies at The Ohio State University maintains Minerva, which is open to the public, although teaching areas may sometimes be closed. Student work is showcased in various areas of the island, and the open-air auditorium hosts the events of the American Association of University Women's Virtual Community Project.
In Second Life: http://slurl.com/secondlife/Minerva/11/154/22
Alternate link: http://elliebrewster.com/Minerva

Contact in Second Life: Ellie Brewster (Dr. Sharon Collingwood)

OSU Medicine

This site is used by the Ohio State Department of Obstetrics and Gynecology to train medical students through observation of giant anatomical models, as well as through roleplay with "robot" avatars scripted to play the role of patients. Open to the public. http://slurl.com/secondlife/OSU%20Medicine/214/130/26

Contact in Second Life: drdoug Pennell (Douglas Danforth, OSU)

SLENZ Midwifery Clinic

The Nelson Marlborough Institute of Technology, New Zealand, funded this replication of a working clinic to provide a virtual classroom for the training of midwives. A Creative Commons Attribution-Share Alike copy of the SLENZ Midwifery studies Build is available at the central landing point.
http://slurl.com/secondlife/Kowhai/144/125/32
Video tour of the SLENZ Midwifery build: http://youtu.be/YjzxxIqax_c
On the web: http://slenz.edumuve.ac.nz/

Contact in Second Life: Petal Stransky

St Isabella's Isle

Due to financial constraints, this privately-funded site has recently closed, but exhibits from the site are shown periodically in Second Life.

Contact in Second Life: Indea Vaher

Texas State University Virtual Field School Project

Texas State has modeled the real-life village of El Cerrito, New Mexico, to provide a virtual interdisciplinary experience for their students.
http://slurl.com/secondlife/TXSTATE%20II/213/233/23

On the web: http://id.its.txstate.edu/elcerrito/second_life/projectoverview.html
Contact in Second Life: Phaeris Bueller

Virtual Ability Island

Virtual Ability has one of the best orientation sites in Second Life, designed for people with disabilities. http://slurl.com/secondlife/Virtual%20Ability/170?99/23

Extensive web presence: http://virtualability.org/va_history.aspx

Contact in Second Life: Gentle Heron

Virtual Harlem

Dr. Bryan Carter of the University of Central Missouri founded this site and its sister project, Virtual Montmartre, to showcase the experience of African Americans in the age of the Harlem Renaissance. Students can dance at the Cotton Club or take a streetcar tour of the project. This is a large and intensively built site; visitors should expect to wait a minute or so for all objects to come into focus. http://slurl.com/secondlife/Virtual%20Harlem/178/194/30
Contact in Second Life: Bryan Mnemonic (Dr. Bryan Carter)

Virtual Macbeth

Created by Angela Thomas of the University of Tasmania, this sim is a recreation of Shakespeare's fortress of Dunsinane on a full island in Second Life. The site is open to the public, and there is a great deal to be explored here. Touching some objects allows students to receive notecards with reading questions that help them put the play in context. http://slurl.com/secondlife/Macbeth/47/50/55

Contact in Second Life: Anya Ixchel (Dr. Angela Thomas)

Virtual Native Lands

This group of islands in Second Life showcases the art and culture of Native North Americans. This site is beautifully landscaped, and very informative. http://maps.secondlife.com/secondlife/Virtual%20Native%20Lands/108/123/24
On the web: http://www.virtualnativelands.org

Contact in Second Life: Nany Kayo

Yoruba Light Project

Cleveland State University hosts this faculty/student collaboration on the art and culture of the Yoruba people of Nigeria and the Republic of Benin. http://maps.secondlife.com/secondlife/Africa%20Illuminated/166/101/22

Contact in Second Life: Tamsin Barzane

Groups and Organizartions

AAUW Virtual Community Project

Hosted on Minerva, The Ohio State University's research and study space in Second Life, The American Association of University Women's Community Project presents a series of lectures, readings, workshops, and concerts in Second Life, designed to foster community, activism, personal creativity, and a spirit of inquiry, with the goal of encouraging women and girls to explore new frontiers in technology. Events are posted here:
http://people.cohums.ohio-state.edu/collingwood7/minerva/events.html

Contact in Second Life: Ellie Brewster

Gimp Girl

A support group for women with disabilities in Second Life. Members who are not in Second Life can join meetings through IRC chat; some meetings are limited to women with disabilities, but there are many open ones as well.
On the web: http://www.gimpgirl.com/

Contact in Second Life: JennyLin Arashi

Second Pride

Second Pride is an international LGBT organization in Second Life; their virtual Pride events raise donations in real-world currency.
On the web: http://www.secondpride.com/

Contact in Second Life: Zack Preminger

SLed, The Second Life Educators List

This is a very large and active listserv, the most important resource for educators in Second Life; many active teachers contribute to the list, and questions are answered at all levels of expertise.
Register: http://lists.secondlife.com/cgi-bin/mailman/listinfo/educators

Sixteen Days of Activism Against Gender Violence

The Sixteen Days of Activism against Gender Violence in Second Life parallels the actual event maintained by Rutgers University and features panel discussions, workshops, presentations, art exhibits, poetry readings, and live music. It is fueled by the participation of over a dozen activist SL groups, and many dozens of individuals.

Second Life contact: Ledoof Constantineau, Scylla Rhiadra, or Ellie Brewster

The Virtual Worlds Educators Roundtable

This group is active in many virtual worlds, including Second Life. Regular meetings are held in Second Life, hosted by Bowling Green University.
VWER Facebook page:
http://www.facebook.com/home.php?sk=group_159154226946

Second Life contact: Sorry.AFK

Bibliography

Blascovitch, Jim and Jeremy Bailenson. 2011. *Infinite Reality: Avatars, Eternal Life, New Worlds, and the Dawn of the Virtual Revolution.* New York: William Morrow.

Boellstorff, Tom. 2008. *Coming of Age in Second Life: An Anthropologist Explores the Virtually Human.* Princeton: Princeton University Press.

Costello, Cary (Rivka Rau). 2010. "Avatars, Identity and Expression of Disability." *Gimp Girl Community.* Accessed October 23.
http://www.gimpgirl.com/mod/resource/view.php?id=12.

Danforth, Douglas. 2009. "OSU Medicine in Second Life." *YouTube.* Accessed June 15, 2011.
http://www.youtube.com/watch?v=7y-B2urR8kM.

Fox, Jesse and Jeremy Bailenson. 2009. "Virtual Self-Modeling: The Effect of Vicarious Reinforcement and Identification of Exercise Behaviors." *Media Psychology* 12, no. 1: 1-25.

Hayes, Gary. 2008. "MacBeth Island Flythrough." *YouTube.* Accessed May 22, 2011. http://www.youtube.com/watch?v=cicIpd1Xp3A.

McGonigal, Jane. 2011. *Reality is Broken: Why Games Make Us Better and How They Can Change the World.* New York : Penguin Press.

Nesson, Rebecca. 2006. "The First Class in Second Life." *CyberOne: Law in the Court of Public Opinion.* Accessed 15 January 2011.
http://blogs.law.harvard.edu/cyberone/2006/09/22/the-first-class-in-second-life/.

Pharr, Suzanne. 1988. *Homophobia: A Weapon of Sexism.* Inverness, CA : Chardon Press.

Rau, Rivka. Pseudonym. See Cary G. Costello.

"Relay For Life of Second Life." 2011. *American Cancer Society.* Accessed August 1. http://main.acsevents.org/site/TR?pg=entry&fr_id=34810.

Schroeder, Ralph. 2011. *Being There Together: Social Interaction in Shared Virtual Environments* (Human Technology Interaction Series). Oxford: Oxford University Press.

Turkle, Sherry. 2011. *Alone Together: Why We Expect More from Technology and Less from Each Other.* New York: Basic Books.

"What is OpenSimulator?" *OpenSimulator.* 2011. Accessed April 24. http://opensimulator.org/wiki/Main_Page.

Yee, Nick. 2008. "Maps of Digital Desires: Exploring the Topography of Gender and Play in Online Games." In *Beyond Barbie and Mortal Kombat: New Perspectives on Gender and Gaming, edited by* Yasmin Kafai and Carrie Heeter, 83-96. Cambridge: MIT Press.

Notes

[1] I would like to thank the Ohio Learning Network and the Office of Continuing Education at the Ohio State University for grants that helped me to develop our teaching and research space in Second Life. The Department of Women's, Gender and Sexuality Studies at OSU has been very receptive to my work; I would like to thank in particular Dr. Jill Bystydzienski, Chair of the department, for her sound advice and tireless support.

[2] Groups and locations mentioned here are listed in the Appendix to this chapter.

[3] Second Life is the largest virtual world; it has the largest educational community and is the richest resource for collaboration, but other companies are beginning to provide comparable environments at much lower cost. The software is open source; institutions can mount a study space on their own server at no cost, although there will inevitably be maintenance costs (Open Simulator).

[4] I would like to thank the American Association of University Women for their generosity in supporting the Virtual Women's Community project, which provides an international meeting place to foster the growing women's community in Second Life.

[5] Boellsdorff (2008) is the best general introduction to the possibilities of virtual worlds for social interaction. His chapter on personhood discusses the use of alternate avatars to express discrete aspects of personality. Schroeder (2011) has a final chapter arguing that the strong sense of social presence in virtual environments allows users more control; he predicts increased participation in these spaces.

Nick Yee lists much of his work on social interaction and self-representation on his website: http://www.nickyee.com/cv.html. Blascovich and Bailenson (2010) note the profound psychological changes that can result from experiencing a virtual environment and point out the potential for positive change, as well as the very real dangers of virtuality. Turkle (2011) has an even bleaker view of the isolating nature of virtual environments, while McGonigal (2011) is relentlessly optimistic about the value of virtual play to improve real lives.

[6] See the Appendix for details on groups and sites.

Chapter Fourteen

Layered Literacies and Nuanced Identities: Placing Praxis from MOO Space to Second Life

Radhika Gajjala, Sue Ellen McComas, Franklin Yartey, Anca Birzescu, Heather Sloane and Yahui Zhang

I felt disabled in Second Life both physically and as a person unwilling to risk my imagination....I ended up at a place called Virtual Ability Island....I spent time there working on my avatar and learning how to negotiate Second Life. I struggled with my appearance, my mobility and my communication. When I explored the literature in disability studies there was mention of the idea that all of us experience times of disability. We don't tend to recognize these moments as temporary disability or how these moments can help raise our awareness about those with disabilities. The literature also suggested that it is in these moments of disability that we often learn about ourselves and our community. This feeling of being off kilter is also prized in ethnography. We know that we learn more about a culture if we are put in unfamiliar spaces. The disability community would like to change the image of disability by looking at how disability might be good. It might also be suggested that those with disabilities are better at observing culture and adapting to new environments. In Second Life it seemed to me that the disability community was proving this idea. They were mastering a new culture quickly and utilizing it to their advantage.
—Heather Sloane, Graduate Student in Radhika Gajjala's class online/ offline in 2009

Feeling disabled in Second Life creates a reciprocal shaping of experience and learning for students. This online world empowers an individual with a disability, while the off-line decisions made by this individual in turn shape his/her online identity. Here, as the authors engage in feminist pedagogies online, the "virtual" is hardly "not real." Indeed, routes leading into digitalized global networks require layered and nuanced literacies developed within socio-economic contexts offline. In this paper, we view contextual literacy as an ability to interpret, produce, and consume information within a specific cultural context.

Literacy, or a lack thereof, is dependent upon one's level of experience, knowledge, and familiarity in a particular context. But those who are literate in one context are not necessarily literate in another; thus literacies are always situated and ultimately incomplete. Acquiring new literacies in an unfamiliar culture requires an adaptation of the ways we previously interpreted and disseminated information. Without re-negotiating and revising familiar literacies in a global culture in which changes occur daily, identity and agency are left to rely on social structures of power and hegemony. While technology can extend our communicative possibilities beyond local, regional, and global borders, it also simultaneously produces opportunity for inclusion *and* exclusion. In the margins are those who have adhered to power structures that serve to (dis)empower some at the expense of others as empowerment is ultimately an issue of literacy (Blair, Gajjala, and Tulley 2009). Constraints then are made visible when the ways in which we communicated with confidence in the past must be renegotiated within a new cultural context.

Toward a Critical-Cyber-Feminist Pedagogy

Weaving offline and online cultures can produce networks of resistance against structures that limit knowledge to selected populations. However, the paradox lies in the dependency upon reconciling the new literacy necessary to reach a point of resistance. Until such/necessary literacies are acquired and practiced at the intersection of online and offline spaces, voices are under/mis-represented in accordance with one's techno-cultural (il)literacies. The complexities surrounding communication technologies continue to create contested spaces wherein situated (il)literacies affect incomes and (in)equities. Addressing such inequities at the online/offline interface affords critical feminist pedagogues an opportunity to introduce alternative ways of knowing through "locations of possibility" (hooks 1994, 207) wherein participants engage in self-reflexivity to uncover personal connections within a socio-political economy. Furthermore, as technology becomes more and more absorbed into everyday communication acts, one's opportunities to contribute to a local/global economy are determined by the skills displayed at the interface.

In this article, we examine how literacies and their lack shape experience and learning in global networks and digital place. Particular socio-cultural and technical literacies come to be privileged in digital places and global networks which become potential transitional places (Naficy 2001) that assist in the formation of transnational subjects. These transnational subjects acquire the ability to work within the increasing digital global economy through socio-cultural processes facilitating the further intellectualization of labor. Therefore it is appropriate that our examination of these experiences begin in university class contexts where our challenge is to educate labor-forces for a global work environment. Based on understandings produced in dialogue with various graduate and undergraduate students in classes taught at online/offline intersections by Radhika Gajjala (henceforth RG),[1] we look at identities formed in online environments ranging from Multi-user Object Oriented (MOO) environments[2] to Web 2.0 and three-dimensional social networking environments such as Facebook and Second Life[3].

A critical feminist pedagogic praxis works to open up different ways for examining how we are *placed* and in turn *place* ourselves in a "cyber*space*" while revealing how we are clearly situated in unequal power relations manifested within current "global" spaces through hierarchies of literacies and connectivity. This includes an examination of how identities come into being through local and global everyday practice, culture, and politics. In the interplay of layered literacies and nuanced identities, the user at the interface is forced into re-negotiating his/her technocultural agency within (un)familiar spaces and practices. Thus, seemingly multiple, yet firmly and temporally located and placed, subjectivities can be mapped through signifiers of offline literacies, knowledge, and praxis that are situated in specific wholly offline as well as wholly online socio-cultural, linguistic, and geographic configurations. Drawing on specific examples from class exercises in which principles of feminist pedagogy are emphasized, we complicate some existing arguments concerning (trans)gender, race, ethnicity, and community in cyberspace, particularly those arguments that see the digital divide as a simple lack of material access to computer technology and a lack of relevant technical or linguistic skills.

As critical feminist pedagogues, we encourage students to question presuppositions, to engage in self-reflexivity, and to promote social activism that interrupts systems of oppression based on gender, class, race, sexuality, and age. Critical feminist praxes focus on participatory learning that values personal experience and encourages social awareness through deeper understandings of issues surrounding privilege and power that are embedded in knowledge production and consumption. In addition, feminist classrooms cultivate open-mindedness, critical thinking, and sensitivity to disability, post-colonial criticism, multi-culturalism, and globalization. Such critical learning environments disrupt traditional ways of transferring knowledge from teacher to student in a top-down fashion and, instead, strive to reflect an egalitarian, collective, interactive, and empowering space where acquiring and imparting knowledge is a reciprocal act among facilitators and students as they engage one another dialogically and dialectically.

As we conceptualize networked identities (drawing from Jilliana Enteen's 2009 *Virtual English: Queer Internets and Digital Creolization*) and placed bodies online/offline (drawing from Anada Mitra's 2006 "Towards Finding a Cybernetic Safe Place: Illustrations from People of Indian Origin" as well as from Tom Boellstorf's 2008 *Coming of Age in Second Life: An Anthropologist Explores the Virtually Human*), we do so in an effort to continue the project of problematizing the placing of bodies in fragmented local and global locations found off and online (Enteen 2005). As we describe each of the examples from class settings, we engage the continuum of possibilities along key dialectics of space/place, virtual/real, embodied/disembodied, membered/dismembered and voice/voicelessness to talk about technocultural identity. These identities are produced at various online/offline and global/local intersections through visual performance and discursive self-representation, through dis- and multiply-embodied performativity, and through layered socio-cultural, linguistic and technical literacies, and access. Students from RG's classes engage as amateur ethnographers in various virtual worlds and online social networks. As anthropologist Boellstorff has shown, immersion in the context allows an understanding and familiarity that in turns reveals multiple modes of meaning-making in these contexts.

This interesting partialness of agency and this ability to act as an individual while simultaneously being disciplined by the structure and invisible hierarchies of the network permits the voicing of various thus-far marginalized identities. Further, this leads to the formation of "media-spaces created by diverse global civil society actors to communicate issues of concern to them and to further their aims" (Clifford et al. 2005, 1). An interesting convergence between actor and audience forms in an almost theatrical sense as performances of possibility and resistance are shared openly to promote an exchange of diverse perspectives and experiences that contribute to a deeper understanding of how personal lives are socially constructed through political and historical hegemonic structures (Gajjala forthcoming). At this intersection of placing ourselves in a computer mediated space and performing for networks of friends, current manifestations of online voice and agency emerge as students explore multiple realities within various contexts. Here, implicit knowledge gained through a "play of identities" is realized while adapting to and reflecting on new situations and changes that occur at the online/offline interface (Gee 2007, 55). This in turn helps to further the techno-cultural literacies students need to negotiate future online domains and contexts within an ever-changing labor force that has cultural, economic, and political implications on how the body is placed in society.

Online spaces become learning platforms for critically exploring social issues related to disenfranchisement, identity/gender performances, and inequities as subjectivities are uncovered through an engagement of (im)possibility while negotiating multi-modal-mediated spaces. The placing of the self relationally leads directly to the production of representative avatars[4] that are constructed and narrated technically, textually, and relationally through the encounter of individual affects and online social contexts that connect through multiple senses experienced by the individual. The individual's response is instinctive, yet nuanced and layered, as s/he learns to live and work in yet another global social world. In this manner subjects are *placed* historically, contextually, relationally in online networks, leading to a reconfiguration of identity, labor, and literacies in sync with transnational cultural and capital flows. This simultaneous travel between online and offline identities shifts meanings and requires participants to have different contextual literacies and skills in order to re-place and re-negotiate them. The present article will thus weave through communicative spaces formed through mediascapes (Appadurai 1990) and offline class-based interactions as well as cybernetic spaces that illustrate the materiality of virtual spatial practices.

In what follows we focus our examples on specific instances of re-negotiations in meaning making that arise of discomfort and displacement through encounters at the online/offline interface through classroom exercises. The examples are narrated in the first person by students/co-authors Anca Birzescu (Birzi), Sue McComas (henceforth SM), Heather Sloane (HS), Yahui Zang (YZ), and Franklin Yartey (henceforth FY), who were members of RG's classes.

Points of Entry

I entered Second Life not very sure of what I will be doing; it was for a
class, and I had never heard of this virtual world. My familiarization
process in Second Life at "Orientation Island" did not last long because I
was eager to explore this new world and to create a new identity for
myself. The learning curve for me was very steep; for the first few days I
struggled to move around, my computer kept crashing, and it still crashes
when I am on Second Life.
—Franklin Yartey (FY)

A new interface oftentimes poses challenges for students who are not
familiar with it. The new environment, the new techno literacy required,
and the need to interact with people, though virtually, all contribute to the
uneasiness many users feel when they are first introduced to MOO,
Facebook, or Second Life. Feelings of uneasiness are not uncommon when
entering an unfamiliar environment, and regardless of whether the new
culture is online or offline, actors in that space must negotiate techno-
literacies alongside identity performances. From registration to the
creation of avatars, Second Life guides users through a journey of having a
digital being that participates in meaning-making processes in a virtual
world that has material anchors and material consequences. As Stuart
Boon and Christine Sinclair point out, not everyone will find the
possibility of creating an online being exhilarating. The computer crash,
the dilemma of deciding one's appearance, the perceived "stripping of real
identity" can all lead to a feeling of "disquiet" and anxiety. But this does
not erase the opportunity for learning to occur, as uneasiness and
ambiguity often foster deeper inquiry into critical feminist principles
through a "pedagogy of discomfort" in which students question what and
how they have acquired present knowledge (Boler 1999, 176).

For instance, FY's eagerness to participate in SL created a contested
space between certainty and uncertainty, as it required certain skills and
better computer reception. Both were unlikely in the moment and
uncertain for the future. He writes about his struggles in creating an
identity for himself. It is one thing to place one's self in cyberspace, and it
is another to know how to navigate that space. FY faces an unfamiliar
environment that demands some level of literacy to know what to do and
how to do it. He describes the learning curve as being very steep. Why is
FY experiencing such disengagement with this new environment? Why
does he feel a sense of displacement? In this space FY is forced to re-learn
how to walk, talk, and perform tasks he finds easy to do off-line. Thus,
identity performances and subjectivities brought to the off/online interface

are reflected upon through an ongoing negotiation of these layered literacies.

Narratives of struggle in regards to global online literacy reflect an ongoing revision and renegotiation of prismatic places in *and* out of a computer screen. Mechanical interruptions confounded FY's quest, but the unexpected rupture pointed to how a lack of technical updates, fast machines, powerful video cards, etc. work together to influence participation and thus shape literacy and access. Narratives of struggle in online spaces complicate the notion that computer literacy is linked primarily to accessing machinery, especially when we consider how class, gender, race, age, and location are increasingly impacted by ever changing technical updates.

YZ and SM have similar reactions to the text-based multi-user environment of the MOO. They assert that entering this world is associated with various challenges and frustrations, and although they have gained access to the technology, without the appropriate literacy, struggles become inevitable. According to YZ, our vulnerabilities are manifested in our encounters *with* cyberspace. We get to know more about ourselves, our weaknesses, strengths, and what is unknown to us is made visible through the obstacles we encounter. We are forced to re-negotiate our cultural and technocultural knowledge in these new environments. Knowledge that could be easily applied off-line had to be modified to be applicable in this new environment.

SM, on the other hand, was torn between curiosity and caution back in 2004 when MOO was the environment for exploring the materiality of virtual spatial practices. With only a sparse amount of computer experience, SM's negotiation between admiration and fear of the interface of MOO's text based world produced more anxiety than what she experienced later in SL's visual environment. That we process information in multiple ways impacts how we experience particular online and offline cultures as well as what types of online cultures we enter and reside in. Just like SL and MOO, off-line scripts can be easily adapted online because for some users their off-line scripts still apply online. For example, the scripts one uses when meeting somebody for the first time off-line may be used in these two mediums. The main difference between SL and MOO lies within the graphical user interface. MOO, which is fully text-based, is easier to use in particular ways; for example, not everyone could fully access it because it was mainly used by coders and not very user-friendly. SL and other 3D worlds on the other hand have been framed by the current generation as easy to use; however, interacting in 3D learning cultural environments is not as easy when one first enters such an environment. For example, when SM was required to choose a digitally modeled image in SL to establish her online persona (avatar), her illiteracy regarding how graphics appear on a computer screen initially left her feeling exposed and embarrassed. Even so, through a process of participation, observation, interpretation, and application, SM discovered connections between her experiences in SL and issues of body politics in offline/online cultures:

> My avatar, Audry, entered SL naked and vulnerable, possessing only the items given to her by the program and its master. She struggled to walk in this new space but continued the journey. Other avatars walked past, narrowly avoiding collision, but when I saw others walking through her virtual body, I was reminded of Audry's invisibility.

SM's feeling of "invisibility" and vulnerability when Audry's naked virtual body appeared on the screen[5] reflects SM's layered relationship not only with computer knowledge and skills but also with appropriated literacies wrapped in offline performances that she brought to the learning experience. At the time, SM was a newly divorced woman in her mid 50s entering a college environment after being a homemaker for nearly half her life. Here, she participated in class activities that not only brought her into an unfamiliar culture offline but that also introduced her to an online interface that she describes as "viscerally uncomfortable." Negotiating new techno-literacies revealed to SM how narratives from past patriarchal ideologies in which she was once skilled had (in)formed gendered performances by teaching that "machines were for men not women, and virtuality was either a religious experience or a game for children, not adults."

In addition to her (dis)comfort with the interface, SM felt doubtful that she could acquire the necessary skills to contribute to this networked global society. Encountering new cultural contexts offline and online, while learning new computer literacies, resulted in SM struggling, stumbling, and learning new "way[s] of being" (Markham and Baym 1999, 8) in a space/place of perceived marginalization. SM as subject/object embodied a blur between "real" and "virtual" through converging offline/online narratives that inform situating the self relationally and performatively in a global economy. More specifically, socio-economic structures that frame inclusion and exclusion intersect with location and quality of material access; however, lack of computer experience is not the only factor in causing discomfort and problems of proficiency. Nor is there only one type of discomfort, feeling of inadequacy, and decreased self-efficacy.

From Discomfort to Discovery at the Interface

I was alone in a solid structure wondering where to go to find other digital beings when the sudden appearance of a strong man figure startled my physical self and the digital self. Instead of approaching him and having some meaningful interactions, I chose to back off and quickly located the nearest door.
—Yahui Zang (YZ)

Encountering the unexpected, the frightening, or the unknown in three-dimensional online worlds raises an issue of performing vulnerability inside socio-cultural norms that have been reinforced through offline behaviors. YZ's instinct to flee was provoked by the fear of being a woman "alone" with a "strong man figure" in an empty structure that appeared "solid." This situation signaled discomfort on various levels. Though offline YZ was not placed in physical danger, her connection with her online persona triggered an emotion, a fight or flight response that directed her away from perceived threat.

I met a vampire for the first time on Second Life; she wanted to turn me into a vampire, she wanted me to be a part of her family of vampires, but after finding out what the process entailed, I was uncomfortable. My explorations in Second Life made me realize that my off-line scripts were interfering with my on-line scripts.

FY: can I turn back again?
VL: No
FY: what????????
FY: why?
VL: You would betray the one who made u
FY: so l will be a vampire forever?
VL: Because u work for the family, making it bigger with more vampires

I refuse to change into a vampire…that I cannot separate my off-line identity from my online-identity plays a huge role in switching identities. I have been caught in the intersection of two worlds, being dragged in two directions at the same time and living in two worlds at the same time.

Though we do have agency to decide how to represent and behave ourselves in the virtual spaces, our representations of our digital selves are devoid of any real meaning if our (inter)actions work to reinstate the "heterosexual matrix" (Butler 1990, 45), a grid of gender rules and sexual laws that supports procreative heterosexuality. As Robert Brookey and Kristopher Cannon observe, "Indeed, when it comes to the construction of gender and sexuality in SL, the users exercise a great deal of control. These users, however, represent subjects whose identities have been formed by the way gender and sexuality are disciplined in society" (148). Melissa Altman, a graduate student in Radhika Gajjala's 2004 online/offline class, commented:

> I hadn't started out interested in "computer" technology at all but was interested in the production of subjectivity in relation to existing dialogues of identity. What I found was that the introduction of a new technology, like the introduction of a new category of identity, functions as the introduction of a new interface [that] disrupt[s] the notion of the self resting in a particular place/category/definition.

Students expressed themselves in the virtual spaces by creating their own avatars. They had both a physical and a digital self to explore; they wanted to find out who they were and what they stood for. However, what they found is that their digital expressions and interactions did not "move beyond the gender roles and sexual norms that created the 'self'" (Brookey and Cannon 149). YZ's submissive virtual movement to the nearest door in the presence of a virtual male body, and FY's uneasiness of not being able to turn back into a recognizable and socially acceptable digital being are all moments that illustrate the point that docile virtual bodies perpetuate established norms of gender and sexuality as powerfully as their physical sisters.

Crossing Boundaries

B: you want to go somewhere else ?
FY: like where?
B: japan
B: you need to re rez your self
FY: rez?
FY: more cloths
B: no
FY: ok what
B: hold down ctrl alt r
FY: did that nothing happened
B: your here as just smoke
B: might need to relog
FY: ok will do that. be back
FY: soon
B: k
(FY logs on again)

FY: so...?
B: look behind you
B: the trees are beautiful
FY: beautiful!
FY: it is
FY: lets go for a walk
B: deer
B: do u have lots of trees where you are
FY: quite a few

We see here from FY's conversations with B that Second Life is giving them the agency to cross geographical boundaries within its space as they consider going to Japan to encounter another culture. This encounter epitomizes how residents on Second Life are encouraged by the interface to engage with other cultures either by visiting "places" virtually or by talking with SL residents who physically live elsewhere. B and FY seem to be content with the environment they find themselves in, but because they have so many other options at their disposal, they are consciously or unconsciously compelled to explore these other options, hence thinking about going to Japan. We also see that they refer to their SL location and surroundings as beautiful. Is there some interplay of realities going on here? Are they applying offline standards of beauty to SL or vice versa?

FY and B exemplify the different literacy levels that exist on Second Life as B, who has obviously more experience and has more agency, shows FY how to "rez" himself on the interface. For FY, this may have been a moment that revealed his vulnerability in this virtual world, a moment that showed the unequal power relations of skill and ability that exist off-line and online.

Materiality of Virtual Students

To this point, we have been referring to "real" students – they could be located in the university enrollment records. Though they were asked to become "virtual" for class participation, they still remained locatable in a definite hierarchy of grading and credit required for the completion of a degree at a university.[6] However in the case of learners who wander in and are permitted to stay with us as we mutually learn – the reality of studenthood or teacherhood is less well defined.

In 2007, RG a young lady met (or so the avatar said she was) who told her she was on Second Life because she had heard of the jobs available there and had seen an advertisement in a regional vernacular newspaper in India. She started to type to me in a roman script version an Indian vernacular language – saying she felt more "at home" in Second Life now that she had found someone who understood the same vernacular Indian language as the one she spoke in her everyday offline.

She eventually became a guest member in some of RG's classes. learning through observing some global cultural practices. The skills she acquired from lurking in online environments cannot clearly be coded in the language of resumes and job requirements, but these are immaterial skills that are implicitly required in global environments. Interacting within digital learning environments, she was quick to learn. She commented on class activities and occasionally interacted with class members. Some instant messages she sent RG in her Indian vernacular suggested mild surprise, while others suggested contempt at what "she" saw as privilege that allowed the lack of literacy and the lack of skill on the part of young people from the Western World (at that time she did not understand the diverse nature of people logging on from this Western location).

She had found a job on Second Life that would pay her about the equivalent of a dollar a week. She said she was annoyed at all the male type avatars that kept asking her for sex. However, about two years later when RG met her alternate avatar in Second Life, it was clear, based on the visual transformation of her avatar, that she implicitly understood the role that a gendered and sexed appearance played in the global work environment. Initially she had only wanted to learn more of the technical aspects in Second Life. Along the way she certainly made some interesting discoveries. She encountered versions of "America," "China," "Netherlands," and even "Australia" as she interviewed for jobs in SL. Yet what did she learn, and what evidence do we have that this process of self-globalizing is real?

> Do I believe the "truth" of the story about this young lady I met on Second Life? What are the truths I believe about her and why? Does the fact that she linked to my profile on Orkut where she has several friends from the region she claims to hail from and that they all seem to think she is a young woman mean that she is "real"? What are the common points of shared meaning that allows our relationship to be real and not imaginary as in a dream? What are the common points of dialogue locatable as interactions between the one who learns and the one who teaches. Where are the lines when the classroom merges with the unenrolled digital avatar? (RG)

Without external witnesses, only the people who met and conversed can verify the reality of an event. Thus most learning that comes out of such relational encounters is immaterial. The global subject that eventually merges with a global labor force thus emerges as an individual with individually self-learned skills. The process of creating or producing an identity in the virtual world is dependent on the interaction between online and off-line scripts. (Dis)comfort amongst intersecting identity scripts and online performances reflect a culmination of various (il)literacies at the interface that the authors revise and renegotiate in changing contexts. For example, creating an identity online may depend on our online and off-line values. It may depend on what we deem wrong or right depending on culturally accepted notions or practices off-line or online. So if it is deemed okay to transform into a vampire online, an individual with an off-line script that contradicts this may have issues transforming into a vampire. Along the same lines of thinking, one may feel uncomfortable approaching someone on SL for the first time and start disclosing personal information. This is because that person's off-line scripts (values, interactional rules/guidelines created by society or my culture) may not agree with the online scripts that may suggest that this person should disclose personal information to a total stranger. Therefore the productions of identity online are dependent on the interactions and reciprocity between online and off-line experiences.

Even those who gain the required knowledge for navigation find themselves in a tug of war with their online identity. FY feels trapped in two worlds by the conflation of his two identities. Choices he makes online are dictated by his off-line values, and though he sees this as a disadvantage, there is interrelated shaping going on through these split worlds. SM considers connections between an aging labor force and the representation of middle age in Second Life as she tries to find stores that offer more than copies of stereotypical offline models. HS realizes that in various situations we are all disabled because we depend on past literacies to inform our choices. The authors are simultaneously trapped in worlds that constantly require them to renegotiate their identities. HS, FY, YZ and SM's struggles with navigation, communication, and appearance clearly problematizes the notion put forward by numerous scholars that the digital divide is perpetuated by the lack of access to technology. From the narratives presented, we see that acquiring digital technology tools or entering digital socio-cultural environments does not automatically make one digitally or globally literate, as global digital environments such as MOO and Second Life exist against the background of global commercialization driven by unprecedented and layered technological developments. Nonetheless, teachers and students find themselves unable to avoid participation in a socio-economically global machine that determines their place in a technically driven labor force. We fear being inside – but we also fear being left out – as we see a so-called new world order unfold at online/offline intersections producing global space through offline displacements of bodies, skills, literacies and abandonments. Jodi Dean writes:

> Fear, desire, and perfection are vital characteristics for reproduction of cyberian subjectivities. And these characteristics remain, of course, inflected by gender, race, ethnicity, and sexuality even as they are part of technocultural reconfigurations of gender, race, ethnicity, and sexuality. (42)

Literacy and Pedagogic Value in Global Online Space Finally – What Makes Virtuality "Real?"

Birzi (AB's Second Life Avatar) watches the class encounter Second Life.

We are waiting for the ITS person to unlock the computer lab door so that we can take our seats, turn on the Macs, and thus start the class discussion about their first contact with Second Life in the previous class. While waiting, one of the students voices his confusion and feelings of helplessness in relation to SL: "I've no clue about this stuff or about blogging...I'm just going to fail this class. I will make an appointment with her during her office hours next week." I calmly smile at him and assure him that I've been through the same feeling of confusion at the beginning of my SL journey and that he should not worry: "Things are going to get normal once you get the gist of it."

I'm taking notes while Dr. G. is encouraging the students to share their thoughts about SL, more specifically about what SL stands for in their view. I see some puzzled faces; others putting together the thoughts they are going to express, and finally, the frustrated look of the student I just tried to appease a few minutes ago. The silence is broken when one student compares SL to a computer game. Another student calls this experience "creepy" (to have an avatar that moves around other weird figures), and even more, another thinks of it simply as a waste of time, as if one has "nothing better to do on a workday" and asks, "What is the whole point of this computer game?" I smile, and I see Dr. G. smiling as well... It seems to me that their first impressions are unquestionably anchored in a thinking frame delineated by the real versus virtual (imaginary, non-real) dichotomy.

Nevertheless, as I'm about to see while the exchange of ideas gets more spirited, they are going to find themselves answers to their initial questions about SL...

A student notices you can change your avatar's clothes as you wish, but clothing items do cost real money: "You have to pay in SL for clothes." This statement prompted other questions from others: "What? You use money in SL?" or "What's then the point to be there if you don't have money?" "No way! So this means real money, like you have to use credit cards and all that stuff?"...step by step they start realizing that SL is not as far from their everyday "reality" as they had imagined at first...they see how the social context in SL has similar economic foundation and values.

Another tells us how, while he was having a conversation with a colleague in SL, the SL avatar's boyfriend showed up and cut short their dialogue – "Hey, stop nudging my girlfriend!" – and the guy shot him; this affected the student to a certain degree, he admits... Note that this was the same student that questioned the whole meaning of entering an entirely imaginary world that has no connection to reality.

"How serious can it get in SL?"

And questions start pouring from others ("Can you get married in SL? Is there a SL marriage license valid in RL as well? Can you earn a living in SL? What is the currency in SL? What's the exchange rate?"); it seems like a constant check against everyday "normalcy" which obviously stems from our natural need of dichotomies during cognitive processes. When feelings of frustration or confusion start fading away, when the unknown becomes less "virtually" unsafe, as it happens in everyday commodified life, questions more or less related to the possibility for self gratification are raised.

"Can we make money in SL?" or "Can we own houses in SL?"...at some point a guy – the same student that was feeling helpless about SL at the beginning of the class – asks a question that instantly triggers shocked and offended looks on the faces of female students in the class: " Can we impregnate women in SL?" To calm the atmosphere and at the same time to make students aware of the RL outcomes that SL experiences can have, Dr. G. brings into discussion the gender assumptions in SL, the expectations that a female avatar must have a different experience in comparison to a male avatar when entering SL, and on this occasion introduces to the students Dibbel's "Rape in Cyberspace."

At this point, I believe female students in the class grasp the similarity of gender relations in RL and SL. Next time when they log on SL, some may want to reconsider the identity of their avatars. Questions now take on a slightly different aspect, namely the ways in which economic values and practices operate in SL. I see students voicing informed opinions about how big RL corporations target SL as their prospective market; they talk about Nissan, Mercedes and other companies that sell SL model vehicles and also about real estate firms that can take advantage of the SL boom. The class is about to finish, and quite frankly I do not notice the usual agitation specific to the last minutes of a class (closing backpacks, turning back on cell phones, and so forth); this means that they are captivated by the world of SL...the class ends on an interesting note when a student asks about the ways economists might view SL as a testing ground to try out or even improve RL economic models....I bet they are leaving the class but not their own thoughts and queries emerging at the intersection between RL and SL...

Conclusion

The narratives that appear on these pages come from various times and places, but they still bring their own histories, positions, and nuanced identities. The authors have sought to show that literacy or lack of literacy in various cultures is dependent upon experience, knowledge, and familiarity in a given context. Those who are literate in one situation are not necessarily literate in another setting. During the transitional time of re-negotiating literacies, agency is often minimized and dependent upon social structures of power and hegemony within the new culture. Until new/necessary literacies are acquired and practiced, some women may be caught in a double bind as they reconcile past narratives of patriarchal privilege that have appropriated socio-cultural positions and daily gender roles. Uncovering and addressing the complexities of how suppressive ideologies are produced on the body and the mind requires feminist teachers from various cultural backgrounds to explore relationships between local and global practices that have served to limit certain populations the world over in both online and offline literacies. Immersing students in such offline/online interfaces as we have discussed in this chapter, coincides with feminist epistemologies and pedagogies that encourage critical research and the uncovering of inequities based on class, race, gender, location, age, and economics.

The classroom as a laboratory in which students are encouraged to be self-reflexive, civic minded, socially active, and curious creates a human skills laboratory where theoretical understandings are realized as students' offline interests emerge in new cyberspaces. SM was well aware of the "epistemologies of doing" associated with Dr. G's classes, and though she had been frustrated by her lack of techno-literacy, she still felt that she had experienced deep learning in MOO and hoped to experience it again in SL.

The sun was setting behind me as I shuffled into Hayes Hall and up the stairs to the computer lab. Apprehension reminded me that my neophyte status in regards to computers had not changed much from my LinguaMOO experience in 2004. Yet, it was that very neophyte status in MOO that created uncomfortable learning moments as I observed my "self" performing at the interface. Now here I am again, on a warm evening, June 26, 2007, to (re)cast myself into yet another "real" and "virtual" identity performance in Dr. G's class. This class, Feminist Research Methods, will surely feed my queries about online and offline subjectivities and literacies. I will again narrate and reflect critically on my journey. Let's see where we go...
...we arrived here with multiple voices.

Appendix A

As cyberfeminist pedagogues, we purposefully take our students into "virtual labs," knowing they may feel somewhat apprehensive and initially perplexed by methodologies that support and encourage growth through uncertainty. Students are not equally familiar with computers, and those who engage in online (auto)ethnography, which involves observation/participation, group cooperation, and individual reflection, must negotiate situated literacies inside "virtual/real" spaces. Virtual spaces offer students an ongoing process of negotiating socio-political issues of communication, mobility, and cultural capital, all of which influence their opportunities, or lack thereof, within a given space. Second Life is a virtual world that simulates offline "real" life in many ways. There are a variety of topics to explore in SL, and inquiries surface from the users' online and offline experiences and narratives. The "real" and the "virtual" blend together into learning moments by bridging virtual and real affects of uncertainty, power, and positionality that surround situated literacies online *and* offline. The following transcripts of some of Dr. Gajjala's undergraduate and graduate courses from 2007 and 2008 illustrate shared "epistemologies of doing" in virtual worlds. Dr. Gajjala's syllabus, available online, also demonstrates students' critical examination of oppressive social structures in local and global contexts. But there was more...

Sitting at neatly lined computer desks in room 107, we perused the syllabus. Dr. G smiled, welcomed everyone, and proceeded to explain class objectives and requirements. Eyes peered above rows of computer screens. Some were familiar; others were not. We were connected... awaiting our boarding passes. This is where we will meet each week, where we will privately and publically perform inquiries at the intersection of virtual and real worlds.

Graduate course overview: "This course will examine theoretical and methodological issues and engage epistemological and ontological concerns at the intersection of feminist theory, methods, and communication."

I better buckle up.

Semester long activity: Working with Second Life and/or with a local community near campus, students engaged ethnographic research methods. They recorded their experiences in offline and online contexts, paying attention to themes and intersections that questioned the situatedness of certain terms in everyday life. "Expect to do a lot of thinking, reading, writing – articulating."

Weekly: Each week we read one book alongside articles written by feminist scholar-authors. Readings provided additional material for discussing various research methods and concerns in relation to globalization and identities. The first portion of class was devoted to unpacking readings from feminist perspectives and the second to entering SL. These discussions and questions were preludes to entering our computer mediated virtual worlds.

The writing component of the class emphasized to students the importance of thinking critically in order to analyze, apply, and articulate their knowledge in written form. More specifically, each week after students read assigned books and articles such as Elizabeth Potter's *Feminism of Philosophy of Science: An Introduction* (2006), John Sloop's *Disciplining Gender: Rhetorics of Sex Identity in Contemporary U.S. Culture* (2004), Judith Butler's *Bodies that Matter* (1993), and Gyatri Reddy's *With Respect to Sex: Negotiating Hijra Identity in South India* (2005), they participated in computer-mediated discussions that contributed greatly to classroom (offline and online) interactions.

Online discussions: Each week all students were responsible for contributing at least one initial post and three thoughtfully written responses to questions posed by the teacher or by other class members.

Journal entries: At the end of each class period, we recorded any thoughts and/or questions that related to issues raised in class, and we submitted them before we left the room.

Biweekly papers: Engaging course content and weekly readings, students developed deeper analytic skills while becoming more adept at articulating how theories and methods work in tandem and then connecting feminist methods to our ethnographic experiences.

Class reading presentations: Each student presented two or three chapters and/or articles at different times during the semester. Handouts for fellow students encouraged the writer and the reader to focus on central questions, important issues, key concepts, and cross-disciplinary connections.

Individual project: Submit a well-developed research proposal at the end of the semester. A few topics that students explored in Dr. Gajjala's classes included Chinese mothers and blogs; technology and aging/gendered bodies; global and local consumption and production of technologies; virtual identity; narratives and techno-literacies; and a variety of issues that examined how local and global computer mediated cultures produce subjectivities that intersect and influence agency, (il)literacy, and positionality online and offline.

But graduate students weren't the only ones who benefited from this type of instruction.

Undergraduate Course Description: "This course examines how digital media shape and structure interpersonal and intercultural communication. Drawing on theories of interpersonal communication, performance studies, cultural studies, race and gender theories, this course exposes students to a variety of digitally mediated socio-cultural spaces and engages them in an in-depth critique and understanding of such communication contexts. Students will therefore examine the performance of identity in digital mediated socio-cultural spaces in relation to race, gender, class, sexuality and geographic location through theories of gender, culture, performance and interpersonal communication through a hands-on engagement with digitally mediated environments. We will examine three dimensional virtual worlds such as Second Life as well as some social network sites."

Goals and objectives: "After completing this course students should be able to understand and articulate: a)main theoretical concepts regarding identities in technospaces and digitally mediated cultures; b)theories of gender, race, sexuality, communication and culture in the context of the production of race, gender, sexuality, geography and class in digitally mediated spaces; c)the power-structures shaping the access to and use of such digitally mediated communicative spaces; d)how to navigate multiple kinds of digitally mediated spaces; e)students should have learned to deliver assignments in a variety of digitally mediated formats."

Semester Projects

Group Project I: For the first 5 weeks of the semester, students carried out general Second Life ethnographies, wrote analysis papers based on their virtual ethnography experiences, and continued blogging of experience via the university blogging space, and sharing of images and videos based in Second Life ethnographies via Flickr and YouTube.

Group Project II: Until last week of classes, each group of students chose and carried out a separate business project in Second Life. Each group wrote a research paper based on research done in group work and had at least one graduate student leader for their group directing their project. The first group designed a clothing store in Second Life; the second group created an art and furniture store; the third chose to open a speed dating business; and the fourth decided to start a swim up bar business. Through experimenting with Second Life building tools and devices and thus creating objects and being exposed to Second Life social rules, students acquired further technological literacies. The "epistemologies of doing" learning model helped students gain an in-depth understanding of how digital media production, use, and consumption shape everyday life practices, identities, and cultures.

Weekly feedback for Group Project II:

Group clothing store project – Dr. Gajjala frequently gave weekly feedback to students to encourage further exploration. "You are on a roll – building both store and clothes. Great self-motivated inquiry into learning how to make what you need for your business. Excellent research skills so far in finding tutorials – websites etc,. easily available if you spend the time – and working on learning the skills needed. Keep up the good work!"

Emphasizing global/local and on/offline marketing, ethics, and practices, Dr. Gajjala reminded the art and furniture group that "on Wednesday one of your group members learned preliminary basics of making and putting an art object out for sale. Her object is sitting in rad Zabibha's store set for sale for 10 Linden dollars. However it is not selling at all. This means you need to create art...that will sell.. and research the rules on copyright etc – you cannot steal art from websites or you will get into trouble and besides no one will buy anything from your store – bad press."

When students were slow to start, as was the case with the speed dating group, Dr. Gajjala directed members to organize tasks and to consider how networking skills impact a group's credibility within a particular culture. "I don't know where you all are with your planning. I arranged for a friend of mine to rent a stall for you at the 'Taste of India' location. I am going to try to get you membership to the group that will allow you to place objects there. Meanwhile you need to be planning and building and saving to your inventories. Please submit a report on your progress. The cost of renting the location is about 300 Lindens a week. If you do not start your work soon – CC Jewell will be wasting money by leaving it empty for you to use and may decide not to let you use it after all. So it is important that you report your progress and show me what you have learned on Wednesday and Friday in Lab classes so I can reassure CC that you are all working towards use of that space. Hopefully by Wednesday or Friday rad Zabibha can help you set stuff up there – since she has membership in the group."

The group building a swim-up bar business was recognized for their enthusiasm. "Exciting ideas so far. It seems like a lot of freebie shopping going on. Cyb Tabla has given you permission to build on her location. I hope to see work started."

Bibliography

Appadurai, Ajun. 1990. "Disjuncture and Difference in the Global Cultural Economy." *Public Culture* 2: 1-24.

Blair, Kristine, Radhika Gajjala and Christine Tulley. 2009. Introduction to *Webbing Cyberfeminist Practice: Communities, Pedagogies and Social Action*, edited by Kristine Blair, Radhika Gajjala and Christine Tulley, 1-19. New Jersey: Hampton Press.

Boellstorff, Tom. 2008. *Coming of Age in Second Life: An Anthropologist Explores the Virtually Human*. Princeton, NJ: Princeton University Press.

Boler, Megan. 1999. *Feeling Power: Emotions and Education*. New York, NY: Routledge.

Brookey, Robert Alan and Kristopher Cannon. 2009. "Sex Lives in Second Life." *Critical Studies in Media Communication* 2: 145-164.

Butler, Judith. 1990. *Gender Trouble: Feminism and the Subversion of Identity*. New York: Routledge.

Clifford, Bob. 2005. *The Marketing of Rebellion: Insurgents, Media, and International Activism*. New York, NY: Cambridge University Press.

Dean, Jodi. 2001. "Feminism in Technoculture." *The Review of Education/Pedagogy/Cultural Studies* 23: 23-47.

Dibbell, Julian. 1998. *My Tiny Life: Crime and Passion in a Virtual World*. New York: Henry Holt.

Enteen, Jillana. 2006. "Spatial Conceptions of URLs: Tamil Eelam Networks on the World Wide Web." *New Media & Society* 8, no. 2: 229-249.

—. 2009. *Virtual English: Queer Internets and Digital Creolization*. New York, NY: Routledge.

Gajjala, Radhika. Forthcoming. "Placing South Asian Digital Diasporas in Second Life." In *Blackwell Reader on Critical Intercultural Studies*, edited by Rona Halualini and Tom Nakayama.

Gajjala, Radhika, Natalia Rybas and Yahui Zhang. 2010. "Producing Digitally Mediated Environments as Sites for Critical Feminist Pedagogy." *The SAGE Handbook of Communication and Instruction*, edited by Deanna Fassett and John Warren. USA: Sage Publications.

Gee, Paul, J. 2007. *What Video Games Have to Teach Us about Learning and Literacy*. New York, NY: Palgrave MacMillan.

hooks, bell. 1994. *Teaching to Trangress*. New York: Routledge.

Markham, Annette, N. and Nancy K. Baym, eds. 2009. *Internet Inquiry: Conversations about Method*. Los Angeles: Sage.

Mitra, Ananda. 2006. "Towards Finding a Cybernetic Safe Place: Illustrations from People of Indian Origin." *New Media and Society* 8: 251-268.

Naficy, Hamid. 2001. *An Accented Cinema: Exilic and Diasporic Filmmaking*. Princeton: Princeton University Press.

Nakamura, Lisa. 2008. *Digitizing Race: Visual Cultures of the Internet*. Minneapolis: University of Minnesota Press.

Turkle, Sherry. 1995. *Life on the Screen: Identity in the Age of the Internet*. New York: Simon and Schuster.

Notes

[1] The primary author wishes to thank members of various courses I have taught from fall 1997 till the present for permission to use their assignments and for the insightful discussions in those classes. I have had Human Subject Review Board approval for all the classes referred to in this chapter. Some past and current graduate students and research assistants are specifically listed as co-authors because the work used from their observations is more than just one or two paragraphs – they were invited back to write more specifically for this article. Each of the authors put in equal amount of work and are listed alphabetically.

[2] MUDs are internet/online text-based computer games. More specifically, this generic name is an abbreviation of "Multi User Domains" or "Multi User Dungeons" since they were created in resemblance with the well known (offline) role-playing game Dungeons and Dragons. Designed on different kinds of software, MUDs allow the players, by typing a range of coded commands, to be a part of a virtual environment where they can "navigate, converse, and build" (Turkle 1997, 11). As Turkle explicates: "you join a MUD through a command that links your computer to the computer on which the MUD program resides…Basic commands may seem awkward at first but soon become familiar. For example, if I am playing a character named ST, any words I type after the command 'say' will appear on all players' screens as 'ST says.' Any actions I type after the command 'emote' will appear after my name just as I type them, as in 'ST waves hi' or 'ST laughs uncontrollably'" (11). In MOOs, which are more elaborate forms of MUDs (MUD Object Oriented), users can build interactive objects that can be used by other participants in this virtual environment. Most importantly, inhabitants of this interactive text-based virtual space "become authors not only of text but of themselves, constructing new selves through social interaction" so that knowledge and agency are acquired by "doing" language at the human/machine interface (12).

[3] Second Life (SL) is a multi user virtual environment called a MUVE and is accessed online. MUVEs and MOOs have similar characteristics but are not the same. Both MOOs and MUVEs are in the family of multi user domains (MUDs), and both require a reworking of offline communication skills while negotiating computer literacies. However, specific differences between the two include the visio-centric emphasis and the user made graphics that encourage ownership in SL. Second Life is almost entirely designed and built by its participants. Additionally, and perhaps most importantly, virtual personas in MOOs are defined and recognized by typing coded text; whereas in SL, virtual personae (avatars) appear as a body on the computer screen, giving the SL user a visual experience of bodily presence at the "real"/"virtual" interface.

[4] The Sanskrit term "Avatara" originally referred to the incarnation or embodiment of the Hindu god, Vishnu. In present computer culture, the term "avatar" denotes an embodying of digitally modeled personae that (re)present the physical self in virtual spaces. Weaving immaterial and material identities extends the mind/body connection from "virtual to actual" and back again (Boellstorff 2008, 128). The

avatar, as a "self" that transcends physical form, characteristically blurs boundaries that attempt to separate offline and online identities and experiences.

[5] The core graphics download program in SL is designed so that digitally produced images gradually appear on the computer screen one layer at a time. When a digitally designed avatar "body" appears on the computer screen, the user at the keyboard sees a "naked" body image. Subsequent layers of clothing overlap, but SM was not aware of this when she first entered SL. So she sat uncomfortably next to others in the computer lab and watched as her avatar slowly became exposed on the screen.

[6] Please see the Appendix for course details.

AFTERWORD

TECHNOLOGY, CHANGE, AND FUTURE COLLABORATIONS

ALVINA E. QUINTANA AND CAROLINE J. SMITH

Historically, women's and gender studies have been ideologically grounded in movements devoted to resistance and social change. Today's challenge builds on the work of the past, for once again we find ourselves in the position of dismantling essentialist notions based on patriarchal systems of oppression and control. Unlike the social struggles of the past, the central issues confronting us today involve moving beyond academic comfort zones that rely solely on conventional approaches to learning. Computer science and new digital technologies offer creative tools useful for transgressing outdated gender stereotypes that continue to dominate our culture. Sharon Collingwood's introduction to our anthology explains why technology is so vital to women by providing a number of studies indicating that women have not participated in "highly-paid technology that is rapidly restructuring society" (Tapia 2004, Walton 2009). The statistics, however useful, should not be interpreted in a way that reinforces the idea that women are, by virtue of genetics, unable to function successfully in evolving new technological domains that move beyond shopping and emotional connections.

In order to develop an appreciation about why and how traditional women's studies programs have been slow to actively participate within new technologically oriented approaches requires an in depth interpretation of the issues at hand. What contributes to fear of the unknown or resistance to new approaches? Adrienne Rich's "Notes Toward a Politics of Location," were written for a different time, but they ring true today:

> A few years ago I would have spoken of the common oppression of women, the gathering of women around the globe, the hidden history of women's resistance and bonding, the failure of all previous politics to

recognize the universal shadow of patriarchy, the belief that women now, in a time of rising consciousness and global emergency, may join across all national and cultural boundaries to create a society free of domination, in which "sexuality, politics,...work,...intimacy...thinking itself will be transformed." (1986, 210)

As we re-read Rich's words, we cannot help but consider them within the context of our contemporary dilemma as we continue to struggle with the common oppression of women across the globe. Just as Rich calls for women to gather and be aware of the failure of all previous politics to recognize "the universal shadow of patriarchy," we cannot resist making connections between the "rising consciousness and global emergency" we confront today. In our minds the key to understanding our reluctance to retool and redefine our approach to gender studies can only be deconstructed if we take the time to solicit the personal accounts of those involved in women's studies.

Bettina Aptheker's *Tapestries of Life: Women's Work, Women's Consciousness, and the Meaning of Daily Experience* provides a useful discussion about the significance of women's personal narratives:

Stories are one of the ways in which women give meaning to the things that happen in a lifetime, and the dailiness of life also structures the telling, the ordering of thought, the significance allocated to different pieces of the story. (1989, 44)

We concur with Aptheker, and offer the following story about how we were inspired to work on this volume and how we came together as an editorial team.

Although Alvina and Caroline had worked together when Caroline was a graduate student at the University of Delaware and although Alvina and Sharon had encountered one another in the virtual world Second Life, it was not until the spring of 2009 that we embarked on a research agenda that would culminate in the production of this volume. Communicating solely through the internet, we collaborated on organizing a panel entitled "Cybergrrls: Negotiating Past, Present and Future Feminisms" for the 2009 National Association for Women's Studies Convention. To our delight, our panel was received with great enthusiasm, filling the room with students and faculty. The session gave us the opportunity to speak about feminist pedagogy and reflect on the courses we had taught at our respective universities. Caroline's presentation reflected on collaborative writing practices, demonstrating how blogs facilitate a deeper awareness of the writing process. Sharon, who is also known "in-world" as Ellie

Brewster, provided an introduction to the virtual world Second Life giving concrete examples on how Second Life can be employed to enable in-depth discussions about representation and the dynamic relationship between the categories of race, class and gender. Alvina's presentation highlighted a capstone course she developed aimed at introducing students to the world of digital storytelling. The session's success provided ample inspiration for us to move from oral to print culture in our effort to create meaning for a broad audience.

The positive reception prompted us to draft a call for papers, soliciting essays that discussed feminism, teaching, and new technology. As noted in the introduction, women are seen to be more tentative when it comes to asserting their presence in digital culture and more hesitant to pursue careers in computer science. Yet we found our response to our call for papers to prove otherwise. The proposals we received indicated a tremendous interest in experimenting with new technologies in the women's studies "classroom." The contributors to this collection are doing exciting pedagogical work across the board. Some are including new media – from blogs to digital storytelling – in their traditional classroom space. Others are using these technologies to enhance online classroom experiences. And, still others are using non-traditional classroom spaces, such as Second Life, to create a different kind of classroom community – one that transcends physical boundaries. All of the contributors show a thoughtful consideration for the best way to implement these technologies. Their commitment to experimenting with digital culture in the classroom will hopefully, in turn, inspire subsequent generations of students to actively participate in new media.

Many of the challenges that we faced during the editorial process paralleled those challenges that our contributors encountered when they implemented new technologies into their "classrooms." Like Michelle McGibbney Vlahoulis and Marcella Gemelli, we were faced with the task of reimagining the editorial process – replacing face-to-face collaboration with collaboration that occurred entirely online. For us as editors, this process was not easy; each of us came to the project with different comfort levels in regard to using various technologies. We discussed and debated the best ways to "meet" online to review abstracts, provide feedback for the contributors, and proofread final copies of the essays. During our editorial process, we soon realized that we needed to think critically about what we wanted to accomplish using technology – a point that Susan Smith Nash makes in her essay for this volume. While chatting in Second Life would be fun, we recognized that checking in via Skype each week actually achieved the same goals. And, while email was more familiar to us all, sending files back and forth for comments would be a much more complicated process than simply creating a Google group where we could post versions of each essay. We assessed our "learning outcomes" and adjusted our technology use accordingly, relying primarily on Google Docs to comment on and edit the essays that we received and Skype and email to communicate with one another effectively and efficiently.

Our engagement in the process of producing this volume has been both challenging and invigorating. The process has made us all the more aware of the value of social networking and new technologies and the way in which this new media can foster connections. As the essays in this anthology reveal, the principal goal for many feminist pedagogues is creating community. L. Ayu Saraswati discusses how her digital gender story project allowed for students in her face-to-face classroom to explore the way in which gendered ideologies had shaped their identities. Students in Radhika Gajjala's class worked with one another to navigate Second Life, and their online encounters prompted thoughtful discussions regarding the ways in which that space both reinforces and subverts social constructions of gender that they encounter in their daily lives. And, other contributors, like Kimberlee Staking, describe the rich, cross-cultural exchanges that occurred between students when technologies enabled them to traverse geographical borders and communicate with people across the globe. The authors of these essays describe how – in face-to-face class meetings, in hybrid courses, and in online classes – they and their students challenged one another to think more deeply about gender ideologies and how, in turn, these academic exchanges fostered a strong sense of community.

As editors, when we began this endeavor we had not realized how our connection would lead to new discoveries and opportunities, to connections with kindred spirits from across the globe. The production of *Feminist Cyberspaces* provided the platform we needed to communicate across disciplines and university campuses. Through the process we have formed new friendships in both real and virtual worlds. A direct result of our initial call for papers came forth when Sharon and Alvina were invited to conduct a workshop on new digital technologies at the Gender and Women's Studies Department at the University of Kentucky in the spring of 2011. And, in working with one another and in working with these authors, we created our own online feminist community. Despite our disparate locations (Ohio, Delaware, and Washington, D.C.), as editors, we still came together virtually, meeting online to exchange ideas, to select essays for publication, to provide authors with feedback, and to proofread the final product. While our authors are geographically scattered, we were able to defy those borders, again coming together online and creating a community among the editors and writers. Together, we worked to create for readers a feminist, teaching community within the pages of this anthology. On this journey we have collected many stories and reflected on a variety of issues related to feminist pedagogy. To say that this has been an exciting and rewarding journey would simply be an understatement.

In her 1994 book *Teaching to Transgress: Education as the Practice of Freedom*, bell hooks writes:

> ...learning is a place where paradise can be created. The classroom with all its limitations remains a location of possibility. In that field of possibility we have the opportunity to labour for freedom, to demand of ourselves and our comrades, an openness of mind and heart that allows us to face reality even as we collectively imagine ways to move beyond boundaries, to transgress. This is education as the practice of freedom. (207)

This quote represents the spirit of *Feminist Cyberspaces: Pedagogies in Transition,* whose essayists work within their classrooms to realize the possibilities that new technologies offer their students. As these essays have shown, new media enables feminist instructors and their students to move beyond the physical limitations of the classroom space and enter into the cyber frontier – a place where the feminist classroom is filled with exciting possibilities.

We hope to develop and sustain this excitement through interdisciplinary collaboration on the web, and we have created a public wiki to encourage dialogue and experimentation. We invite you to contribute to the wiki, whether you are an experienced user of technology or just beginning your classroom explorations. We are living in a time of tremendous change, and for many of us the challenges of using technology may seem overwhelming. Many hands make light work.

Please join us at http://adarocks.wikispaces.com/

Bibliography

Aptheker, Bettina. 1989. *Tapestries of Life: Women's Work, Women's Consciousness, and the Meaning of Daily Experience.* Amherst: University of Massachusetts.

hooks, bell. 1994. *Teaching to Transgress: Education as the Practice of Freedom.* New York: Routledge.

Rich, Adrienne. 1984. "Notes Towards a Politics of Location." *In Blood, Bread and Poetry: Selected Prose 1979-1985* by Adrienne Rich, 210-231. London: Little Brown & Co.

Tapia, Andrea and Lynnette Kvasny. May 22-24, 2004. "Recruitment Is Not Enough: Retention of Women and Minorities in the IT Workplace." Proceedings of the ACM SIGMIS CPR Conference, Tucson, Arizona. Accessed June 10, 2010.
http://ist.psu.edu/faculty_pages/ lkvasny/publications.html.

Walton, Marsha. 2009. "IT Jobs Offer Growth, but Women Are Bailing Out." *Women's eNews*. Accessed June 24, 2010.
http://www.womensenews.org/story/women-in-science/100623/it-jobs-offer-growth-women-are-bailing-out.

CONTRIBUTOR BIOGRAPHIES

Karen Keifer-Boyd is a professor of art education and affiliate professor of women's studies at The Pennsylvania State University. Her writings on feminist pedagogy, visual culture, cyberNet activism art pedagogy, action research, and identity speculative fiction are in more than 45 peer-reviewed research publications, and translated into several languages. She co-authored *InCITE, InSIGHT, InSITE* (NAEA, 2008), *Engaging Visual Culture* (Davis, 2007), co-edited *Real-World Readings in Art Education: Things Your Professors Never Told You* (Falmer, 2000), and served as editor of the *Journal of Social Theory in Art Education* and guest editor for *Visual Arts Research*. She has co-edited the journal, *Visual Culture and Gender*, since 2005. Keifer-Boyd has presented at more than 50 international and national conferences, and at universities in South Korea, Taiwan, Hong Kong, Austria, Germany, Uganda, and Finland. Her research focuses on feminist strategies for teaching critical and creative inquiry with dynamic/interactive technologies. She has been honored with leadership and teaching awards including a 2006 Fulbright Lecture and Research Award in Finland from the Council for International Exchange of Scholars, the National Art Education Association (NAEA) Women's Caucus Connors Teaching Award in 2005, the Texas Outstanding Art Educator in Higher Education Award in 2001, and the Arts Administrator of the Year National Art Education Association Award for the Pacific Region in 1994.

Lisa Child graduated from University of Toronto with a BA in Caribbean Studies and Women's Studies. Her family comes from the islands of St. Vincent and the Grenadines, and Barbados, while she was born and raised in Ontario. Compiling an oral history of her family began with discussions with her Aunty Candy, who is the eldest of the sisters on her mother's side, and the only one who still lives in Barbados. These discussions were only the beginning of a much bigger personal project of learning more about herself through getting to know her ancestors.

Sharon Collingwood received her Ph.D. from The University of Western Ontario and teaches in the Department of Women's, Gender and Sexuality Studies at The Ohio State University. In 2007 she received grants from The Ohio Learning Network and the Department of Continuing Education at Ohio State to develop a teaching and research space in the virtual world Second Life; she has been teaching distance courses there since that time. In 2010 a grant from the American Association of University Women allowed her to develop the Women's Virtual Community Project, a series of lectures, concerts, workshops and other events that encourage dialogue and collaboration in Second Life communities.

Deena Dadachanji's interest in the intersections of immigration and spirituality were encouraged by Dr. Jacqui Alexander's 'Migrations of the Sacred' course at the University of Toronto. Her discovery of the extraordinary parallels between her own journey of migrating from Pakistan to Canada and her grandmother's journey of migrating from India to Pakistan led to the unearthing of her grandmother's intricate life history, and a strengthening of her own belief and trust in the Sacred in ways unimagined.

Kandace Creel Falcón earned her Ph.D. in Feminist Studies from the University of Minnesota; she currently teaches in the Women's Studies Program and American Multicultural Studies Department at Minnesota State University Moorhead. Her teaching interests include Chicana feminisms, Chicana and women of color epistemologies, feminist pedagogy, feminist media making, and storytelling/oral history methodologies, and she blogs about these interests on a collaborative feminist pedagogy blog project http://teachingblogs.room34.com/ and on her personal cooking/storytelling blog La Kitchen Chicana http://lakitchen chicana.blogspot.com/.

Christine Ward Gailey is Professor of Women's Studies and Anthropology at The University of California, Riverside. She was Chair of UCR's Women's Studies Department from 1999-2006. Professor Gailey's research centers on gender hierarchies in the context of state dynamics, viewed comparatively and historically. Professor Gailey has published on feminist methods in anthropology, on comparative issues of gender in reproductive policies and practices, on gender and colonial state formation, on gender and nationalism, and on community and familial responses to gendered violence. Her latest research focuses on gender, race, and class dynamics in U.S. domestic and international adoption. Several of her anthropological publications focus on the history of critical ethnology. In addition to her scholarly writing, Professor Gailey is a published ethnopoet.

Radhika Gajjala received her Ph.D. from The University of Pittsburgh and is the Director of the American Culture Studies Program at Bowling Green University. Her research interests include Digital Media (ICTs) and Globalization, Gender, Race and Technology, South Asian Diasporas, Critical Development Studies, Affect and Placement in Digital Space, Transnational Labor, Women and NGOs. She is the author of *Cyber Selves: Feminist ethnographies of South Asian Women* (2004) and is collaborating on a collection of essays titled *Global media, cultures, and identities*, to be published by Routledge.

Marcella Gemelli received her Ph.D. in Sociology from Arizona State University, completing her dissertation, *Bridging the Digital Divide: Homeless Women Participate in Internet Life,* in 2007. She is a Lecturer in the School of Social and Family Dynamics at Arizona State, and is Associate Director for Research and School Quality at The Arizona Charter Schools Association.

Isela González received a Masters in Public Administration, with a Health Services Emphasis from the University of San Francisco in 2004, and holds a B.A. in History and Latin American Studies from Notre Dame de Namur University. She is the HIV Prevention Services Coordinator for the Forensic AIDS Project, a program of Jail Health Services, and has over 16 years experience providing HIV prevention and care services, the past 13 years working specifically with incarcerated adult men, women and transgenders. She has worked closely with the Jail Health Services staff to ensure a Medical Model HIV Testing program is successfully implemented within Jail Medical Services, and is the technical assistance lead for this project ensuring HIV prevention services are delivered in a culturally, linguistically and client centered manner to all prisoners. In 2009 she concluded her work as Co-Principal Investigator on the *Jailed Women and HIV Education: A Collaborative Investigation*, a participatory action research study conducted in the San Francisco county jails with incarcerated women of color, by facilitating a final report back session to women incarcerated in the SF jail. She currently serves as a Community Co-Chair of the San Francisco HIV Prevention Planning Council and is the San Francisco steering representative on the Urban Coalition for HIV/AIDS Prevention Services (UCHAPS). She is also a member of San

Francisco HIV Prevention Section's Transgender Advisory Group (TAG); she is a CAB member of TRANS:THRIVE, and is a CAB member of the Transgender Economic Empowerment Initiative.

Mervi Heikkinen is a graduate student in the Faculty of Education at the University of Oulu, Finland. Her areas of expertise are gendered and sexual harassment, gendered organizations, violence against women, and gender-sensitive education. She is also a project coordinator of the *From Violence to Caring, a* study program in the Department of Women's Studies at the University of Oulu that works to increase competence in organizations and provides new insight for interdisciplinary research around the themes of violence and non-violence. She is the editor, with with Suvi Pihkala and Vappu Sunnari, of *From Violence to Caring – Gendered and Sexualized Violence as the Challenge on the Life-span* (2008).

Katie King received her Ph.D. in the History of Consciousness at the University of California, Santa Cruz. Her interdisciplinary scholarship is located at the intersection of feminist technoscience studies, cyberculture and media studies, and LGBT Studies. Her first book was *Theory in its Feminist Travels: conversations in U.S. women's movements.* In press with Duke for Winter 2011 is *Networked Reenactments: Stories transdisciplinary knowledges tell,* while two others are in progress: Speaking with Things, an introduction to writing technologies, and Demonstrations and Experiments: Quakers, plain style, and the Scientific Revolution.

Jarah Moesch has an MFA in Integrated Media Art from Hunter College and is currently a PhD student in American Studies at the University of Maryland. She is a digital media and performance artist activist whose current research and creative practice investigates and disrupts concepts of normativity in public spaces. Her work lies at the intersection of gender performance, queerness and everyday life. Prior to returning to school, she taught media theory and practice at Hunter College for a number of years. Jarah's work has been exhibited internationally at museums, galleries and festivals.

Sara Mohammed is a graduate of the University of Toronto, with a double major in Women Studies and Psychology. She currently works at a community women's health organization and is a Masters candidate at York University in Environmental Studies focusing on how social, structural and other environments affect the physical, mental and spiritual well-being of women. She has a particular interest in arts-based approaches to research and healing. Sara is a child of immigrants, born and raised in Toronto, Ontario, Canada and has undertaken the process of familial healing by digging into her families past to uncover ancestral stories, histories and the multiple inherited effects of colonization, migration and silence.

Susan Smith Nash received her Ph.D. in English from the University of Oklahoma and also did graduate work in Developmental Economics. She is the Director of Education and Professional Development for the American Association of Petroleum Geologists, and is responsible for administration of education conferences, short courses, field courses, distance education, as well as the design and deployment of new education products (e-symposia, webinars, geotechnology workshops and innovative use of mobile technologies for learning settings). Her most recent publications on technology and education are *Moodle 1.9 Teaching Techniques,* co-authored with William Rice, 2010; The E-Learner Survival Guide, 2009; and *Excellence in Teaching and Learning: Classroom and Online,* co-authored with George Henderson, 2007.

Suvi Pihkala received her M.A. from the University of Oulu, Finland, where she is a researcher in *Openrisk – social media in professional collaboration regarding safety and wellbeing at work* (Information Processing Sciences). She is also the project planner in ALLIES: Teachers' and Parents' Alliance for Early Violence Prevention, an international two-year (2010-2012) research and development project that aims to develop caring, community-based measures to prevent school violence. She is the editor, with Mervi Heikkenen and Vappu Sunnari, of *From Violence to Caring – Gendered and Sexualized Violence as the Challenge on the Life-span* (2008).

Sara L. Puotinen received her Ph.D in Women's Studies from Emory University and teaches in the Gender, Women and Sexuality Studies Department at the University of Minnesota. Her areas of research interest include: feminist and queer ethics, feminist pedagogies, blogging and troublemaking. She frequently writes about feminist pedagogy and blogging on my three blogs: (making/being in/staying in) Trouble (http://trouble.room34.com), Unchained (http://unchained.room34.com) and It's Diablogical! A Collaborative Diablog on Feminist Pedagogy.

Alvina E. Quintana received her Ph.D. from the History of Consciousness Department at the University of California at Santa Cruz, and teaches in the Department of Women's Studies at the University of Delaware. Her publications include articles on multicultural literature and cinema studies. Aside from book chapters and articles, she has published two books: *Home Girls: Chicana Literary Voices*, Temple University Press and *Reading U.S. Latina Writers: Remapping American Literature*, Palgrave/Macmillan Press. Her research interests focus on feminist theory; sexuality and difference; new technologies, transnational gender studies with a particular emphasis on the intersections between U.S. Latino/as and Latin American cultural practices; multiculturalism in the U.S.A and abroad; the internationalization of American Studies. She is currently working on a book that reconceptualizes American literary practices and a documentary film that explores notions of transculturation and the Black Pacific. Association, Quintana has served as Chair of the Women's Committee, the Minority Scholar's Committee, the 2006 Program Committee's Chair in Chief, a member of the the Nominating Committee, the International Women's Task Force, Executive Committee and Council. She was also elected to serve a three-year term as the Modern Language Association's delegate for Ethnic Studies. Aside from her academic appointment in Women's Studies, she holds secondary appointments in Black American and Latin American Studies at the University of Delaware.

Margaret Rhee is a doctoral student at the University of California, Berkeley. Her field of interest is Ethnic Studies with a designated emphasis in New Media. Her scholarly work is interdisciplinary, focusing broadly on representation and race, gender, and sexuality. Her pedagogical projects include feminist-based participatory action research and arts, particularly in partnership and mentorship with the SF Department of Public Health Forensic AIDS Project. Additionally, as a 2009 HASTAC scholar, she co-organized the first online forum on Queer Feminist New Media Spaces. As an activist and artist, she has worked extensively with community based media organizations such as Berkeley Community Media, Center for Digital Storytelling, and the Queer Women of Color Media Arts Project. Her scholarly, artistic, and pedagogical work is dedicated to feminism(s) and social justice.

L. Ayu Saraswati is an Assistant Professor of Women, Gender, and Sexuality Studies at the University of Kansas. Her research interests are feminist media and new media studies, race and racial formation studies, transnational feminism, women and diaspora, affect and cultural studies of emotion, gender and globalization, gender and consumption, and Indonesian studies.

Caroline J. Smith is assistant professor in The George Washington University's Writing Program, where she teaches freshmen writing classes themed around her interests in women's literature and popular culture. Her book, *Cosmopolitan Culture and Consumerism in Chick Lit*, published by Routledge Press in 2007, focuses on how the genre of chick lit interfaces with magazines, self-help books, romantic comedies, and domestic-advice publications. Her current book project, *The Politics of the Kitchen: Postfeminism and Women's Food Writing*, is a scholarly analysis of the work of contemporary female food memoirists, looking specifically at the way in which these women construct their identities in relation to the kitchen.

Danielle Smith works in the health care field as a body worker using a multidisciplinary approach. She returned to school mid-career to complete the Caribbean Studies Program at the University of Toronto. Interested in her family tree from an early age, Danielle has bridged the worlds of bodywork and Caribbean Studies to explore some of the sacred migrations in her own ancestry. She is currently a key collaborator with Diane Roberts and Heather Hermant in the Personal Legacy Process, a workshop series involving ancestral research, in-studio physical and vocal exercises, and 'Afrisporic' influenced performance traditions, all designed to awaken ancestral histories stored in our bodies, and to serve as gateways for the emergence of historic, transgenerational truths from critically anchored personal places. It is this work which resonates so closely to Professor Alexander's focus of Sacred Migrations.

Kimberlee Staking is an ABD student in the Women's Studies Department at the University of Maryland. Her contribution to this anthology will form the nucleus of a chapter in her dissertation exploring the use of active learning partnerships in the humanities classroom. The recipient of a University award for Outstanding Graduate Teaching Assistant (2004), and of a Center for Teaching Excellence (CTE) grant for the preparation of curricular materials engaging diversity (2005), Ms. Staking teaches courses on women's health, gender and sexuality, and women in visual culture. She also participated in a second CTE grant developing a website resource for faculty in the College of Arts and Humanities to support their teaching with images and to facilitate student acquisition of visual literacy skills (2006). With a Ford Foundation grant to develop web-based pedagogies in the support of transnational teaching collaborations, Ms. Staking worked with colleagues in Africa, Israel, and Jamaica to design and teach an online course bringing students together from all four sites in a cross-institutional, transnational exploration of women's health (2007).

Vappu Sunnari received her doctorate from the University of Oulu, Finland, and is a lecturer in Women's and Gender Studies and the Faculty of Education at the Unviersity of Oulu. Her areas of interest are gender equity, gendering in schools and in teacher education, education in the North, and sexualized and gendered violence and bullying. She is the editor, with Mervi Heikkenen and Suvi Pihkala of From *Violence to Caring – Gendered and Sexualized Violence as the Challenge on the Life-span* (2008).

Chikako Takeshita received her Ph.D from the Virginia Polytechnic Institute and State University and teaches at the University of California, Riverside. Her forthcoming book, "The Biopolitics of Contraceptive Development: Population, Women's Bodies, and the IUD," traces the development of the intrauterine device from the 1960s to the present. Her work demonstrates that various social interests, including the desire to restrict global population grown, the threat of medical malpractice litigations, attacks from parties opposed to abortion, and women's aspiration for better reproductive control have all played a significant role in directing scientific research on the device. She was awarded the 2010-2011 American Fellowship Short-term Research Publication Grant from the American Association of University Women (AAUW) to support the completion of this work. Her current project explores how Internet health information mediates women's sense of embodied self while experiencing illness.

Michelle McGibbney Vlahoulis is a Lecturer in Women and Gender Studies at Arizona State University. She teaches a variety of courses including large lecture, hybrid and online courses, particularly classes on social change, media and film. She was a member of the original grant team who was responsible for the large hybrid redesign of the introduction to women's studies course, Women, Gender and Society, and has been developing multiple online course offerings, content and curriculum for the program.

Courtney Lee Weida is an assistant professor of Art Education at Adelphi University in Garden City, New York. Her research centers on gender, craft, and ceramic art. She has a background in English Literature, Visual Art, and Education. She holds teaching licenses in Art, English, and Elementary teaching. Courtney has served as a teaching artist in schools, camps, museums, and afterschool programs. She has collected and created zines since high school.

INDEX